Programming for Parks, Recreation, and Leisure Services:

A Servant Leadership Approach

by

Donald G. DeGraaf
Calvin College

Debra J. Jordan
Oklahoma State University

Kathy H. DeGraaf

Programming for Parks, Recreation, and Leisure Services:

A Servant Leadership Approach

by

Donald G. DeGraaf
Calvin College

Debra J. Jordan
Oklahoma State University

Kathy H. DeGraaf

Venture Publishing, Inc.
1999 Cato Avenue • State College, PA 16801

Production Manager: Richard Yocum
Manuscript Editing and Design: Michele L. Barbin
Cover Design and Artwork: ©1998 Sikorski Design

Library of Congress Catalogue Card Number 98-88780
ISBN 0-910251-99-1

This book is dedicated to those professionals in parks, recreation, and leisure services who are living models of the servant leader.

Table of Contents

They know us by our programs. The activities, special events, games, instruction, sports, and entertainment we offer to constituents provide a glimpse into the beliefs, values, and assumptions of our organizations. Furthermore, programs and services are the visible, tangible media through which we reach out and touch the lives of others. Thus, program planning and the resultant programs are critically important to what we do and how we present ourselves in the field of parks, recreation, and leisure services. We can never learn enough about the program process!

The values that undergird our efforts to facilitate and provide recreation and leisure programs for our constituents provide guidance and direction in the hundreds of program-related choices we make each day. We present just such a philosophy in this text—one that provides guidance and direction in the way we present material and in making suggestions about the *best* way to do something. This underlying foundation is that of *servant leadership*.

Through a Servant Leadership philosophy we suggest that the work we do in parks, recreation, and leisure services ought to be values-based. By this, we mean that our efforts should focus on providing the best possible situations and scenarios for our constituents, and involving them in as much of the decision-making processes as possible. We want to listen to and empower those we serve, rather than dictate and direct their leisure opportunities. So, as you work your way through this text, you will find specific references to the notion of servant leadership, as well as statements and suggestions that reflect a servant leadership approach to programming.

Conceptually, this book is organized into three parts. Part One lays the foundation for the book and is about the art of programming. In this section we offer information related to program development from a servant leadership perspective. We also offer theoretical information to serve as a foundation for subsequent sections of the text, and examine the relationship between service and quality in the programming process.

Parts Two and Three relate to the science of programming. In Part Two we examine the pre-program process of planning. We begin with material about gathering information from potential constituents, and continue with issues about diversity, program design, and facilitating the pre-program experience.

In Part Three of the text we get into what some might call the "nitty-gritty." This section looks at important programming issues such as pricing, marketing, staffing, program implementation, and evaluation. In the last chapter of the text we provide a variety of resources to assist programmers in designing and implementing programs.

In addition to this text, we feel particularly excited about offering students an accompanying student manual that correlates with the material in the book. The student manual is designed to encourage active learning where students are challenged to think for themselves and to integrate theory with practice. The chapters in the student manual correlate to each chapter in the text and include learning objectives, identification of key concepts and terms, questions for reflection and study, suggested applications and practice, and a step-by-step approach to developing a program. We hope you enjoy using the student manual as a personal learning tool.

In undertaking a project such as this there are a number of people to whom we are indebted. First, we would like to thank the people who have assisted us (both directly and indirectly) in completing this text. Michele Barbin, our production editor at Venture Publishing, was absolutely fabulous in pulling this book and the student manual together. In addition to providing invaluable assistance in editing, layout, design, and content, and with keeping us on schedule, Michele also made wonderful contributions to the appendix of this book. From each of us, Michele, thank you.

The evolution of knowledge in a profession such as ours is an ongoing process; with this in mind, we'd like to thank the authors of programming texts which have preceded this one. The influence of such people as Gay Carpenter, Dan Corbin, John Crompton, Chris Edginton, Susan

Edginton, Pat Farrell, Geof Godbey, Carole Hanson, Chris Howe, Dick Kraus, Herberta Lundegren, Bob Rossman, Ruth Russell, and Ellen Williams is evident throughout this book. In addition, our colleagues throughout the country have been supportive and willing to critique ideas and offer suggestions through the writing process. We are appreciative of Wendy Hultsman who provided a critical review of early material, and provided excellent feedback. Colleagues at the University of Northern Iowa, Oklahoma State University, and Calvin College supported this writing endeavor by sharing ideas and giving us space, when needed.

Finally, and always in our thoughts, we would each like to express our appreciation and love to our families and close friends who offered their enduring support, love, and encouragement.

—D.G.D., D.J.J., K.H.D., 1999

About the Authors

Deb Jordan has worked in outdoor and wilderness education, special events, military recreation, and in a nonprofit organization working with adjudicated youth. She has published numerous articles and made presentations about leadership, group dynamics, programming, and gender issues; authored a textbook about leadership in leisure services; and coauthored an introductory textbook for parks, recreation, and leisure services. Deb earned her degrees from Slippery Rock State College, Western Illinois University, and Indiana University.

In her house, you'll find two very cute kittens—Machai and Ripley. Deb enjoys reading, playing in the mountains, and riding a motorcycle. She currently is an associate professor of Leisure Studies at Oklahoma State University.

Don and Kathy DeGraaf have worked in a variety of recreation and social service organizations including camps, after-school programs, outdoor education centers, schools and hospitals. Don has published numerous articles and has been involved in many presentations and workshops dealing with issues such as programming, environmental ethics, adventure education, and the management of leisure services. In addition, Don has coauthored an introductory textbook for parks, recreation, and leisure services. Don earned his degrees from Calvin College, Indiana University, and the University of Oregon. Kathy has published articles and manuals and given presentations as well in the areas of programming, leadership, and management. Her degree is from Valparaiso University; she has also completed additional coursework at Northern Illinois University.

Both Don and Kathy enjoy water sports, camping, reading and "hanging out" with their family. Together they have two children, Isaac and Rochelle, and a dog named Lantau. The DeGraaf family enjoys traveling, and recently spent a year in Hong Kong while Don worked for a nonprofit youth serving organization. Don is currently an associate professor in the Physical Education and Recreation Department at Calvin College in Grand Rapids, Michigan. Kathy is a teaching assistant at New Branches Charter Elementary School.

About the Cover

The artist conceptualizes the idea of duality of the servant leader on the cover. The half sheet of paper, representing research and writing, turns into a sprig of flowers that symbolizes parks, recreation, the outdoors, and growth. The paper and flowers are tied together in the center by a CD-ROM, a contemporary symbol of the computer, and a useful tool in leisure management and promotion of programs. The CD-ROM also echoes the circular motif of the process of leisure programming as does the pocket watch on the back that represents both leisure time and the time process while implementing a program. Spears' definition of servant leader is prominently displayed over the pocket watch on the back. The musical score in the background adds a touch of harmony to the programming process and represents interaction between people and the art of listening while in itself being a form of leisure activity. Of the many natural elements that appear in the cover, the water symbolizes the outdoors, movement and motion.

Chapter One

Basic Concepts

The idea of the servant as leader came out of reading Hermann Hesse's Journey to the East. *In this story we see a band of men on a mythical journey ... . The central figure of the story is Leo who accompanies the party as the servant who does their menial chores, but who also sustains them with his spirit and his song. He is a person of extraordinary presence. All goes well until Leo disappears. Then the group falls into disarray and the journey is abandoned. They cannot make it without their servant Leo. The narrator, one of the party, after some years of wandering finds Leo and is taken into the Order that had sponsored the journey. There he discovers that Leo, whom he had known first as servant, was in fact the titular head of the Order, its guiding light, a great and noble leader. ... to me this story clearly says that the great leader is seen as servant first, and that simple fact is the key to his [sic] greatness. Leo was actually the leader all of the time, but he was servant first because that was what he was, deep down inside. Leadership was bestowed upon a man who was by nature a servant. It was something given, or assumed, that could be taken away. His servant nature was the real man, not bestowed, not assumed, and not to be taken away. He was servant first.*

Greenleaf, 1977, pp. 7–8

Meeting the needs of customers through servant leadership is imperative if leisure service organizations are to survive and prosper in the twenty-first century. One means by which leisure service professionals provide value and meet customers' needs is through their programs. *Programming, a continual process of planning, implementing, and evaluating leisure experiences for an individual or a group of individuals is unique to the body of knowledge in parks, recreation, and leisure services* (Carpenter & Howe, 1985). Thus, programming is an important concept for all leisure service professionals to grasp and understand. Whether a leisure service professional is working for a municipal recreation department providing recreational sport leagues for adults, or for a nonprofit organization providing day camp programs for children, or as a commercial tour operator offering wilderness backpacking trips, programming is a central part of her or his job.

Most are well-aware that quality leisure programming does not just happen—it's hard work. And, to complicate things a bit, programming is viewed as both an art and a science. The art aspect of programming comes from experience and creativity while the scientific aspect of programming includes the systematic study of preparing, delivering, and evaluating programs. The purpose of the early part of this book is to examine the philosophical and scientific aspects of programming in order to provide a strong foundation on which the intuitive (art) aspect of programming can be developed, nourished, and grown (see Figure 1.1, page 2).

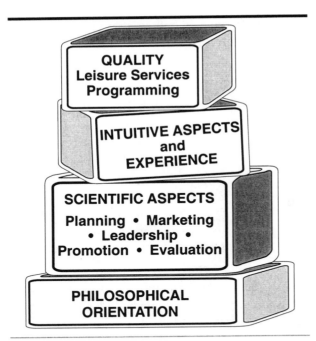

Figure 1.1   The Building Blocks of Programming

Through the underlying theme of this book we would like to encourage parks, recreation, and leisure professionals to take on the role of servant leader as described in the opening quote. The importance of servant leadership is based on the premise that all recreation, parks, and leisure professionals serve their customers through programs. Thus, servant leadership is an integral aspect of programming. In describing the importance of servant leadership, Greenleaf (1977, p. 49) stated

> ... if a better society is to be built, one that is more just and more loving, one that provides greater creative opportunity for its people, then the most open course is to raise both the capacity to serve and the very performance as servant of existing major institutions by new regenerative forces operating within them.

This chapter begins to lay the foundation for the remainder of this text. Definitions of leisure and recreation are presented along with a glimpse of the history of recreation programming and the relevance of programming in today's world. Individual and societal benefits of recreation programming are examined with an emphasis on helping the reader understand a benefits-based management

approach to programming. In addition, the chapter examines the role of the parks, recreation, and leisure service programmer in the programming process with special emphasis placed on helping the reader gain an understanding of the relevance and importance of servant leadership to programming. As the opening quote about servant leadership suggests, parks, recreation, and leisure professionals are often the *spirit and song* of society.

Definitions

An important starting point for understanding leisure programming is understanding what is meant by the terms *leisure* and *recreation*. Defining the terms leisure and recreation is a complex task due to the individual nature of the leisure experience. What one person considers a leisure experience (i.e., gardening, jogging, reading) might be viewed as work by someone else. Throughout history, leisure has been identified in a number of different ways including time, activity, a state of mind, a symbol of social class, and as a holistic concept (Edginton, Jordan, DeGraaf & Edginton, 1998).

Leisure as Time

The easiest and most popular way economists and lay people define leisure is by describing it as discretionary time; that is, time left over from work and other life maintenance activities. Discretionary time implies that individuals have choice, autonomy, and freedom to exercise their will to experience leisure.

Leisure as Activity

This definition pays no attention to the concept of leisure as it relates to what happens within an individual's mind; rather, leisure is defined by categories of activity such as sports, social activities, travel, and outdoor activities (i.e., rock climbing, canoeing, camping). This view is most closely aligned with the term *recreation*.

Leisure as State of Mind

Defining leisure as a state of mind suggests that the leisure experience is a function of one's subjective understanding of leisure. In this case, leisure is an attitude based on an individual's own perspective, feelings, values, and past life experiences.

Leisure as a Symbol of Social Status

The evolution of a "leisure class" where people use leisure as way of claiming or demonstrating social status in society by virtue of the products and services that people consume or purchase can be seen throughout history. For example, the brand of gym shoe and type of recreational equipment a person buys can express their desire to be aligned with a particular social group.

Leisure as a Holistic Concept

The holistic perspective suggests that leisure has the potential to be present in many forms of human endeavor. This focus of leisure is on an individual's ability to shape an integrated lifestyle in which opportunities to operate creatively, expressively, physically, and intellectually exist. Leisure as a holistic concept considers all aspects of one's life.

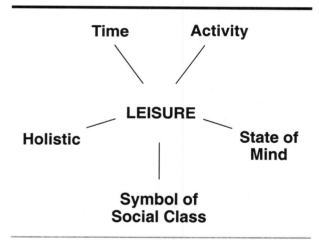

Figure 1.2   Definitions of Leisure

As can be seen from the above explanations, there is no one definition of leisure that can capture all that leisure represents. *Leisure is a societally-based phenomenon.* This means that there is no such thing as one universal definition that explains what leisure is in every society or in every situation. Thus, this can present a challenge to leisure programmers.

Whereas little consensus exists in defining the term *leisure*, the term *recreation* has commonly been viewed as an activity that is freely chosen and has the potential of many desirable outcomes.

Thus, *recreation is an activity that takes place during one's free time, is enjoyable, freely chosen, and benefits the individual emotionally, socially, physically, cognitively, and spiritually.*

Because these terms are closely related and readers generally understand both terms, in this text we will use the terms *leisure* and *recreation* interchangeably. Both terms will represent experiences that include the following five factors. These factors have been shown to relate to satisfying leisure experiences (Csikszentmihalyi, 1975; Ellis, 1973; Gunter, 1987; Neulinger, 1974; Samdahl, 1988), and are often achieved through recreation (see Figure 1.3, page 4).

Freedom

To be free means to be able to act without interference or control from another, or to choose or act in accordance to one's own will. No one else makes (or forces) us do something. We are free to choose to do anything. In order for a successful leisure experience to occur, there must be some element of choice exercised by participants.

Perceived Competence

The perception of having skills and abilities necessary for successful participation leads to a satisfying leisure experience. Thus, in order for a successful leisure experience to occur, individuals must perceive themselves to have a degree of competence equal to the challenges of the intended leisure experience. People match their skill levels to a particular game, or experience.

Intrinsic Motivation

Beyond having the element of choice in leisure activities, participants must choose their involvement because they are moved from within and not because they are influenced by external factors. This means that the drive for leisure comes from within each person, the activity itself motivates an individual to act (and not a desire to lose weight, be with friends, and so forth).

Locus of Control

The concept of locus of control refers to the need to exert influence within the context of the leisure experience. Individuals need to have some control or influence within the leisure process in order for a successful leisure experience to occur. This does not mean that participants need to be involved in the planning of every aspect of every event, but they should feel some degree of control as the experience unfolds. For instance, they might choose their teammates, influence the day and time or place, or decide to modify rules.

Positive Affect

The remaining factor that relates to a satisfying leisure experience is that of positive affect. This refers to enjoyment—people who have positive affect are happy, upbeat, and pleasant. Recreation and leisure experiences have inherent affect and if they are truly recreation and leisure, result in positive affect for the participants.

Understanding these five factors as they relate to satisfying leisure experiences is very important if leisure service programmers are going to design and implement leisure programs and services to meet the needs and demands of a variety of people. When leisure professionals plan programs to help individuals experience these elements, they can facilitate a positive leisure experience.

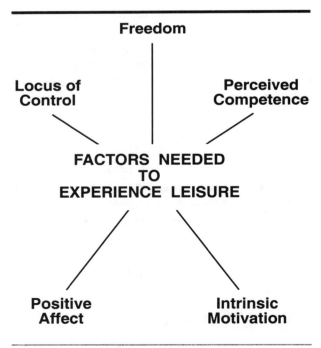

Figure 1.3   Factors of a Satisfying Leisure Experience

Recreation Programs

A wide range of agencies and organizations are involved in delivering recreation programs to an increasingly diverse clientele. Thus, great diversity exists in the type of recreation and leisure programs offered today. These agencies and organizations are found in the public, nonprofit, and commercial sectors and include the following types of leisure service organizations:

1. Public or governmental agencies at the federal, state, and local levels;
2. Voluntary nonprofit organizations, both nonsectarian and sectarian;
3. Private membership associations;
4. Commercial profit-oriented recreation businesses;
5. Armed forces (although this is a branch of government, it does constitute a distinct form of recreation programming);
6. Campus recreation programs serving college and university students and staff members;
7. Corporate recreation programs serving company employees; and
8. Therapeutic recreation services for people with special needs (Kraus, 1985).

In addition to these types of organizations there has been a continuous increase in partnerships between organizations to better meet the needs of participants. For instance, across the United States new programs are appearing as a result of collaboration between therapeutic recreation services and campus recreation programs. As an example, at Oklahoma State University wheelchair basketball and tennis leagues are beginning to develop.

The scope and breadth of recreation programs in all of these settings continue to expand to meet the needs and demands of a variety of participants. For example, it is not uncommon to find senior citizens demanding high-risk activities like alpine skiing, adolescents wanting opportunities to travel, blended families who are looking for bonding opportunities, and singles flocking to adventure travel programs. The common tie between all these groups and activities is programming.

Recreation programs have long been the lifeblood of leisure service organizations in that programs are the vehicle professionals use to deliver leisure benefits to both individuals and society. Programs are where people and parks, recreation, and leisure services organizations meet. *Recreation programs are purposeful interventions which are deliberately designed and constructed in order to produce certain behavioral outcomes (e.g., having fun with family and friends, meeting new friends, learning new skills, increasing fitness levels) in an individual and/or group.* A key element to remember is that programs are not an end in themselves; rather people (and the benefits they desire) are the true reasons for the existence of leisure services organizations. This commitment to people through leisure can be seen throughout the history of the organized parks, recreation, and leisure movement in the United States which dates back to the late 1800s, and is the reason we call for a servant leadership approach to programming.

The Beginnings of Leisure Programming

Recreation organizations emerged during the late 1800s to address the tremendous social, psychological, and general welfare needs that grew out of the Industrial Revolution. Social reformers saw the potential of using play and recreation to improve people's quality of life. For instance, the Boston Sand Gardens (the first playground) were established to meet the play needs of disadvantaged children and give them a safe place to play. Also, many of the first organized camps were designed for and targeted at "sickly boys." Large city parks (e.g., Central Park in New York) were designed in an attempt to regain the rural countryside in the middle of the city and thus give people who lived in crowded slum tenements a place to relax and get away from it all. Further, the settlement house movement used recreation as a means to ease the transition of immigrants to living in large urban American cities. Sessoms and Stevenson (1981) have written that

> Adult education, recreation, and social group work all have a common heritage. Each is a product of the social welfare reforms that occurred in our cities and

industries at the turn of the nineteenth century. Their founders shared a belief— they were concerned with the quality of life and believed that through the "proper" use of leisure it could be achieved. (p. 2)

Initially, many aspects of the recreation movement were focused on providing *places* for leisure— parks, playgrounds, and recreation centers. As the movement progressed the importance of organized programs was acknowledged. Curtis (1915) wrote "the playground that has no program achieves little" (p. 163). Boden and Mitchell (1923) suggested that "programs are necessary to make playgrounds more interesting and efficient" (p. 264). The expansion of leisure service programs has been a major factor in the growth and development of public recreation departments. As the profession matured and diversified, the philosophy that views leisure as an end in itself was adopted by most public recreation agencies across the country (Gray, 1969). In other words, public recreation drifted away from a social welfare model (with specific social service goals) and adopted a model of providing services to all.

The last half of the twentieth century has seen tremendous growth in all sectors of parks, recreation, and leisure services. Public, private nonprofit, and commercial leisure service organizations have all grown at a rapid rate. In addition, leisure service organizations have dealt with phenomenal social change. On one hand, the demand for leisure experiences has skyrocketed. People from all walks of life are seeking and demanding leisure experiences in their lives. At the same time, the environment in which these experiences can be created is also changing. For example, both public and private nonprofit organizations are being asked to be more financially accountable and do more with less. Commercial organizations are being asked to be more ethically responsible in the programs they offer (e.g., ecotourism); and all organizations are being asked to respond to greater diversity in potential customer groups.

In examining the wide range of leisure service organizations that have developed over the last 120 years, Godbey (1997) notes that three factors have shaped all forms of leisure services: the desire to help people, an entrepreneurial spirit, and changes in technology which facilitate, or necessitate, such intentions (see Figure 1.4, page 6).

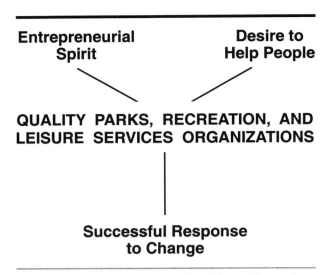

Figure 1.4   The Factors That Have Shaped Leisure Organizations

The Desire to Help People

Whether it be public agencies responding to the play needs of children by creating playgrounds, private nonprofit organizations developing summer camps to help children experience the great outdoors, or Thomas Cook (a commercial tour operator) creating traveler's checks to help people feel secure when they travel, leisure service professionals have always demonstrated a desire to make people's lives better. This is an important element of the servant leadership philosophy.

An Entrepreneurial Spirit

The entrepreneurial spirit may be defined as a belief in innovative ideas that result in quality products or services which will benefit both those who use the product and those who developed it. It also implies creativity, a willingness to take risks, and innovation.

Changes in Technology

Successful parks, recreation, and leisure service organizations have always been able to respond to societal changes that are going on around them. As Jane Addams in 1893 wrote, "the one thing to be dreaded in the settlement (house movement) is that it lose its flexibility, its power of quick adaptation, its readiness to change its methods as its environment may demand." Technology is growing and changing at an astonishing rate; it has been increasing in usability and accessibility for the masses, and because of this, it impacts leisure.

To be successful, leisure service programs must build on their past by going forward to meet and create their future. Programs will need to continue to respond to societal changes in innovative ways to empower individuals and communities to grow and develop.

Understanding the Benefits of Leisure Programs

Today's complex world demands that parks, recreation, and leisure service providers understand societal changes as well as the specific benefits customers expect from recreational programs. This knowledge is vital for programmers when planning and developing programs to meet constituent needs. In an attempt to accomplish this task many leisure services organizations (especially public leisure service organizations) are embracing a benefits-based approach to providing services.

A benefits approach to leisure has evolved from benefits-based management (BBM) theory which encourages recreation providers to consider a broad model for explaining benefits in which funders and managers understand the long-term benefits of participating in leisure and recreation programs. Within such a model, benefits are defined as:

- The realization of desired and satisfying on-site psychological experiences;

- Changes that are viewed to be advantageous or improvements in condition (gains) to individuals (i.e., psychological and physiological), groups, society, or even to another entity such as an endangered species; and

- The prevention of a worse condition (Driver, Brown & Peterson, 1991).

In this regard, benefits-based management is turning out to be a major catalyst in helping to dispel a popular myth: that parks, recreation, and leisure agencies provide something of value, but only as long as the pleasurable experience lasts. Benefits-based management moves the leisure profession forward by integrating the concept that value is added to people's lives *following* on-site recreation participation (Driver, Brown & Peterson, 1991). For example, Figure 1.5 identifies a variety of immediate benefits and potential long-term benefits of a couple hiking together in a natural area.

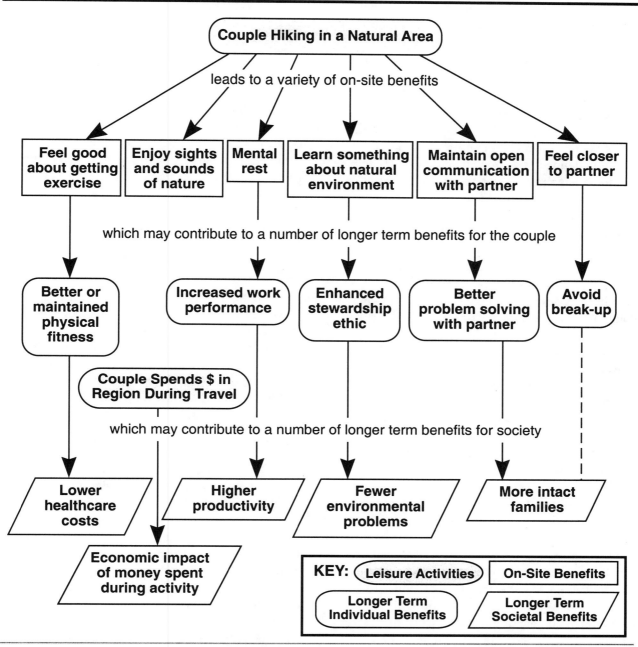

Figure 1.5   Benefits Chain of Causality (Adapted from Driver and Bruns, in press)

According to Driver and Bruns (in press) the fundamental question raised by a benefits approach to leisure is

> [W]hy should a particular leisure service be provided? The answer to this question is formulated in terms of clearly defined positive and negative consequences of delivering that service with the objective being to optimize net benefits—or to add as much value as possible. To do this, leisure policy analysts and managers must understand what values would be added by each leisure service provided, articulate those values, and understand how to capture them (p. 4).

Thus, it is important for programmers and managers to understand the immediate and potential long-term benefits connected to their programs and work to maximize these benefit opportunities.

Individual Benefits of Leisure

There are signs everywhere that people are concerned with improving the quality of their lives. They want a higher degree of life satisfaction—typically defined as a stronger sense of well-being and more happiness (Shichman & Cooper, 1984). In a Time/CNN poll conducted in the late 1980s, seven out of ten people indicated that they wanted to slow down their lives—"Earning a living today requires so much more effort that it is difficult to find time to enjoy life" (as cited in United Way, 1992, p. 22). Leisure can play an important role in meeting this desire for a better quality of life by contributing to the daily well-being of an individual.

In examining the actual benefits of leisure participation Driver and Bruns (in press) have identified five categories of both individual (e.g., psychological, psychophysiological) and social benefits of leisure (e.g., sociological, economic, environmental). Table 1.1 presents a variety of specific benefits in each of these categories. Many of these benefits were substantiated by a 1992 study which asked 1,305 respondents about specific activities they had participated in during the last 12 months, and then asked about the benefits they received from that participation. The results of that study are presented in Table 1.2 (page 10). In examining the results, Godbey, Graefe and James (1993) call attention to what respondents did *not* mention. While respondents clearly saw parks, recreation, and leisure service organizations as benefiting the entire community, not one of the respondents mentioned services to the poor, the disadvantaged, or ethnic minorities as a benefit. Similarly, the study found environmental benefits secondary to personal and social benefits. These are both areas needing to be addressed by leisure professionals.

Despite wanting the benefits of leisure, many individuals find obtaining them difficult. Thus, leisure service programs are needed to help people experience leisure. For example, lack of time is often cited as one of the major constraints for individuals in experiencing leisure (Jackson, 1994; Jackson & Henderson, 1995; Lankford, DeGraaf, Edginton &

Neal, 1996). This seems to be related to what many sociologists have identified as time famine for many Americans. There is some disagreement over the cause of time famine. While Schor (1991) has proposed that free time has evaporated over the last two decades as a result of Americans working more hours, Robinson and Godbey (1997) argue that free time has continued to increase. They do acknowledge, however, that people feel more rushed and believe they have less free time now than in the past. Many attribute this to the rapid pace of contemporary society. Regardless of the cause, people are feeling a time crunch, and this has led to a paradox inherent in leisure. In the past it may have been possible to allow leisure experiences to "just happen;" today individuals need to consciously make time for leisure.

The implications of time famine for leisure service programs are diverse and include helping individuals create time for leisure, as well as preparing and educating individuals to use their free time wisely. According to Robinson and Godbey (1997) leisure service programmers can create programs that help individuals "back up and see what they have missed, accepting the gift of time" (p. 318).

Social Benefits of Leisure

In addition to meeting personal needs, leisure also enhances satisfaction in community life. In fact, leisure opportunities within a community have been found to be the strongest predictor of overall satisfaction with the community (Allen & Beattie, 1984). Leisure experiences have also been identified as an ideal medium for helping participants gain a multicultural perspective in their lives. Through ethnic festivals, travel, involvement with different people and new leisure experiences, many participants are helped to move past the biases of prejudice. In this way, the free flow of ideas and sharing through the medium of leisure benefits all of society. For example, in the United States, sharply contrasting leisure interests, values, and patterns of involvement help to make American society a rich mosaic of nonwork experiences and personal enrichment across a variety of subcultures. People learn a tremendous amount through leisure.

Dustin (1989) identified leisure experiences for children (in the form of organized camping) as an environment where children and youth can prepare

Table 1.1 Specific Types and General Categories of Benefits Which Have Been Attributed to Leisure by Research (Source: Driver & Bruns, in press)

Personal Benefits — Psychological	Personal Benefits — Psychophysiological
Better Mental Health and Health Maintenance Holistic sense of wellness Catharsis Positive changes in mood and emotion Stress management (i.e., prevention, mediation, and restoration) Prevention of, or reduced, depression/anxiety/anger *Personal Development and Growth* Self-confidence　Self-reliance Self-competence　Self-assurance Values clarification　Humility Leadership　Aesthetic enhancement Adaptability　Creativity enhancement Spiritual growth　Cognitive efficiency Problem solving　Nature learning Tolerance　Balanced living Environmental awareness/understanding Balanced competitiveness Independence/autonomy Improved academic/cognitive performance Sense of control over one's life Prevention of problems to at-risk youth Acceptance of one's responsibility Cultural/historic awareness/learning/appreciation *Personal Appreciation and Satisfaction* Sense of freedom　Self-actualization Flow/absorption　Exhilaration Stimulation　Sense of adventure Challenge　Nostalgia Creative expression　Aesthetic appreciation Nature appreciation　Spirituality Quality of life/Life satisfaction Positive change in mood and/or emotion	Improved control and prevention of diabetes Increased bone mass and strength in children Prevention of colon cancer Reduced spinal problems Decreased body fat/obesity/weight control Improved neuropsychological functioning Reduced incidence of disease Improved bladder control for the elderly Increased life expectancy Management of menstrual cycles Management of arthritis Improved functioning of the immune system Reduced or prevented hypertension Reduced serum cholesterol and triglycerides Reduced consumption of alcohol and use of tobacco Increased muscle strength and healthier connective tissue Cardiovascular benefits (including prevention of strokes) Respiratory benefits (increased lung capacity, benefits to people with asthma)

Social and Cultural Benefits	
Ethnic identity	Community satisfaction
Social support	Family bonding
Reciprocity/sharing	Social mobility
Cultural identity	Cultural continuity
Enhanced world-view	Community integration
Reduced social alienation	
Pride in community/nation (pride in place)	
Community/political involvement	
Social bonding/cohesion/cooperation	
Conflict resolution/harmony	
Support democratic ideal of freedom	
Nurturance of others	
Understanding and tolerance of others	
Environmental awareness, sensitivity	
Socialization/acculturation	
Prevention of social problems by at-risk youth	
Developmental benefits of children	
Cultural/historical awareness and appreciation	
Greater community involvement in environmental decision making	

Environmental Benefits

Environmental ethic
Maintenance of physical facilities
Stewardship/preservation of options
Public involvement in environmental issues
Maintenance of natural scientific laboratories
Preservation of particular natural sites and areas
Improved relationships with natural world
Understanding of human dependency on the natural world
Preservation of cultural/heritage/historic sites and areas
Environmental protection—Ecosystem sustainability and species diversity

Economic Benefits	
Reduced health costs	Increased productivity
Decreased job turnover	Less work absenteeism
Reduced on the job accidents	
Local and regional economic growth	
Contribution to net national economic development	
International balance of payments (from tourism)	

Table 1.2   Benefits of Leisure (Source: Godbey, Graefe & James, 1993)

Specific Individual Benefits	Count	Percent
Exercise, Fitness, Conditioning	236	11.5
Relaxation and Peace	125	6.1
Open Space	88	4.3
Place for Kids to Go	67	3.3
Nature	63	3.1
Family Time Together	57	2.8
Fun and Entertainment	56	2.7
Enjoy Being Outdoors/ Natural Resources	52	2.5
Place to Go	51	2.5
Place for Recreation	51	2.5

Specific Household Benefits	Count	Percent
Exercise, Fitness, Conditioning	144	13.5
Relaxation and Peace	58	5.4
Fun and Entertainment	53	5.0
Place for Kids to Go	46	4.3
Place to Play	41	3.8
Facilities, Play Area for Kids	33	3.1
Family Time Together	32	3.0
Keep Kids Busy/Occupied	27	2.5
Open Space	26	2.4
Enjoy Being Outdoors/ Natural Resources	25	2.3

Specific Community Benefits	Count	Percent
Exercise, Fitness, Conditioning	136	6.4
Place for Kids to Go	132	6.2
Gathering Place	87	4.1
Activities	79	3.7
Community Awareness	79	3.7
Place for Recreation	75	3.5
Fun and Entertainment	68	3.2
Family Time Together	66	3.1
Good for Kids	65	3.0
Place to Go	63	2.9
Play Organized Sports	63	2.9
Keep Kids Off Streets	61	2.9

for an active adult role in democracy. The premise of Dustin's argument is that children live in an increasingly complex world which is difficult for them to understand. Because of this it is easy for young people to lose perspective, and remain unable to see the connections between their actions and the consequences of these actions when the consequences are global in scale. For instance, if a youngster wastes water resources by letting the water run while brushing her teeth, the water reserves for the globe are reduced, yet the youth rarely notices a change in her own life. However, in camp settings (a leisure venue) it is a different story. The link between an individual's actions and the consequences of those actions is brought down to a scale that is more easily understood by the youth.

For healthful living most people agree that the process of learning to work and play as a member of a group is an extremely important part of a child's overall development. Becoming active, accepted members of a subgroup contributes to positive self-concept and sound mental health (Kraus & Scanlan, 1983). Small group experiences help children accept differences among their peers and encourage them to learn how to function in the democratic system (DeGraaf & DeGraaf, 1994).

As society changes, adults may find it increasingly difficult to build the "social capital" needed to create a sense of community. Putnam (1995) defines social capital as "features of social life—networks, norms, and trust—that enable participants to act together more effectively to pursue shared objectives" (as cited in Robinson & Godbey, 1997, p. 168). This is a critical element to the success of democracy. Putnam documented the decline of social capital in America as reflected by decreased membership in voluntary organizations, such as the Boy Scouts, the League of Women Voters, Parent Teacher Associations, and the American Red Cross.

From the context of a benefits approach to leisure, the concept of social capital is an important component of recreation programming. Finding ways to reinvent and encourage social capital is important and may ultimately determine whether democracy, as our society knows it, will continue on a local level. Building social capital is one of the major ways in which all parks, recreation, and leisure organizations whatever their service orientation—private, public, commercial—serve society. Commercial leisure service organizations may be involved on an individual level assisting individuals in building social capital with family and friends. Public organizations, on the other hand, might be more involved at a community level. Strengthening the social fabric of communities through leisure experiences can help build neighborhood ties and strengthen intergroup and intergenerational relations (Kraus, 1990). This enables leisure professionals to rebuild the social capital of the communities they serve.

Leisure Service Professionals

Many people feel that the increasing number of leisure choices for participants, the declining social capital in communities, and growing time famine are just some of the challenges that must be overcome in planning, implementing, and evaluating leisure service programs. Addressing problems such as these takes a tremendous commitment on the part of leisure service organizations. In addition to commitment it takes energetic, skilled professionals who desire to serve others and live with a servant leadership orientation.

Leisure service programmers may be found working in a variety of agencies and organizations including public agencies (e.g., local, state and federal government), private, nonprofit agencies (i.e., religious sponsored organizations, youth serving organizations, nonsectarian sponsored organizations, organizations serving special populations, relief organizations, social service organizations, hospitals, conservation organizations, service clubs), and commercial organizations (e.g., travel tour operators, entertainment services, theme parks). Because of leisure programmers' widespread impact, their role as leisure service professionals is to understand the power and potential of leisure service programs to meet desired ends (benefits) of constituents. Whether the leisure services professional is involved in direct leadership, organizing a specific aspect of a program or event, or managing a leisure facility, she or he is pivotal to the organization's success.

Characteristics and Skills of Leisure Service Professionals

First and foremost, the leisure services programmer is a professional. According to Edginton, Hanson, Edginton and Hudson (1998) the efforts of a professional are directed toward service rather than simply financial remuneration. The professional is concerned about the overall well-being of participants and works for their growth and development. For example, in a study about youth leaders, McLaughlin (1994) identified the characteristics of leaders who make a difference in the lives of youth in American inner cities (see Sidebar 1.1). Some of the characteristics the leaders exemplified were an ability to

see potential in youth rather than pathology; to commit to help youth by giving back to the community; and to believe in themselves that they could make a difference in the lives of others. Although specific to youth, these characteristics may be generalized to programming for all populations. Focusing on the potential of participants rather than their problems; focusing on the needs of participants first; seeing work as a mission or vocation instead of a job; and finding a personalized style may all be

---

Sidebar 1.1 The Characteristics of Wizards
(McLaughlin, 1994)

Wizards See Potential, Not Pathology

The youth of inner cities are not people to be fixed, remediated, or otherwise controlled but as young people with promise, largely ignored, wrongly perceived, and badly served by society at large. (p. 96)

Focusing on Youth

Successful leaders' commitment to youth also means that they focus on youth before organization, program, or activity. Wizards' personal agendas contrast with those of well-intended leaders whose primary passion is their program or institution.

A Sense of Efficacy

Wizards have a firm conviction that they can and do make a difference in the lives of teenage youth from even the bleakest urban settings. *They do not believe it is too late to save "these kids."*

Giving Back

Part of a Wizard's consuming commitment to youth results from their wanting to give back what others gave them as they grew up. Wizards also hope that their adolescents, in turn, will develop a commitment to give opportunities and brighter futures back to others. All of them see their work as a mission and vocation, not simply a job or even a career in the traditional sense.

Authenticity

Each Wizard manifests a different personality and programmatic interest to make programs that make a difference. There is no one-size-fits-all program. Wizards try to mesh their personal talents with their work.

considered important elements to be successful in programming for and with a variety of individuals and groups. This focus also supports the premise of servant leadership.

Skills for leisure service professionals are often grouped into three areas: technical skills, human relation skills, and conceptual skills (Jordan, 1996). Technical skills are those that are specific to accomplishing tasks. They enable a person to do a particular job or task. Examples include managing a pool at an aquatics center, leading a game, and recording a city festival on videotape. Human relation skills are those skills and techniques that involve relationships with people. Understanding group dynamics, facilitating cooperation and trust, and communicating with participants all fit within the human relations realm of leadership. Conceptual skills include the ability to analyze, anticipate, and see the big picture of programs and activities. Critical thinking, problem solving, creativity, and being able to handle ambiguity are commonly considered conceptual skills.

In developing these skills, Godbey (1997) has identified a number of personal strategies for those who will work in leisure services in the 21st century. These strategies center on being flexible and innovative in serving others (see Figure 1.6). The strategies include:

Serving Others

An ethic of service will continue to distinguish leisure services in the public, private nonprofit, and commercial sectors. As a leisure services programmer the emphasis must always be on the people served and the benefits provided rather than the program itself. Leisure programs should not be thought of as an end, but rather

> …a means to an end—a higher quality of life, increased learning, better health, improved physical fitness, more appreciation and understanding of nature, improved morale, and less crime are among the many benefits . . . the worth of the profession (and the professional) is not linked to recreation, but to the benefits recreation, under some conditions and in some circumstances, can provide. (Godbey, 1997, p. 228)

Becoming an Entrepreneur

Peter Drucker, a noted management theorist, believes that entrepreneurship involves systematic innovation. According to Drucker (1985), systematic innovation consists of the purposeful and organized search for changes and systematic analysis of the opportunities such changes might offer for economic or social innovation. A new entrepreneurial spirit has emerged in the United States and Canada, reflected by the number of new jobs that emerged over the past few decades. These new jobs result from entrepreneurial ventures in the service and information sectors of society, with many in the leisure services area. "Entrepreneurs serve as pacesetters of opportunity, a challenging and demanding role. Their work is dynamic, diverse, inventive, and creative. Entrepreneurs produce new ways of meeting needs, work to improve existing products

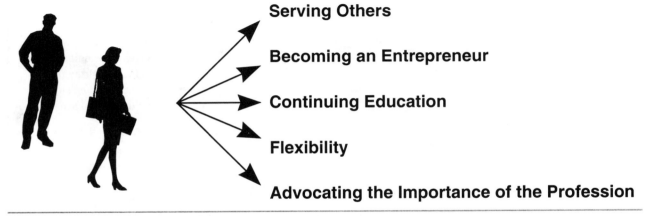

- Serving Others
- Becoming an Entrepreneur
- Continuing Education
- Flexibility
- Advocating the Importance of the Profession

Figure 1.6   Personal Strategies for Leisure Services Professionals in the 21st Century

and services, and respond to changing demographic conditions" (Edginton, Jordan, DeGraaf & Edginton, 1998, p. 296).

Seeking Continuous Learning Opportunities

As the primary basis of the economy becomes knowledge, it becomes imperative that parks, recreation, and leisure service professionals stay current with the world around them through lifelong learning. Professionals seek out these experiences at professional meetings, conferences, through opportunities provided by university extension programs, and through self-education.

Becoming More Flexible

In a world of rapid and continuing change, the ability to adapt to changing circumstances is critical. One of the worst ways that professionals in leisure services sometimes lose flexibility is to assume that an issue doesn't concern them because it doesn't have 'leisure' as a central theme.

> Leisure is among the more diverse and complex ideas in the world and, perhaps unfortunately, it relates to the myriad of issues that concern freedom, pleasure, human growth and understanding, health, nature, spirit, learning and other huge ideas. Becoming more flexible means the boundaries of what is relevant to you must become more flexible. (Godbey, 1997, p. 226)

Calling Attention to the Importance of What We Do

Leisure services professionals must believe in the power and potential of leisure programs to affect change in the lives of individuals and society. Leisure services are critical components of society, not just "frosting on the cake." Leisure services can contribute to the creation of an environment that nourishes the human potential (Dustin, McAvoy & Schultz, 1995). Leisure service professionals must also believe in their own ability to make a difference in the world. Little things do matter.

Leisure programmers blend these skills and strategies in order to design programs that facilitate leisure experiences for participants. In the programming process programmers manipulate a variety of variables in the physical, natural, and social environments which help participants experience the conditions needed to produce a leisure experience (i.e., freedom, perceived competence, intrinsic motivation, locus of control, and positive affect). Within this framework it is important to remember that programmers do not produce recreation experiences and benefits, but instead produce *opportunities* for recreationists to produce these experiences and benefits for themselves. Thus, leisure services managers produce recreation opportunities, just as teachers produce learning opportunities and doctors produce health-restoring opportunities. Identifying the process of creating, implementing, and evaluating programs, and understanding how programmers can manipulate the variables associated with this process is a recurring theme throughout this text.

Programming: A Servant Leadership Approach

In designing opportunities for leisure we believe there is a need for a new type of leadership and programming model, a model that puts serving others—including customers, employees, and the community—as the number one priority. As a result, we advocate a servant leadership approach as the foundation upon which leisure and recreation programming should be based for all types of recreation and leisure organizations. We believe this emphasis on serving others stresses the similarities between various commercial, private nonprofit, and public organizations rather than their differences. Although the philosophy of each of these types of organizations will impact programming decisions, the underlying desire to serve will remain constant.

The term *servant leadership* was first coined in 1970 by Robert Greenleaf. Since then this concept has been utilized as a specific leadership and management approach in a variety of fields. Spears (1995) identified servant leadership as an approach that

> attempts to simultaneously enhance the personal growth of workers and improve the quality and caring of our many institutions through a combination of teamwork

and community, personal involvement in decision making and ethical and caring behavior (p. 4).

Table 1.3 identifies ten characteristics of a servant leader.

A servant leadership approach to delivering services encourages partnerships between constituents and professionals. Unfortunately, professionals are often too busy dealing with day-to-day crises and issues rather than listening to customers and finding innovative solutions to problems as they develop. Within a servant leadership model, parks, recreation, and leisure professionals need to remember to listen, realizing:

that our field is experimental, should be experimental and will not survive unless it continues to be experimental. It is not written in stone what a playground should

---

Table 1.3   Characteristics of Servant Leaders (Spears, 1995)

Listening	Traditionally, leaders have been valued for their communication and decision-making skills. Servant leaders must reinforce these important skills by making a deep commitment to listening intently to others. Listening, coupled with regular periods of reflections, are essential to the growth of the servant leader.
Empathy	Servant leaders strive to understand and empathize with others. People need to be accepted and recognized for their special and unique spirits. The most successful servant leaders are those who have become skilled empathetic listeners.
Healing	Learning to heal is a powerful force for transformation and integration. Many people have broken spirits and suffer from a variety of emotional hurts. Although this is a part of being human, servant leaders recognize that they have an opportunity to help make whole those with whom they come in contact.
Awareness	General awareness, and especially self-awareness, strengthens the servant leader. Awareness also aids in understanding issues involving ethics and values. It enables one to view most situations from a more integrated position.
Persuasion	Servant leaders rely on persuasion rather than positional authority, in making decisions. Servant leaders seek to convince others, rather than coerce compliance. The servant leader is effective at building consensus within groups.
Conceptualization	Servant leaders seek to nurture their abilities to dream great dreams. Servant leaders must seek a delicate balance between conceptualization and day-to-day focus.
Foresight	Foresight is a characteristic that enables servant leaders to understand lessons from the past, the realities of the present, and the likely consequence of a decision for the future.
Stewardship	Stewardship is defined as holding something in trust for another. Servant leadership, like stewardship, assumes first and foremost a commitment to serving the needs of others. It also emphasizes the use of openness and persuasion, rather than control.
Commitment to the Growth of People	Servant leaders believe that people have an intrinsic value and must be included in decisions affecting their lives.
Building Community	Servant leaders are aware of the need to build community and actively seek to involve people in the process.

look like, or that there should be playgrounds. Nor can we say what a park should look like, how and to whom leisure skills should be taught or who should teach them. As Cranz (1982) so wisely observed, many recreation and park professionals have developed the mistaken idea concomitant with professionalization that providing park and recreation services is a matter of technology when in reality it is a process of cultural discovery. Said another way, it is a process rather than a product. (Godbey, 1991, p. 5)

Within recreation and leisure organizations, the metaphor of servant leader is a powerful model to guide the recreation programming process. Today, constituents want leaders and programmers who will listen and empower rather than dominate and dictate.

In some ways the term servant leadership is an oxymoron since people commonly view a leader as one who leads and a servant as ones who follows. Yet, this is part of the inherent value of the concept of servant leadership; the importance of both leadership and followership are emphasized. All of us both lead and follow. One is not better than the other; in the course of our lives we are called to do both. Leisure professionals must learn to be good leaders by learning to be good followers, by listening to participants and by helping them lead so we as leisure professionals can follow. This is also true in programming. We must truly listen to our constituents and follow their lead before we make global statements about appropriate programming.

Summary

All parks, recreation, and leisure s_ tions are concerned with programming. After all, programs are the vehicle professionals use to deliver leisure benefits to both individuals and society. This chapter has laid the foundation for understanding the recreation programming process by presenting a number of important concepts. First and foremost, recreation programmers must understand the five prevailing factors that characterize the leisure experience—freedom, perceived competence, intrinsic motivation, locus of control, and positive affect. Freedom implies choice, spontaneity, and being free from constraints that inhibit participation. Perceived competence refers to the skills that an individual believes she or he possesses that will contribute to successful participation. Intrinsic motivation refers to an individual's desire to participate in leisure experiences based on personal needs and desires, rather than external motivation. Locus of control refers to the need of an individual to control elements of the leisure experience once she or he is engaged in the process, and positive affect refers to a sense of enjoyment. Understanding these factors as they relate to satisfying leisure experiences is imperative if leisure service programmers are going to design and implement leisure programs and services to meet the needs and demands of a variety of people.

Second, the concept of benefits-based programming was introduced. A benefits approach to leisure encourages a broad understanding of the long-term and short-term benefits provided by the leisure experience. These serve as the driving force behind programming approaches.

Finally, servant leadership was presented as a philosophical approach to programming leisure experiences. Servant leadership emphasizes increased service to others by encouraging shared decision making and a sense of community. Such an approach emphasizes the three factors that have shaped all forms of leisure services at their best: the desire to help people, an entrepreneurial spirit, and the ability to respond to societal changes.

References

Addams, J. (1893). The subjective necessity for social settlements: A new impulse to an old gospel. In T.Y. Croswell (Ed.), *Philanthropy and social progress*. New York, NY: Thomas Y. Crowell and Company.

Allen, L. and Beattie, R. (1984). The role of leisure as an indicator of overall satisfaction with community life. *Journal of Leisure Research, 16*(2), 99-109.

Boden, W.P. and Mitchell, E.D. (1923). *The theory of organized play*. New York, NY: Barnes.

Carpenter, G. and Howe, C. (1985). *Programming leisure experiences*. Englewood Cliffs, NJ: Prentice Hall.

Csikszentmihalyi, M. (1975). *Beyond boredom and anxiety*. San Francisco, CA: Jossey-Bass.

Curtis, H. (1915). *The practical conduct of play*. New York, NY: Macmillan.

DeGraaf, D. and DeGraaf, K. (1994). *Planning and supervising camp programs*. Washington, DC: U.S. Army Youth Services.

Driver, B.L. and Bruns, D.H. (in press). Concepts and uses of the benefits approach to leisure. In E.L. Jackson and T.L. Burton (Eds). *Leisure studies: Prospects for the twenty-first century*. State College, PA: Venture Publishing, Inc.

Driver, B.L., Brown, P.J. and Peterson, G.L. (Eds). (1991). *Benefits of leisure*. State College, PA: Venture Publishing, Inc.

Drucker, P. (1985). *Innovation and entrepreneurship*. New York, NY: Harper and Row.

Dustin, D. (1989, September/October). Magical outcomes of organized camping: The total camp environment, *Camping Magazine, 62*(1), 31-35.

Dustin, D., McAvoy, L. and Schultz, J. (1995). *Stewards of access/Custodians of choice*. Champaign, IL: Sagamore Publishing.

Edginton, C., Jordan, D., DeGraaf, D. and Edginton, S. (1998). *Leisure and life satisfaction: Foundational perspectives*. Dubuque, IA: McGraw-Hill.

Edginton, C., Hanson, C., Edginton, S. and Hudson, S. (1998). *Leisure programming: A service centered and benefits approach*. Dubuque, IA: McGraw-Hill.

Ellis, M. (1973). *Why people play*. Englewood Cliffs, NJ: Prentice Hall.

Godbey, G. (1997). *Leisure and leisure services in the 21st century*. State College, PA: Venture Publishing, Inc.

Godbey, G. (1991). Recreation and leisure in the 1990s: They are playing our song. *J. B. Nash Lecture* presented at the American Alliance of Health, Physical Education, Recreation and Dance National Convention, 6 April, San Francisco, CA.

Godbey, G., Graefe, A. and James, S. (1993). Reality and perception—Where do we fit in? *Parks and Recreation, 28*(1), 76-83, 111-112.

Gray, D. (1969). The case for compensatory recreation, *Parks and Recreation. 4*(4), 23-24.

Greenleaf, R. (1977). *Servant leadership: A journey into the nature of legitimate power and greatness*. New York, NY: Paulist Press.

Gunter, B. (1987). The leisure experience: Selected properties. *Journal of Leisure Research, 19*(2), 115-130.

Jackson, E. (1994). Activity specific constraints on leisure participation, *Journal of Park and Recreation Administration, 12*(2), 33-50.

Jackson, E. and Henderson, K. (1995) Gender-based analysis of leisure constraints, *Leisure Sciences, 17*, 31-51.

Jordan, D. (1996). *Leadership in leisure services: Making a difference*. State College, PA: Venture Publishing, Inc.

Kraus, R. (1990). *Recreation and leisure in modern society, 3rd ed*. Glenview, IL: Scott, Foresman & Co.

Kraus, R. (1985). *Recreation program planning today*. Glenview, IL: Scott, Foresman & Co.

Kraus, R. and Scanlan, M. (1983). *Introduction to camp counseling*. Englewood Cliffs, NJ: Prentice Hall.

Lankford, S., DeGraaf, D., Edginton, C. and Neal, L. (1996). A comparison of barriers to leisure and sport participation in the United States: Implications for Hong Kong. *Hong Kong Recreation Review*, pp. 43-46.

McLaughlin, M. (1994). *Urban sanctuaries: Neighborhood organizations in the lives and futures of inner-city youth*. San Francisco, CA: Jossey-Bass.

Neulinger, J. (1974). *The psychology of leisure*. Springfield, IL: Charles C. Thomas Publisher.

Putnam, R. (1995, January). Bowling alone: America's declining social capital. *Journal of Democracy*, *6*(1), 65-78.

Robinson, J. and Godbey, G. (1997). *Time for life: The surprising ways Americans use their time*. University Park, PA: The Pennsylvania State University Press.

Samdahl, D. (1988). A symbolic interactionist model of leisure: Theory and empirical support. *Leisure Sciences*, *10*(1), 27-29.

Schor, J. (1991). *The overworked American: The unexpected decline in leisure*. New York, NY: Basic Books.

Sessoms, D. and Stevenson, J. (1981). *Leadership and group dynamics in recreation services*. Boston, MA: Allyn and Bacon.

Shichman, S. and Cooper, E. (1984). Life satisfaction and sex role concept, *Sex Roles*, *11*(3/4), 227-240.

Spears, L. (1995). Servant leadership and the Greenleaf legacy. In L. Spear (Ed.). *Reflections on Leadership: How Robert K. Greenleaf's Theory of Servant Leadership influenced today's top management thinkers* (pp. 1–16). New York, NY: John Wiley & Son.

United Way of America. (1992). *What lies ahead: A decade of decision*. Alexandria, VA: United Way Strategic Institute.

Chapter Two

Service and Quality in Programming

The servant-leader is servant first. It begins with the natural feeling that one wants to serve, to serve first. Then conscious choice brings one to aspire to lead. The difference manifests itself in the care taken by the servant first to make sure that other people's highest priority needs are being served. The best test is: do those served, grow as persons; do they, while being served become healthier, wiser, freer, more autonomous, more likely themselves to become servants? And, what is the effect on the least privileged in society: will he [sic] benefit; or at least, will he not be further deprived?

Greenleaf, 1991, p. 7

Programming leisure experiences for or with people can be done in a variety of ways and requires a holistic view of both the individual and the community. This chapter examines some of the overarching tenets to providing leisure services, as well as how recreation programs have been planned in the past. In addition, an entrepreneurial and empowerment model are offered as approaches to delivering recreation programs.

John Muir, the great American naturalist, once stated, "When we try to pick out anything by itself, we find it hitched to everything else in the universe" (Sierra Club Staff, 1992, p. 73), and so it is with programming leisure experiences. There are a vast number of factors parks, recreation, and leisure service programmers must be aware of in planning recreation programs including demographic, political, economic, and societal factors. As was stated in Chapter One, one of the characteristics of successful leisure service organizations is the ability to respond to societal changes going on around them. For example, the National Recreation and Park Association (NRPA) has been engaged in a process of identifying critical issues and trends in society and identifying a public parks and recreation agenda (see Table 2.1, page 20). This information is then made available to all in the profession so that decisions appropriate to the local community might be made on a local level.

In examining the list of critical issues and trends that are applicable to all aspects of leisure services, one sees that many focus on the need to deliver quality services. They also identify a mission or values orientation for providing programs. As a result, this chapter will focus initially on examining the leisure experience as a service, considering the role of quality in providing leisure programs, and understanding the importance of serving both individuals and society through programs. It will also address various approaches to the delivery of leisure services.

The Leisure Experience as a Service

The most marked change in the structure of developed economies in the last half of the twentieth century has been the societal transformation from a manufacturing to a service economy. In the United States alone, the percentage of workers employed in the service sector has risen from a mere 30% in

Table 2.1   Public Parks and Recreation in the 21st Century (Source: Mobley & Toalson, 1992)

Critical Issues and Trends	Parks and Recreation Agenda
Change is the norm.	Parks and recreation professionals must be able and willing to identify, analyze, promote, and respond to change in society.
There is a strong trend toward greater participation in the decision-making process by citizens and employees.	New leadership techniques will be required of park and recreation professionals to facilitate consensus building.
The field may be losing its mission orientation.	Parks and recreation must return to its heritage of serving all people. Renewed attention must be given to the poor and their impact on recreation and parks.
Multicultural diversity will continue to grow rapidly.	Parks and recreation must find ways to celebrate the variety of cultures within the community.
Substance abuse will continue as a major problem.	Parks and recreation programs must provide alternatives to the use of drugs and develop self-esteem in our youth.
The wellness movement will continue to grow.	Parks, recreation, and leisure services must facilitate and identify directly with the growing wellness movement.
Success will depend on an organization's ability to build cooperative relationships and establish rewards and coalitions with other organizations.	Park and recreation organizations must work with other agencies building networks and coalitions to achieve success.
Lifelong learning will become necessity.	Parks and recreation must make a commitment to continuing education and professional development.
Success depends on quality of service.	The success of parks and recreation will depend on the quality of service provided to the people we serve. It is essential to improve the image of the profession so that the relationship between recreation and parks programs, and values and contemporary issues is clearly apparent.
Tourism has emerged as one of the world's growing industries and an increasingly important part of leisure expression.	Parks and recreation must be involved in mutually beneficial partnerships with tourism.
The environment will increasingly become a focus of international concern.	The park and recreation profession must take its rightful place as a leader in shaping environmental policy.
The mission of parks, recreation, and leisure services is extremely broad and loosely defined.	The park and recreation profession must develop and articulate clearly defined mission statements, goals, and objectives for the field.

1900 to an estimated 80% in 1995 (Rust, Zahorik & Keiningham, 1996). Within the broad framework of service sectors the following classification of services is offered by Payne (1993): retail and wholesale; transportation, distribution and storage; banking and insurance; real estate; communications and information services; public utilities, government, and defense; healthcare; business, professional, and personal services; recreational and hospitality services (leisure services); and education and other nonprofit causes.

The service nature of leisure service organizations as well as the increasing demand for leisure services cannot be denied. People are now collecting experiences (services) as they once collected things. For example, Holloway (1986) writes that tourism experiences

> are, in my view, to become deeper and more meaningful over time, so that tourists instead of merely collecting visits to sites in a whirlwind tour of Europe will begin to collect interactive experiences, in which people will become as important as places. This desire to meet people at an individual and meaningful level will help to encourage the movement of tourists away from the present centers of mass tourism, where relationships between hosts and guests are ephemeral and impersonal. (p. 10)

To be prepared to give individual customers the experiences they seek, leisure providers must first understand the nature of delivering services. Because service is not a single dimension item, it can be difficult to define and understand. A traditional starting place for defining services is understanding how they differ from products. It is frequently argued that services have unique characteristics that differentiate them from goods or manufactured products. The four most commonly identified characteristics ascribed to services are:

Intangibility

In services what is actually purchased is the experience rather than a tangible thing. As a result, criteria on which to evaluate the experience can be complex and difficult to capture. For example, a participant involved in a tour of a museum takes nothing tangible home beyond the personal value she or he placed on the experience. Because it comes from within each person, measuring the satisfaction of that intangible experience can be difficult.

Heterogeneity

This refers to the potential for variability in service delivery. This is especially prominent when a large number of employees is involved. The quality of services is largely dependent upon the actions of people. Therefore, the quality of interactions between personnel and customers is likely to vary among staff members. In addition, for individual staff members the quality of interactions may differ from day to day. For example, within aerobic classes some instructors are more requested than others as a result of how participants perceive the class experience.

Inseparability of Production and Consumption

Services are often delivered and experienced simultaneously. This usually requires the presence of both the consumer and the provider during the delivery process, and the service cannot be taken back and exchanged if the customer is not satisfied. The provider can show various examples of the service, but the customer's own ceramic creation, for example, does not exist and cannot be shown.

Perishability

It is not possible to store services in inventory. For example, a camping experience (service) is not like a can of soup which can be produced and stocked for later consumption. Services are consumed as they develop.

Using these characteristics by no means fully describes the differences between leisure goods and services—some products have one or more of the above characteristics and not all services display all of these characteristics. For example, in identifying the degree of intangibility of a service Kotler (1991) distinguished four categories along a continuum ranging from a pure good to a pure service.

- A pure tangible good such as sporting equipment (e.g., tennis rackets, golf clubs, and sports shoes) where no services accompany the product.

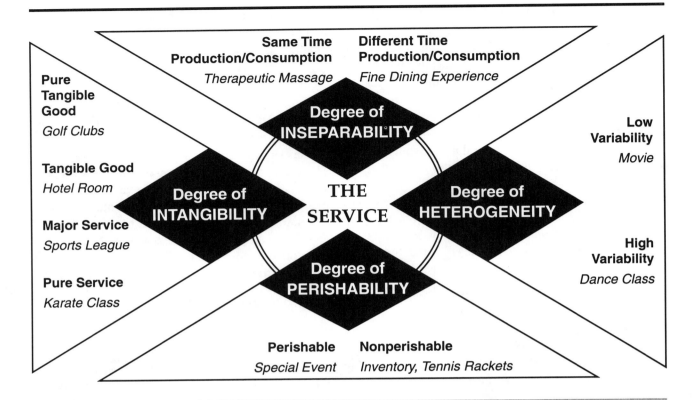

Figure 2.1   The Four Characteristics of a Leisure Service

- A tangible good (e.g., motel or hotel room) with accompanying services to enhance its consumer appeal.

- A major service with accompanying minor goods and services such as a week at camp or an adult sports league.

- A pure service such as a painting class, fitness membership, or childcare.

This categorization helps make it clear why it is difficult to define or generalize services. Services vary considerably over a range of factors. Four of these factors have been presented as continua along which various services differ (Payne, 1993). Services can only be described as having a *tendency* towards intangibility, heterogeneity, inseparability, and perishability. Any given service will display a different combination of each of these four characteristics as illustrated in Figure 2.2. For example, programming in an ice arena is high on tangibility, highly standardized (homogeneous), performed near to the customer, and is perishable. Childcare is less tangible, highly varied (ranges from day camps to baby-sitting), is performed with the customer, and is perishable. Understanding the position of a particular service on each continuum is an important step in not only providing services, but also in incorporating the emerging dimension of quality.

The Concept of Quality

Quality and value have become increasingly important elements in delivering services in the past twenty five years. *Quality—a perception of excellence—is the extent to which the products and services received by the customer equal or exceed expectations.* As Albrecht (1993) notes "the most fundamental change in management's thinking going on today is the shift from managing the boxes on the organizational chart to managing customer outcomes" (p. 10). This quality revolution can be traced back to the years following World War II. This is when American quality control expert, William Deming, began sharing his approach with

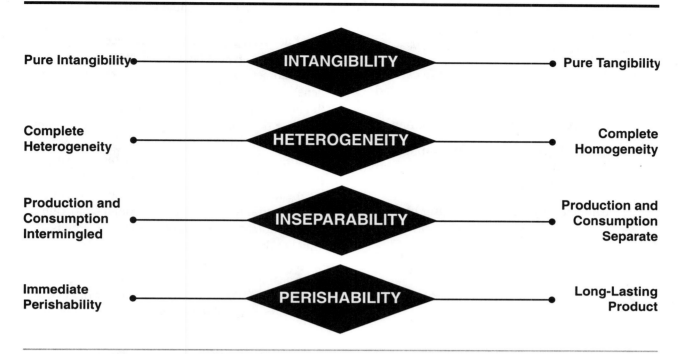

Pure Intangibility	**INTANGIBILITY**	Pure Tangibility
Complete Heterogeneity	**HETEROGENEITY**	Complete Homogeneity
Production and Consumption Intermingled	**INSEPARABILITY**	Production and Consumption Separate
Immediate Perishability	**PERISHABILITY**	Long-Lasting Product

Figure 2.2   The Continua of Service Characteristics

Japanese firms to focus on quality rather than focusing on cutting costs to increase profit margins. Deming asserted that higher quality leads to lower costs and higher productivity, which in turn leads to higher profits, higher share price, creation of more jobs, and more security for everyone involved (Aguayo, 1990). Deming presented 14 points for management to follow which concentrate on removing major roadblocks to quality improvement (see Figure 2.3, page 24).

The essence of Deming's 14 points is focusing on preventing errors before they appear by involving everyone in the organization. The aim is to have employees take pride in their work skills. The early work of Deming and others was focused on product quality, and set the stage for the emergence of a revolution in the way organizations deliver goods and services.

> Call it the customer revolution, the quality revolution, or the service revolution, or whatever you like. All of the various energies and lines of action that businesses are putting forth now are beginning to converge to a single focus: winning and keeping the customer's business by doing

the right things outstandingly well.
(Albrecht, 1993, p. ix)

As recreation programmers, we suggest taking this concept one step further by realizing the importance of delivering customer value; moving beyond customer satisfaction to customer delight.

In this light, it becomes more apparent that the old distinction between product and service is obsolete. Both the service and the product are incomplete pieces of the same element. Only when leisure services programmers combine them into a single, composite entity can we think about quality as a competitive advantage and a way of operating a business. What exists is total customer value—the combination of the tangible and the intangible experienced by the customer during all points of contact with the organization. These shape the participants' perceptions of doing business with that particular organization. The importance of understanding the perceptions of customers cannot be overstated. After all, perception of quality is crucial to the success of a service-oriented business. "It is not enough just to give good service; the customer must perceive the fact that he or she is getting good service" (Albrecht, 1985, p. 48).

1 Create consistency of purpose toward improvement of products and service.

2 Adopt a new philosophy. We can no longer live with commonly accepted levels of delays, mistakes, defective materials, and defective workmanship.

3 Cease dependence on mass inspection. Require instead statistical evidence that quality is built in.

4 End the practice of awarding business on the basis of price tag.

5 Find problems. It is management's job to work continually on the system.

6 Institute modern methods of training on the job.

7 Institute modern methods of supervision of production workers. The responsibility of foremen [sic] must be changed from numbers to quality.

8 Drive out fear, so that everyone may work effectively for the company.

9 Break down barriers between departments.

10 Eliminate numerical goals, posters, and slogans for the workforce; ask for new levels of productivity without providing methods.

11 Eliminate work standards that prescribe numerical quotas.

12 Remove barriers that stand between the hourly worker and his [sic] right to pride in workmanship.

13 Institute a vigorous program of education and retraining.

14 Create a structure in top management that will push every day on the above 13 points.

Figure 2.3   Deming's 14 Points of Quality
(Aguayo, 1990)

Although the intangible nature of delivering leisure services should not be forgotten, the emphasis of delivering quality leisure services must be on the *product* (i.e., the benefits or values received by the customer) as well as the *process* by which those benefits are delivered. In order to concentrate on the total customer experience organizations must embrace the tenets of a new "customer value paradigm." Comparing this new paradigm (i.e., way of looking at the world) to that of the old industrial paradigm allows us to see where organizations have been and where they need to go. The concepts of the industrial revolution differ from the emerging information age in terms of service and adding value to the customer experience—see Table 2.2.

Many leisure service organizations are making the transition to the customer value paradigm. McCarville (1993) identified a number of keys to quality programming which have emerged from the quality services literature.

- *Establish programming priorities.* Programmers must remember to serve constituents rather than simply operate programs. This is the core of servant leadership.

- *Discover customer needs.* Understand what customers want and expect from the recreation and leisure programs the organization provides. Leisure professionals do this through needs assessments and other forms of data gathering.

- *Develop programs from customer needs, wants and expectations.* This requires that leisure professionals utilize the information they learned from data gathering and needs assessments.

- *Identify key program providers.* By making program staff and customers partners in the programming process leisure professionals help identify key people, they empower constituents, and they enhance their responsiveness to constituents.

- *Identify key encounters with clients.* These key interaction points occur between customers and staff, customers and facilities, and between customers

Table 2.2   The Changing Quality Management Paradigm (Adapted from Albrecht, 1992, p. 40)

INDUSTRIAL PARADIGM	DIMENSION	CUSTOMER-VALUE PARADIGM
Pushing programs	**Business Mission**	Adding value Providing benefits
Efficient use of labor Capital drives profit	**Profit Principle**	Customer response to values drives profits
Seen as expendable or replaceable	**Customers**	Seen as appreciating assets with whom organizations must partner to provide programs
Obedient doers: Cogs in a wheel	**Employees**	Highly empowered quality strategists: Optimal discretion
Taskmasters or Presiders	**Supervisors and Executives**	Leaders, Enablers, and Supporters
Evidence of outputs (e.g., number of participants)	**Measurements**	Evidence of customer approval (e.g., Are benefits provided?)
Structure and systems define work life	**Organization**	Structure and systems serve people Agile: Able to respond to change

and other customers. They occur at all phases of program development.

- *Train staff for flexibility*, but when in doubt establish, maintain, and hold to standards.
- *Ask for help.* Successful programs result from endless innovation. As programmers, we should not miss the opportunity to gather input from staff, customers, and other programs in an attempt to increase the quality of programs.

According to McCarville (1993):

the search for program excellence never ends. Excellent programs remain in a state of constant development. Once they cease to develop, they will cease to meet the changing needs of their clientele. (p. 23)

It is one of our responsibilities as leisure services professionals to continually seek this level of excellence.

The Limits of Individual Quality— The Need for Social Responsibility

The importance of delivering quality leisure services within a customer value paradigm is clear; yet such a paradigm is still not complete for several reasons. First is the issue of being able to satisfy all expectations of customers. Many businesses, nonprofit agencies, and other entities that serve others believe that "the customer is always right." This approach—that the customer is always right—is certainly a way to stress quality and guide staff behavior with customers. As a guide it is simple, easy to remember, and clear on what the staff should do. However, as Jandt (1995) has noted,

[A]s an ideal it seems clear, but in practice it doesn't work . . . If a customer makes impossible demands ... the customer leaves dissatisfied, may never return, and probably tells others about your failure. (p. 2)

Jandt (1995) argues that as a result, organizations must look to develop a win-win approach by using negotiation skills in the interaction between a service provider and the service customer. For the service interaction to be successful for both parties over the long term, both the service provider and the customer must feel that each has won. Customers must believe that they received the service they expected at a price they accepted. Furthermore, the service provider must also feel good about providing the service—and that often includes making a profit on the transaction.

Another perspective on quality and excellence is provided by Kouzes and Posner (1993) who note that

> excellence is a noble goal ... to surpass the average and to become superior is what makes for high quality services and products. But one can go too far. One can go beyond excellence to excess. (p. 261)

The result of such excessive emphasis may mean the short-term triumph of an organization, but at a costly long-term price for the individual, organization, and larger community.

A third perspective on the limits of the customer value paradigm is based on meeting individual needs of participants which may conflict with meeting collective societal needs. As Machan (1986) points out

> people do not in fact automatically seek out what is best for them—if it were only so we would live in a wonderful world. Nor do they always know what is best for them—that too would be very helpful if it were so. Rather people must work very hard to learn what is best for them and then try hard to obtain it. (pp. 272–273)

Therefore, there must be a balance struck between the freedom of the individual to pursue her or his goals and the responsibility the individual has in living as a member of a common society. Thus, for parks, recreation, and leisure service organizations there must be a balance struck between delivering quality leisure experiences and maximizing individual freedom while also being socially responsible to both the local and global community (see Figure 2.4).

This tension between promoting both individual freedom and responsibility is found in all aspects of recreation programming. Assisting individuals in experiencing leisure is balanced by decisions about who we serve, how we serve, what we provide, and so on. Different leisure service organizations will approach these questions differently as their basic values differ. Yet one constant remains—the desire to serve both the individual and society. For some organizations the emphasis may be on serving the individual rather than the community, for others the opposite may be true, while still others will try to serve both individuals and the community equally.

Historically, a service ethic has been associated more with public (government) and private, nonprofit organizations than with commercial ventures. As Schultz, McAvoy and Dustin (1988) note,

> [S]houldn't public recreation be governed by a social service ethic that rises above the bottom-line thinking? How can we serve all people—not just those who are willing to pay? Who will look out for minorities, the environment, the poor, society's underprivileged? (p. 53)

Figure 2.4   Scales of Balance

Yet in today's changing environment there is a blurring of the traditional lines between public, nonprofit, and commercial organizations. Public and nonprofit organizations are being asked to be increasingly innovative and entrepreneurial while commercial firms are being asked to be more socially responsible than in the past.

As a result, society is seeing more collaboration and cooperation between all types of organizations to meet the demands of financial and social responsibility. As one recent CEO from a major Fortune 500 electronics firm stated

> my philosophy is this; we don't run our business to earn profits. We earn profits to run our business. Our business has meaning and purpose—a reason to be here. People talk today about businesses needing to be socially responsible as if this is something new we need to do, on top of everything else we do. But social responsibility is not something that one should do as an extra benefit of the business. The whole essence of the business should be social responsibility. It must live for a purpose. Otherwise, why should it live at all? (Kiuchi, 1997)

Leisure service organizations are uniquely positioned to prosper in such an environment for several reasons.

First, all leisure and the delivery of it is value laden. Our profession believes in leisure as a requirement for a basic quality of life where individuals and society both prosper because of it. We have an orientation toward others that is based on doing good things for people which encompasses all elements of living—economics, political success, the environment, and so on. In addition, the key for leisure service organizations to be successful in balancing the needs of the individual and society is to examine the benefits that people are seeking from programs and activities and then find ways for participants to experience these benefits. This is within a context of simultaneously demonstrating a caring attitude toward others as well as the environment. This process involves two critical components: (1) listening to and understanding the needs of participants, and (2) assisting participants to understand and take responsibility for their actions. According to Edginton, Jordan, DeGraaf and Edginton

(1998), leisure professionals are in the life satisfaction business. When thought of in these terms, programs are not important. The focus is on the benefits that each program provides to increase the quality of life of participants. It is these benefits that are important.

Developing an Understanding of the Importance of Planning

Committing to both quality leisure experiences for individuals as well as serving the needs of society is a difficult task requiring leisure service professionals to understand the basic planning process. We know we want parks, recreation, and leisure service organizations to be responsive to both individual and community needs; what we are lacking is a blueprint or plan for how to get there. According to Russell (1982), much of what recreation programmers know and use of planning theory comes from other disciplines such as social work, which sees planning as a means for problem solving; and from corporate or business fields, which see planning as a way of managing change. Over the past decade, interest in planning has increased as a result of a scarcity of resources (e.g., staff, economic, tangible goods) and by the belief that greater accountability comes with using a planning process. In this way the planning process becomes a mechanism for managing and controlling.

Today, planning may be defined as *the process of determining what an agency or organization intends to be in the future and how it will get there.* Thus, planning involves choices about the mission or goals to be pursued; the programs, services, or products we will offer; and how we will attract and utilize the various resources we need—people, money, expertise, facilities, equipment, and so on (Barry, 1993).

How does an organization chart a wise course for the future as well as remain flexible enough to be able to change course as needs demand? The answer to this question may be found in planning. Planning acts as a tool or process through which leisure service organizations navigate the uncertain waters of delivering leisure experiences. Traditionally, planning was viewed as finding the "right fit" between the mission of an organization, opportunities and threats (forces outside the organization), and strengths and weaknesses (forces within the organization). Figure 2.5 adds an additional component to the strategic planning process for leisure service organizations—programs that address the issue of how we are going to get where we want to be.

In addressing the question of what is needed and feasible in delivering leisure experiences, we have focused on two overarching principles for leisure service organizations: (1) delivering quality to individuals while (2) responding to the collective needs of society. In addition to this, we also need to examine the many approaches or strategies used in programming leisure experiences. These help us to understand the framework from which programmers operate and are sometimes used as programming "recipes."

Strategies for Delivering Leisure Programs

Historically, a number of different approaches have been employed by leisure service organizations to plan and provide programs and services to a wide variety of constituent groups—see Table 2.3. A basic distinguishing characteristic between these approaches is the extent that customers or constituents are involved in the planning process, and conversely the amount of planning and supervision provided by the leisure service programmer.

At one end of the spectrum, leisure service professionals take on all the responsibility of planning leisure experiences. We serve as experts and develop leisure service programs based on what we think or believe is best for our constituents. Planning then becomes a task oriented strategy directed toward

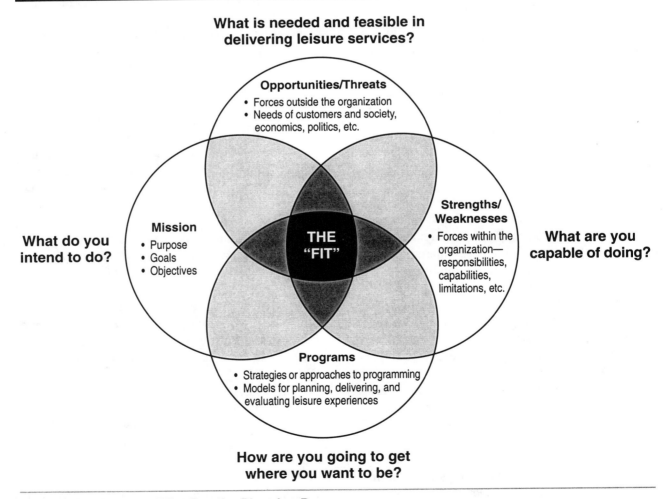

Figure 2.5   Factors Effecting the Planning Process

Table 2.3	**Strategies for Delivering Recreation and Leisure Services**	
Danford and Shirley (1964)	**Traditional approach**	Provides services that have been offered in the past, relying on former successes.
	Current practice approach	Use of current trends to understand program needs.
	Expressed desires approach	Use of participant information for program development.
	Authoritarian approach	Professional executives make decisions regarding program design.
Tillman (1974)	**Reaction approach**	Professionals wait and respond to demands generated by participants.
	Investigation plan	Uses fact-finding methods to determine needs.
	Creative plan	Promotes an interactive relationship between the participant and the professional for joint problem solving and sharing.
Murphy (1975)	**Cafeteria approach**	Creates a menu of services and many program opportunities from which customers can choose.
	Prescriptive approach	Professionals diagnose the needs of participants in an attempt to improve their leisure functioning.
Edginton and Hanson (1976)	**Trickle-down theory**	Bureaucratic activities result in services trickling down through the organization.
	Educated guess theory	Professional hunches are used to plan programs.
	Community leadership input theory	Advisory and policymaking boards assist in program planning.
	Identification of need theory	Involves analyzing demographic and psychographic information to determine need.
	Offer-what-people-want theory	Involves reflecting "what participants want." Promotes communication and interaction between professionals and participants.
	Indigenous development theory	Promotes grassroots program development which uses community resources.
	Interactive discovery	Encourages joint problem solving; no subordinate/superior relationship, rather a process of assisting others without imposing a value system.
Kraus (1985)	**Sociopolitical approach**	Recognizes the influence of social and political pressures on the program planning process.
	Quality of life/Amenity approach	Promotes leisure programs as a way of improving community life.
	Marketing approach	Views programming as finding out what "target groups" want and providing it to them.
	Human service approach	Promotes a social ethic, and views programs as purposeful; linked to other community-health related programs.
	Prescriptive approach	Sees programming as an instrumental activity; a form of therapy.
	Environmental/aesthetic and preservationist approach	Views programming as a mechanism to preserve the natural environment and protect historical heritage.
	Hedonistic/individualist approach	Stresses the pursuit of excitement and pleasure as focus of leisure programs; promotes creative expression.
Farrell and Lundegren (1978, 1991)	**Programming by objectives**	Establishes the use of performance or behavioral objectives to guide program development.
	Programming by desires of participants	Built on the assumption that participant needs can be identified and linked to program development.
	Programming by perceived needs of participants	Promotes anticipatory planning and understanding the interests of individuals.
	Programming by cafeteria style	Creates a menu of services and many program opportunities from which customers can choose.
	Programming by external requirements	Promotes utilization of normative standards or external criteria.

solving problems (Edginton, Hanson, Edginton & Hudson, 1998). At the other end of the spectrum the leisure service programmer is more of an enabler and collaborator empowering people to plan for their own leisure needs. In this context, planning utilizes a community development approach, a process oriented strategy directed toward helping individuals identify their own problems and assisting them with resources necessary to solve them (Edginton, Hanson, Edginton & Hudson, 1998). In Table 2.4 all of the approaches to delivering recreation programs are presented on a continuum between these two extremes.

To assist the reader in understanding the continuum presented in Table 2.4 we will discuss the following five general strategies found on the continuum: social advocacy, social planning, social marketing, marketing, and community development or grassroots empowerment. In discussing each of these strategies a general overview will be presented, along with a discussion about the role of the programmer and an example of a leisure service program that might fit into this strategy for delivering services.

Social Advocacy

As a programming approach, social advocacy has a strong history in the parks, recreation, and leisure field. Social reformers advocated for the rights of disadvantaged populations, worked to right social injustices, and to force organizations to change the way they were distributing resources, hence services. Today, social advocacy continues to be important to serve underrepresented groups and entitle those who cannot speak for themselves (e.g., the mentally and emotionally disabled, children). Within a social advocacy framework the leisure services programmer often works outside the established system to advocate for the rights of a specific group or issue.

Table 2.4   Social Planning to Community Development Continuum

Programming Approach	Social Advocacy	Social Planning		Social Marketing	Marketing Approach		Community Development
	PROGRAMMER AS EXPERT						PROGRAMMER AS ENABLER
Danford and Shirley (1964)	Authoritarian Approach	Traditional Approach	Current Practice Approach			Expressed Desire Approach	
Tillman (1974)					Reaction Plan	Investigation Plan	Creative Plan
Murphy (1975)	Prescriptive Approach		Cafeteria Approach				
Edginton and Hanson (1976)		Trickle-Down / Educated Guess		Community Leadership	Offer What People Want / Identification of Needs		Interactive Discovery / Indigenous Development
Kraus (1985)	Prescriptive Approach	Human Service Approach		Environmental Approach / Sociopolitical Approach	Marketing Approach	Hedonistic Approach	
Farrell and Lundegren (1991)			Cafeteria Approach	External Requirements / Programming by Objectives	Perceived Needs of Participants / By Desires of Participants		

SAGE, Senior Action in a Gay Environment, established in 1978 in New York, is an excellent example of an organization that uses a variety of programming strategies, including a social advocacy approach, in serving customers. This community-based organization has multiple purposes. It provides social services especially designed for seniors who are gay or lesbian (e.g., medical services, legal services, bereavement counseling, financial counseling). SAGE also provides social recreation and leisure opportunities designed for seniors (events include movies, antiquing, supper clubs, traveling, and book clubs). In addition, SAGE strives to educate participants and community members to act as advocates for the rights of individuals who are both seniors and gay, to train new and existing professionals, and to develop innovative programs that meet the ever changing, leisure related needs of this element of the population (see Figure 2.6).

S A G E

Senior Action In A Gay Environment

A unique idea, unlike any other organization of its kind,
a model for the country in service, professional training - and caring.

Like other older Americans, senior gay

men and lesbians face daunting problems of illness, reduced income, loss of friends and family and increased isolation from society at large as they age.

Many older gay people do not seek or find help - either because they are old, or are gay, or because they are both. Sometimes it seems simpler not to ask than to risk rejection.

SAGE was established to make sure that high quality, professional help is available for gay and lesbian seniors. Since 1978, SAGE's staff and volunteers have provided hands-on services at little or no cost to thousands of older gay men and lesbians - in their homes, in medical institutions, over the phone and in SAGE offices. Intergenerational and culturally diverse, SAGE works to insure the future of the lesbian and gay community.

SAGE has pioneered in creating a remarkable service for lesbians and gay men of all religious, racial, cultural and ethnic backgrounds which is a model for the country.

Professional Social Work Services

The heart of SAGE is its social services program. A staff of professional social workers and counselors provides direct services to more than 1,500 senior lesbians and gay men each month.

Social Services.
Case management and counseling on all government entitlement programs for seniors. Direct help accessing medical services, physicians, clinics, legal services, Social Security programs and community services.

Friendly Visitors.
Periodic visits to homebound gay elderly by trained volunteers to run errands, chat, play cards, take walks, share hobbies, establish friends and maintain links to the outside world.

Therapy.
Individual, family, and group psychotherapy, including a special bereavement counseling program.

Women's Support Services.
Outreach to older lesbians to provide individual and group support specific to their needs, such as issues of invisibility, sexuality and health.

AIDS and the Elderly Program.
A national model for older people with HIV/AIDS, combines assessment services, Friendly Visitors, support groups and individual and partner counseling under the guidance of MD's, RN's and MSW counselors. SAGE is licensed by the New York State Office of Mental Health as a clinic treatment program for persons 50 and older with an HIV/AIDS diagnosis.

Figure 2.6   An Example of Social Advocacy through Leisure Services

Social Planning

Social planning is a task-oriented strategy directed toward rationally and logically distributing community resources. Participants are viewed as consumers of services that programmers create. It is a process of using the knowledge and expertise of professionals to plan, organize and deliver services (Edginton, Hanson, Edginton & Hudson, 1998). At its worst, social planning can mean simply providing programs based upon knowledge of past successes. When this happens, we do not respond well to social changes as they develop. At its best, social planning can be a systematic approach to identifying the needs of the individual, community, and organization and then creating recreation programs that the programmer believes will meet these needs.

An example of a recreation program from a social planning approach is Gates Park Youth Basketball League in Waterloo, Iowa. A group of concerned community individuals identified a need to provide a program that would be of interest to adolescent males, and which would keep the youth out of trouble late at night (community need). Responding to these perceived needs the citizens organized a late-night basketball league which uses the resources of the newly formed organization in an effective manner (organizational needs). Many communities have offered similar programs.

Social Marketing

Created as a way to produce social change, social marketing differs from other areas of marketing (as described below) only with respect to the objectives of the marketers and their organizations. By this we mean that social marketing *seeks to influence social behavior not to benefit the marketer, but to benefit the target audience and general society.* Kotler and Andreasen (1996) have identified a number of possible responsibilities of organizations involved in social marketing. Those relevant to parks, recreation, and leisure organizations include the following:

- *We are often asked to influence negative demand.* It is sometimes the case that social marketers are asked to promote a behavior for which the target market has negative perceptions. For example, driving 55 MPH, exercising, and recycling are all 'costly' behaviors that most consumers would rather avoid.

- *The behaviors to be influenced often have invisible benefits.* In the private sector it is relatively clear what benefits we are likely to receive (i.e., with an expensive hotel room or a new jet ski), yet social marketers often encourage behaviors where nothing "happens." For example, individuals with high blood pressure are told it will be lowered if they exercise and take their medicine. Leisure service professionals know that positive leisure experiences contribute to emotional and mental health, yet it can be very difficult to market positive leisure behaviors without visible benefits.

- *The behaviors to be influenced often have benefits only to third parties.* Some behaviors advocated by social marketers have payoffs for third parties such as the economically disadvantaged, youth, or society in general and not to the person engaging in the behavior. Examples of these behaviors include energy conservation, recycling, and fundraising. It can be very challenging to motivate people to take actions if they do not directly and uniquely benefit from those actions.

- *The behaviors often involve self-rewards.* The social marketer cannot ensure benefits because the type and amount of benefits requires the discipline of the individual (i.e., exercising) if the benefit is to be realized. Thus, the nature and quality of the benefits are largely out of the marketers' control and are very difficult to manipulate.

At one time, social marketing was considered to be exclusively for public and nonprofit organizations. It was used for designing public awareness campaigns to promote social causes or to introduce behavior change. Social marketing, however, is also used by commercial organizations. For example, fitness clubs are often utilized not only as places to exercise, but also as opportunities for restoring balance to one's life (O'Sullivan, 1991). As another example, Figure 2.7 highlights the efforts of the National Recreation and Park Association to

Figure 2.7   NRPA Example of Social Marketing

position parks and recreation departments as an alternative for youngsters and drugs. This campaign, "Exercise the Right Choice," is an example that incorporates a social marketing approach to promote desired behavior.

Marketing

Marketing means many different things to different people. To some the term is synonymous with sales and to others, advertising. Yet neither of these terms serve as accurate or complete definitions of marketing. For the purpose of this discussion, *marketing is defined as a process of human exchange whereby people exchange something of value for something they need* (Stern, 1992). Thus, marketing is the umbrella for all management functions which foster desired exchanges. Exchanges only take place when a target audience member takes an action, thus the ultimate goal of marketing is to influence behavior. An inherent component of marketing is determining what specific customers or groups of customers (a target market) need and then providing programs that meet those needs. This is done by manipulating the price of the service, the place the service is delivered, and how the service is going to be implemented and promoted to meet the expressed needs of customers.

Marketing is a very customer-oriented approach to delivering services and requires extensive knowledge of who is going to be served in programs. In addition, a customer-oriented approach means going beyond discovering *what* people need and want to do in their leisure time. We must also identify *how* they wish to participate (O'Sullivan, 1991).

An example of a recreation program offered through a marketing approach is presented by Kotler and Andreasen (1996). The Buffalo Philharmonic Orchestra had a serious problem in trying to broaden its audience. Marketing research revealed that many people who indicated they might like to attend a concert did not do so because they expected the occasion to be very formal. The orchestra itself was seen as distant, formal, and forbidding. As a result, the Philharmonic began to humanize the orchestra and the concert-going experience. Select members of the orchestra began playing "short sleeve" chamber music programs at neighborhood events, art fairs, and outdoor festivals. Contact was made with primary and secondary school children. The orchestra even performed at half-time at a Buffalo Bills football game. "Concert going never again had the sense of formality that was clearly keeping many potential patrons away. Attendance

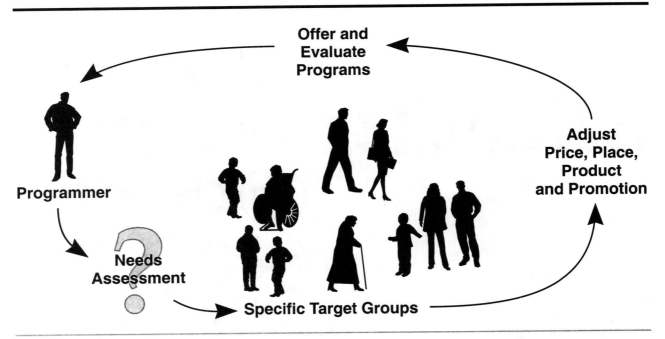

Figure 2.8   The Marketing Approach

figures clearly reflected this new customer-centered orientation" (Kotler & Andreasen, 1996, p. 42). Being willing to change how and where the service was offered contributed greatly to eventual success of the organization.

Community Development/ Empowerment

Community development or grassroots empowerment is process-oriented and rests on the basic assumption that individuals should be partners in the process of determining their leisure destiny (Edginton, Hanson, Edginton & Hudson, 1998; Rossman, 1995). It suggests that individuals are partners in the planning process. As partners, they can learn the processes and strategies necessary to plan, organize, and implement their own recreation services based on their perception of their own needs. The aim of community development is empowering communities and individuals to (a) stimulate local initiative by involving people in community participation, specifically the process of social and economic change; (b) build channels of communication that promote solidarity; and (c) improve the social, economic, and cultural well-being of community residents (Christianson, Fendley & Robinson, 1989).

Within a community development approach to providing services the leisure service programmer takes on the roles of enabler, encourager, and cheerleader. Thus, the programmer listens and assists individuals and communities in identifying their own needs as well as planning and organizing programs to meet these needs. Within this framework, "leadership is a dialogue not a monologue ...where leaders breathe life into the hopes and dreams of others and enable them to see the exciting possibilities that the future holds" (Kouzes & Posner, 1995, p. 11).

An example of a community development planning model is presented in Figure 2.9. The model has been used in a southern rural community school district to develop programs which bring together latchkey children and older adults who wish to remain active, contributing community members (Carter, Keller & Beck, 1996). After identifying specific needs (with constituents), a planning and advisory committee consisting of teenagers and seniors planned and implemented a program called TEA Time. The program used older volunteers to instruct and mentor latchkey children, teaching skills in folk arts and craft skills. At the end of the year, an evaluation of the program by participants resulted in a wide variety of findings including:

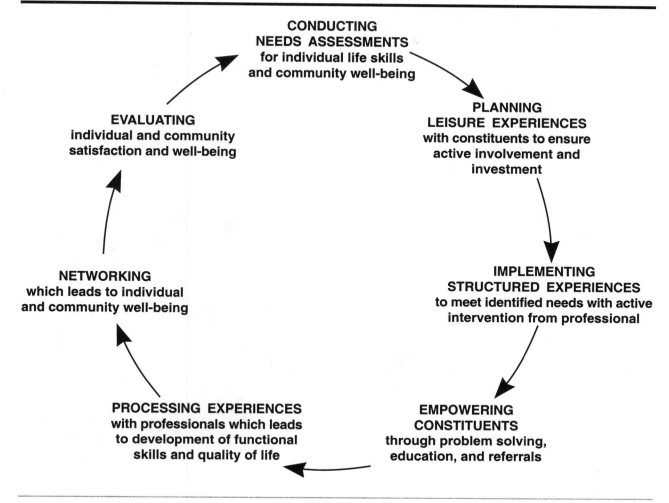

Figure 2.9   Model of Community Development (Adapted from Carter, Keller & Beck, 1996)

(a) the majority of TEA Time participants deepened their appreciation for persons of different ages;

(b) the majority of older adults felt more useful and indicated they learned new ideas;

(c) all participants rated the overall program effectiveness as excellent or good, as did the school and recreation administrators;

(d) the more individualized the interactions between young and old, the higher the level of satisfaction with the program by both age groups" (Carter, Keller & Beck, 1996, p. 49).

Evaluators attributed the overall success of the program to the commitment and involvement of participants as well as the commitment of the park and recreation district to the betterment of individuals and the enhancement of the overall community well-being.

Building a Strategy/Philosophy of Recreation Program Planning

It is important to remember that there is no single consensus about the proper way to plan. Each plan has to be unique, tailored to the particular situation and planner(s), and use a blend of strategies and approaches (Burch, 1996). Within this constraint, there is a move toward involving customers as much as possible in the planning process. This tends to lead to increased programmatic success.

Lappe and DuBois (1994) put forth the idea that human services (which include recreation and leisure) are moving away from simply providing services to creating a living democracy model. Figure 2.10 provides an overview of these changing concepts in human services which seem to indicate that collectively human services are moving toward a community development and empowerment approach to delivering services. The challenge inherent in this approach is that it takes time to develop the relationships needed to build partnerships between programmers and participants, and time is a limited commodity. As Russell (1982) noted, participant involvement can be seen as an "additional burden to the already hectic and cumbersome job of [recreation] planning" (p. 54).

While a variety of strategies and approaches exists under the umbrella of community development, citizen participation is perhaps the approach that is most familiar in leisure services (Ari & Pedlar, 1997). Citizen participation is *a process in which individuals take part in decision making related to the organization and its programs and services which affect them in some manner.* Russell (1982) stressed the importance of customer participation in the planning process, yet acknowledged that there is no single technique to achieve this goal. It is up to leisure service programmers to identify the appropriate strategy that works with the other elements of the strategic planning process as presented in Figure 2.11.

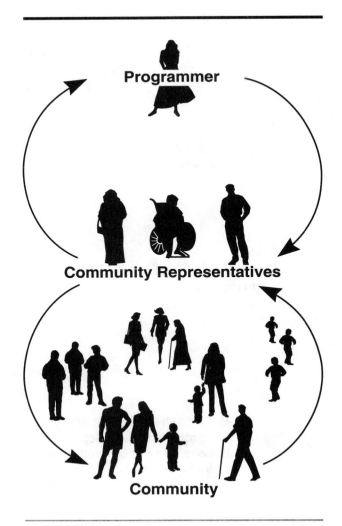

Figure 2.11 Empowerment and Community Development Approach to Programming

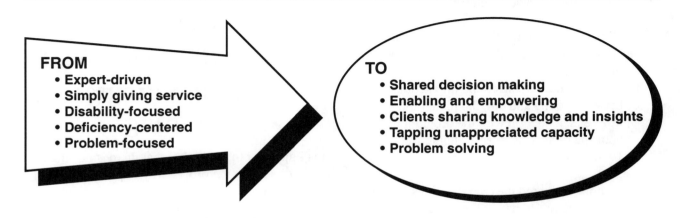

Figure 2.10 Changing Principles in Human Services (Source: Lappe & Dubois, 1994, p. 146)

The strategy we will emphasize throughout this text is that of an entrepreneurial and community empowerment approach to providing services. It is entrepreneurial from the standpoint that parks, recreation, and leisure service organizations must be willing to take risks in order to take advantage of opportunities brought on by change to produce a good or service which will benefit both the giver and receiver. In many cases, this will include empowering individuals to make their own choices about the types of recreation and leisure experiences they desire. Yet, in many settings (especially public and nonprofit organizations) it is important to move beyond individual empowerment to community empowerment. This not only encourages social responsibility, but also looks to involve everyone in improving the collective community quality of life.

An entrepreneurial and empowerment strategy blends well with the concept of servant leadership. Through involving a wide range of constituencies, working to help create leisure experiences that meet their needs as well as raising issues for those who cannot speak for themselves (e.g., children), leisure service professionals begin to balance the need to deliver quality experiences to customers with the responsibility to meet the general needs of society. As Carter, Keller and Beck (1996) remind us

> professional practice should be driven by our constituents' needs; the satisfaction and well-being of our participants are cornerstones of what we do. By using participatory management, we can incorporate service providers and participants in a strategic planning process. (p. 45)

Summary

Delivering quality leisure experiences should be the primary goal of all parks, recreation, and leisure service organizations. Committing to quality demands that park, recreation and leisure service organizations understand the dynamic nature of delivering services. A traditional starting place for defining a service is understanding how services differ from products. The four most commonly identified characteristics ascribed to services are their intangibility and perishability, the potential variability inherent to service delivery, and the inseparability of production and consumption in delivering services.

Quality of service is an important concern of leisure services professionals. In delivering quality programs, the ability to meet the wants and desires of participants is extremely important, yet maximizing individual choice must also be tempered with a sense of social responsibility for the collective community. In addition, we should focus on both the product and the process of programming. This requires an understanding of the planning process.

Historically, the parks, recreation, and leisure profession has used many different approaches and strategies to plan and deliver recreation programs. These may be visualized along a continuum of programmer and participant involvement. The five major approaches include social advocacy, social planning, social marketing, marketing, and community development. There is little consensus about the proper way to plan because different situations demand different approaches. There does seem to be a movement towards encouraging more involvement of participants in planning their own programs with programmers acting as enablers and resources to participants.

References

Aguayo, R. (1990). *Dr. Deming: The American who taught the Japanese about quality*. New York, NY: Carol Publishing Group.

Albrecht, K. (1992). *The only thing that matters: Bringing the power of the customer into the center of your business*. New York, NY: Harper Business.

Albrecht, K. (1985). *Service America*. Homewood, IL: Dow Jones-Irwin.

Ari, S. and Pedlar, A. (1997). Building communities through leisure: Citizen participation in a healthy communities initiative. *Journal of Leisure Research, 29*(2), 167-182.

Barry, B. (1993). *Strategic planning workbook for nonprofit organizations*. St. Paul, MN: Amherst H. Wilder Foundation.

Burch, H. (1996). *Basic social policy and planning*. New York, NY: Haworth Press.

Carter, M., Keller, M. and Beck T. (1996). A vision for today: Recreation and leisure services. *Parks and Recreation, 31*(11), 42-49.

Christianson, J., Fendley, K. and Robinson, J. (1989). Community development. In J. Christianson and J. Robinson (Eds.), *Community development in perspective* (pp. 3-25). Ames, IA: Iowa State University Press.

Danford, H. and Shirley, M. (1964). *Creative leadership in recreation*. Boston, MA: Allyn and Bacon.

Edginton, C. and Hanson, C. (1976). Appraising leisure service delivery. *Parks and Recreation, 11*(3), 27, 44-45.

Edginton, C., Hanson, C., Edginton, S. and Hudson, S. (1998). *Leisure programming: A service-centered and benefits approach*. Dubuque, IA: McGraw-Hill.

Edginton, C., Jordan, D., DeGraaf, D. and Edginton, S. (1998). *Leisure and life satisfaction*. Dubuque, IA: McGraw-Hill.

Farrell, P. and Lundegren, H. (1978). *The process of recreation programming: Theory and technique*. New York, NY: Wiley and Sons.

Farrell, P. and Lundegren, H. (1991). *The process of recreation programming: Theory and technique, 3rd*. State College, PA: Venture Publishing, Inc.

Greenleaf, R. (1991). *The servant as leader*. Indianapolis, IN: The Robert K. Greenleaf Center.

Holloway, J. C. (1986). International tourism—Some future structures and orientations, *World Leisure and Recreation, 28*(5), 8-13.

Jandt, F. (1995). *Contrary to what you've been told . . . What you know to be true! The customer is usually wrong*. Indianapolis, IN: Park Avenue Publishing.

Kiuchi, T. (1997). *What I learned from the rain forest*. Keynote from World Future Society, September 16. San Francisco, California.

Kotler, P. (1991). *Marketing management: Analysis, planning and control, 7th ed*. Englewood Cliffs, NJ: Prentice Hall.

Kotler, P. and Andreasen, A. (1996). *Strategic marketing for nonprofit organizations*. Englewood Cliffs, NJ: Prentice Hall.

Kouzes, J. and Posner, B. (1995). *The leadership challenge: How to keep getting extraordinary things done in organizations*. San Francisco, CA: Jossey-Bass.

Kouzes, J. and Posner, B. (1993). *Credibility: How leaders gain and lose it, why people demand it*. San Francisco, CA: Jossey-Bass.

Kraus, R. (1985). *Recreation program planning today*. Glenview, IL: Scott Foresman.

Lappe, F. M. and DuBois, P.M. (1994). *The quickening of America: Rebuilding our nation, remaking our lives*. San Francisco, CA: Jossey-Bass.

Machan, T. (1986, July). The ethics of privatization. *Freeman's Idea on Liberty, 36*(7), pp. 270-273.

McCarville, R.E. (1993, October). Keys to quality leisure programming, *Journal of Physical Education, Recreation & Dance—Leisure Today*. pp. 34-35, 46-47.

Mobley, T. and Toalson, R. (Eds). (1992). *Parks and recreation in the 21st century: Chapter I.* Arlington, VA: NRPA.

Murphy, J. (1975). *Recreation and leisure service: A humanistic perspective.* Dubuque, IA: William C. Brown.

O'Sullivan, E. (1991). *Marketing for parks, recreation and leisure.* State College, PA: Venture Publishing, Inc.

Payne, A. (1993). *The essence of services marketing.* New York, NY: Prentice Hall.

Rossman, R. (1995). *Recreation programming: Designing leisure experiences, 2nd ed.* Champaign, IL: Sagamore Publishing.

Russell, R. (1982). *Planning programs in recreation.* St. Louis, MO: C. V. Mosby.

Rust, R., Zahorik, A. and Keiningham, T. (1996). *Service marketing.* New York, NY: HarperCollins.

Schultz, J., McAvoy, L. and Dustin, D. (1988). What are we in business for? *Parks and Recreation, 23*(1), 51-53.

Sierra Club Staff. (1992). Sierra club centennial. *Sierra, 77*(3), 52-73.

Stern, G. (1992). *Marketing workbook for nonprofit organizations.* St. Paul, MN: Amherst H. Wilder Foundation.

Tillman, A. (1974). *The program book for recreation professionals.* Palo Alto, CA: National Press Books.

Chapter Three

Programming Theories

"The fact is," said Rabbit, "we've missed our way somehow." They were having a rest in a small sand-pit on the top of the Forest. Pooh was getting rather tired of that sand-pit, and suspected it of following them about, because whichever direction they started in, they always ended up at it, and each time, as it came through the mist at them, Rabbit said triumphantly, "Now I know where we are!" and Pooh said sadly, "So do I," and Piglet said nothing....

"Well," said Rabbit, after a long silence in which nobody thanked him for the nice walk they were having, "We'd better get on, I suppose. Which way shall we try?" "How would it be," said Pooh slowly, "if, as soon as we're out of sight of this Pit, we try to find it again?" "What's the good of that?" said Rabbit. "Well," said Pooh, "We keep looking for Home and not finding it, so I thought that if we looked for this Pit, we'd be sure to not find it, which would be a Good Thing, because then we might find something that we weren't *looking for, which might be just what we* were *looking for, really."*

Hoff (1982, pp. 12–13)

As mentioned in the introductory chapter, programming is the essence of what parks, recreation, and leisure service professionals do. We develop a process, which results in a product, that enables the interaction of participants to achieve some benefit through leisure. We can undertake this effort in a variety of manners—by using a cafeteria style, a traditional approach, programming by objectives, and others (refer to Table 2.4, page 30). In the previous chapter we suggested an entrepreneurial and empowerment approach whereby constituents are integral to and involved in the program planning process from beginning to end. The many approaches to leisure services programming and the way providers view themselves as leisure service practitioners are theories (or interrelated concepts) that help to explain the programming process.

Theories are ideas and concepts connected through a thoughtful process that help leisure professionals to understand the reasoning behind doing what they do. *Model* is another word that captures the essence of theory. It provides a mental picture of a concept. Theories and models are crucial to the complete understanding of the profession, and in this particular case, programming. As such, theories serve as the underpinnings for our efforts. Therefore, this chapter will present several different theories to parks, recreation, and leisure services programming. In addition, we present a programming *process* to help understand what happens (the tasks) as providers design, implement, and evaluate recreation and leisure programs.

Systems Theory

The systems theory of recreation programming has been in existence for a long time. Systems theory is based on the premise that by adhering to a defined process (system) a variety of individuals, working independently, can follow similar paths and achieve similar products or outcomes. One obvious benefit to utilizing this theory of programming is that it suggests something all practitioners can follow and achieve similar results.

The basic systematic process is one of *input* (determining where you are going), *process* (determining the best way to get there), and *output* (knowing how you arrived). It implies wholeness and interrelationships throughout the programming process (Peterson & Gunn, 1984). This process or method is very much like what happens when we use a computer. We input data (type in words or figures on the keyboard), the computer processes that information and does something at our request (translates the keystrokes into words or calculates mathematical formulas), and then we receive an output (a screen picture or printout of the product). If each one of us were to input similar data and tell the computer to do the same function, our outputs would also be similar. This is also true when developing recreation programs from this model.

Programming approaches that are examples of this theoretical model include programming by standards and programming by objectives (Farrell & Lundegren, 1978; 1991). In both of these cases we begin with standards, criteria, or objectives (input), work toward achieving them through program planning (process), and end up with a program (output) that meets those standards or criteria. The leisure experience that is a result of this systems process is well-defined before the delivery of the program. This means that we usually have some idea of what the outcome (program) will look like prior to its implementation, and this can be very helpful in preparing for contingencies (see Figure 3.1).

Many therapeutic recreation settings use systems theory for programming. Objectives are developed for each client based upon her or his needs; several program ideas are generated to achieve these objectives, and once engaged in, client success is measured. To illustrate this theory, Playright is an agency in Hong Kong that provides play services to children who are hospitalized. In general, they help children regain skills lost through the effects of illness and hospitalization and try to provide for normal development in an abnormal situation. Individual goals and objectives are identified for each child to achieve these larger aims, activities are implemented, and the success of programming for each child is then measured against those goals. It is a highly successful recreation and leisure program for children in need.

Ropes course programs are another example of a setting that typically uses a systems approach to programming. For example, at Vision Us, Inc., which has a 29-element high-and-low ropes course, corporate groups define their goals and learning objectives (e.g., develop teamwork, build trust, establish better communication) through customized group planning. The ropes course elements are introduced and facilitated, the group engages in the various activities, and client success is measured upon completion to see if they met their goals.

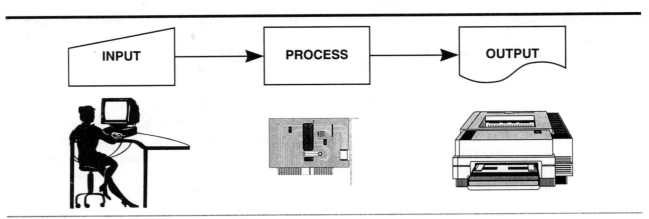

Figure 3.1   Systems Theory

Playright Volunteer Programme

Where do the volunteers go to work ?
- in hospitals
- in institutions
- in the community

What do they do ?
- Play with children with 100% time and attention
- Programme planning
- Have fun

How much time of commitment ?
- Regular commitment (e.g. once every or every other week)
- Work for a period of time, depends on the nature of service

Is there any training before they go ?
- Yes, each volunteer will receive a playwork training
- Training includes: play values & concepts, play skills, communication skills, topics related to particular service

How can I become a volunteer?
- If you are over 15 and love to play with children

I would like to join, what should I do?
- Contact our Volunteer Coordinator

Playright

Address: 18A Blk. F. Senior Staff Quarters,
Pamela Youde Hospital,
3F Lok Man Road, Chai Wan,
Hong Kong.
Telephone: 28982922   Fax: 28984539

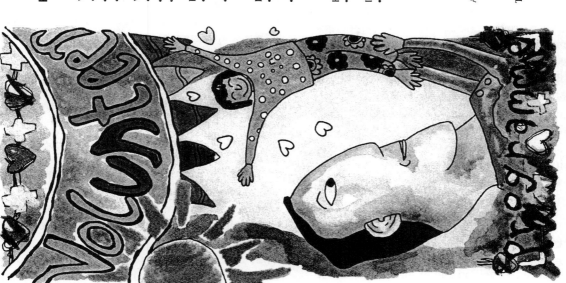

Figure 3.2   An Example of Systems Theory (Playright, Hong Kong)

Benefits-Driven Model

A benefits-driven model or theory of understanding programming is a relatively new conceptualization of recreation and leisure programming. Kraus (1997) has integrated the concepts associated with benefits-based management (BBM) and programming in his view of benefits-driven programming. This theory involves a strong movement to identify and document parks, recreation, and leisure service outputs in terms of benefits gained from engagement in various leisure programs. In other words, we first identify the possible benefits to be gained from participation in parks, recreation, and leisure services experiences. Next, we identify those as outcomes and then seek to achieve those outcomes through some form of programming. This model may be viewed as a combination of three approaches mentioned in Chapter Two: quality of life, human services, and the marketing approach.

Parks, recreation, and leisure service outcomes are typically identified as being found in the physical, emotional, and cognitive domains for individuals. We also know that both individuals and communities receive social, economic, environmental, and other quality-of-life benefits from participation in leisure experiences. In this theory of programming emphasizing benefits as outcomes becomes the driving force shaping the program planning, implementation, and evaluation processes.

The Office of Youth Development in the City of Aurora, Colorado, is an excellent example of a benefits-driven program (see Figure 3.3). A program designed to build positive life-enhancing skills for youth, the Office of Youth Development is involved in direct services, community education, grant procurement, and consultation services. The benefits of this program include an increase in emotionally healthy youth, more youth with improved social and personal skills, and a more accepting and supportive community networks. The youth benefit, their parents benefit, and the community benefits from these programmatic efforts.

Special Events Model

Special events as recreation and leisure programs are unique in that they usually have readily identifiable tasks to be completed and follow a well-defined event life cycle. Special events may occur monthly, annually, or as once-in-a-lifetime programs. They are specific to a time and place, are viewed by communities as "extras," and tend to draw people both from within and outside of a local area to participate.

The model of programming that best suits special events stands alone from other theories of programming (although it can be used in other types of parks, recreation, and leisure service programs, and often is). Commonly, the special event program model follows a flow chart format to guide the tasks to be accomplished in the special programming efforts. It is relatively straightforward, and may appear to look like a recipe of sorts. Furthermore, this particular programming theory has a visible time or calendar element. This allows for easy task identification, task delegation, and task evaluation (for completion).

The special events programming model is often seen as an offshoot of the traditional or current practice approaches to programming. Special events are often held because of their successful past history, thus a type of "tradition" surrounding the event has been established. Other times special events are the result of being responsive to current issues and trends. For instance, many communities put together annual "festivals of lights" around the Christmas holiday season. These light decorations are highly traditional, often held in the same location year after year, and draw large crowds. On the other hand, the festivals and parades that developed in small towns across the world as the 1996 Atlanta Olympic Games torch passed through the areas were in response to a current international event. Both of these types of special events follow similar models as they are developed.

The Program Evaluation and Review Technique (PERT) and the Gantt chart are examples of the special events theory of programming (see Figure 3.4, page 46). These models are actually used in evaluation, but have been adapted for use as program design models. Both the PERT and Gantt chart processes allow for the examination of "interrelationships among tasks and the time required to complete both subsets of tasks and entire projects" (Worthern, Sanders & Fitzpatrick, 1997, p. 287). They have been translated into use as a program theory to enhance program planning, design, implementation, and evaluation.

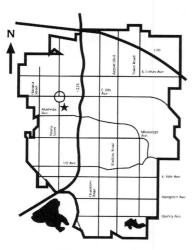

FACILITY LOCATIONS

★ Office of Youth Development
North Branch Library, Lower Level
1298 Peoria Street
Monday - Friday
8:00 A.M. to 4:30 P.M.
361-2990
361-2954 Fax

Aurora Recreation Services is committed to creating a community in which everyone helps build positive life-enhancing, skills, attitudes, and behaviors in our youth and families.

Office of Youth Development
North Branch Library,
Lower Level
1298 Peoria Street
361-2990

The Office of Youth Development's mission is to create a community in which everyone helps build positive life-enhancing skills, attitudes and behavior in our youth. These qualities are called developmental assets.

We work toward this mission in four ways:
▶ By weaving asset building throughout City of Aurora youth programs.
▶ By educating the community on asset building to inspire everyday acts of asset building.
▶ By working with community groups to develop a unified effort toward community change.
▶ By developing collaborative grant projects that provide positive asset development opportunities for youth in Aurora.

Services Available
▶ Prevention Information and Resources
▶ Asset Building Speakers
▶ Consultation on Prevention and Asset Building

Assets for Aurora Youth
Research has identified 40 assets that are essential for youth to blossom into productive citizens. Just as financial assets allow an individual to invest in the future, the more "developmental assets" a young person has, the more likely he or she is to succeed and become a productive citizen. The less assets available to a youth, the more likely he or she is to try alcohol or drugs, commit a crime or do poorly in school. Parents, teachers, church members, business leaders, everyone, can help build assets in our youth. For information on the 40 assets or to obtain a speaker on asset building, call the Office of Youth Development at 361-2990.

Each of us can build assets by:
▶ Supporting and loving the children in your life.
▶ Setting clear rules and boundaries for youth.
▶ Encouraging education.
▶ Providing positive ways for youth to use free time.
▶ Instilling positive values.
▶ Building social and interpersonal skills in youth.

Figure 3.3   An Example of a Benefits-Driven Program (Office of Youth Development, Aurora, Colorado)

PERT Chart

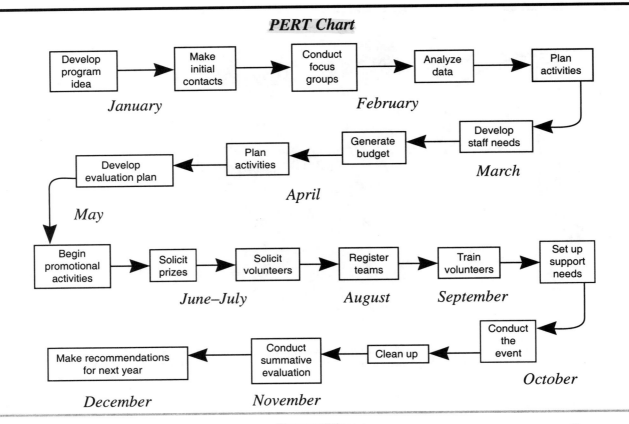

Gantt Chart

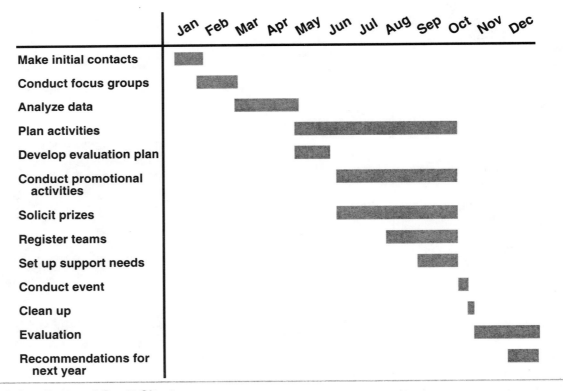

Figure 3.4   Pert and Gantt Charts

Flow Theory

Flow is a concept that has been embraced by the parks, recreation, and leisure services profession since the late 1980s. Very simply put, flow describes the state of mind one experiences when skills and challenge levels are well-matched (a variety of other elements are also involved and discussed below). As a program theory flow depicts the driving force behind leisure services programming as the desire to match, as best possible, participant skill and challenge levels in all activities and events.

Developed by Csikszentmihalyi in the early 1970s, flow includes several elements (1990). First, the activity one undertakes must be challenging and require some level of skill. Skills and challenge must be matched to achieve flow. If a participant does not have skills commensurate with the challenge, she or he will likely feel anxious. On the other hand, if the participant is not challenged enough to meet her or his skill levels, boredom may occur. When skills are matched with the challenge of an activity the individual's attention is merged with that activity. When this occurs, people can lose conscious thought of themselves and become totally immersed in the activity—their actions feel almost automatic (see Figure 3.5).

People can achieve such immersion in activity because activity-related goals are usually clear and feedback is immediate. These are two additional elements of the flow model—a participant knows what she or he wants to do, sets out to do it, and receives immediate feedback throughout the activity (related to success or failure at each step of the activity). While in flow, people report that they concentrate totally on the task at hand—all distractions are forgotten. This leads to a feeling of being in control; as such there is no fear of losing control or of failing. The last two elements of flow are a loss of self-consciousness—we become unaware of ourselves because "we are one with the activity"—and a transformation of time. The adage, "time flies when you're having fun" applies here. Those experiencing flow have no sense of time as measured by the clock. For some, time seems to go by very quickly; for others it seems to almost stand still.

Borrowing the theory of flow and applying it to programming in parks, recreation, and leisure services leads leisure practitioners to use it as a guide in shaping their programming efforts. Practitioners who follow this theory use their desire to facilitate flow experiences for participants as the driving force behind program design, planning, implementation, and evaluation. To be effective, programmers need to have a clear understanding of human development. This is necessary because in this model they do what they can to aid participants to: experience a match of skills and challenge, feel one with the activity in which they are engaged, have clear goals and receive immediate feedback, be totally immersed in and concentrating on the event, lose the worry about possible failure, experience a loss of self-consciousness, and lose all sense of clock time (see Figure 3.6, page 48). Examples of programs designed with flow as the driving force might include indoor climbing walls, 5K and 10K fun runs, art classes, and music shows/recitals. These types of programs have great potential in terms of facilitating flow experiences for people.

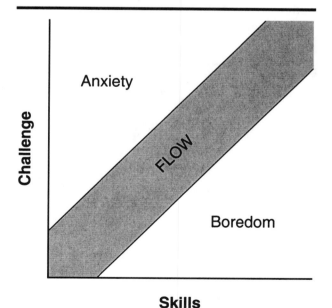

Figure 3.5   Csikszentmihalyi's Flow Theory (Adapted from Csikszentmihalyi, 1990)

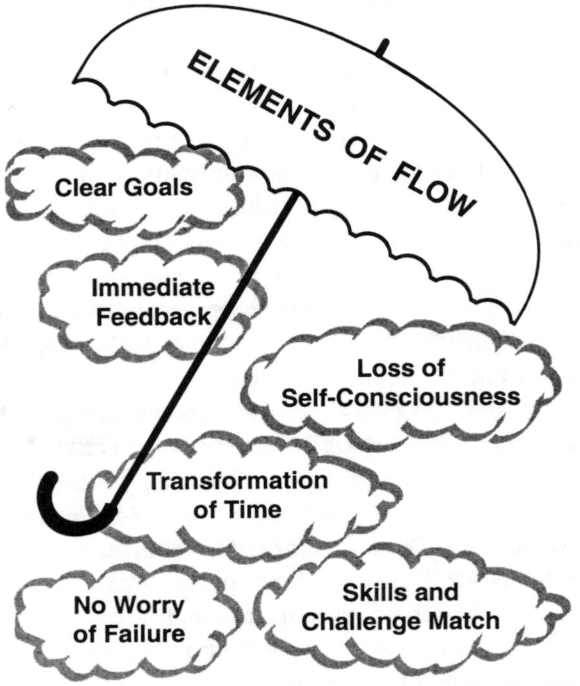

Figure 3.6 Elements of Flow

Motivation-Based Theories

Motivation-based theories are those models that suggest recreation and leisure programs should be an outgrowth of, or response to, individual and group needs. Needs are viewed as motivators, or factors, that influence the drives people have in making decisions about involvement in leisure programs. This means that as long as individuals have unfulfilled needs, they will be motivated to meet those needs.

Most people are familiar with Maslow's Hierarchy of Needs—a pyramid shaped model that depicts various levels of needs (see Figure 3.7). According to Maslow, higher order needs are ignored until lower order needs are met. At the bottom of the pyramid are those needs that drive all people—food, water, air, sleep, sex—and until these needs are met, individuals will be motivated to do what they can to meet them. Next, people have a need for physical, emotional, and psychological safety. Once these needs have been met, the need for love, affection, and belonging becomes the primary motivator of actions. The next motivator is achievement, and once an individual has met this need, she or he is then motivated by a drive for self-actualization.

If we were to use Maslow's Hierarchy as a driving force behind leisure services programming, we would be well-aware that various needs drive people's actions and preferences (Murphy, Niepoth, Jamieson & Williams, 1991; Niepoth, 1983). It has been suggested that the need for self-actualization drives human behavior. Thus, we might suggest that recreation and leisure programs should be designed to facilitate self-actualization. We should bear in mind, however, that according to Maslow, if lower order needs are not met, an individual's actions and attentions will be toward making that happen. An example of addressing this need to meet lower order needs prior to higher order needs is the breakfast programs offered in public schools. It is well-known that in order for children to learn (a high order function), their lower order needs (eating) must be met first. Otherwise, hunger and discomfort will drive children's behaviors (which will likely be in conflict with their learning program's goals).

If we follow motivation theory as the driving force behind recreation programming, we need to remember that as leisure service providers, we do not motivate people. Rather, we create and manipulate environments to facilitate people to motivate themselves. True motivation is intrinsic—it comes from within an individual. Thus, our goal is to develop social, psychological, and physical settings

Figure 3.7 Maslow's Hierarchy of Needs

that support individual motivators. For instance, we know that lighting (subdued or bright) and colors (pastels or neon) affect people's moods, and thus, motivate people to behave in certain ways.

A lot of adolescent and teen programs are developed from a base of motivation theory. From human development we know that adolescents are motivated to experience a sense of belonging with their peer group. When alternatives are not provided, this may manifest itself in terms of gang membership, or other antisocial groupings. Many urban areas provide special outdoor adventure programs for teenage youth where group bonding can occur in an atmosphere of excitement and risk.

Symbolic Interaction Theory

Symbolic interaction theory comes from the field of social psychology (Blumer, 1969; Denzin, 1992). It has been used to understand and interpret human behavior in areas such as qualitative research for quite some time, and has recently been proposed as a parks, recreation, and leisure services programming theory (Rossman, 1989; 1995). From this theoretical perspective

- People interact with and gain meaning from others, equipment, facilities, rules, and so on;

- The meanings come from communication between and among individuals, because through communication people create symbols that have shared meanings; and

- The meanings are established and revised through an interpretive process (Schwandt, 1997).

In addition, human beings are said to engage in "self-reflexive" behaviors. This means that people make choices about how they act and respond within a situation rather than just passively reacting to it [the situation]. See Figure 3.8.

In considering parks, recreation, and leisure services programming as symbolic interaction the program planner must come to understand participants and their behaviors. To do this she or he must

first actively enter the setting or situation of the people ... to see their particular definition of the situation, what they take into account, and how they interpret this information (Schwandt, 1997). In other words, the program planner must view the situation as potential participants might. Professionals must see programming through the participants' eyes, determine what the participants find

People gain meaning from interacting with others and equipment.

We share meanings and symbols.

Meanings are established through interpretation.

Figure 3.8   Three Elements of Symbolic Interactionism

important, and how the participants interpret the situation in which they find themselves. According to Rossman (1995)

> A theory of recreation and leisure programming derived from symbolic interactionism should explain and predict how programmers will design, develop, and operate leisure programs to facilitate individual's leisure experiences. (p. 22)

From this perspective programmers need to bear in mind that participants play a role in shaping the nature of all recreation and leisure experiences in which they participate. This is done through their interactions with others, equipment, and facilities as well as the meanings they give to these interactions. No matter the program, each individual will experience the event differently from others. If programmers understand how people shape meanings, they will better understand how that meaning also shapes actions.

To illustrate this theory consider the following: If we were planning a theme park ride we would want to keep in mind that different people give different meanings to the structure of the ride (some might ascribe excitement and thrills meaning to a ride while others see it as having meanings of personal lack of control and fear). These views are affected by interactions with others, the structure of the ride, signage, and other sensory input. For example, while waiting in line for a theme park ride we can influence a person's view of the upcoming experience by what we say and how we say it. In addition, certain colors (of the equipment and structure), and smells in the air, can increase or decrease the anxiety levels of those waiting. These different perceptions affect the way people view the ride, their desire to participate on it, and the nature of the leisure experience they derive from it. By understanding, planning for, and being responsive to these meanings, programmers can best meet a variety of participant needs.

Disney does this extremely well. For instance, while standing in line for a virtual reality movie ride about the human body at Disney World, customers are moved through an environment that gives the impression of moving through a biological sanitation and cleansing zone. There are white, sanitized walls; moving sidewalks with scientific-looking grids; voices in loudspeakers that remind

"biologists" (customers) to be sure and go into the "cleansing hydrospray;" and Disney cast members (employees) attending this ride are dressed like physicians and biologists. All of this preparation and lead-in sets the tone to make even waiting in line part of the "ride." It also is a wonderful example of how leisure professionals can influence the way people interact with their environment in leisure settings.

Sociocultural Theory

Recognizing the influence of social (e.g., education, gender, culture, age, religion) and political (i.e., demands from constituents with money or large lobbying support) issues on program activities, choices, and opportunities is reflective of the sociocultural theory of programming. Kraus (1977; 1985) presented a sociopolitical approach which set the groundwork for this theoretical presentation of programming. In it, Kraus saw community recreation programming as heavily influenced by such factors as the demands of pressure from groups for facilities and programs, and the varying social needs of different neighborhoods and communities (see Figure 3.9).

In the expanded sociocultural theory of programming the social events of contemporary culture influence and impact upon the nature of parks, recreation, and leisure services programming. For

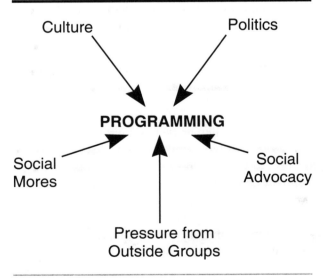

Figure 3.9   Social and Cultural Influences

example, community recreation services for people with disabilities have increased tremendously over the past ten to fifteen years. This is due, in part, to the social and political (as well as legal) forces of people with disabilities and their advocates. It is not only "the right thing to do," but it is also socially advantageous to offer programs and facilities that are accessible to people with disabilities.

This sort of influence is also apparent in the culturally relevant programming that has become popular in the past five to ten years. Parks, recreation, and leisure service agencies are becoming more and more interested in serving people of all cultural groups. Culturally relevant programming makes good business sense and agencies are socially encouraged or pressured to do so. Various cultural groups, whether they are based on religion, ethnicity, sexual orientation or another demographic variable, influence the very nature of recreation programming. For instance, the type of music played and the type of food served at an event will draw people from one age or ethnic group over another. Furthermore, in communities where large numbers of a particular cultural group live (e.g., Cuban Hispanics in Miami, Florida) we will find parks, recreation, and leisure programs that are culturally relevant to these constituents. The games, sports, special events, and facilities offered by leisure services professionals are reflective of the cultural needs and preferences of this constituent group. Therefore, from this theoretical perspective, programming is developed from one's knowledge of and responsiveness to a particular group's cultural needs. It might be viewed as a combination of the authoritarian and expressed needs approaches to programming (as presented in Chapter Two).

Comprehensive Theory

The last theory we will present here is one that encompasses the most important elements of several models just discussed—we call it the comprehensive theory of programming. From this viewpoint, programming is the intersection of the following elements: participants, equipment and resources, facilities, and staff. As these four elements come together one can see the art and science of leisure services programming. Of course, nothing exists in

a vacuum. Therefore, these four elements both influence, and are under the constant influence of outside factors (see Figure 3.10, page 52).

These influences include historical factors (e.g., traditions, past experience); environmental factors (e.g., time, temperature, lights); cultural factors (e.g., preferences based on ethnicity, gender, age, religion); social factors (e.g., fads, trends, current events); and organizational factors (e.g., values, budget, philosophy). The combination of outside factors defines the unique nature of the program or event to be provided to various constituent groups.

For example, let's say we know that our constituent group consists of participants who are urban, ethnically mixed, family groups. We have a facility that includes a gymnasium and a multipurpose room along with limited outdoor space including an outdoor basketball court. In addition, we have a variety of balls and other miscellaneous play equipment. We also have a good mix of arts and crafts supplies. Finally, our staff consists of parks, recreation, and leisure service professionals who have been in the field for an average of eight years, and at this agency for an average of five years. Our staff to participant ratio is 1:35, and several of the staff are highly skilled in sports and social recreation activities.

From the information we have so far, the program we would likely develop would be one that utilizes the resources we have as described. In this case, we might offer open recreation opportunities for families; an ethnic festival featuring a mix of ethnic groups, and perhaps highlighting traditional crafts or sporting activities; family recreation activities that encourage mixed family participation; or programs for children to encourage social skill development. The programs would likely be offered after school, in the evenings, or on weekends. Furthermore, they would be offered at facilities that are easily accessible with public transportation.

Outside influences, such as the environment, might change the nature of the program. For instance, if we were holding the program outdoors and the weather was poor, we would either need to move it indoors or change the date of the event. Either of these two responses would change the atmosphere, perhaps the activities, and certainly, the experience of participants.

Organizational factors such as available budget and philosophy, could also impact the event. The

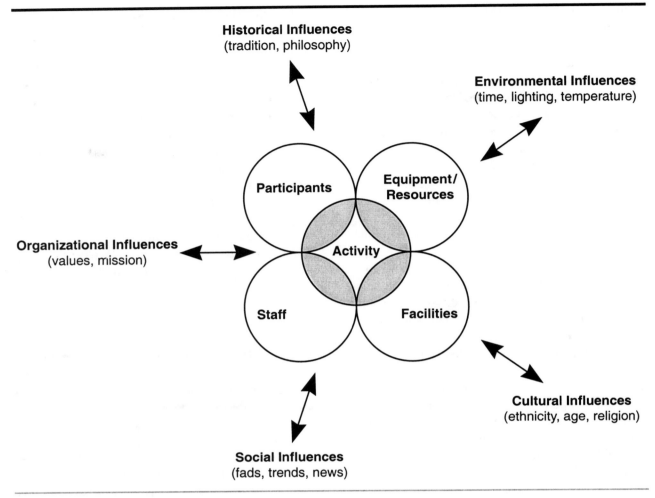

Figure 3.10   Comprehensive Model of Programming

budget might constrain (or enhance) the event, or it might event dictate that the program be offered at a minimum fee. Organizational philosophy could very well demand that a primary goal be the inclusion of all interested participants no matter their skill level, financial status, or personal needs. Social influences such as what is trendy (e.g., music, colors) might impact the decorations and mood setting program elements. Similarly, historical factors such as organizational and community tradition might influence the activity by suggesting that it always be offered on the same day and time, at the same location, and be sponsored by the same entities as in the past.

Program theories are the underlying structure of what we do as parks, recreation, and leisure service professionals. The theory we utilize to help us understand programming provides the framework on which we fashion and accomplish our programming tasks. The theory we buy into drives the focus and direction of our work. No matter the theoretical underpinnings, all recreation programs involve specific tasks for accomplishment—identifying the organization's philosophy and mission, assessing participant needs, planning or designing a program/event, implementing the program/event, and evaluating the program/event. It is through these tasks that a program or activity comes to fruition. These tasks define the *programming process*.

The Cyclical Programming Process

As we might imagine, a cyclical process of programming presents the tasks to be accomplished as ongoing, without end. The process begins at one point, and returns to that same point, continuing in the cycle for as long as the organization continues to conduct and offer recreation and leisure programs. Farrell and Lundegren (1978), as well as Carpenter and Howe (1985), have used this structure as the foundation for the parks, recreation, and leisure services programming process.

Typically, this process is characterized by identifying specific tasks to be done in order to put together a program or event, and following those tasks through. At the heart of this process is the organizational philosophy and mission—this drives the very nature of the other process components. Once we have identified the organization's philosophy, mission, and vision, we move outward to:

1. Assess participant needs;

2. Plan or design a program/event;

3. Engage in pre-program tasks such as pricing, promotion, and staffing;

4. Implement the program/event;

5. Conduct formative evaluations;

6. Continue implementation with adjustments (based on the information gained from the formative evaluation); and

7. Conduct the summative evaluation. This last step then leads to a revisiting of the organization's mission, new participant assessments, improved program planning and design, new program implementation, revised program evaluation, and so on (see Figure 3.11).

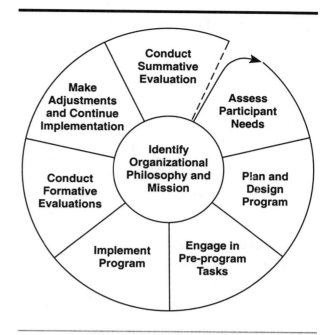

Figure 3.11   The Programming Cycle

A graphic representation of the programming process might look like a stretched-out coil or spring (see Figure 3.12). The process is moving forward, and not simply repeating itself. A key element of the program process is that it is *not* a start-and-stop type of activity. It is ongoing, and based on what has been learned from previous program efforts. The cyclical nature of this process also enables practitioners to be responsive to social, cultural, and individual changes in needs and desires. Because of this, followed well, the process allows for continuous program improvement and innovation. Throughout this text and in the accompanying workbook, we will be basing our program examples on this cyclical program process.

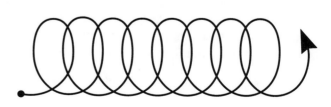

Figure 3.12   Program development is both circular and cyclical.

Summary

The various theories of programming include a systems model which resembles a computer process, the cyclical model which is Slinky-like in its representation of the programming process, and the benefits-driven theory which suggests that programming is driven by the sought after and expected benefits of recreation participation. Other theories presented here included the flow theory which suggests the facilitation of optimal experiences as the goal of all parks, recreation, and leisure service programming efforts; motivation theory which explains recreation programming as being driven by the motivations of participants; and symbolic interaction theory which arises out of social psychology and examines human behavior. Lastly, the sociocultural and comprehensive theories were presented. Sociocultural theory speaks to the influences of social, political, and cultural elements on the program process. The comprehensive theory represents programming efforts as an outgrowth of the intersection of participants, equipment and resources, facilities, and staff. All of these four comprehensive elements are influenced by external forces that change the "flavor" of the program process.

In addition to building programming on a theoretical framework, all programs have various tasks in common. These tasks, when defined in a cycle, define the programming process. All programmers engage in the same tasks when designing and implementing programs. Those tasks include: being knowledgeable about the organizational mission and philosophy; conducting a needs assessment; planning and designing the program; engaging in pre-program activities such as pricing, promotion, and staffing; implementing the program; conducting formative evaluations; making adjustments in the program based on those evaluations; and conducting a summative evaluation. The cycle is then continued by conducting another needs assessment, and continuing the programming process from there.

References

Blumer, H. (1969). *Symbolic interactionism: Perspective and method.* Englewood Cliffs, NJ: Prentice Hall.

Carpenter, G. and Howe, C. (1985). *Programming leisure experiences: A cyclical approach.* Englewood Cliffs: Prentice Hall.

Csikszentmihalyi, M. (1990). *Flow: The psychology of optimal experience.* New York:, NY HarperCollins.

Denzin, N. (1992). *Symbolic interactionism and cultural studies.* Cambridge, UK: Basil Blackwell.

Farrell, P. and Lundegren, H. (1978). *The process of recreation programming: Theory and technique.* New York, NY: Wiley and Sons.

Farrell, P. and Lundegren, H. (1991). *The process of recreation programming: Theory and technique, 3rd ed.* State College, PA: Venture Publishing, Inc.

Hoff, B. (1982). *The Tao of Pooh.* New York, NY: Penguin.

Kraus, R. (1997). *Recreation programming: A benefits-driven approach.* Boston, MA: Allyn & Bacon.

Kraus, R. (1985). *Recreation program planning today.* Glenview, IL: Scott, Foresman & Co.

Kraus, R. (1977). *Recreation today: Program planning and leadership, 2nd ed.* Santa Monica, CA: Goodyear.

Murphy, J., Niepoth, E. W., Jamieson, L. and Williams, J. (1991). *Leisure systems: Critical concepts and applications.* Champaign, IL: Sagamore Publishing.

Niepoth, E. W. (1983). *Leisure leadership.* Englewood Cliffs, NJ: Prentice Hall.

Peterson, C. and Gunn, S. (1984). *Therapeutic recreation program design: Principles and procedures, 2nd ed.* Englewood Cliffs, NJ: Prentice Hall.

Rossman, J. R. (1989). *Recreation programming: Designing leisure experiences.* Champaign, IL: Sagamore Publishing.

Rossman, J. R. (1995). *Recreation programming: Designing leisure experiences, 2nd ed.* Champaign, IL: Sagamore Publishing.

Schwandt, T. (1997). *Qualitative inquiry: A dictionary of terms.* Newbury Park, CA: Sage.

Worthern, B., Sanders, J. and Fitzpatrick, J. (1997). *Program evaluation: Alternative approaches and practical guidelines, 2nd ed.* New York, NY: Longman.

Chapter Four

Program Philosophy

While he sat at the café in the Fredericksberg Garden in Copenhagen one afternoon smoking a cigar, as was his habit, and turning over a great many things in his mind, Kierkegaard reflected that he had not really begun a career for himself, while a good many of his friends were already making names for themselves, getting set up in business or getting published…. The cigar burned down, he lit another, the train of reflection held him. It occurred to him then that since everyone was engaged everywhere in making things easy, perhaps someone was needed to makes things hard again, and that this too might be a career and a destiny…. to go in search of difficulties, like a new Socrates.

*Schoel, Prouty, and Radcliffe
(1988, pp. 145–146)*

The term philosophy often evokes an image of old men espousing their interpretation of the meaning of life in terms that the average person cannot understand. In reality, each individual, regardless of age, gender, or education has their own philosophy, although it may vary greatly in complexity and content from person to person. Factors that shape an individual's philosophy are the people, events, and circumstances that shape her or his values and beliefs. These factors include our families, teachers, friends, and coworkers; physical, mental, and emotional health; culture, history, education; and so on. Philosophies provide individuals with direction and affect all aspects of individual behavior.

Organizations also have philosophies which are shaped by the principal parties that guide the organization. These parties include advisory boards, boards of directors, executive directors, CEOs, presidents, administrative staff, service delivery staff, and service recipients or consumers. It is imperative that recreation programmers understand the philosophy of the leisure service organization and how the organization's philosophy impacts creating and implementing recreation programs for participants. In so doing, the programmer increases the clarity and continuity of programs and services provided, thus increasing the likelihood of their success.

This chapter introduces several key concepts by providing explanations and examples of terms related to the foundation of leisure service organizations. We explain the importance of each concept and provide applications to facilitate the reader's understanding. The relationship between concepts is also addressed so that recreation programmers will be able to assess the interface between these concepts in their own organizations as well as begin to see connections between the organization and their own professional philosophy. Furthermore, we present and interpret these concepts from the perspective of servant leadership.

Foundation, Direction, and Reflection (FDR) Concepts

The concepts presented in this chapter collectively serve several functions. The first is to provide a *foundation* for the work of the leisure service organization and recreation programmer. Specifically, philosophy, values, and traditions combine to provide the building blocks for service delivery. The second function is to provide the leisure service organization and recreation programmer with *direction*. Most critical to this endeavor are organizational mission, vision, goals, and objectives. Finally, all of these concepts are *reflected* in the services provided to participants. In other words, the programs, facilities, and staff serve as mirrors which reflect the philosophy, values, traditions, mission, vision, goals, and objectives of the organization. For the purposes of this text, these concepts, which are tied together by the functions of Foundation, Direction and Reflection, will be referred to as FDR concepts (see Figure 4.1). The following definitions, examples, applications, and discussion of how FDR concepts interact, and implications for the recreation programmer as a servant leader, should provide the reader with a thorough understanding of the meaning and importance of program philosophy.

Philosophy

A philosophy is a framework which reflects the values and beliefs of an individual or organization. A philosophy is usually characterized by both breadth and depth as seen in the following examples:

- Humanity's purpose is to take care of the earth.

- People were created to serve each other.

- The purpose of humanity is to glorify God.

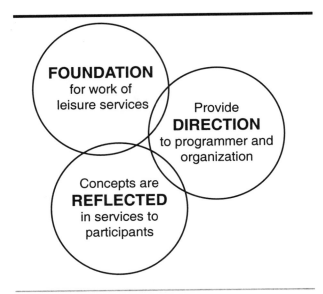

Figure 4.1   Functions of Philosophical Foundations

- Our purpose is to become the best individuals we can, developing each aspect of our being to its fullest potential.

- There is no overriding reason for our existence.

Each philosophy statement, which offers its own unique explanation of who we are and why we exist, could serve as a foundation for organizations and individuals to develop their mission and vision.

Values

Values may be defined as those things one holds to be important or as having worth. All of us have them even though we may not be aware of them. Some examples of values include power, money, progress, conservation, service, equal opportunity, quality services, parental authority, fitness, cooperation, self-discipline, competition, and freedom. Values are also enduring. While they are subject to change, they are not fleeting whims or preferences. We see values in people's thoughts, words, and actions. The leisure programmer is in a unique position to teach values through programs. In fact, it is not just the programmer's role to teach values, it is her or his responsibility. All decisions about facilities, staff, equipment, activities, rules, and other program functions reflect values, and consequently become the foundation for teaching values.

Traditions

Many times when participants are asked to reflect on a particular leisure experience, they recall memories which may have occupied little of their actual time, but have made a significant impact on them nonetheless. We tend to think that such recollections will undoubtedly reflect the unusual or exotic components of a program. However, many of these memories focus on what seem to be the opposite—traditions. Traditions are activities, interactions, or occurrences which are repeated through time and convey something meaningful about the program or organization and its participants (including the recreation leaders). Traditions are often anticipated and even expected to occur. In fact, some of the power of a tradition is its predictability.

Mission

A mission statement conveys the essence of an individual or organization and answers the question "What am I (or we) about?" The mission reflects an organization's essential reason for being, its unique identity that sets it apart from others (Hensler & Brunell, 1993). It clarifies for participants, employees, and the community what the organization considers important and in what areas they are likely to invest energy and resources. A mission statement is generally a succinct, declarative statement of being.

Vision

A vision statement addresses what an individual and organization want to do and where they want to be. "The vision . . . is a description of the organization's most desirable future state and a declaration of what the organization needs to care about most in order to

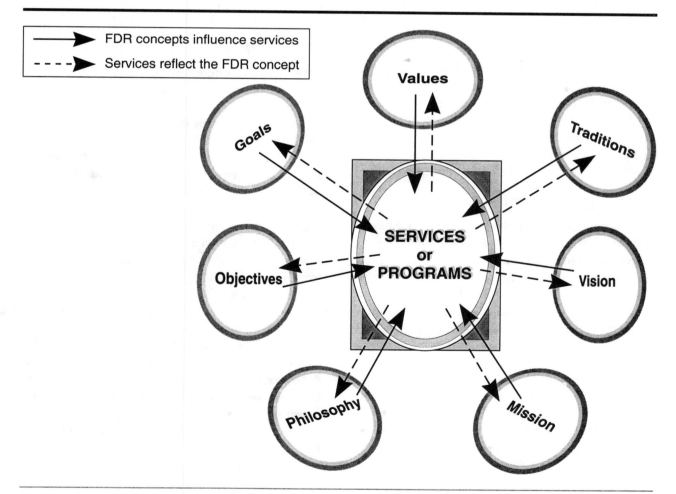

Figure 4.2   The Reflective Relationship Between FDR Concepts, and Programs and Services

reach that future" (Hensler & Brunell, 1993, p. 168). The term *vision* comes from *visualization*, the process a person goes through when they see images which represent the steps they need to take to reach a particular goal. One example of this is athletes who mentally visualize themselves completing their race, performance, or event just prior to competition (Rust, Zahorik & Keiningham, 1996). Vision reveals the direction that an organization or individual is heading and answers such questions as:

- Whom do I wish to serve?
- What resources do I wish to utilize?
- What customer benefits do I strive to reach?

Kouzes and Posner (1995) use the metaphor of a magnetic compass to characterize vision because it "provides others with the capacity to chart their course toward the future" (p. 24).

Also characteristic of a vision statement is that it contains high hopes and aspirations for the future. To some it may seem idealistic and impractical, but vision by its very nature needs to focus on far reaching possibilities. A vision statement is "a dramatic picture of the future that has the power to motivate and inspire" (Hensler & Brunell, 1993, p. 168). This element of vision is critical since a leader who is unable to draw others into her or his dream will not be able to move toward the desired future state.

Goals and Objectives

Goals are broad-based statements of intent. They indicate what an individual or organization wishes to accomplish in the future. They may be short-term, to be accomplished within a few months, or long-term, to be accomplished in a few years. When writing goals, all entities to whom the programmer has some accountability should be considered. Consequently, the programmer's goals will likely reflect some benefit to, or involvement with, the leisure service organization, self, coworkers, participants, and community members.

Objectives are specific statements of intent which give focus to service delivery and provide a basis for subsequent evaluation. Consequently, they must be measurable. When writing objectives the programmer takes a general statement and puts it into language that reflects specific behavior that is

going to be undertaken. Similar to a good journalistic article, the objective should answer the questions "Who?" "What?" "When?" "How?" and "To what degree?" in a succinct manner. Each goal will have one or more corresponding objectives which will specify how it is going to be accomplished. Goals and objectives are discussed in detail in later evaluation chapters, and in the accompanying workbook.

Importance and Application of Concepts

Goals and objectives, along with all the other FDR concepts, play an integral role in determining the programs an organization provides and influence decisions about participation, funding, location, timing, staffing, benefits, and so on. By examining how this occurs, we can understand the importance of each concept and how recreation programmers are influenced by, as well as influence, each of them.

Importance of Philosophy

For recreation programmers, it is imperative to develop a personal professional philosophy as well as understand the philosophy of the organization in which they work. One of the best reasons for investing time in identifying and developing one's philosophy is for the recreation professional to remain grounded in her or his professional endeavors. The link between personal and organizational philosophies provides a connecting point for the recreation programmer.

The leisure services field has undergone considerable changes in the past century. We have moved from a foundation of social services to a society described by quickly changing technology. Thus, it is the task of every professional to balance her or his loyalties to tradition and historical roots with flexibility and responsiveness to trends and the ever-changing world in which we live. Each recreation programmer's philosophy should reveal some of the reasons she or he chose the leisure services field as a career. It also can help a leisure services professional to keep priorities and commitments in focus while addressing the current needs of society and participants.

Application of Philosophy

If we look upon philosophy as a framework of attitudes and beliefs we can begin to see how significantly it affects the decisions of parks, recreation, and leisure service professionals. For instance, the statements presented earlier that depict the purpose of humanity and our reason for being may seem a bit remote and abstract to hold much meaning for the daily operations of an organization and its employees. If we look at the following sample statements, however, we can start to see the connections in the chain of FDR concepts.

- People will rise and fall to meet expectations.

- As people age they become more resistant to change.

- People are motivated most by money and power.

- All persons should have equal access to basic human rights under the law.

- Persons with disabilities are unable to take care of themselves.

- Children have no respect for authority.

- Granting freedom and rights to individuals breeds responsibility.

- The reward of providing quality services is the service itself.

- Leading is better than following.

- New is better.

- All people are prejudiced.

These beliefs and attitudes will dramatically influence the decisions a recreation professional makes in areas such as standards of quality of service, expectations of participants, adherence to tradition and routine versus variety and change, resource distribution, behavior management strategies, participant empowerment, innovation in searching for funding sources, strategies for participant and staff recruitment, and all other aspects of programming. This is the nature of philosophy. Figure 4.3 presents a section of the philosophy statement of "I Will Not Complain," a commercial organization that provides

"I Will Not Complain"

Our Philosophy

At "I Will Not Complain," we believe there is a continual need to improve teamwork and communication within an organization. The greatest challenge to ensuring corporate success is to motivate employees to effectively work together in pursuit of organizational goals.

We believe employees are committed to their company and want to do their best. What we aim to do is to develop an open culture within organizations where employees know new ideas are welcomed and taken seriously.

The best source of information and ideas about how to improve team performance is the team members themselves. In today's business environment this source of wisdom, knowledge and experience is an asset that needs to be recognized and developed. We want to help you unlock this potential.

Figure 4.3   The Importance of Philosophy— "I Will Not Complain" Philosophy Statement

management training through team-building exercises and outdoor adventure activities to businesses throughout Asia.

Importance of Values

Values are an integral part of what makes each of us human, and serve as a common denominator between people. Researchers have found that companies that possess shared values are far more productive and successful than other firms. In fact, researchers found that it was less important what values each company adopted than the fact that each had a "core ideology" within the organization (Kouzes & Posner, 1995). Furthermore, when disparity in values is high and tolerance for these differences is low, divisiveness between people can occur. Consequently, the leisure programmer must be able to identify the values of all relevant parties and deal with anticipated conflicts.

Leisure service providers must be careful that they do not just give "lip service" to values, but are actually taking a stand for what they think is right and important. This may require very specific actions such as confronting a participant who demeans another person during a program rather than simply ignoring it and moving things along. This may also take the form of more far-reaching behaviors such as standing by a commitment to serve all participants. As discussed in Chapter Two, the adage "the customer is always right" tends to serve primarily as an *ideal* rather than actual practice. In reality, how businesses put this professed value into action is very telling relative to their philosophy. Far too often business practices seem to reflect an adherence to profit rather than customer satisfaction. The challenge many face is to maintain their values in spite of outside pressures.

To extrapolate from Snyder, Dowd, and Houghton (1994), in order for leisure programmers to truly be servant leaders, they must profess and, more importantly, live out three basic values:

- *Service to others*, having a genuine interest and orientation to other people;

- *Humility*, putting aside pride long enough to listen to someone even if she or he is wrong; and

- *Integrity*, establishing a relationship with participants based on "truthfulness, honor and responsibility in acting out these beliefs" (p. 168).

Application of Values

It is Sam Walton's "deceptively, simple vision that is credited for his huge success as the founder of Wal-Mart" (Snyder, Dowd & Houghton, 1994, p. 49). We should note that "embedded in Walton's vision for Wal-Mart was his rock-solid set of personal values, including humility, honesty, frugality, and trust. . . . Walton's personal values were translated into three key business principles: provide the customer with value and service in a clean and friendly shopping environment, create a partnership with the associates, and maintain commitment to the community" (Snyder, Dowd & Houghton, p. 53). Although he was just one person, by utilizing these values in policy development and disseminating them throughout his company, Walton's *product* or *service* reflects his founding principles.

Because leisure programmers are in leadership roles, they are naturally in positions of influence which provide the opportunity to model and teach values. In fact, this will occur regardless of whether or not the programmer does so consciously. This dynamic is similar to the experience of professional athletes who find their behavior scrutinized because they are role models whether they want to be or not. Likewise, by the very nature of the relationship between programmer and participant, and the value laden society in which we live, programmers are in the business of teaching values every day.

Suppose a leisure organization receives a donation from a former participant; a message will be conveyed by how the organization chooses to allocate those funds. For example, if it is used to build a ramp into a facility the organization demonstrates a priority on accessibility for persons with disabilities; if it is used for a new weight machine in the gym, it shows a priority for physical fitness; and if it is to be used to establish a scholarship fund for youth from the inner city for leadership training, community development is prioritized. Regardless of whether or not recreation professionals are thinking about the underlying values that are communicated with each of these decisions, a message is being sent.

It is also true that an action or decision may be interpreted as placing a higher value on one thing over another when this is not the intent or even accurate. People are not always aware of the values they have or that they are expressing them through their behavior and decisions. One of the most obvious examples is the activity leader who selects the energetic, talkative child in the group to be a helper rather than the child who is quiet and mild mannered. The assumption on the part of the leader is that the talkative child will make a better helper, perhaps because she or he assumes talkative people are more willing to take on additional roles. In reality, however, the other child may be equally or better skilled at helping with a particular task.

While it may seem unjust at times, leisure professionals need to realize the importance of impressions and the consequences that can result. For instance, a day care provider who recently received bad news about the health of a family member may have a legitimate reason for greeting her or his preschoolers with little animation or enthusiasm; nonetheless, that action may be interpreted by participants as a lack of care or concern and have far-reaching effects on what transpires later.

In order to stay focused and be sure leisure professionals are teaching the values that they want, it is helpful for individuals and organizations to formalize a values statement. Such a statement reflects what the person or organization holds to be most important and these values need to be considered when developing programs. An example of such a statement written for NOLS—National Outdoor Leadership School—a private nonprofit organization, is presented in Figure 4.4.

Importance of Traditions

When we think about traditions, we often think about patterns of behavior or customs that our families engage in during holidays. Most of us associate different holidays with an array of traditions such as turkey on Thanksgiving, candle lighting during Chanukah, and fireworks on Independence Day. Many of these we take for granted until they are suddenly missing or changed for some reason. Such a change in a tradition often evokes an emotional response. Somehow our feelings about the holiday are not quite the same. The reason for this is because traditions are a means of establishing

---

NOLS Values Statement

The NOLS community—its staff, students, trustees and alumni—shares a commitment to:

Wilderness

We define wilderness as a place where nature is dominant and situations and their consequences are real. Living in these conditions, away from the distractions of modern civilization foster self-reliance, judgment, respect, and a sense of responsibility for our actions. It can also be a profoundly moving experience that leads to inspiration, joy, and commitment to an environmental ethic.

Education

We believe that education should be exciting, fun, and challenging. With this in mind, our courses are set up to help people develop and practice the skills they need to live, travel, and play safely in the outdoors. On our expeditions, people learn by accepting and meeting real challenges. Our instructors are educators, not guides. They are committed to inspiring students to explore and develop their understanding of wilderness ethics, leadership, teamwork, natural history, and technical skills.

Leadership

We believe that leadership is a skill that can be learned and practiced. With students and staff, we encourage the evolution of judgment, personal responsibility, and awareness of group needs—key leadership traits— through practical experience and timely feedback. We value integrity, experience, accountability, and humility in our leaders.

Safety

We accept risk as an integral part of the environments through which we travel and of the learning process itself. The recognition and management of risk is critical to both the development of leadership and to the safety and health of our students and staff. We believe successful risk management stems from good judgment based on experience, training, and knowledge.

Community

NOLS is an international community composed of talented individuals who care deeply about what they do. We value diversity, integrity and personal responsibility while recognizing that our strength lies in teamwork and commitment to our mission and each other. We appreciate creativity, individuality and passion among our staff and institution. We take our jobs seriously and pursue our mission with enthusiasm, but we cherish our sense of humor and our ability to laugh at ourselves.

Excellence

We seek excellence in all we do. We recognize that maintaining excellence requires that we question decisions, learn from failures, and celebrate success. We are committed to high quality experiences where every moment and every relationship counts. We evolve and adapt with new technology, changing techniques and differing circumstances.

Figure 4.4   The Importance of Values—The National Outdoor Leadership School (NOLS)

bonds and loyalty between family members. A study at the Ohio State University Extension revealed that the more importance families placed on traditions, the higher they ranked on a scale of family strength (Coady & Beckham Mims, 1998). Similarly, traditions are also a way of building a sense of community and loyalty within organizations and in communities.

All this is not to suggest that change is not a good thing; to the contrary, change and the resulting adaptations are necessary for any family or recreation program to survive and certainly to thrive. Even traditions undergo change through the years, but the essence of each one continues. Historian A. N. Whitehead noted that we must simultaneously respect the value of tradition and stability while responding to societal changes (Bennis, 1993).

Application of Traditions

One example of a tradition that has changed significantly since its inception, but has survived the test of time is the *Rags* and *Leathers* program conducted at many of the YMCA camps on the west coast. Begun in 1914 as a way to recognize the character of a camper with a disability who had inspired others, rags are colored coded (see Figure 4.5) and symbolize an area of character development. The program is used to challenge youth ages 12 and older to focus on an area of self-improvement during the camp experience.

At the beginning of the camp session, counselors meet with each youth to help them write goals in the area of development they have chosen. On the last night of camp, each camper is blindfolded with their rag (a YMCA rag bandanna) and led up a trail. Every 100 yards, a reading is shared that pertains to the particular rag that individuals in the group have worked on and more readings are shared when they reach their destination on the top of the hill. Counselors share comments about each camper and then rags are removed; campers emerge from a world of total darkness to find themselves in an area that is lit by candles that are arranged in patterns forming the YMCA symbols. Then campers have an opportunity to address the group.

This program tends to be quite powerful and emotional. One former director of Camp Silver Creek recalls a particular evening when one of their "toughest kids broke down crying and told about how he had made his first real friend—his counselor." The *Leathers* program was developed for campers ages 9 to 11 and is simpler, but similar to *Rags*. Each camper selects one area of self-improvement that corresponds to one of the YMCA symbols (see Figure 4.6). During a closing ceremony each participant is presented with a leather symbol that corresponds to the area they have worked on during the session (LaBarre, 1998).

This tradition is an example of being participant focused, an important aspect of servant leadership. In *Rags* and *Leathers*, campers are involved by choosing whether they want to participate, selecting their challenge area, and developing their own goals. There are also provisions for non-Christian participants to adapt the challenge description to meet their own belief system. It is always important when developing and implementing a program to maintain the integrity of participants and to protect their feelings at all costs. This requires that programmers be able to empathize with their constituents.

YMCA Rags Program

Color	Challenge Area
Blue	Loyalty to God, country and one's best self
Silver	Rededicate to Christian way of life and values
Brown	Service to others
Gold	Understanding, concern and acceptance of others
Red	Sacrifice of time, talents and personal will
Purple	To lead the best life possible
White	Life of full-time Christian service to youth

Figure 4.5   An Example of Traditions—The YMCA Rags Program

YMCA Leathers Program

Symbol	Challenge Area
Triangle	To grow in mind, body and Spirit
Square	To grow and become a better friend and keep good friends
Circle	To become close to God through the earth He created

Figure 4.6   An Example of Traditions—The YMCA Leathers Program

Importance of Mission

Before an individual or organization can determine where they want to go, there must be some understanding of where they are and what they are about (i.e., What is the mission?). Imagine a scuba diver submerged in the ocean at an unknown depth. Perhaps she was very clear in her dive plan that she was going to descend to 15 meters and stay submerged for 40 minutes. But suppose in the process of descending the diver was so entranced in looking at marine life that she had no idea after 15 minutes how far she had descended. While the diver knows she wants to be at 15 meters, if she does not know her current depth, she does not know whether to swim up or down to achieve this. In this analogy, the diver's depth gauge serves the same function as a mission statement by providing bearings so the goal can be pursued.

Lack of a clear mission can be seen as the demise of some organizations. Sears Roebuck and Company is cited as a classic example of a business that lost their mission when they switched from being a prominent mail-order company to a chain of retail stores. Sears "seemed to target both everybody and nobody. Low-priced goods and high-priced goods were offered haphazardly and the store's image became confused" (Rust, Zahorik & Keiningham, 1996, p. 77). Sears lost a good deal of the market share.

In a leisure services organization, mission provides unity, focus, and a starting point for future endeavors. The bottom line is that without such a common purpose, recreation programmers are likely to find themselves simply scheduling activities rather than serving their communities by developing and providing quality programs.

Application of Mission

While the content of a mission statement may vary depending on the type of leisure service organization (i.e., commercial, public, or nonprofit), the process of writing one is essentially the same for all. Most importantly, the fact that a written mission statement should exist is undeniable. One example of a mission statement that does a superb job of serving the essential function of reflecting the organization's values can be seen by looking at Ben and Jerry's Homemade, Inc., an ice cream company that is also the number one tourist attraction in

Vermont. Their mission consists of three interrelated parts (see Figure 4.7, page 66).

This mission statement addresses the need of the organization to make money, but goes further by emphasizing a commitment to product quality and social responsibility. It explains why their ice cream is relatively expensive (only the finest ingredients), why they are not manufacturing and selling ice cream in Asia (profits of tapping this market are outweighed by the environmental cost of natural resources consumed), and why they have increased their product line to include non-fat yogurts and new flavors (increasing revenue). Like Ben and Jerry's, each leisure service organization must ask what mission(s) they wish to adopt whether it be to make money, increase health and fitness in the community, enhance the lives of the elderly, or some other benefit of servant leadership.

Importance of Vision

The word *vision* has roots in biblical history; "When there is no vision, the people perish" (Proverbs 29:18). It has also become a buzz word in business as managers note that "a person leads through a vision, a shared set of values, a shared objective" (Bennis, 1993, p. 92). Think about a jigsaw puzzle and how difficult it is to put the pieces together if no one has seen "the whole picture"—a vision of the whole picture is lacking and the task is nearly impossible. Kouzes and Posner (1995) view the absence of vision as similar to giving a slide presentation with the projector out of focus. When they experimented with this in leadership seminars, they found that the reaction of participants included impatience, confusion, frustration, anger, even nausea. All consumers want to know what an organization is going to be doing in both the near and far future so they can make appropriate decisions to facilitate getting there (Kouzes & Posner, 1995). The importance of vision is most clearly seen when viewed from the perspective that it is vision that moves an organization from "doing things right to doing the right thing" (Hensler & Brunell, 1993, p. 168).

Application of Vision

David Hillard, executive director of the Wyman Center, a leisure service organization that operates Camp Wyman in Eureka, Missouri, gives strong testimony to the importance of vision for camping

BEN&JERRY'S STATEMENT OF MISSION

Ben & Jerry's is dedicated to the creation and demonstration of a new corporate concept of linked prosperity. Our mission consists of 3 interrelated parts:

PRODUCT MISSION

To make, distribute and sell the finest quality all natural ice cream and related products in a wide variety of innovative flavors made from Vermont dairy products.

ECONOMIC MISSION

To operate the company on a sound financial basis of profitable growth, increasing value for our shareholders and creating career opportunities and financial rewards for our employees.

SOCIAL MISSION

To operate the company in a way that actively recognizes the central role that business plays in the structure of society by initiating innovative ways to improve the quality of life of a broad community: local, national and international.

UNDERLYING THE MISSION

Is the determination to seek new and creative ways of addressing all three parts, while holding a deep respect for individuals inside and outside the company, and for the communities of which they are a part.

© Ben & Jerry's Homemade Holdings, Inc. 1999. Ben & Jerry's is a trademark of Ben & Jerry's Homemade Holdings, Inc.

Figure 4.7   An Example of Mission—Ben & Jerry's Ice Cream
Used with permission of Ben & Jerry's Homemade Holdings, Inc.

organizations to survive at a time when so many are being sold and disbanded. In the process of restructuring and redefining the services offered by Wyman Center a new vision was created for both the community and the organization. The community vision statement says, "Every home, every classroom, every neighborhood will be a safe harbor and an environment that nurtures, educates, and guides children to reach their full potential and to live successful lives" (Hillard, 1994, p. 16). Supporting this is the vision statement for the Wyman Center,

> We will become a worldwide enterprise designing and delivering programs that offer solutions to kids at-risk in all parts of the world" (Hillard, 1994, p. 16).

These seem to express very lofty ideas, but as Walt Disney, one of the great visionaries of the twentieth century, wrote, "If you can dream it, you can do it" (Bennis & Nanus, 1985, p. 33).

Developing Vision

"To do it," leisure professionals must somehow visualize a desired outcome for the future. How have individuals and organizations been able to accomplish this? Bennis and Nanus (1985) examined the

successes of a variety of business and world leaders in search of the answer to this question. They found that individuals have many different strategies and sources of inspiration as they approached this task. Some of the sources people credited in developing their vision statements are identified below:

- An administrator at UCLA received inspiration from the faculty;

- John F. Kennedy looked to historical accounts and philosophers for his vision;

- Martin Luther King, Jr. utilized religious and ethical ideologies in the development of his visionary ideas;

- An early manager of General Motors examined the idea of the "American Dream" and the role of capitalism as he captured his notion of vision; and

- Executives at Apple and Polaroid utilized a logical process of seeking and expanding technological limits.

What this wide range of sources shows us is that there is no one way to develop vision; it is very individualistic. However, part of the vision-building process must include looking to the past, present, and future. We could begin by reflecting on our own experiences as well as talking with others in the field to benefit from their experiences. Secondly, leisure providers can look around at what is currently happening in the field. They can look to the resources that are available and what actions they might undertake to test the market. They should also examine the trends and changes that are likely to occur in the future which may affect their vision (Bennis & Nanus, 1985). Once a vision statement is completed, it should be assessed and evaluated continually to be sure that it accurately reflects the philosophy and values of the individual or organization. Additional samples of vision statements are included in Figure 4.8.

Active Australia:

"The vision of Active Australia is all Australians actively involved in sport, community recreation, fitness, outdoor recreation and other physical activities."

Pima County Community Resources, Parks, and Recreation:

"It is the vision of Pima County Parks and Recreation Department to serve the taxpayers of Pima County by providing leisure services, new park facilities, and well-planned natural resource areas through community partnerships and neighborhood input."

Ann Arbor District Library:

"The Ann Arbor District Library continues to lead and inspire by providing ever-expanding opportunities to enrich and inform users' lives. The library sets the standards for excellence and innovation."

City of Pasadena:

"...to aim at nothing less than a vision of a TOTAL RECREATION ENVIRONMENT that encompasses not only the physical, educational, and social dimensions of traditional programs but also the aesthetic and environmental assets which Pasadena is so richly endowed, and to establish Pasadena's recreation programs and approaches as the CLEAR STANDARDS OF INNOVATION AND EXCELLENCE in local government and to LEAD AND INSPIRE the entire community to become involved in the pursuit of these goals."

Figure 4.8   Sample Vision Statements

Communicating Vision

In addition to developing a vision statement, leisure professionals need to be able to enlist the support of others in their quest for attainment. As mentioned earlier, the vision itself should be inspirational. The statement must also be communicated in a clear and interesting way in order to draw others into the journey. Bennis and Nanus (1985) refer to former U.S. President Jimmy Carter as an example of someone who lacked the ability to successfully communicate his vision. President Carter is cited as "one of the best-informed presidents since Woodrow Wilson" but according to one of his loyal cabinet officers,

> working for him was difficult because she never knew what he stood for. '[It] was like looking at the wrong side of a tapestry—blurry and indistinct.' (1985, pp. 36–37)

In contrast, one of the most memorable and inspiring moments in American history is the "I Have a Dream" speech delivered by Martin Luther King, Jr. His "enlivening influence is rooted in fundamental values, cultural traditions, and personal conviction" (Kouzes & Posner, 1995, pp. 126–27). An analysis of how King inspired his listeners has been conducted many times in leadership development workshops. The results focused less on any particular characteristic of the person himself (such as charisma) and more on specific skills or strategies of effective communication. They include:

- Using images and word pictures;
- Using examples that people can relate to;
- Talking about traditional values;
- Appealing to common bonds;
- Getting to know your audience;
- Using repetition;
- Being positive and hopeful;
- Shifting from "I" to "we;"
- Speaking with passion and emotion; and
- Having personal conviction about the dream. (Kouzes & Posner, 1995, p. 128)

It is not just through effective communication or charisma that leaders are able to draw others toward their particular vision. Also important are two factors toward which all recreation programmers should strive: (1) quality, and (2) dedication or love of our work. Organizations and leaders who foster these characteristics are more likely to experience collective support for their vision (Bennis, 1993) and the subsequent energy and spirit which is likely to evolve than others.

We know that one of the most important characteristics of a leader is a powerful vision and the ability to communicate that vision to others. It is not enough, however; we must also act in such a way as to achieve that mission. One action taken by Wyman Center after the process of developing a vision included starting a program called Camp Caravan. In response to the realization that Camp Wyman was not in touch with the inner-city youth they had vowed to serve, program equipment was loaded into a truck and services were taken to school playgrounds. Services include teaching history experientially, teaching environmental science through a field laboratory, team building, and conflict resolution (Hillard, 1994).

Importance of Goals and Objectives

While the Foundation, Direction, and Reflection (FDR) concepts all have a role in guiding individuals and organizations, one of the concrete tools that recreation professionals can actually "hang onto" are goals and objectives. It is the goals and objectives that serve as a path toward the organization's vision and dictate the actions needed to get there. By ignoring this step in the chain of concepts, we run the risk of "spinning our wheels" in spite of having a well-developed mission and vision. Goals and objectives also provide accountability and, using a servant leadership model, ensure that services delivered are targeted to meet constituent needs.

Application of Goals and Objectives

When writing goals it is important to remember that they should reflect desired benefits to be achieved for individuals as well as the organization. The following statements serve as examples of possible goals for a leisure service organization.

- To provide before- and after-school care for all families in need.

- To decrease juvenile delinquency in the neighborhood.

- To attend professional conferences in the field of health and fitness promotion.

- To ensure paid planning time for all service delivery staff.

- To become the most visited resort in the region.

Each of these goals has a particular beneficiary although there may be overlap since what benefits one entity is often beneficial to another. The first addressees the needs of participants; the second addresses the community; the third addresses the employee; the fourth goal addresses coworkers; and the fifth addresses the organization.

The next step in the process is to take each of the goals and write at least one objective which will indicate the action to be taken, and by whom, in order to meet the goal. Using the goals listed in the previous paragraph, possible objectives include:

- The program manager will meet with principals at least once at the five neighborhood schools by January 1st to discuss networking and combining resources to provide before- and after-school care in the district.

- The program manager will schedule bimonthly retreats for youth ages 12–15 at Camp Algonquin beginning in May.

- The program manager will attend the RCRA conference each October at the organization's expense.

In actuality, most goals will require several objectives to increase the likelihood of success and utilize available resources to maximum benefit. Figure 4.9 conveys the goals of a public park and recreation department.

Interface of FDR Concepts

The reader should now understand the FDR concepts which shape the decisions and actions of each individual as well as the organization in which she or he works. Likewise, the resulting programs and services

---

Goals of the City of Southlake Parks and Recreation Department

*GOAL ONE:

Conserve and enhance Southlake's remaining natural resources to maintain the City's environmental health and quality of life.

GOAL TWO:

Develop a system of improvements and programs that provides a wide range of park and recreational opportunities to meet the diverse recreational needs of Southlake's citizens.

GOAL THREE:

Provide for the involvement of the general public, and educational and business communities in the planning, design, and development of the park and recreation system.

* The city of Southlake, Texas, follows the goals and objectives of the Parks, Recreation and Open Space Master Plan.

Figure 4.9   An Example of Goals—The Goals of the City of Southlake Parks and Recreation Department

---

reflect the philosophy, values, traditions, mission, vision, goals, and objectives that they have adopted.

As an example of this, let's look at a situation in which a consumer approaches a fitness trainer at a private health club pleading, "I can't stand myself anymore. I've tried everything to lose weight and get in shape and nothing works. Do something!" How the trainer responds to this request reveals a great deal about her or his professional philosophy, mission, vision, values, goals and objectives. Suppose she or he responds saying, "You can be successful. I can help you, but within you is a trainer who can provide the motivation and discipline to make the changes you want."

From such a statement we can extrapolate some of the driving beliefs and attitudes that influence this trainer. One philosophical statement we might attribute to the trainer is that human beings are incredibly resourceful and talented creatures. Her or his mission may be described as helping individuals feel better about themselves. The trainer's vision might include something such as endeavoring to help each person reach her or his greatest potential and

discover inner resources. Values might include such things as empowerment of others, self-determination, and physical fitness. An example of a goal would be to help the customer develop realistic objectives for weight loss and fitness improvement. Examples of objectives would be for the customer to read (insert name of motivational book here) within one week and for the trainer and customer to cooperatively complete the organization's forms which document details of previous attempts at fitness improvement within three days.

Think about this response in relation to a trainer who promises, "Don't worry about those other attempts. We can shed those pounds and inches off you." This trainer's FDR will be very different than the first trainer. Therefore, it is very important for the recreation programmer to think through, design, develop, and evaluate a program plan with thoughtful consideration of the FDR concepts.

Implications for Recreation Programmers

When a parks, recreation, and leisure services professional applies and interviews for a job, it is the responsibility of both the employer and employee to make a hiring decision that will result in a good fit between all parties. A written mission and vision statement for the organization should be shared as well as a verbal statement of a personal mission and vision of the profession by the applicant. Regardless of how creative and skilled the applicant is, an obvious incongruence between the organization and programmer will undoubtedly present problems.

Suppose the organization, an art museum in a white-collar, urban neighborhood perceives its mission to be to provide a safe and aesthetic environment to working professionals. In particular, the museum supports small area businesses by providing a convenient and pleasant environment for employees, thus reducing stress and improving health. Furthermore, the art museum benefits the businesses as well as their employees. In contrast, the job applicant is committed to increasing the cultural and social skills of urban adolescents, particularly through hands-on discovery activities. While both parties may value what the other is doing, they may not be able to be part of the same leisure service delivery system due to differing priorities. On the other hand, an applicant who wishes to challenge business executives by providing art education classes, may be able to mesh this vision with that of the agency given the common variable of the population served and benefits to small businesses in the community.

The Servant Leadership Perspective

At this point we would like to examine the FDR concepts from the perspective of servant leadership in more detail. Let's first look at a diagram which captures some of the relationships between FDR concepts as defined by a servant leadership philosophy (see Figure 4.10). In this diagram, servant leadership serves as the core foundation of developing a program and leisure organization. It affects the values and vision that are developed as well as how other aspects of the organization are designed.

Specifically, participants are empowered, organizational structure is responsive to changes (i.e., agile), the community is utilized and supported through networking and partnerships, and leaders demonstrate empathy and compassion. The result of this is the delivery of quality services and energized staff, participants, and programs. The following section further illustrates how to apply this philosophy to parks, recreation, and leisure programming by describing several servant leadership values: accountability, empathy, diversity, empowerment, community, integrity, and service.

Accountability

One factor closely tied into the FDR concepts is organizational structure. For example, is the organization a strict hierarchy or is peer management utilized? How does the structure reflect and influence program philosophy? Are consumers part of the structure in any way? Godbey (1997) proposes that all organizations need to become more "agile" in response to the rate of change we face in our society. He characterizes an agile organization as one that deals with customers' changing needs and desires; develops the knowledge, skills and creativity of staff; distributes authority, decision-making expertise, initiative, and expertise throughout the organization; and fosters leadership, trust and motivation rather than control and command.

If we apply the perspective of servant leadership to organizational structure, we may recognize that at times mission and vision need to start at the "top of the organizational pyramid." However, during implementation, it is essential that the pyramid be inverted. This ensures that energy and attention continue to flow toward customers rather than management. If, for instance, in a traditional hierarchical structure staff perceive themselves working for the person above them, when we invert the pyramid, staff quickly realize they are now "working for" the customer. Traditionally, top management is perceived as *responsible* with staff being *responsive* to those at the top. By turning the pyramid upside down, the constituents or consumers become *responsible* and the staff are *responsive* to them (Hesselbein, Goldsmith & Beckhard, 1996). This structure enables the servant leader to give the needs and desires of constituents primary consideration in all she or he does.

Empathy

In addition to conducting a formal needs assessment (see Chapter Five), one dimension of knowing consumer needs and desires is being able to empathize with them. Servant leaders must be willing to listen and learn; to walk a mile in the other person's shoes. Once we as leaders know what others want or need, we need to mobilize ourselves to act accordingly, including being prepared to get in the trenches and do what we ask of others (Hesselbein, Goldsmith & Beckhard, 1996). This can be quite a challenge as it involves identifying and understanding cross-cultural issues, and putting aside some of one's own preconceived ideas and prejudices.

Diversity

Since servant leadership is committed to the dignity and worth of all people and promotes diversity, recreation programmers must search to find ways to accommodate participants of a variety of abilities and varied backgrounds and beliefs. This includes actions such as hiring a diverse staff that represents people of various ethnic backgrounds in marketing materials; confronting participants and coworkers when they tell an ethnic joke; scheduling programs at times and locations that are accessible to a variety of constituents; and other actions which protect the rights of all participants for equal access and participation in leisure programs.

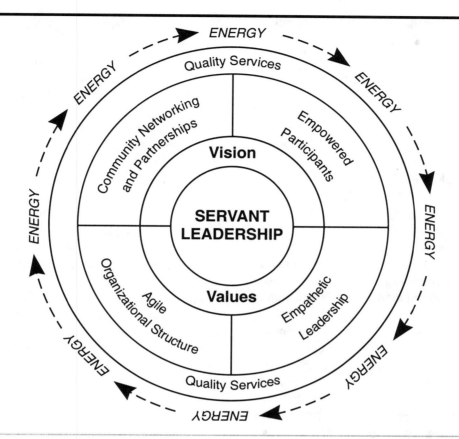

Figure 4.10 Servant Leadership as Applied to FDR Concepts

Empowerment

Programmers of leisure experiences can use a variety of techniques to empower participants. This may take the form of compiling customer opinions through surveys, interviews, and group meetings and using that information in decision making. Participants may also be included on governing committees and boards. Even very young participants can be involved in the development and implementation of programs by offering suggestions about what they want to do and selecting programs from choices offered. By involving participants in every way possible, they gain a sense of ownership and services become more responsive to customer needs.

Community

A leisure service organization that adopts a servant-leadership philosophy must consider benefits of service to the community in addition to the organization and constituents. This responsibility to community reflects the servant leader's value of relationships

between people and commitment to "a greater whole." This will take the form of networking with other leisure organizations, forming partnerships in all sectors of society, and referring constituents to the most appropriate organization—even competitors. By maximizing resources, not just within an organization, but within the entire community, recreation programmers will be able to provide more variety and creativity in their programs.

Integrity

In a world that seems to be increasingly bombarded with accusations of impropriety and challenges to standards of ethics, it is critical that servant leaders in the parks, recreation, and leisure service profession maintain a high level of integrity. Most importantly this involves being forthright, truthful, and responsible to constituents. Regardless of how dazzling a brochure, creative an idea, or exciting an event, a program is only as valuable as the leader's ability to be forthright and honest with constituents. Furthermore, it is this kind of behavior that reinforces the participants' own sense of dignity and being treated fairly.

Service

While the component of service to servant leadership may seem quite apparent, it is still helpful to examine this value and how it can be incorporated into leisure programs. Service involves a conscious effort to help those who are less privileged in our society. This should not be misinterpreted as a call to "charity work." Recognizing and acknowledging that we live in a world plagued by disparity of resources is a good beginning.

While we as servant leaders want to empower all of our constituents, we also must make a commitment to improving the quality of life of those who are less advantaged than most in some area of their lives. This includes characteristics such as physical, mental or emotional disabilities; economic hardship due to unemployment or underemployment; cultural limitations such as language barriers, racism, and so forth. Servant leadership reminds us that it is not just the public and nonprofit sector that are called upon to do this. The leisure services programmer who works at a commercial amusement or theme park (for example) can serve others in such ways as initiating senior discounts, translating brochures and signs into more than one language, and providing transportation on designated days to migrant workers.

Summary

A philosophy statement should reflect the values and beliefs that individual(s) deem important. Philosophies of staff, participants, and organizations need to be considered by staff when planning, implementing, and evaluating programs. If done consistently, such programs will reflect not just attitudes about leisure, but attitudes about time, communication, authority, diversity, and other areas, and will minimize conflict caused by incongruent philosophies. It is important to remember that what is excluded from a program is also indicative of an individual and/or organization's philosophy. Philosophy statements need to be the foundation for developing mission and vision statements as well as goals and objectives. The programmer is challenged to find ways, using limited resources, to address the needs of all parties—organization, employees, and participants—while placing highest priority on serving those she or he leads.

References

Bennis, W. (1993). *An invented life: Reflections on leadership and change.* Reading, MA: Addison-Wesley Publishing.

Bennis, W. and Nanus, B. (1985). *Leaders: The strategies for taking charge.* New York, NY: Harper and Row.

Coady, S. and Beckham Mims, K. (1998). *Celebrating traditions can strengthen family ties* [Online]. Available: http://www.ag.ohio-state.edu/-uhioline/lifetime/lt-1a.html

Godbey, G. (1997). *Leisure and leisure services in the 21st century.* State College, PA: Venture Publishing, Inc.

Hensler, W. and Brunell, K. (1993). Creating a world-class service quality management system. In E. Scheung and W. Christopher (Eds.), *The service quality handbook.* New York, NY: American Management Association.

Hesselbein, F., Goldsmith, M. and Beckhard, R. (1996). *The leader of the future: New visions, strategies, and practices for the next era.* San Francisco, CA: Jossey-Bass.

Hillard, D. (1994). The traditional camp out of touch out of time. *Camping Magazine, 66,* March-April, 14-21.

Kouzes, J. and Posner, B. (1995). *The leadership challenge: How to keep getting extraordinary things done in organizations.* San Francisco, CA: Jossey-Bass.

LaBarre, F. (1998). Rags and leathers. A telephone interview. January 15.

Proverbs 29:18. In R. Carroll and S. Prickett (Eds.) (1997). *The Bible: Authorized King James Version.* Oxford, UK: Oxford University Press.

Rust, R., Zahorik, A. and Keiningham, T. (1996). *Service marketing.* New York, NY: HarperCollins College.

Schoel, J., Prouty, D. and Radcliffe, P. (1988). *Islands of healing: A guide to adventure-based counseling.* Hamilton, PA: Project Adventure.

Snyder, N., Dowd, J. and Morse Houghton, D. (1994). *Vision, values and courage: Leadership for quality management.* New York, NY: The Free Press.

Chapter Five

Needs Assessment: The First Step

When you cannot see what is happening in a group, do not stare harder. Relax and look gently with your inner eye. When you do not understand what a person is saying, do not grasp for every word. Give up your efforts. Become silent inside and listen with your deepest self. When you are puzzled by what you see or hear, do not strive to figure things out. Stand back for a moment and become calm. When a person is calm, complex events appear simple. To know what is happening, push less, open out, and be aware. See without staring. Listen quietly rather than listening hard. Use intuition and reflection rather than trying to figure things out.

Heider, 1985, p. 27

Programming theories serve as the undergirding or foundation of the programming process. As mentioned earlier, the theory or model people buy into determines the driving force behind all of our programming efforts. Also, closely linked to this theoretical foundation is the organization's philosophy, mission, and vision. In the program process cycle (which identifies the *tasks* to be undertaken in program development) the agency philosophy, mission, and vision are at the center, or heart, of all programming tasks. In this text we are taking the approach that servant leadership and participant empowerment are important foundations upon which all parks, recreation, and leisure services entities build recreation and leisure programs.

In this light, it becomes critically important that we involve participants in the programming process. The first step in the program process cycle is designed just for this type of input. Needs assessments enable leisure professionals to seek out participant and citizen input about programming ideas, desires, and needs of various constituent groups. That's because a needs assessment is *a systematic inquiry about needs, attitudes, behaviors, and patterns of both participants and nonparticipants* (in this case, related to parks, recreation, and leisure services).

Conducting a needs assessment is the first step of the programming cycle and is repeated often throughout the program process. As you will see in this chapter, there are many reasons why needs assessments are conducted. In addition to discussing the importance of needs assessments, we will also present several definitions of terms related to needs assessments, and discuss a variety of ways in which needs assessment data can be gathered.

Needs assessments are used in all parks, recreation, and leisure settings. Professionals in therapeutic recreation, outdoor recreation, the military, public or community settings, commercial venues, nonprofit entities, tourism-based services, and other settings all gather information about constituents and use that information in their planning and programming efforts. Because the information needed is dynamic (it constantly changes) needs assessments should be comprehensive and ongoing. For instance, we might conduct a needs assessment at the beginning of an annual program (sports league), and then conduct a similar needs assessment in each subsequent year. In addition, when leisure providers recognize that a significant portion of their constituent base has changed, they should conduct a needs assessment update.

While needs assessments are absolutely necessary, they do have limitations. First, needs are infinite—there is no way we could ever satisfy every person's every need. Next, it is quite common for multiple groups to have conflicting needs (e.g., hunters and hikers) and leisure providers have to negotiate that. Thirdly, there will continue to be a lack of consensus on definitions, values, and priorities as related to parks, recreation, and leisure (Benest, Foley & Welton, 1984).

All leisure professionals need to recognize these limitations of needs assessments and do their best to address them in their efforts. As we begin the process of attending to the early steps of the programming cycle we must first agree on common meanings. To aid in the effort of developing some common understanding, this chapter begins with definitions, provides rationale for why leisure providers conduct needs assessments, and then delves into the type of information collected, as well as how it is done.

Definitions

It is our firm belief that before beginning any effort to explain why and how something is done it is important to come to an agreement on terminology. In this section we provide an overview of the meanings for common terms used in needs assessments as related to the field of parks, recreation, and leisure. These are the meanings we will use throughout the remainder of the text. In addition, they will set the stage for further explanation of the program process cycle.

Need

Most of us probably think we know what a need is—we get a certain feeling when we are in need, and we tend to act in a certain way to satisfy the need. People believe that needs drive us to go running, buy something, call someone, or go on vacation. With the very complex society in which we live, however, and the wonderful marketing efforts of manufacturers and producers, people often think they *need* something when, in fact, that need is really a strong desire. Most of us could live quite well, for instance, without that new pair of athletic shoes we saw on television that we think we "need."

Many parks, recreation, and leisure services professionals have worked to differentiate the meaning of *need* from desire or want. In a concise and succinct fashion, Carpenter and Howe (1985) defined need as an innate trait which people are motivated to satisfy. Adding to this definition, and emphasizing the biological nature of a need, other authors have defined need as a lack of some physical (physiological) (Rossman, 1995), psychological, or social requirement (Edginton, Hanson, Edginton & Hudson, 1998). Farrell and Lundegren (1991) noted that needs are interrelated—that people's minds and bodies work in concert to express a need. Once a need is met, it no longer motivates a person to act.

In general, we agree with all of these thoughts. *A need is, indeed, something that drives individuals to act in a certain way; and, once the need is met it no longer serves as a driving force for behavior. Furthermore, a need is born out of a physical, psychological, emotional, spiritual, or social deficiency an individual is currently experiencing.* These are basic human need categories and affect all people in all cultures. Servant leadership would have us address needs in programming efforts. In addition to this overarching definition of need, there are specific types of needs that affect constituents of parks, recreation, and leisure services.

Expressed Need

Expressed needs are the easiest to define because they are also the most visible. *These needs are defined by the activities in which people are currently participating* (Edginton, Hanson & Edginton, 1992; Edginton, Hanson, Edginton & Hudson, 1998; Rossman, 1995). Therefore, if you participate in your university intramural program you are expressing a need to do so. Current involvement is considered an expressed need because if an activity were taken away from participants, a need would be created. So, to determine expressed needs leisure providers can examine registration records, ticket sales, purchases, count participants through observation, or ask people what activities they currently engage in.

Felt Need

A felt need is an expressed need that hasn't happened yet. In other words, these are desires a person has, but has not yet actively expressed (Edginton, Hanson & Edginton, 1992; Edginton, Hanson, Edginton & Hudson, 1998). Rossman (1995) believes these are the same as interests, wants, and desires. So, a person who wants to join a cooking class, but has not yet attended, has a felt need for that activity.

Comparative Need

It is very common for individuals from one community or geographic area *to compare parks, recreation, and leisure opportunities available to them to those available to others living in nearby geographic areas.* These are considered comparative needs. Comparative needs may exist due to differences in leisure opportunities because of geographic location, work shift differences, differing ranks in the military, or due to social values (e.g., girls and boys are often offered different athletic opportunities). Through this comparison, an individual may discover that she or he is lacking in parks, recreation, and leisure opportunities, and thus, a comparative need is created (Edginton, Hanson & Edginton, 1992; Edginton, Hanson, Edginton & Hudson, 1998; Rossman, 1989; 1995).

Created Need

A fourth type of need identified by Edginton and colleagues (1998) is *determined by the agency or organization and accepted by participants without question. Clever marketing and promotion creates a need where none existed and is supported (and identified as a need) by constituents.* Children often are targets of created needs as they have a good deal of influence over their parents' responses to this new need. An example of a created need is the overwhelming created need for "official" NBA, WNBA, and NFL clothing and gear that children have. In some schools, not having this very expensive clothing and gear can result in teasing and even physical assaults. A need, where none existed before, was created in the minds of consumers.

Normative Need

The last type of need we will discuss are normative needs. Normative needs are *"objective" needs established by experts in the field and relate to what humans require for good health and a modicum of quality of life* (Edginton, Hanson, Edginton & Hudson, 1998; Rossman, 1995). These needs are sometimes defined by a discrepancy method (i.e., what is needed minus what exists) based on expert opinion (Rossman, 1995). One example that relates directly to our field is that of the NRPA open space standards that outline (for instance) how much of a particular type of green space is needed for a specific number of people living in a community (e.g., a large park of five acres per 1,000 people should serve citizens living within a three to five mile service zone). These standards also recommend a certain number of swimming areas per capita (e.g., one pool for every 20,000 persons with 8,000 to 10,000 square feet of surface water), museums, golf courses, campgrounds, and other parks, recreation, and leisure amenities.

Normative needs are often used in city or community planning when issues of master planning arise. As different lands are zoned commercial, residential, or agricultural, these normative needs may be used to define the need to preserve space for parks, recreation, and leisure services to enhance the population's quality of life. Normative needs are also used to justify changes in physical resources (e.g., new construction) for various leisure organizations.

Want/Desire

As mentioned earlier, many of us have difficulty in discerning the difference between a need and a want, or desire. Part of our difficulty is that a want or desire is typically something that we perceive as being needed. However, it does not necessarily address the physical, psychological, emotional, spiritual, or social needs of being human. Wants and desires are culturally learned and are influenced by social fads and trends. In addition, they are often based on previous experience and knowledge (Edginton, Hanson, Edginton & Hudson, 1998; Rossman, 1995). One of the dilemmas of satisfying a want or desire is that satisfaction often leads to wanting more.

For example, we might experience a *need* for physical activity. Whether one *wants* to play racquetball or go for a walk is influenced by one's interests, past experiences, skills, existing social mores, and current trends. Another example might be having a need for achievement. To meet that need one person might want to paint a picture while another prefers to engage in a competitive activity.

Interest

Closely related to a want or desire is interest. This has been explained as an attraction to or identification with some type of experience (Carpenter & Howe, 1985; Kraus, 1985). An interest is a relatively low-level notice of desire to engage in a particular activity. People may be interested in many things, but actually participate in very few. Interests are often reflections of a person's identity or personality, and are influenced by outside factors. They are not predictive of peoples' behaviors.

Intention

One level higher on the "notice of desire" scale is intention. This has been described as the commitment to engage in specific actions that will address what a person wants under given market conditions (Rossman, 1995). This means that a person expresses an intention to do something at a particular time, place, and price. Rossman (1995) notes that while intentions do not always lead to actions, they are stronger than interests, and thus, better predictors.

It is important for leisure service providers to understand the difference between interests, intentions, wants, and needs, because depending upon the

comparative need

(kəm par´ ə tiv nēd), *n.* To compare parks, recreation, and leisure opportunities available to oneself to those available to others living in nearby geographic areas.

created need

(krē āt´ id nēd), *n.* Determined by the agency or organization and accepted by participants without question. Clever marketing and promotion creates a need where none existed and is supported (and identified as a need) by constituents.

expressed need

(ik spres´ d nēd), *n.* These needs are defined by the activities in which people are currently participating.

felt need

(felt nēd), *n.* A felt need is an expressed need that hasn't happened yet. In other words, these are desires a person has, but has not yet actively expressed.

intention

(in ten´ shən), *n.* This has been described as the commitment to engage in specific actions that will address what a person wants under given market conditions.

interest

(in´ tər ist, –trist), *n.* This has been explained as an attraction to or identification with some type of experience.

need

(nēd), *n.* A need is, indeed, something that drives us to act in a certain way; and, once the need is met it no longer serves as a driving force for behavior. Furthermore, a need is born out of a physical, psychological, emotional, spiritual, or social deficiency we are currently experiencing.

normative need

(nôr´ mə tiv nēd), *n.* "Objective" needs established by experts in the field and related to what humans require for good health and a modicum of quality of life.

want/desire

(wont, wônt; di zī° r´), *n.* Wants and desires are culturally learned and are influenced by social fads and trends.

Figure 5.1   Definitions of Needs

questions they ask in their needs assessments they will get different types of responses. An intention to act is stronger than an interest in activity, so if programmers want to know what people are likely to participate in, they would want to ask about intentions, rather than interests. On the other hand, if they wanted to know about peoples' broad interests, they would cast a wider net with their questions. In addition, leisure service providers would want to be sure they learned about needs in addition to learning about wants. Understanding these many characteristics of their constituents will greatly influence their programming efforts. Without knowing something about their constituent base they may be "programming in the dark."

Why Conduct Needs Assessments?

As mentioned at the beginning of this chapter, once one has a firm understanding of their organizational philosophy, a needs assessment is the first step in the cyclical programming process. It has become relatively apparent, however, that many practitioners in the field begin the programming process without ever having conducted a needs assessment. This can be problematic because without the information gathered from a needs assessment, recreation and leisure services programmers are missing a vital aspect of providing appropriate programs and services *for* participants. For instance, programmers will not know if their efforts truly meet the needs and desires of constituents. Programs will be offered "because it's always been done that way" or out of convenience rather than based on any knowledge of constituent interests, wants, or needs. A parks, recreation, and leisure services professional has a duty to learn as much as possible about all constituents— both those who currently participate in activities, and those who do not participate in activities—so the services provided are meaningful and result in benefits for all.

Needs assessments are conducted for a variety of reasons. All of those reasons should be reflective of a commitment on the part of the professional to best serve all of her or his constituents, within the scope of the organizational mission or philosophy. Several reasons for conducting needs assessments are provided in the following section.

Service Orientation/Participant Empowerment

We strongly believe that parks, recreation, and leisure services professionals have an opportunity to make a profound impact on people from all walks of life. From a position of servant leadership and with an attitude of empowering participants through

leisure, needs assessments are the medium through which leisure professionals begin to effectively and meaningfully engage others in dialogue. By empowering individuals to contribute to meeting their leisure needs, leisure programmers participate in the program process *with* them (rather than *for* them). This is true no matter what an organization's profit orientation, or leisure setting (e.g., military, commercial, therapeutic recreation).

Constituent Input

A desire for input by constituents is one driving force behind the conduct and use of needs assessments. If providers act on their desire and belief in constituent empowerment as servant leadership demands, they must provide opportunities for meaningful input by all of their constituents. Needs assessments allow for this input. Assessments serve as an opportunity for current users and nonusers to influence the programming cycle (Benest, Foley & Welton, 1984). Input might be solicited regarding pricing, promotion, allocation of resources, purchases, facilities, activities, and other elements of programming.

Needs assessments are also used as a way to generate new program ideas (Carpenter & Howe, 1985; Russell, 1982). By asking the people who are in one's service area about ideas they have for enhancing, changing, or developing new programs, leisure programmers can greatly improve what they do. All of us increase the diversity of ideas and viewpoints by asking people outside of our agency or organization for ideas.

By asking our constituents about their interests, wants, intentions, and needs we provide an opportunity for ongoing dialogue. This type of focused conversation generally enhances our relationships with individuals and groups in the community. This can be crucial in times when an agency needs support for a new endeavor, bond issue, or an increase in resources. One thing is certain in this dialogue effort—if we ask for input, we must show we are utilizing that input. If the information we gather is not evident in our efforts, people will feel used and stop responding to us.

To Solicit Responses to New Ideas

Parks, recreation, and leisure services professionals tend to be creative people who desire to be innovative in their work. One way we do this is to develop and test new programming opportunities for various people in our communities. By trying out and asking for feedback about creative program ideas, we gain from the knowledge of others. Needs assessments are one tool that enable us to do this. We can solicit feedback about program ideas prior to implementation or conduct a pilot test of a program and then gather input about it.

Inclusion

Serving people (i.e., providing parks, recreation, and leisure services) is the crux of our profession, whether as part of a nonprofit, commercial, or community venture. In this respect inclusion of all people is critical to meeting our goals of service and empowerment. By being inclusive of all people, regardless of sex, age, physical abilities and qualities, sexual orientation, race/ethnicity, religion, education level, socioeconomic status, and other aspects of diversity, leisure professionals promote inclusion and equality.

Inclusion can only occur once we have determined the needs of the many constituent groups in our community—this is accomplished by involving them in the needs assessment process (Smith, Austin & Kennedy, 1996). It is especially important for parks, recreation, and leisure services professionals to learn about various cultural groups (based on *all* the elements of diversity). Learning about others' values, beliefs, preferences, and cultural influences enables us to be culturally responsive in a way that is meaningful.

For instance, it is too easy for an individual who is able-bodied and ambulatory to think that the reason there are never any people who use wheelchairs in the fitness/weight room facility is that they are not interested in lifting weights. It is not until we either put ourselves in a chair to experience the facility, or have a guest who uses a wheelchair come in and try it, that we realize that there is no way to transfer out of a chair and onto the equipment. In this scenario, people who use wheelchairs don't use our facility because they cannot, not because they don't want to. This, of course, should change our entire view of programming is this area—there may very well be a need for an accessible fitness room. A needs assessment that solicits information from *all* constituents can be quite revealing.

Meet Real Needs of Constituents

A servant leadership approach to programming requires that we be in tune with the real needs of people. These needs may include physiological needs such as food, air, and water; psychological needs of achievement, self-esteem, and identity; socioemotional needs of belonging, love, and affection; and spiritual needs of knowing a greater power than ourselves. Some of the needs such as health, economic standing, status, and personal skill development can easily be addressed through our programming efforts. By orienting ourselves toward the entire constituent base, we are attentive to and responsive to the real needs of our community. The only way for us to determine the needs, desires, and preferences of our constituents is to ask them.

One aspect of our field in particular—therapeutic recreation—uses needs assessments (often at intake or initial screening) to identify client health status, strengths, family and friend support structures, and interests to determine the appropriateness and use of selected activities in therapy. In addition, needs assessments are used to determine the specific tasks

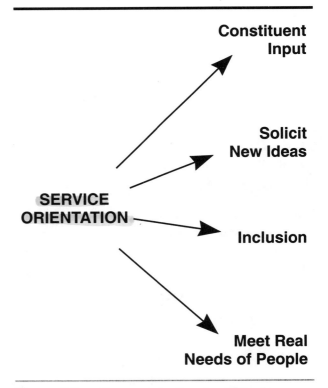

Figure 5.2   Reasons to Conduct Needs Assessments: Service Orientation

or activities needed for successful task intervention at various levels (Austin & Crawford, 1996). In this capacity needs assessments are extremely individualistic and recreation therapist responses to what is learned are client-specific. Individuals are helped to achieve their goals by utilizing information collected from the needs assessment.

Desire for Quality and Exceeding Expectations

Dedicated professionals have a concern for quality in all that they do. Quality in interactions with customers, programming, leadership, and all efforts of one's organization is of primary concern to individuals who care about others and target ways to meet their needs. Quality may be described as a level of excellence that meets or exceeds customer expectations (as well as needs). In order to know our customers' expectations and needs, we must conduct a needs assessment and respond to what we discover.

Professional Commitment

A personal commitment to the profession of parks, recreation, and leisure services demands high ethics and standards from leisure services practitioners. A hallmark of a professional is one who is ethical, well-educated (and seeks ongoing education), exceeds standards as set by the profession, and constantly strives to do the best possible job. One aspect of that commitment, then, is following through on all tasks that have potential to improve services to our constituents. Leisure professionals do this by adhering to "best practices" which, in programming, requires that providers conduct needs assessments as part of the cyclical process. It is through following the steps of excellent practices that we most contribute to our field.

Accountability

Accountability is a term that refers to being publicly responsible for our actions and choices. By conducting needs assessments we can determine, in advance, what is desired and needed by the people in our service area and respond to those expressions. Thus, when the time comes to indicate how we utilized our resources, we have the necessary data to support our programming decisions. Needs assessments provide a very good basis for the evaluation process (another necessary and oft forgotten element of the program planning cycle) and as such aid in addressing accountability (Benest, Foley & Welton, 1984; Carpenter & Howe, 1985).

Appropriate Resource Allocation

Another reason to conduct needs assessments is that they help to inform us about where we need to focus our resources (Benest, Foley & Welton, 1984; Hudson, 1988). With the information we gather from our constituents, we can tell if we should increase staffing in one area and facility maintenance in another. We can often predict where future needs will be based on the information gathered from a needs assessment. Resource allocation includes issues of staffing, finances, equipment, facility use and facility maintenance, and other elements required to conduct the business of our organization.

Increase Profits

In the upcoming millennium the amount of revenue raised by various programs will probably become increasingly important in various decision-making processes. As it stands now, almost every agency or organization has some programs that make money,

Figure 5.3   Reasons to Conduct Needs Assessments: Desire for Quality

some that break even, and some that lose money. Those that make money subsidize the programs that lose money to help cover expenses. As budgets continue to be cut and resources shrink, generating revenue in programs will become increasingly important. By planning and offering programs in which people intend to participate, we can better ensure revenue generation.

For those parks, recreation, and leisure services businesses that have a for-profit orientation, needs assessments are a very important element of the decision-making process to increase company profits while maintaining customer satisfaction. Through use of needs assessments we can maintain customer loyalty while at the same time work to recruit new customers.

Program Management

Program management is one of the primary reasons we conduct needs assessments. The intent is to understand our constituents well enough so that the programs we design and implement are both appropriate and appealing to a wide constituent base. Needs assessments provide the information we use to initiate the program cycle; they can be also used to set goals and objectives around which the remainder of the program cycle builds.

Manage Duplication of Services

Duplicating services within an agency or with another community agency can result in a waste of resources (Benest, Foley & Welton, 1984; Hudson, 1988) and unhealthy competition. By conducting a needs assessment we can see if people are getting some of their needs met elsewhere. We then can make educated decisions about either providing similar services (if the service is considered a "core" service) or using our resources in other program areas. In this way we manage our agency resources wisely.

Maintain and Address Safety Issues

Safety is an ongoing concern of all programming efforts. By asking questions in a needs assessment that relate to how facilities, equipment, and programs are used, we can better understand where potential hazards might exist. This is particularly important in therapeutic recreation and outdoor recreation settings (Schleien, McAvoy, Lais & Rynders, 1993). By understanding peak use times, traffic patterns,

and attitudes toward other participants we can structure programs for maximum safety and enjoyment. This raises the quality of programming efforts in all areas.

Help Prioritize Program Plans

By understanding our constituents' interests, wants, intentions, and needs, we can do the most effective job of prioritizing the implementation of program plans (Benest, Foley & Welton, 1984; Edginton, Hanson, Edginton & Hudson, 1998; Hudson, 1988; Rossman, 1995). We can learn how many people want and need which type of program and respond in-kind. Bear in mind that there are times when programs will be offered that serve only a very small portion of our constituent base. It is imperative that we do not fall into the trap of only offering programs and services to members of a majority group. Special programs and services have a definite place in programming efforts, and all members of our constituency have equal rights to have their leisure needs met.

Plan a Variety of Enjoyable Programs

People want to enjoy their recreation and leisure experiences. In fact, this is a requisite element of the definition of recreation and leisure. Needs assessments help us to design and implement a wide variety of enjoyable programs because we have so many individuals involved in the programming process. By asking lots of questions about various elements of parks, recreation, and leisure services we can augment and make more enjoyable the programs we currently have, as well as those being planned (Corbin & Williams, 1987; Farrell & Lundegren, 1991; Rossman, 1995). Participant involvement in planning contributes to a sense of ownership in the program—this often heightens enjoyment.

Develop and Meet Individual Goals

Finally, yet another reason for conducting needs assessments is that the information we gather can aid us in developing and meeting individual goals (Howe, 1989; Kraus & Shank, 1992; Schleien, McAvoy, Lais & Rynders, 1993; Schleien, Ray & Green, 1997). This is especially pertinent in therapeutic recreation, yet it also has applicability in other settings. Participant goals might include skill development, broadening of leisure experiences, personal enhancement, health, or simple enjoyment.

PROGRAM MANAGEMENT

→ Manage Duplication

→ Address Safety

→ Help Prioritize Program Plans

→ Plan a Variety of Programs

→ Develop and Meet Individual Goals

Figure 5.4   Reasons to Conduct Needs Assessments: Program Management

There are many excellent reasons for conducting needs assessments in the programming process. If we believe in a service orientation and in participant empowerment, we have to give all of our constituent groups the opportunity to participate in continuous dialogue related to services. As professionals in parks, recreation, and leisure services we are committed to enhancing the viability of our profession—conducting needs assessments is one way to augment our professional position. Finally, what we learn from needs assessments aids tremendously in program management—it is an integral and necessary part of the programming cycle.

Whom to Ask, What

We've established a shared meaning for a variety of terms and established the need for conducting needs assessments as an integral component to the programming cycle. Now we need to examine whom we ask and what to ask—Just how do we go about the needs assessment process? Who do we involve in the needs assessment process? What kind of information do we solicit from them?

Constituents

Current users of parks, recreation, and leisure services are easily identified. They are all the individuals who are actively participating in one or more leisure programs. Their frequency, intensity, and duration of participation might vary, but they are currently engaged in some form of recreation and leisure pursuit. *Nonusers*, on the other hand, are all those people within our service area who, for some reason, are not currently participating in our programs or services. Because there is something distinctly different between users and nonusers, it is important that in any needs assessment, both groups be fairly sampled. These two groups form our constituent group and both are important in the needs assessment process.

We include users in the needs assessment process because we want to keep their business. We try to determine how we can address the loyalty of these individuals so as to retain their business. We include nonusers in needs assessments because we wish to add these people to our user list. Being service-oriented, we want everyone to participate and have an opportunity to have their leisure needs met through efforts of our agency.

Constituent Information

One of the major categories of information we want to gather from our constituents are data about themselves. These data help us to better understand who our constituents are, what interests and desires they have, and what they are currently doing (if anything) in parks, recreation, and leisure services. We can collect several different types of data as seen in this next section.

Demographic Data. Demographic data include factual information that describe a person and their style of living. Typical demographic items include:

Figure 5.5 **Constituents include both those who use and those do not use our programs and services.**

age, sex, race/ethnicity, physical disabilities, religion, income, level of education, marital status, parental/family status, occupation, and zip code (or some other indication of where they live). This type of information gives us a feel for some, but not all, needs. For example, we can be fairly certain that those individuals with children would be interested in and have a need for family recreation while those who do not have children would not have that need.

Current Activity Involvement. Similar to the demographic data we collect, this section of a needs assessment is factual; we want to know in what events or experiences people currently participate. We also might ask how often they participate, with whom, where, what days of the week, for how long, during what time period, and at what cost. This provides a picture of who the users are, and may be reflective of how expressed needs are being met in existing programs. The information we gather about what people are *not* doing is also telling. As we collect information we begin to see patterns and reasons for various levels of participation.

Needs and Skills Information. In addition to asking about physical, emotional, psychological, social, and spiritual needs, it is often helpful to get a picture of the perceptions people have of their own skill levels. This helps in planning appropriate levels of activities and in matching participants based on skills. This is good information to have whether developing athletic leagues, cooking classes, or arts and crafts sessions. It is important to note that by asking constituents (called self-reporting) about their skill levels we will not always get accurate results. Some people have a tendency to underestimate their skills, while others overestimate their abilities. In some instances (i.e., water-based programs) skill testing may be necessary prior to assigning individuals to program groups.

Attitudes, Beliefs, and Values of Constituent Groups. Needs assessments are used to help us gain information about our constituents so we can best meet their needs and wants. Needs and wants are both influenced by attitudes, beliefs, and values (although wants are influenced much more heavily than needs); thus, asking about these characteristics of constituents gives us a more complete picture of who they are and what they might want. Questions about the importance of various recreation and leisure experiences fall under this category. An example of such an item is: "It is important that every child be exposed to sports before the age of twelve." Scores from this item would be indicative of respondents' beliefs about the need for youth sports.

Preferences, Opinions, Interests, and Intentions. Other data we want to collect from constituents is about their preferences, opinions, interests, and intentions. This information can provide us with straightforward background data to help us better plan programs. We might ask about when they would prefer to participate in a certain activity (e.g., season, time of day, day of week), where they would want to participate (e.g., indoors or out-of-doors), and with whom (e.g., friends, family, alone). This information is particularly important for nonusers. In addition, it would be helpful to know what recreation and leisure opportunities the respondent is interested in and whether or not they have an intention to participate in activities we currently offer or that we are in the process of designing and planning.

The following questions will help us to get a profile of what women at the workshop are like. Please answer all questions so that we may have the most complete picture possible.

1. What is your age?
   ❑ under 25 years
   ❑ 25–35 years
   ❑ 36–45 years
   ❑ 46–55 years
   ❑ over 55 years

2. What is the highest education level you completed?
   ❑ grade school
   ❑ high school
   ❑ some college work
   ❑ college degree
   ❑ graduate work

3. What is you marital status?
   ❑ single
   ❑ married/partnered
   ❑ widowed or divorced

4. What is your household income level?
   ❑ less than $25,000 per year
   ❑ $25,001 to $50,000 per year
   ❑ more than $50,001 per year

5. What is your occupation? _____

6. What is your ethnicity? _____

7. Children— Number: 0 1 2 3 4 5+

8. Children— Ages: under 5 yrs 5–12 yrs 13–17 yrs over 18 yrs

9. If you have a disability, please identify: _____

10. What state/province do you live in? _____

11. What is your zip code? _____

Figure 5.6   Sample Demographic Questions

Data Gathering

To conduct a needs assessment we need to ask users and nonusers different types of questions. The asking of questions is considered data gathering and there are many ways to accomplish this. This section of the chapter will present resources and techniques through which data collection can occur. Each element can yield rich data for use in one's program planning efforts.

External Inventory

An external inventory occurs when we look outside of our organization to determine what resources exist, as well as what markers exist in identifying the needs of constituent groups. The resources in our community might be found at other leisure service agencies, the environment at large, the local tax base, and so on. Markers include those social indicators that tell us our community might need something. By taking a "read" on the surrounding environment we begin to get a picture of who is in our service area, the needs they might have, and the types of interests they might share. This type of inventory is very much like taking inventory at a department store. What do we have (stock) and at what price (cost)?

Comparative Inventories

Comparative inventories are just that—identifying and counting the physical resources and parks, recreation, and leisure programs in a variety of communities. Usually these inventories are compared across cities or towns of similar sizes. If a discrepancy exists in terms of programs and resources, it could be indicative of a need for the lacking community. Comparative inventories relate well to identifying normative needs. As with all needs assessment tools, comparative inventories are conducted by commercial, nonprofit, and public parks, recreation, and leisure services organizations.

Environmental Resources

By taking an inventory of community resources we get a feel for program, open space, and facility discrepancies that might exist between what is and what should be. This is particularly useful if we are utilizing normative needs in determining program plans. For instance, we would want to gather information about available resources in the community (e.g., number and location of playgrounds, pools, parks, campgrounds) as well as about other organizations and their resources (e.g., facilities, equipment, staff) and programs. In this process we develop inventory lists of what is available to our constituents in the community.

In addition to counting the physical resources, identifying the resources that are accessible (and those that need retrofitting to become accessible), those that need repair or replacement, safety concerns, and where resources are located are also important. It could very well be that we have "enough" resources in terms of numbers, but that they are all clustered at one end of town and do not serve all people equally well. We need to strive to gather complete data.

Social Indicators

Social indicators are pieces of data that are typically gathered and maintained by governmental or non-profit agencies. They include such statistics as juvenile arrest rates, mortality and birth rates, population and age group information, education levels, rates of disease, vaccination rates, income, and other factors that attest to the general health of a community. This information is relatively objective and can be helpful in our assessment and efforts to program for unstated needs in the community. Typically, these indicators are relatively stable, and we need to remain attentive to when changes occur—change could be indicative of new needs. State and federal governments distribute these reports and much of this information is available on the Internet.

Social Values

Understanding the social mores and values of a community is very important when developing program plans. Some communities have strong religious ties and the influence of the church is quite strong throughout community institutions. Other communities have social mores that attribute a great deal of importance to the extended family; yet other communities manifest strong values toward and an emphasis on youth development. Each of these community types would have different needs, in part driven by the social mores of the surrounding area.

Figure 5.7   An external inventory occurs when we look outside of our organization.

Internal Inventory

An internal inventory is conducted from the vantage point of having a good look at oneself. In this inventory process, an organization conducts a thorough review of itself—its facilities, staff, financial resources, open space, existing programs, equipment, and so on. During this inventory process personnel look for evidence of areas that need attention, an infusion of new ideas, or ideas or programs that need to be retired. In this effort, we should strive to conduct an unbiased self-audit—these efforts are often very revealing and can uncover unhealthy patterns.

Philosophy/Mission

Continual and periodic checks of the organizational philosophy, mission, and vision are the only way to stay focused and be sure that program efforts are leading toward the achievement of the mission. Knowing that staff continue to support and buy into the organization mission is important in ensuring a well-focused and cooperative staff. Examining the mission and vision statements, as well as the philosophy for their viability, timeliness, and appropriate direction is an effort to be revisited frequently. This provides the focus for all programming efforts.

Staffing

Knowing a bit about who constitutes our staff (support staff, program staff, and administrative staff) is an important component of needs assessments. To program effectively we need to know how many staff we have; their strengths, limitations, interests, skills, and needs; availability; where they are assigned; and other information that would be helpful in determining the best use of these very important resources. In addition, knowing their level of training and certification in various areas is often a necessity (e.g., pool operations, advanced first aid, C.T.R.S.). This information is found in employee files and on resumes. In addition, some organizations keep training files for all staff in one location. This allows for quick identification of individuals who have training in a specific area so they may be appropriately utilized.

Recent and Past Programs

Internal reviews are not complete without a review of recent and past programs implemented by one's organization. In this process we identify a variety of characteristics: programs that are traditional, those that are held periodically, those that generate revenue, the types of participants attracted to each program, programs that flopped or were successful, the goals the programs addressed, and other program traits that help us to identify needs of constituents.

The success of this effort is incumbent upon detailed programming records and documentation.

Equipment, Facilities, and Supplies

Part of our internal review should include an objective inventory of what is available in terms of supplies (i.e., office as well as program planning supplies), equipment (i.e., what needs to be repaired, what needs replacing), and facilities (i.e., amount of space, strengths, and shortcomings). Each of these elements have an impact on what we can offer, how often, the prioritization of resource allocation, and more. Before we begin, then, we must know what we have.

Budgetary Issues

Lastly, in the internal component of a needs assessment we must come to know and understand the financial situation of our organization. Whether we have an unlimited budget, are required to have programs break-even or generate revenue, or are operating on a "shoestring" budget, we must include this component in a complete needs assessment process. Whether we are tax-supported, profit-driven, or supported by grant funds is also important to know—each of these has a different impact on programming efforts.

Are our philosophy and mission statements up-to-date? Do they serve our constituents' needs?

How many staff do we have? What are their skills?

What programs have we run that were successful? What programs have we run that were not successful?

What equipment, facilities, and supplies do we have access to?

What is our budget situation like?

Figure 5.8   An internal inventory includes asking tough questions of our organization.

You Are Invited to a Needs Assessment

WHY?

WHAT?

HOW?

WHERE?

WHEN?

FROM WHOM?

WHO
will use it?

Figure 5.9   Questions in the Development of Needs Assessment

The Process of Gathering Needs Assessment Information

Now that it is quite clear why we conduct needs assessments, and we know the types of information we want to collect, we next must consider how we are going to go about this. You already know that one of the characteristics of the cyclical program process is that it begins with assessment and "ends" with assessment ("end" assessment is usually called evaluation). Because program evaluation is so important, a great deal of time is spent in later chapters of this text discussing the various steps of developing a data collection, analysis, and reporting system.

The steps for conducting needs assessments are the same as for program evaluation; therefore, we will not repeat the information here. Instead, in this section we will discuss the various avenues through which input from constituents can be gathered, as

well as other sources from which we obtain information. The primary questions to bear in mind prior to beginning a needs assessment are: *Why* are we doing this needs assessment (i.e., what is the purpose)? *What* information do we want to collect? *How* are we going to obtain these data? *From where* will we get the information we seek? *When* will we gather the information? *From whom* will we collect information? And, *who* will use the information once we obtain it? After answering all of these questions, we then begin the data collection process.

People as Resources

We know that to best serve all constituent groups we need to collect information from both users and nonusers of our programs and services. We can use similar techniques for collecting data from both of these groups. There are advantages and disadvantages for each method, and this should be taken into consideration when deciding upon a technique to use. Any written type of data gathering (paper-and-pencil survey) should be relatively simple and straightforward. Jargon and technical language often act as barriers to respondents and should be avoided.

Comment Cards

Comment cards can be useful ways to gather information if they are used appropriately. If we only make them available at our facility, only the individuals who use that facility will have the opportunity to share their thoughts. To be effective, comment cards need to be widely distributed (perhaps as an insert with a utility bill or some other mass mailing). In addition, respondents should have the option of putting it in the mail (at the organization's expense) or dropping it in a "suggestion box." If the box drop-off method is an option, the receptacle must be in an easily accessible location. It is counterproductive to have a suggestion box kept behind the staff counter where recreation participants rarely see it. See Figure 5.10 for a sample comment card.

Surveys (Mail, Telephone, In-Person, Electronic)

As with program evaluations, we can gather needs assessment data through the use of paper-and-pencil (or electronic) surveys. Whether we do so by mail, telephone, or in person depends upon available resources and the time and talents of our staff. Mail

Got A Timely SUGGESTION?

To: Management, Campus Recreation
From (optional): _____
Campus/Home Address: _____
Phone: _____

I would like to make the following observation/suggestion.
_____
_____
_____
_____
_____
_____
_____

Thank you for sharing your concerns with us. If appropriate, action will be taken to address/correct your concerns in a timely manner.

Figure 5.10   Sample Comment Card

surveys can be costly and response rates may be low, yet are useful in that they have the potential to reach almost all individuals in our constituent base. Telephone surveys are often perceived as intrusive by those on the receiving end, yet can be done quickly and efficiently. Electronic surveys only reach those who have computers and access to an on-line service and cannot guarantee anonymity, yet are very quick to do.

By handing a survey to an individual or group of individuals in person, we are readily available should questions arise. In addition, this technique usually results in a high response rate. If we choose this method we do need to be sure to survey non-users as well (e.g., distribute the survey to people at a shopping mall rather than our facility to ensure a mix of people). Surveys can be quite useful for collecting information for needs assessments because constituents have time to look them over, consider the information, and respond with some thought. In addition, we can ask a lot of questions at one

time and obtain a good deal of information from a wide variety of people. A sample survey appears in Figure 5.11 (page 90).

Observations

Observing what people do is an excellent method of gathering information about participation rates and behaviors. Through observation we can tell quite a bit about current users of a particular area or facility. External clues about constituents such as sex, approximate age, apparent race/ethnicity, and physical abilities and qualities can be noted. In addition, information about the activity in which the person is participating, with whom, for how long, at what intensity level, and the time of week and day may also be noted. This type of information may also be telling in noting who is NOT using our facility or participating in our programs. For example, if our agency exists in an ethnically mixed area yet we never or rarely observe people of color in our facility, this could be indicative of not meeting the needs of minority group members.

Open Meetings

In the United States, open meetings are a part of every city, county, and state governmental process. Thus, for public parks and recreation organizations open meetings may be utilized to aid with decisions about budgeting, resource allocation, capital improvements, and so on. Organizations that are profit driven and fall into the commercial or entrepreneurial sector also might decide to hold open meetings to solicit input from a variety of constituent groups. In this way agencies are proactive and responsive to the wishes of their constituents.

Advisory Boards

Many parks, recreation, and leisure service organizations have identified advisory boards which consist of people from the community. These individuals serve to aid the organization in decision making, and are often a wonderful source of information about community needs, wants, and interests. While advisory boards differ in how often they meet and in the functions they provide to a particular organization, they do offer an opportunity for staff to better understand the local community and its needs.

Stillwater Parks, Events and Recreation Survey

Section I. **Please check the one that you feel is appropriate.**

1. Do you feel the parks should be mowed:
   ❏ weekly ❏ once every two weeks ❏ once every three weeks ❏ once every four weeks

2. Do you feel the restrooms in the parks should be cleaned:
   ❏ twice daily ❏ every three days
   ❏ daily ❏ once a week

Section II. **Please check all that apply.**

1. What amenities should be provided at a picnic shelter?
   ❏ picnic tables ❏ water spigot to fill up jugs and water coolers
   ❏ drinking fountain ❏ electricity
   ❏ lights ❏ cooking grill
   ❏ outdoor sink to clean pots and utensils ❏ covered trash can

2. Plese check the items that you feel are necessary in a neighborhood park playground area:
   ❏ slides ❏ baseball/softball practice field
   ❏ swings ❏ shelter
   ❏ climber ❏ restroom
   ❏ fire fighters' pole ❏ tennis courts
   ❏ overhead arm rings or ladder ❏ bike trail
   ❏ spiral slide ❏ walking trail
   ❏ baby swings ❏ security lighting
   ❏ benches ❏ electricity
   ❏ picnic table ❏ shade structure
   ❏ sandbox area ❏ access sidewalks
   ❏ drinking fountain ❏ half-court basketball
   ❏ landscaping ❏ other _____

3. Do you feel transportation from home should be made available to:
   ❏ children participating in recreation programs
   ❏ disabled individuals to get to work and doctors
   ❏ older citizens for shopping and doctor appointments

4. Would you or members of your family like to participate in any of the following:
   ❏ music lessons or programs ❏ theater or acting programs
   ❏ book or poetry clubs ❏ family dynamics programs
   ❏ craft classes ❏ art classes
   ❏ nature programs ❏ outdoor concerts
   ❏ exercise programs ❏ out-of-town trips
   ❏ hobby clubs or classes ❏ one-day family day camp
   ❏ child and adult programs (parent-child)

5. Would you or your family prefer to participate in classes that meet:
   ❏ once a week for several weeks ❏ only once in a workshop
   ❏ twice a week for two to three weeks ❏ two-day weeknight workshop
   ❏ two-day weekend workshop ❏ other _____

6. As a parent or participant, do you feel you should pay the full cost of:
   ❏ youth league ❏ senior transportation
   ❏ adult league ❏ local neighborhood playground
   ❏ senior league ❏ fishing
   ❏ youth classes ❏ camping
   ❏ adult classes ❏ swimming
   ❏ senior classes ❏ special events such as Halloween Fest or Fourth of July

7. I feel the city needs more:
   ❏ neighborhood playgrounds ❏ regional parks
   ❏ walking/bicycle trails ❏ shelters
   ❏ soccer and football space ❏ baseball and softball league
   ❏ basketball courts ❏ tennis courts
   ❏ nature trails ❏ youth activities
   ❏ instructional programs ❏ special events
   ❏ adult activities ❏ family activities
   ❏ gym space ❏ indoor recreation facilities
   ❏ beautification ❏ other _____

Thank you for taking the time to help citizens help citizens!

Figure 5.11   Sample Survey

Direct Assessment

The therapeutic side of our profession engages in direct assessment of individual patients and clients. When a new client enters a clinical therapeutic recreation setting an intake assessment is conducted. The recreation therapist must learn as much as she or he can about the client in order to determine the best course of therapeutic intervention for this particular person. This assessment may be repeated later on during that person's stay to determine if needs are being met or have changed. In community therapeutic recreation settings some level of assessment must also be done at intake so as to best serve the individual through recreation and leisure services. By determining strengths, areas of deficits, and level of functioning, the recreation therapist can develop, plan, and implement appropriate leisure activity strategies within the given resources. See Figure 5.13 (pages 92-93) for a sample assessment.

Focus Groups and Interviews

Another form of gathering data directly from constituent groups involves using focus groups. Focus groups are essentially group interviews where groups of individuals are brought together to respond to a particular question. Thus, if we want to know about the interests, wants, and needs of the community, we would bring together several groups of constituents and ask them to discuss that topic. By playing off of one another in their discussion of the question, much information is brought to light. If focus groups are not possible, we can solicit information from individuals through formal or informal interviews. We can even gather data from informal conversations with people we meet.

Records as Resources

In addition to gathering information directly from people it is also possible, and oftentimes desirable, to collect information about constituents from written documents, records, and archives. We can obtain a good deal of background data this way without being an imposition to individuals. See Figures 5.14 and 5.15 for examples.

Registration Information

When people register for programs and services at many leisure service organizations, they must complete some type of paperwork. If we "build in" a mini needs assessment into every registration form we can collect ongoing information from users of our services. Unfortunately, this method of gathering data does not provide any insight into those who have never registered for a program. Depending upon our analysis, the information we glean from registration records can be useful in what is not found as much as what is found. For instance, by asking for information about age of registrants we might find that very few of our constituents are people over the age of 45 years old; or we might find that very few individuals come to our facility from "across the river." This type of information can be very informative in terms of who is *not* using our services. We then may decide to take corrective action of some sort.

Activity Analysis/Program Plans

Every program that is offered should be based on written documentation including goals and objectives, tasks to be completed, staffing and equipment needs, numbers of individuals served, marketing efforts, target populations, and other information. By analyzing these records, and in conjunction with other information, we can identify patterns in our programming efforts. These might point to a particular type of program and/or service where we focus our energies, elements of the constituent group we tend to neglect, how we respond to public fads and trends, how we spend our money, and other program related information.

Census Bureau and Almanacs

The U.S. Census Bureau conducts a nationwide research project every ten years gathering data about individuals. The data are primarily demographic and include such information as: race/ethnicity, number in household, ages, income levels, family and marital status, and so on. These data are then utilized in ongoing projections about the population. We can also find information about the year's most watched television shows, films, and sporting events; where and how often people travel, how we spend our money, and the most common recreation activities in which people participated. This information is updated annually, found in almanacs (in paper and on the Internet), and can be extremely useful in planning new programs.

COLUMBIA SPECIALTY HOSPITAL OF TULSA
ADMISSION DATABASE—THERAPEUTIC RECREATION
THERAPEUTIC RECREATION THERAPIST signature/title _____

Dates of assessment _____

ASSESSMENT DATA	PROBLEMS IDENTIFIED	SHORT-TERM GOALS	INTERVENTIONS
INDEPENDENCE WITH COMPLETION OF LEISURE TASK ___ verbal cues required and/or ___ physical assistance required	___ No functional deficits ___ Functional deficits related to: ___ verbal cuing required ___ physical assistance required	Within ___ week(s) patient will complete ___ with ___ verbal cue(s) and/or ___ with ___ physical assistance	___ Functional therapy ___ Therapeutic group ___ Community reintegration ___ Patient/Family education ___ Other ___
ENDURANCE WITH COMPLETION OF TABLE TOP LEISURE TASK WITHOUT SIGNS/COMPLAINT OF FATIGUE X ___ seated X ___ standing X ___ in bed X ___ bedside	___ No functional deficits ___ Functional deficits related to endurance: ___ seated ___ standing ___ in bed ___ bedside	Within ___ week(s) patient will complete without sign/complaint of fatigue: X ___ seated X ___ standing X ___ in bed X ___ bedside	___ Functional therapy ___ Therapeutic group ___ Community reintegration ___ Patient/Family education ___ Other ___
MOBILITY TO TREATMENT SESSIONS ___ distance physically in wc ___ feet ___ independence with wheelchair ___ walking distance ___ feet ___ walking independently	___ No functional deficits ___ Functional deficits related to: ___ wheelchair independence ___ wheelchair distance ___ walking independence ___ walking distance	Within ___ week(s) patient will: ___ propel wc ___ feet ___ with ___ assistance ___ walk ___ feet ___ with ___ assistance	___ Functional therapy ___ Therapeutic group ___ Community reintegration ___ Patient/Family education ___ Other ___
USE OF THE UPPER EXTREMITIES TO COMPLETE LEISURE TASKS utilized RUE x ___ % utilized LUE x ___ %	___ No functional deficits ___ Functional deficits related to: ___ use of RUE to complete leisure task ___ use of LUE to complete leisure task	Within ___ week(s) patient will utilize: ___ RUE x ___ % ___ LUE x ___ % to complete leisure task.	___ Functional therapy ___ Therapeutic group ___ Community reintegration ___ Patient/Family education ___ Other ___
L/R NEGLECT WITH LEISURE TASKS ___ cues required to attend midline ___ cues required to attend to right ___ cues required to attend left	___ No functional deficits ___ Functional deficits related to attention to: ___ midline ___ right ___ left	Within ___ week(s) patient will complete leisure task with: ___ cues to attend to midline ___ cues to attend to right ___ cues to attend to left	___ Functional therapy ___ Therapeutic group ___ Community reintegration ___ Patient/Family education ___ Other ___
ATTENTION TO LEISURE TASKS ___ cues required to attend to task ___ time patient is able to tend to task	___ No functional deficits ___ Functional deficits related to: ___ cuing required to attend to task ___ time patient attends to task	Within ___ week(s) patient will attend to task with ___ cues x ___ minutes.	___ Functional therapy ___ Therapeutic group ___ Community reintegration ___ Patient/Family education ___ Other ___

Figure 5.13   Sample Assessment

ASSESSMENT DATA	PROBLEMS IDENTIFIED	SHORT-TERM GOALS	INTERVENTIONS
COMMUNITY RESOURCES Patient identifies ___ current resources Patient identifies ___ past resources	___ No functional deficits ___ Functional deficits related to: ___ identification of resources ___ use of resources	Within ___ week(s) patient will identify ___ community resources to assist with maintaining or improving level of functioning present at time of discharge ___	___ Functional therapy ___ Therapeutic group ___ Community reintegration ___ Patient/Family education ___ Other ___
IDENTIFICATION OF LEISURE TASKS Patient identifies ___ current tasks Patient identifies ___ past tasks	___ No functional deficits ___ Functional deficits related to: ___ identification of leisure tasks ___ use of leisure tasks	Within ___ week(s) patient will identify ___ current leisure pursuits to assist with maintaining or improving level of functioning present at time of discharge. ___	___ Functional therapy ___ Therapeutic group ___ Community reintegration ___ Patient/Family education ___ Other ___
ORIENTATION Patient is oriented to: ___ person ___ place ___ time ___ situation	___ No functional deficits ___ Functional deficits related to:	Within ___ week(s) patient will be oriented to: ___ person ___ place ___ time ___ situation	___ Functional therapy ___ Therapeutic group ___ Community reintegration ___ Patient/Family education ___ Other ___
EDUCATION Patient/family knowledge of: adequate inadequate Community transportation ☐ ☐ Sr. Citizen Center ☐ ☐ Sr. Nutrition site ☐ ☐ Adult day health programs ☐ ☐ Purpose of use of leisure activities ☐ ☐ Purpose of use of commun. res. ☐ ☐	___ No functional deficits ___ Requires education in designated areas Barriers to learning: ___ language barrier ___ motivation to learn ___ ability to read ___ emotional state ___ physical limitations ___ financial situation ___ cognitive limitations	Within ___ week(s) patient/family will verbalize knowledge of: ___ Community transportation ___ Sr. Citizen Center ___ Sr. Nutrition site ___ Adult day health programs ___ Purpose of use of leisure activities ___ Purpose of use of community resources ___ Other ___	___ Patient education ___ video instruction ___ 1:1 sessions ___ demonstration ___ Family education ___ video instruction ___ written instruction ___ 1:1 sessions ___ demonstration ___ Home program notebook ___ Community reintegration sessions ___ Other ___

OTHER:

LONG-TERM GOALS: At time of discharge patient will

Figure 5.13   Sample Assessment (continued)

Oklahoma State University
School of Applied Health & Educational Psychology
103 Colvin Center
Stillwater, OK 74078–2021

We hope you are looking forward to an exciting summer as you apply to participate in the National Youth Sports Program (NYSP). This will be the 24th year for NYSP at Oklahoma State University, which will be held on the following dates:

- **Regular Program June 1 through July 3, 1998**
- **Physical exam days May 28 and 29, 1998, provided free to ALL applicants.**

This program is open to children 10–16 years of age and is at no cost to the participants. A free breakfast and lunch will be served each day, along with instruction in sports skills and academic areas. Bus transportation will also be provided from your community.

THERE ARE SOME RESTRICTIONS TO THE PROGRAM. Please review the information and return your application before May 1, 1998.

- **Only 300 students will be allowed to participate in the program, which will be divided among the various age groups.**
- **Positions will be filled on a "first come, first serve, by age" basis.**
- **EVERY question on our application must be completed.**
- **The medical release must be signed by your parent.**
- **The application must be returned to the NYSP office by Friday, May 1, 1998.**
- **You will receive a letter informing you that you have been accepted into the program or placed on a waiting list.**
- **All applicants must have a physical exam in order to participate or to be placed on the waiting list.**

Please complete and return the application below to the following address:

NYSP—Oklahoma State University
103 Colvin Center
Stillwater, OK 74078–2021

If you have any questions, please call 405/744–2819. Looking forward to a great summer.

Dr. Paula Dohoney, Activity Director

======================================cut here======================================

Name _____ **Telephone** _____
Address _____ **M ❏ F ❏ Age** _____
_____ **Birthdate** _____ / _____ / _____

School _____ **NYSP returnee: Yes ❏ No ❏ Number of years in NYSP** ____
Parent or legal guardian _____ **Telephone: Home** _____ **Work** _____
Emergency contact: Name _____ **Telephone: Home** _____
Relationship _____ **Telephone: Work** _____
Address _____
_____

I understand and consent that a medical examination will be required before enrollment in NYSP and that the host institution and/or the NCAA is authorized to obtain medical care or treatment deemed necessary.

Office Use Only

Residing within target area: Yes ____ No ____

Eligible ____   Noneligible ____

Medical examination record: Yes ____ No ____

_____
Parent/Guardian Signature   *Date*

Figure 5.14   Sample of Registration Information

Campus Recreation
Facility Reservation Form

Organization _____ Date Submitted _____
Contact Name _____ Day Phone _____
Description of Activity _____ Number in Group _____

1. If you answer yes to either of the following questions you must see the Asst. Director and make arrangements to rent the facilities:
   ✓ Are you charging others to be in your event?
   ✓ Are there any participants **not** OSU students or Activity Card holders?
2. There are additional charges for staff supervision, setup/cleanup, equipment and damages. Discuss these with the Asst. Director.
3. It is our goal to provide a decision within two working days of receiving your request. Assume nothing—Come back and pick up your request.
4. **The facilities requested below are my first preference but, if available, another room will meet my needs. YES or NO**

I. Activity Area _____ **Days of Week** (Check all that apply) **Weeks of Month**
From Date: _____ Sunday ....❑   (Check all that apply)
To Date: _____ Monday ....❑
From Time: _____ Tuesday...............❑ 1st ....❑
To Time: _____ Wednesday..........❑ 2nd ....❑
                                      Thursday ....❑ 3rd ....❑
                                      Friday.................❑ 4th ....❑
                                      Saturday ....❑ 5th ....❑

II. Activity Area _____ **Days of Week** (Check all that apply) **Weeks of Month**
From Date: _____ Sunday ....❑   (Check all that apply)
To Date: _____ Monday ....❑
From Time: _____ Tuesday...............❑ 1st ....❑
To Time: _____ Wednesday..........❑ 2nd ....❑
                                      Thursday ....❑ 3rd ....❑
                                      Friday.................❑ 4th ....❑
                                      Saturday ....❑ 5th ....❑

III. Activity Area _____ **Days of Week** (Check all that apply) **Weeks of Month**
From Date: _____ Sunday ....❑   (Check all that apply)
To Date: _____ Monday ....❑
From Time: _____ Tuesday...............❑ 1st ....❑
To Time: _____ Wednesday..........❑ 2nd ....❑
                                      Thursday ....❑ 3rd ....❑
                                      Friday.................❑ 4th ....❑
                                      Saturday ....❑ 5th ....❑

IV. Activity Area _____ **Days of Week** (Check all that apply) **Weeks of Month**
From Date: _____ Sunday ....❑   (Check all that apply)
To Date: _____ Monday ....❑
From Time: _____ Tuesday...............❑ 1st ....❑
To Time: _____ Wednesday..........❑ 2nd ....❑
                                      Thursday ....❑ 3rd ....❑
                                      Friday.................❑ 4th ....❑
                                      Saturday ....❑ 5th ....❑

Office Only

Date Approved _____ Recware Reservation #'s _____ Date Denied _____

Modifications to I?   Modifications to II?   Modifications to III?   Modifications to IV?

Figure 5.15   Sample of Program Records

Social Indicators

We talked about social indicators earlier. This information is often maintained by governmental or nonprofit agencies. Again, social indicators speak to the general health and wealth status of an area or state. The information can be helpful to parks, recreation, and leisure service programmers in identifying social deficits to which we can then respond.

Both people and records can serve as resources for gathering data in the conduct of a needs assessment. Each can be a rich source of data and should be well-utilized in programming efforts. The information can be gathered formally or informally, and from a variety of sources. It should be reemphasized that needs assessments should be conducted continually so that new information is constantly coming into the agency providing up-to-date justification for program development.

Summary

Needs assessments are the first step to the program planning cycle. Through needs assessments we gather information about interests, wants, intentions, and needs from a variety of constituent groups and respond to what we find. In this way we remain responsive to our constituents. In addition, needs assessments provide an avenue for ongoing dialogue between an agency and the people in its service area. This allows us to maintain our goal of empowering constituents in affecting the programs and services we offer. There are many reasons for conducting needs assessments and we do so by gathering data from external as well as internal sources. The actual process of gathering and analyzing data is very similar to that done in program evaluation, discussed in Chapter Thirteen.

References

Austin, D. and Crawford, M. (1996). *Therapeutic recreation: An introduction, 2nd ed.* Boston, MA: Allyn & Bacon.

Benest, F., Foley, J. and Welton, G. (1984). *Organizing leisure and human services.* Dubuque, IA: Kendall/Hunt.

Carpenter, G. and Howe, C. (1985). *Programming leisure experiences: A cyclical approach.* Englewood Cliffs, NJ: Prentice Hall.

Corbin, H.D. and Williams, E. (1987). *Recreation programming and leadership, 4th ed.* Englewood Cliffs, NJ: Prentice Hall.

Edginton, C., Hanson, C. and Edginton, S. (1992). *Leisure programming: Concepts, trends, and professional practice, 2nd ed.* Dubuque, IA: Brown & Benchmark.

Edginton, C., Hanson, C., Edginton, S. and Hudson, S. (1998). *Leisure programming: A service-centered and benefits approach, 3rd ed.* Dubuque, IA: WCB McGraw-Hill.

Farrell, P. and Lundegren, H. (1991). *The process of recreation programming: Theory and technique, 3rd ed.* State College, PA: Venture Publishing, Inc.

Heider, J. (1985). *Tao of leadership.* New York, NY: Bantam.

Howe, C. (1989). Assessment instruments in therapeutic recreation: To what extent do they work? In D. Compton (Ed.), *Issues in therapeutic recreation: A profession in transition* (pp. 205–221). Champaign, IL: Sagamore Publishing.

Hudson, S. (1988). *How to conduct community needs assessment surveys in public parks and recreation.* Columbus, OH: Publishing Horizons.

Kraus, R. (1985). *Recreation program planning today.* Glenview, IL: Scott, Foresman & Co.

Kraus, R. and Shank, J. (1992). *Therapeutic recreation service: Principles and practices, 4th ed.* Dubuque, IA: Wm. C. Brown.

Rossman, J.R. (1995). *Recreation programming: Designing leisure experiences, 2nd ed.* Champaign, IL: Sagamore Publishing.

Rossman, R. (1989). *Recreation programming: Designing leisure experiences.* Champaign, IL: Sagamore Publishing.

Russell, R. (1982). *Planning programs in recreation.* St. Louis, MO: Mosby.

Schleien, S., McAvoy, L., Lais, G. and Rynders, J. (1993). *Integrated outdoor education and adventure programs.* Champaign, IL: Sagamore Publishing.

Schleien, S., Ray, M.T. and Green, F. (1997). *Community recreation and people with disabilities, 2nd ed.* Baltimore, MD: Paul H. Brookes Publishing.

Smith, R., Austin, D. and Kennedy, D. (1996). *Inclusive and special recreation: Opportunities for persons with disabilities, 3rd ed.* Dubuque, IA: Brown & Benchmark.

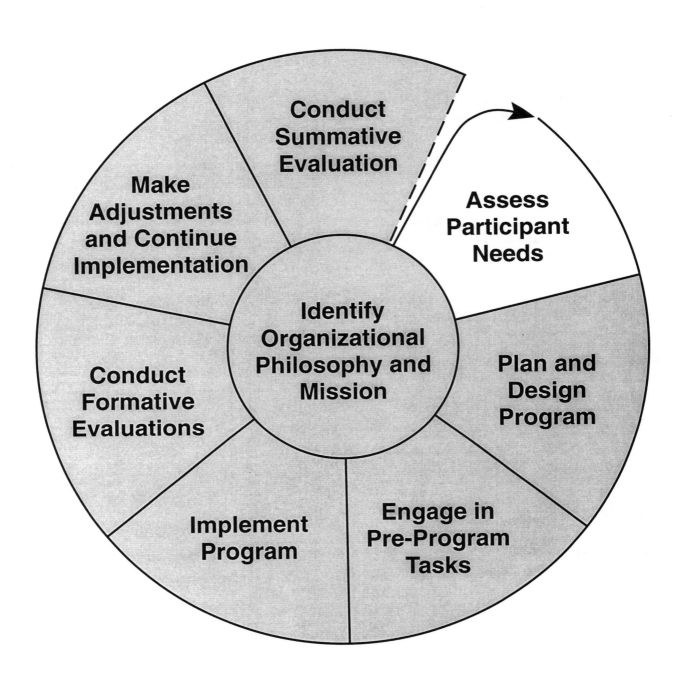

Chapter Six

Programming for People

It is fundamental that leaders endorse a concept of persons. This begins with an understanding of the diversity of people's gifts and talents and skills. Understanding and accepting diversity enables us to see that each of us is needed. It also enables us to begin to think about being abandoned to the strengths of others, of admitting that we cannot know or do everything. The simple act of recognizing diversity ... helps us to connect the great variety of gifts that people bring to the work and service of the organization. Diversity allows each of us to contribute in a special way.... The aim is to embody the concept of persons, for a substantial concept of person must underlie an inclusive system. A belief that every person brings an offering to a group requires us to include as many people as possible. Including people, if we believe in the intrinsic value of their diversity, will be the only open path to us.

DePree, 1989, p. 9, 65

In Chapter Five, we discussed the importance of collecting information from constituents to ensure that leisure programmers offer appropriate and successful programs. This is done to help leisure programmers understand the people they are to serve. To do this, we gather information from needs assessments and relate that information to what is known, generally, about various groups of people. As we discuss generalizations about people it is important to remember that this information is not predictive (e.g., we cannot say that because someone is six years old they will pout if they don't get their way) because individuals differ from the larger group. Nonetheless, generalizations are helpful in that they give leisure professionals a foundation of understanding upon which they can build their knowledge base.

It is likely that material about people (e.g., ages, stages, diversity) has been presented in other courses related to parks, recreation, and leisure services. This is because this type of information helps leisure professionals to understand people, and people are the foundation of the parks, recreation and leisure services business. Thus, the information presented in this chapter is merely a review of material related to understanding people so that we might program appropriately.

Diversity is a concept referring to how we differ from one another—remembering that at the same time, we are also similar to one another. *Dimensions of diversity* refer to the various dimensions, traits, or characteristics on which individuals differ. There are core and secondary characteristics we all have upon which others make assumptions about us, and we about them. They include such things as sex, age, class, level of education, and others (Loden, 1995; Loden & Rosener, 1991).

These assumptions that we and others make, based on the dimensions of diversity, are known as *stereotypes*. Stereotypes are part of a perceptual and thinking process whereby specific traits are ascribed to people based on their apparent membership in a group—they may be positive or negative (Cox, 1993; Gudykunst, 1991). For instance, a negative stereotype might be one where all members of a cultural group are believed to be lazy. A positive stereotype might be when an individual is perceived to be highly responsible and dependable simply because she or he belongs to a particular cultural group. *Prejudice* and *discrimination* are often outgrowths of stereotypes and severely limit the people against whom we are prejudiced or discriminate.

While all of us are unique individuals, people do share cultural traits with one another. As various groups we share assumptions, beliefs and values (usually unspoken); learned responses; and ways of being, knowing, and doing. We transmit culture from one generation to the next through language, material objects, rituals, institutions, and art (Cox, 1993; Hirsch, Kett & Trefil, 1993).

Dimensions of Diversity

Various dimensions of diversity have a large impact on individual perceptions of the world. Core dimensions of diversity cause the strongest reaction and include elements of identity we notice upon seeing and meeting people. These dimensions are extremely difficult, if at all possible, to change. The five *primary dimensions* of diversity include sex/gender, race/ethnicity, sexual orientation, physical and cognitive abilities and qualities, and age. *Secondary dimensions* of diversity include such characteristics as educational level attained, parental status, marital status, socioeconomic status, geographic location (e.g., where a person grew up or currently lives), religion, and military status.

Secondary dimensions of diversity impact on leisure in many ways. For instance, research tells us that people with higher levels of education tend to engage in more and a wider variety of leisure. In addition, those with children are more likely to desire family types of leisure opportunities than those without children. Both primary and secondary dimensions of diversity impact on leisure choices, preferences, and participation.

Sex/Gender

Sex is the biological difference between females and males present at birth; gender is the way we perceive femaleness (i.e., what is feminine) and maleness (i.e., what is masculine) and is taught to people very subtly throughout life. We see evidence of a cultural concern for sex and gender roles in various settings. In parks, recreation, and leisure programming the issue of sex and gender arises in the gendered nature of programs offered. By this, we mean that most people who participate in our programs (especially children) could tell us which activities we offer are "for girls" (e.g., gymnastics, aerobics) and which are "for boys" (e.g., football, martial arts). In programming, we often inadvertently (and sometimes purposively) perpetuate these stereotypes.

Society is recognizing that both sexes benefit from participation in a wide variety of recreation and leisure opportunities. For instance, people recognize the many social benefits of participating

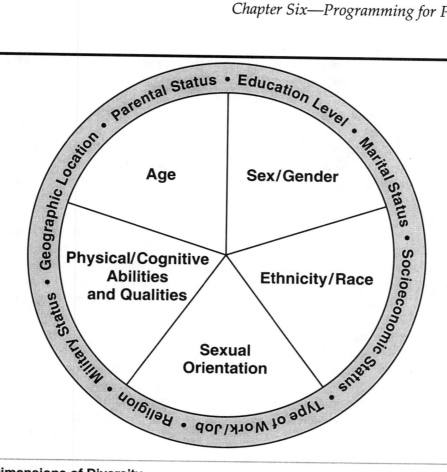

Figure 6.1   Dimensions of Diversity

in team sports (which is predominantly a male domain) and there has been a tremendous rise in girls'
sport involvement because of this. Likewise, it is
becoming more acceptable for males to engage in
traditional female activities such as cooking and
dancing. In programming, the leisure provider influences the way activities and events are gendered
through activity selection (offering only contact
sports such as football and karate) and in the time
of day offered (activities held during the day are not
available to people who work during the day). We
also contribute to "gendering" parks, recreation, and
leisure through promotional efforts (such as when
all flyers only have pictures or graphics of males
on them), thus subtly excluding females, and in customer relations (when a male calls to register for
an aerobics class, the staff inform him that "it is an
activity for ladies").

Ethnicity/Race

Ethnicity refers to the commonalties passed down
through history and tradition from one generation
of people to the next. As a term, ethnicity is a more

accurate description of the culture with which one
identifies than is race. King, Chipman, and Cruz-
Janzen (1994) have identified seven components
that constitute ethnicity: a historical link, shared
geographic beginnings, linguistic commonalties,
shared religious beliefs, common social class status,
mutual political interests, and a joint moral (values)
base. Individuals who have most or all of these
seven aspects of ethnicity in common would be
considered to share an ethnic heritage and culture.

Race, on the other hand, refers to a group of
people who share a genetic make-up which results
in biological characteristics that can be used to distinguish one group from another (e.g., people of
Spanish descent have a darker skin color than people
of Scandinavian heritage).

Programmers should gain information about
ethnic groups with which they might work because
each culture is very complex in its attitudes, beliefs,
values structures, and leisure preferences. It is also
important to recognize that within each culture
individuals are unique; not all Asian women share
the same beliefs about gender roles, for instance.

Gender, age, physical abilities and qualities, and sexual orientation all interact with one's ethnicity to result in differences within ethnic groups. Learning through observations, interactions, and personal research, then, would be important to gain a solid understanding of various ethnic groups.

In programming for people who are of various ethnic backgrounds we should recognize that various ethnic groups are different in their perceptions and use of time, belief in the importance of the individual over the group, use of language and patterns of communication, leisure preferences, and values. Ethnic groups are *not* different in terms of intellectual, physical, or emotional abilities and needs. Learning about specific ethnic groups will reveal appropriate programming approaches. Certainly, going beyond celebrating ethnic festivals, hanging posters in our facility of famous people of color, and eating ethnic foods is required of leisure services programmers. We can use leisure opportunities as a subtle way to teach and learn about various ethnic groups, and develop a greater appreciation of various cultures.

Sexual Orientation

Sexual orientation includes identifying as gay, lesbian, bisexual, and heterosexual. For many, this core dimension of diversity is the most easily hidden of all the core elements (e.g., one cannot tell if someone is straight or gay simply by looking at them), yet it still engenders strong social reactions. People of all sexual orientations engage in a variety of leisure activities and are involved in every type of leisure services organization. Leisure services programmers have long catered to the needs and desires of people who are heterosexual—family programming, husband/wife activities, coeducational dances—yet, the needs of gay, lesbian, and bisexual participants have essentially been ignored.

Gay, lesbian, and bisexual people differ from heterosexuals in terms of emotional and sociosexual attraction, but are similar in leisure preferences. There certainly are no differences based on sexual orientation in physical, cognitive, or emotional abilities. Specific needs of gay, lesbian, and bisexual participants generally fall in the area of emotional support and social opportunities. There are many leisure services providers that specifically cater to the needs of gays, lesbians and bisexuals, particularly in tourism; and there are an increasing number of public agencies responding to the needs of gay youth.

Physical/Cognitive Abilities and Qualities

In this dimension of diversity cognitive and physical disabilities are addressed as are other physical qualities which might foster negative reactions—obesity, wearing thick glasses, having severe acne, or being "ugly" in cultural terms. Too often people with disabilities and other "less than perfect" physical qualities are discriminated against relative to equal access to parks, recreation, and leisure services opportunities. Assumptions and prejudgments about desires and capabilities are often made upon seeing a person who is obese, a person with Down Syndrome, a person with a companion animal (e.g., a Seeing Eye dog) or a person who has prominent birth marks.

An estimated 40 million people in the U.S. are disabled; 44% of those individuals have physical disabilities, 32% exhibit various health impairments, 13% have sensory impairments, 6% are reported to have mental disabilities, and 5% of disabled individuals have other disabilities (Havens, 1992). There is no question that all parks, recreation, and leisure services programmers will be planning and designing activities and events that include people with disabilities and varying physical qualities.

In addition to desiring to do the right thing and program for all the constituents in our service zone, we are also required to do so by law. The Americans with Disabilities Act of 1990 (ADA) has had a profound influence on parks, recreation, and leisure services, as well as on the lives of those with disabilities.

The Americans with Disabilities Act (ADA)

The Americans with Disabilities Act of 1990 makes it illegal to discriminate against a person on the basis of her or his disability. Parks, recreation, and leisure services program directors are responsible to ensure that the spirit of the ADA is followed so as to facilitate a full range of leisure experiences for all people. The ADA states that leisure services providers **shall not**:

- Deny a qualified person with a disability the opportunity to participate or benefit from services available to people without disabilities;

- Offer less effective opportunities for the disabled;

- Provide separate aids, benefits, or services for people with disabilities unless those services are necessary to make services available;

- Aid or perpetuate discrimination in any form; or

- Use facilities or sites that result in the exclusion of people with disabilities.

Furthermore, the ADA states that leisure services providers **shall**:

- Make reasonable accommodations for people with disabilities to enable full enjoyment of services, programs, and facilities; and

- Provide services, programs, and activities with the most interaction possible (Eichstaedt & Kalakian, 1993).

Parks, recreation, and leisure services professionals are required by law to offer programs and services in such a way as to fully include people with disabilities in activities. Furthermore, ethically, it is the right thing to do. Necessary program modifications and adaptations will vary for different types of disabilities, and most involve minimal changes. Information about how to determine the type and level of modification necessary is presented in Chapter Eleven. It requires us all to engage in ongoing professional education.

Life Stages and Age Groups

There is one core element of diversity that we will all experience—stages of development, or aging. This is the only dimension of diversity that we all share, regardless of other personal characteristics. Because of this parks, recreation, and leisure programming needs to be reflective of the changes through which human beings move as we age. While there are many ways to examine human development, and many theories related to development, we will present this information from a life stage development process. It is a relatively common way of thinking and may be familiar to you.

People who are close in age tend to have similar mental, physical, social, and emotional capabilities (Goode Vick, 1989; Howe, 1993; Howe & Strauss, 1993; Schickedanz, Hansen & Forsyth, 1990;). This enables us as programmers to design and implement

Figure 6.2 **The Americans with Disabilities Act mandates that we make reasonable accommodations for people who have disabilities.**

activities that are appropriately matched to these capabilities. By doing this, we can ensure enjoyable and successful leisure programs for everyone.

Behavior results from a combination of physical, cognitive, socioemotional, and moral aspects of a person—it is both a holistic process and a product. Generally speaking, *physical development* includes energy and growth, the acquisition of fine and gross motor skills, activity preferences, and physical co-ordination. *Cognitive development* includes the ability to think abstractly, academic achievement, reasoning and logic, and limitations in mental abilities. *Socioemotional development* consists of relationships with others (peers and adults), fears, worries, self-control, and moods (Howe, 1993).

It is necessary to remind ourselves that as with all generalities about groups of people there are individuals who, although they are in the identified age range, are exceptions to the traits and characteristics representative of a particular life stage. Therefore, while this information can be helpful in many ways, predicting *specific individual* behaviors is not possible.

Young Childhood (5–7 years)

Physical Development

In terms of physical development, children ages five to seven years have lots of energy which comes in spurts, and is often difficult to keep under control. As they continue to practice large motor skills, children at this age enjoy a great deal of running, hopping, skipping, climbing, and catching. In addition, chasing and being chased are favorite activities. Because children at this age struggle with fine motor control there may be frustration surrounding fine motor efforts (such as tying shoes). Their high level of physical activity is balanced by a similar need for rest as youngsters in this age group tend to tire quickly and easily.

Cognitive Development

Five to seven year olds tend to be concrete thinkers and are very literal in interpreting meanings. At this age, children operate from perception and intuition rather than logic. It is difficult for young children to focus on more than one thing at a time and they only see things from their own perspective (and they believe everyone else sees things as they do, as well). Young children can accept and work with

Physical Development

Cognitive Development

Socioemotional Development

Moral Development

Figure 6.3   Behavior results from a combination of physical, cognitive, socioemotional and moral development.

basic rules, but they will change rules when needed to avoid failure or losing. Due to their heavy reliance on concrete thinking, movement is necessary for learning and understanding directions. At this age children have wonderful capabilities for fantasy and active imaginations. In addition, in this stage children are curious and ask a lot of questions—they are trying to figure out how the world works.

Socioemotional Development

Young children do not have strong social skills (e.g., communication, conflict resolution, an other-orientation). They tend to be egoistic with everything centering on themselves. In this age group, children engage in some sharing, but do not necessarily seek out ways to share. In addition, there tends to be a separation of the sexes with boys and girls playing apart from one another. Children at this age generally are very honest; this is due in part to a lack of mastery over the nuances of lying. Organizational skills are not a strong suit for these young children and items are often lost or left lying about.

Youngsters at this stage of development can be overly sensitive to comments and actions of others (e.g., they may be very hurt if a child sticks out her tongue at them). If there is difficulty in understanding directions, youngsters of this age can be easily frustrated. They need a good deal of encouragement and support from adults and seem to crave adult affection. Children of this age are very impulsive and unable to control their emotions; they tend to use physical aggression to resolve problems, and start and stop crying quickly.

Middle Childhood (8–11 years)

Physical Development

As children move into middle childhood physical coordination improves as do abilities in gross and fine motor skills. High energy levels are still apparent, although there is a reduced need for rest as children at this stage do not tire as easily. While children at this age are able to be still for longer periods of time, active participation is still needed for optimum learning to occur. It is not uncommon for early signs of preadolescence to occur in girls at ten or eleven years of age (e.g., onset of menstruation, change in body shape). Youth at this stage are capable of rhythmic movement and begin to show an interest in group activities such as sports.

Cognitive Development

At the middle childhood stage logic, reasoning, and the ability to effectively deal with abstractions develop. One of the characteristics of eight to eleven year olds is that they ask a lot of 'why' questions as they begin to sort out and understand issues of cause-and-effect. It is here that the development of self-concept begins to take shape. Youngsters in this stage of development tend to be easily motivated and are able to work within activity rules. In addition, they have wonderful senses of humor and love challenges (appropriate to their level of development).

Children are now able to consider more than one aspect of a situation at once, and they understand general concepts better than when younger. Problem-solving skills are improving and at this age youngsters are able to work independently for short periods of time. When children ages five to seven often would give up if faced with frustration, at this age children tend to persevere longer—they begin to believe that they can make something happen if they try hard and long enough.

Socioemotional Development

As children move out of the egoistic phase (focused on self-interests) they become interested in their peer group. Because children are beginning to form attachments to groups, they become very concerned about fairness and equality. They share better, yet the sexes (for the most part) remain separate (girls/boys have the "cooties"). Those children in this age group who are maturing more quickly than others may describe girl/boyfriend relationships. As groups develop, so too, do relationship skills; youngsters at this age develop some tact, but are not always sensitive to others' needs. Adults remain important figures in the lives of these youth, although older children are beginning to test adults in their desire for independence.

It is important to remember that children between the ages of eight and eleven years old do not take criticism from peers or adults very well (they tend to be sensitive and defensive), and are easily embarrassed. An increased awareness of peers and others' expectations impacts the development of self-esteem. This may be seen in an increase of girls "primping" and boys striving to look "cool." It has been documented that at about age ten or eleven years self-esteem in girls begins to drop (Howe, 1993; Sadker & Sadker, 1994).

Young Adolescence (12–14 years)

Physical Development

In the early teen years youth experience a balance in their energy output; generally they have calmed down since early and middle childhood. The impulsivity of the previous years has lessened. At twelve to fourteen years of age most girls have experienced the onset of puberty and the development of secondary sex characteristics. There is great variation with boys; some boys have reached puberty, others are just beginning the sexual maturation process. For many young people in this age group, abilities related to coordination and fine and gross motor skills are well-developed. They have a great capacity to try new tasks. Continued opportunities to practice and develop individual skills is still needed. Physical activities that appear to be (and sometimes are) reckless are favorites of young people in this life stage. Risk-taking behaviors are highly desired.

Cognitive Development

Most young teens are gaining experience in logic, reasoning, and problem-solving skills, while also improving in their organizational skills and rules management. Twelve- to fourteen-year-old youth have the capabilities to understand multiple perspectives (i.e., they can see and begin to appreciate others' viewpoints) and to deal with abstractions. Teens begin to develop the ability to formulate and test hypotheses ("what if…" situations). In this period of early adolescence youth are beginning to develop a sense of self-identity. These are years of much exploration (e.g., drugs, sexuality, risk-taking behaviors) as the search for self ensues. Young adolescents are capable of understanding and developing strategy in their play and appreciate knowing reasons for why things are the way they are.

Socioemotional Development

Peers are a very important source of support for young teens as they strive to make the transition from family dependence to independence. This age group is easily influenced by their peer group and the need for belonging seems all important. At the same time, there is a need to have time alone. Sociosexual relationships (attractions to others based on sexuality) begin to develop, as does sexual exploration.

Emotions and moods can range widely as changes in hormones interfere with other cognitive, social, and physical changes. Self-esteem, particularly for girls, fluctuates tremendously in this development stage. Research to determine why self-esteem for teenage girls drops so steeply is ongoing. Concerns with body image (as body shape changes with physical maturity) and embarrassment are important issues to this age group of teens. Boys often work through determining a sense of self through being "cool" and engaging in between-boy competitions. That is, teenage boys often engage in showing off behaviors and spontaneous public competitions (e.g., basketball "jam" contests at the neighborhood court). Teen girls often subscribe to social images of what is beautiful and may experience negative effects on their own psyche (e.g., anorexia, bulimia).

Adolescence (15–17 years)

Physical Development

Well into being teenagers, fifteen to seventeen year olds tend to be very concerned about their physical development and body image. Most males reach puberty during this period; most girls have already reached puberty. As physical growth outpaces their ability to adapt, boys' coordination takes a dip (they may appear gangly—all arms and legs). By this age most girls have accepted their postpubescent bodies. Skills acquisition becomes important and is made possible by physical capabilities—this is the age at which many physical skills are refined. A great deal of sleep is needed during this life stage and many teens are constantly tired; this may be a factor in leisure choices. Reckless behavior (that suggests a sense of immortality) and exploration (e.g., sex, drugs) continue from early adolescence into this life stage.

Cognitive Development

Many teens hold an idealistic view of the world and believe that situations can change if people just try hard enough. At this age the ability to handle abstractions, test hypotheses, and engage in problem solving come together. Cognitive abilities have reached a point of development where further growth results in increasing sophistication rather than the development of new skills. Teens have a wide variety of interests and a strong need to experiment and stretch themselves. They understand the need for rules in games and activities and enjoy sophistication in terms of rules and strategy.

Socioemotional Development

Moving toward young adulthood, older teens strive to achieve self-identity, freedom from adults, and responsibility for themselves. Group affiliation remains important and mixed-sex activities are sought. This stage of development can be difficult for teens as the pull for independence and desire for familial security coexist. Moodiness might reflect the struggle in maintaining changing relationships. Many teens in this age group often seem like two different people—one mature young adult, and one immature youngster. Music becomes important as an avenue for self-expression. It serves as an outlet for moods as well as a sign of growing independence. In addition, for males, competition becomes increasingly important. Females often drop out of team sports during this stage of development.

Young Adulthood (18–25 years)

Physical Development

Young adults are at their physical peak. Most physical abilities are well-developed by this age, and while nuances may be refined, increased physical prowess is unlikely. The activity level of young adults is relatively high, but it can be slowed somewhat by life changes (e.g., beginning a career, relocation, establishing a family). Structured competition and recreation play are desired by most people in this age group. Often a concern for fitness drives physical activity, and activity is often secondary to job or career. Interests in physical activity often include both individual and group activities. Outdoor recreation and other forms of physical recreation are welcomed by young adults. High energy, often high in risk-taking behaviors, and a need to "do" are traits of this group.

Cognitive Development

Building on the cognitive skills of the late teens, young adults are creative and capable of handling abstractions quite well. Cognitive skills are sharp and are often considered at a peak during these years. Problem solving and hypothesis testing are further refined as young adults build on previous knowledge and experience. Intellectual development tends to

increase in sophistication as does an understanding of strategy and complex rule structures.

Socioemotional Development

It is during the young adult years that most people in our culture search for a life partner and a sense of stability; a family orientation is initiated. Enjoyment is often experienced in mixed-sex activities and one's circle of friends expands through work contacts and neighborhood connections. People take risks at this life stage to develop intimate and social connections with others. There is a beginning concern for work and work efforts; competitiveness often reaches a high point in this life stage.

Middle Adulthood (26–40 years)

Physical Development

At middle adulthood, many people are still at their physical peak. Some slowing down is evident as family and career take priority, and finesse generally becomes more important than strength. Those in middle adulthood strive to perfect skills rather than using brawn. Physical activities often take on a family orientation. Personal activity involvement tends to be focused on a few activities in which an individual works to hone her or his skills. Involvement in team sports lessens while individual lifelong sports begin to take on increased importance.

Cognitive Development

Cognitive skills and abilities of human beings are at a peak in middle adulthood. One's creativity, use of logic and reasoning, and understanding abstractions reach a high point and many people enjoy stretching their cognitive skills through mental challenges. An awareness of the influences of greater society and global issues on self and family occurs. Perseverance, the ability to work toward one goal for a prolonged period of time, is characteristic of people at this life stage. A solid understanding of self has typically developed for people in this age range, and individuals are engaged in planning for long-term concerns.

Socioemotional Development

Persons in middle adulthood generally have decided and are settled in their decisions relative to children and family. Often, the family orientation is one that goes in both directions; that is, there is a concern for both one's children and aging parents. For those without children, in the early years of middle adulthood there is often a "couple" orientation, and a focus toward developing one's work and career. Work-related stresses may begin to interfere with one's personal and leisure life. Values are firmly established and a commitment to community is often evident.

Older Adulthood (41–60 years)

Physical Development

As individuals pass middle adulthood, changes in physical abilities become evident. For most people, there is a general slowing down along with some changes in eyesight, strength, and flexibility. Metabolism begins to slow and weight gain is common; for women, menopause occurs. Physical activity tends to decline as personal work and family situations change.

Cognitive Development

As with middle adulthood, people in this age group experience strong cognitive skills and abilities. Much of one's focus is on career; creativity and the use of mental capabilities are focused in that direction. An understanding of global and social issues is increasingly important to individuals and families. It is during these years that people experience a sense of their own mortality. There is often a concern about falling into boredom in both work and leisure. In addition, many fear being put into situations when they will fail; thus, some leisure opportunities are missed.

Socioemotional Development

A focus on social position and security in retirement become issues of interest with people in this age group. Family, grandchildren, aging parents, and extended family also become increasingly important. Social relationships tend to be stable and long lasting. Concern about the future and work-related stresses may influence one's emotional and mental stability. This is the life stage when it is common for adults to experience midlife crises—often a radical change in behaviors and attitudes occurs. Midlife crises are experienced by both women and men, and by people from all walks of life. There is a desire for respect by others and to experience a variety of life experiences by older adults.

Seniors (61+ years)

Physical Development

As medical and lifestyle changes are introduced and accepted people tend to live longer and healthier. Due to longer life spans, there is tremendous variation in physical abilities and limitations of adults aged 61 and older. While everyone experiences changes in balance, eyesight, hearing, strength, and flexibility, how each person is affected by and deals with these changes is based on one's own physical make-up, mental attitude, environment, and opportunities. Some people seem as young and vibrant as those many years their junior, while others are quite frail.

The great disparities between well active seniors (most aged 61–70) and frail elderly (most aged 71–100+) require that recreation and leisure service leaders be careful to avoid categorizing all older adults as having limited physical or cognitive abilities. In fact, many people in their sixties and early seventies are as active and healthy as people in their fifties. We also know that women tend to outlive men in all racial and ethnic groups; therefore, in the senior age group there are higher numbers of women than men.

Cognitive Development

As with the changes and differences in physical condition, there is a similar variation in cognitive and mental processes between individuals at this life stage. Eventually mental processes slow, but as a whole, older adults remain sharp and in control of their mental capacities until well into old age. Some seniors are impacted by diseases such as senility and Alzheimer's Disease which affect their mental capabilities, but these people are exceptions, and not the norm. Work-related stresses are reduced as retirement and life changes are likely to occur. However, as retirement arrives stresses related to a change in life (from worker to retiree) can occur. People at this stage of life tend to be more cautious than in younger years and like to think through new ideas prior to engagement. Health concerns often preoccupy people in this age range.

Socioemotional Development

As people age, social connections become increasingly important. Ironically, this occurs at the same time that people begin to deal with social isolation (as life partners and friends die) and thoughts of their own mortality. Conflict in response to the desire for and lessening of social contacts may occur. Much reflection over one's life is common as people realize their own mortality. Because of this a renewed interest in religion may occur. Furthermore, retirement may result in great joy and an apparent rejuvenation, or it may cause new stresses as financial stability and quality of life become important issues.

There is often a "second wind" where people in this life stage begin or renew leisure activities. Outdoor recreation such as gardening, walking, and bird-watching become common outdoor activities. Fear often increases and is related to physical safety and well-being as well as the fast pace of life lived by young people. There is a danger of boredom setting in for some of these folks.

Summary

This chapter has provided a basis for understanding people—the one common element in all leisure services settings. Elements of diversity and life span issues affect us all. If we are to be true to a servant leadership approach to programming, within our programming efforts we need to consider cultural influences as well as any adaptations or modifications needed by potential participants. By being knowledgeable about general traits of people we can plan and implement programs that are enjoyable, allow for success, and address participant needs.

It is important to remember that while people all pass through the various life stages, not everyone does so at the same chronological age. In their development people are affected by social mores and stereotypes, genetic disposition, opportunities, their own abilities and limitations, and others' expectations. By understanding the basic elements of human development—physical, mental/cognitive, and socioemotional—programmers can make appropriate choices in activity selection, timing, equipment use, and other aspects of program development.

References

Cox, T. (1993). *Cultural diversity in organizations.* San Francisco, CA: Berrett-Koehler.

DePree, M. (1989). *Leadership is an art.* New York, NY: Dell Publishing.

Eichstaedt, C. and Kalakian, L. (1993). *Developmental/adapted physical education, 3rd ed.* New York, NY: Macmillan.

Goode Vick, C. G. (1989). *You can be a leader.* Champaign, IL: Sagamore Publishing.

Gudykunst, W. (1991). *Bridging differences: Effective intergroup communication.* Newbury Park, CA: Sage.

Havens, M. (1992). *Bridges to accessibility.* Dubuque, IA: Kendall/Hunt.

Hirsch, E., Kett, J. and Trefil, J. (Eds.). (1993). *The dictionary of cultural literacy.* Boston, MA: Houghton Mifflin.

Howe, F. (1993). The child in elementary school. *Child Study Journal, 23*(3), 229–338.

Howe, N. and Strauss, B. (1993). *13th Gen: Abort, retry, ignore, fail?* New York, NY: Vintage Books.

King, E., Chipman, M. and Cruz-Janzen, M. (1994). *Educating young children in a diverse society.* Needham Heights, MA: Allyn & Bacon.

Loden, M. (1995). *Implementing diversity.* Chicago, IL: Irwin.

Loden, M. and Rosener, J. (1991). *Work force America: Managing employee diversity as a vital resource.* Homewood, IL: Business One Irwin.

Sadker, M. and Sadker, D. (1994). *Failing at fairness: How our schools cheat girls.* New York, NY: Touchstone.

Schickedanz, J., Hansen, K. and Forsyth, P. (1990). *Understanding children.* Mountain View, CA: Mayfield.

Chapter Seven

Program Design

The world is full of opposites. Any attribute, concept or idea is meaningless without its opposite. In the sixth century B.C., Lao-tzu wrote Tao-te Ching *which stressed the need for the successful leader to see opposites all around:*

> *The wise leader knows how to be creative. In order to lead, the leader learns to follow. In order to prosper, the leader learns to live simply. In both cases, it is the interaction that is creative. All behavior consists of opposites.... Learn to see things backwards, inside out, and upside down.*

Thompson, 1992, p. 89

The program design step in the program planning cycle integrates the philosophy of the organization with the needs and our knowledge of participants into programs and services. In the program design process our focus (as the programmer) turns to the benefits to be produced through a specific program. This process requires that recreation programmers look at a variety of factors. Constant changes in society, participants, and staff dictate the need for a plan as well as require great flexibility by programmers. In addition to this need for constant adaptation in response to external changes, programming is a process which includes far more than scheduling specific activities. In reality, a program includes the interaction of the organization's philosophy, needs of customers, program goals and objectives, activities (i.e., program area), program format, physical environment (i.e., facilities and space), people (i.e., staff and participants), equipment, scheduling, budgets, concern for safety, and other less tangible factors such as policies and procedures, relationships, and stage within the product life cycle. The program design is created to ensure the most positive interface between these components—see Figure 7.1 (page 114). It is important, then, that as we program we understand the resources available to us in each of these areas, and what we want to develop.

Russell (1982) identifies the program design stage as the most imaginative, the most adept in associative thinking, and the step that requires the most creativity. Later steps in program planning require decisions relating to budgets, promotion strategy, staffing, and evaluation. At this point in program planning it is important to let the "creative juices" flow. The development and use of a creative imagination are the keys to using knowledge successfully. The knowledge derived from creatively understood, practical, everyday problems is the most beneficial knowledge available to a programmer. Such knowledge is what links creativity to the idea of best professional practice in the field. The challenge inherent in the program design stage is twofold. First and foremost is how to empower participants to be creative and involved in the program design process. Second, is how the programmer can combine good judgment (which has the potential to hamper innovative ideas) with creative thinking (Russell, 1982).

There are several subcomponents to the program design stage in the overall program planning cycle. First, it is important to evaluate how specific programs fit into the full range of leisure-related activities and services offered by an organization. Later steps concentrate on the fees and charges connected to the program as well as identifying how the program will be promoted. This chapter will focus primarily on the creative process in program design. In addition, we will discuss a variety of factors that impact on the program design process.

Importance of Creativity

Creativity is important in all aspects of the program planning cycle from interacting with customers, to facilitating the actual leisure experience, to dealing with staff challenges, to developing new programs and services. Creativity also assists programmers in dealing with the ambiguity brought on by continual change. All leisure providers in parks, recreation, and leisure services face a work environment that is constantly changing. On one hand we are being asked to document outcomes, respond to the needs of customers, and provide quality services, while on the other hand we are asked to deal with budget cuts and staff reductions. Programmers everywhere must meet the challenge of doing more, doing it faster, doing it better, and with fewer resources.

To meet this challenge managers must learn to build on the renewable resources of their staff. The philosopher William James wrote, "[C]ompared to what we ought to be, we are only half awake. We are making use of only a small part of our physical and mental resources" (Blohowiak, 1992). With this thought in mind, programmers must look for ways to harness their creativity and passion, and apply these resources to designing programs.

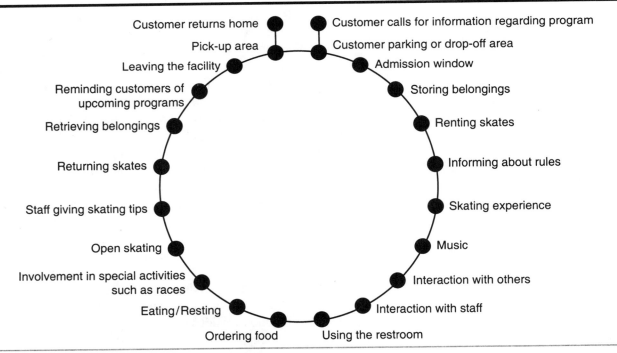

Figure 7.1   Cycle of Service for an Ice Skating Rink

Each of us probably knows someone whom we would label as being creative. In fact, many believe that only some individuals are blessed with this talent. As your authors, however, we believe that everyone has the *potential* to be creative. Creativity is a learned skill which can be fostered and developed in both staff and participants. Creativity implies making something from nothing or using something in an innovative or new way. Being creative means seeing opportunities in problems as well as other unique situations. Creative people are flexible and are not tied to the way things have always been. Wilson (1981) has identified the following characteristics of creativity: curiosity, enthusiasm (passion), persistence, imagination, and discrimination (knowing what ideas to pursue).

Developing these skills and learning to be creative involves recognizing one's blind spots and trying to overcome them (von Oech, 1983). Blind spots are sensory "lock outs" of our environment caused by conditioning or prior expectations. For example, read the quote presented in Figure 7.2.

FEATURE FILMS ARE THE RESULT OF YEARS OF SCIENTIFIC STUDY COMBINED WITH THE EXPERIENCE OF YEARS

Figure 7.2

How many letter "fs" do you count? Research has shown that approximately 50% of the population will see only three "fs," approximately 10% of the population will see all six "fs," while the remaining portion of the population will see either four or five "fs." The reason for this disparity is that we are conditioned to speed read over the small words in sentences and as a result many of us miss or discount the "fs" in the word "of." Research supports the notion that we are conditioned to repress our creativity. One study found that most adults demonstrate only 10% of the creativity they displayed at age five (Shrieves, 1996). This creativity hasn't been lost; it has just been pushed below the surface. Without a conscious effort, many of us lose our ability to use our innate creativity as we grow older. As a result, we need to consciously work to redevelop our creativity. A good place for us to start is to be aware of the mental blocks to creativity presented in Figure 7.3 (page 116).

There are infinite ways to be creative in program design. As individuals remove the mental blocks to creativity they are often empowered to try new and innovative program ideas and approaches. Specific techniques for encouraging creative thought include brainstorming, discontinuity, forced analogy, mental imagery or visualization, mind mapping, and unconscious problem solving. These are discussed in detail throughout this chapter. Figure 7.4 (page 116) presents specific actions each of us can each take in efforts to increase our creativity.

Brainstorming

Creative thought may be divided into divergent and convergent reasoning. Both abilities are required for creative output. Divergent thinking is essential to the novelty of creative products whereas convergent thinking is fundamental to determining appropriateness. *Divergent thinking* is the intellectual ability to think of many original, diverse, and elaborate ideas. In other words, thoughts diverge or separate from the norm. *Convergent thinking* is the intellectual ability to logically evaluate, critique, and choose the best idea from a selection of ideas. This type of thinking requires that a judgment be made about an idea.

The basis of brainstorming is divergent thinking which generates ideas in a group situation based on withholding judgment. The generation (i.e., divergent thinking) phase is separate from the judgment (i.e., convergent thinking) phase of thinking. Research has proven brainstorming to be highly productive in generating a large quantity of ideas which ultimately yield higher quality ideas (Bannon & Busser, 1992). The greater the number of ideas generated, the greater the likelihood of coming up with new and potentially effective program alternatives (Russell,

THE RIGHT ANSWER—By the time the average person finishes college, they have taken over 2,600 quizzes, tests and exams, most of them seeking the one right answer to solve the question. Thus, the "right answer" approach becomes deeply ingrained in our thinking. We need to relearn that life is ambiguous and there are many right answers, all depending on what we are looking for.

BE PRACTICAL—Be a magician… ask "what if" questions and use the provocative answers as stepping stones to new ideas. Cultivate your imagination and encourage "what iffing" in others!

AVOID AMBIGUITY—Look at something and think what else it might be. Pose a problem in an ambiguous fashion so as not to restrict the imagination of the problem solvers. Try using humor to put you and your group in a creative state of mind.

TO ERR IS WRONG—If you make an error, use it as a stepping stone to a new idea you might not have otherwise discovered. Differentiate between errors of "commission" and "omission." Strengthen your "risk muscle" by taking at least one risk every twenty-four hours. Remember the two benefits of failure: first, if you do fail, you learn what doesn't work, and; second, the failure gives you an opportunity to try a new approach.

PLAY IS FRIVOLOUS—It is not so important to be serious as it is to be serious about important things. The next time you have a problem, play with it. If you don't have a problem, take the time to play anyway. You may find some new ideas. Make your workplace a fun place to be!

THAT'S NOT MY AREA—Develop the outlook that wherever you go, there are ideas to be discovered. Schedule idea-hunting time into your day and week. Develop different kinds of hunting grounds. The wider and more diversified your knowledge, the more places you have to draw from.

DON'T BE FOOLISH—In a time when things are changing very quickly, who is to say what's right and what's foolish? Occasionally let your "stupid monitor" down, play the fool, and see what crazy ideas you can come up with.

I'M NOT CREATIVE—Creative people think they are creative. Less creative people don't think they are creative. This is an example of a self-fulfilling prophecy. If you want to be more creative, believe in the worth of your ideas and have the persistence to continue building on them. With this attitude you'll take a few more risks and break the rules occasionally.

Figure 7.3 Mental Blocks to Creativity (Adapted from von Oech, 1983)

PLAY MORE—Get involved with children's activities; you may find that some toys aid the creative thinking process. Jigsaw puzzles (for spatial thinking), building blocks, drawing, role-playing/acting, just talking and asking questions, all contribute to creative thought and practice. Gaming, as a hobby, can improve problem-solving and creative skills. There are many types of games that involve intellectual thought and creative solution; investigate miniatures, board games, card games, computer games and simulations, and so forth. Much creative exercise can be found in such activities.

CREATE YOUR OWN CREATIVE SPACE—Having your special place for creative outlet has many benefits. A very famous creative space is Henry Thoreau's cabin described in Walden. Vance and Deacon (1995) in their book, *Think Out of the Box*, describe a concept called the Kitchen for the Mind which is a room filled with creativity-stimulating objects and decor—a resource rich environment. Vance and Deacon recommend that you take a space in your home or organization and make it a place that stimulates you to think and be creative. Make a conscious effort to surround yourself with the tools and resources you need to be creative. Think about your ideal creative space. What do you need (e.g., computers, art supplies, musical instruments) and where will you locate your space?

KEEP RECORDS—Keep a daily journal and record your thoughts, ideas, sketches, and so on as soon as you have them. Review your journal regularly and see what ideas can be developed.

DEVELOP OUTSIDE INTERESTS—Develop an interest in a variety of different things, preferably well away from your normal sphere of work. For example, read comic books or magazines you wouldn't normally read. This keeps the brain busy with new things. It is a common trait of creative people that they are interested in a wide variety of subjects.

DON'T WORK TOO HARD—You need time away from a problem to be creative after periods of intense focus. Indulge in relaxation activities and sports to give the mind a rest and time for the subconscious to digest information. Relaxation and good health are important to mental and physical health—essential prerequisites to creative thinking. For example, when jogging some individuals are able to clear their minds and think through problems. Some have been able to visualize computer programs, develop ideas, and process solutions to different problems when engaged in various forms of exercise.

Figure 7.4 Steps to Improve Creativity

1982). Thus, the *number* of ideas generated is the goal of brainstorming. Brainstorming is a process that works best with a group of people when the six rules presented in Figure 7.5 are followed. Figure 7.6 also provides a number of idea generating questions for brainstorming related to parks, recreation, and leisure programming.

Discontinuity

The more familiar we are with something, the less stimulating it is for our thinking. When we disrupt our typical thought patterns, those ideas that create

1 Identify a well-defined and clearly stated problem.

2 Arrange the group so each member can see the others (a circle often works well).

3 Trade off the job of writing down all the ideas as they occur. Write on newsprint, overhead transparencies, or some other medium which can be seen by all.

4 Have an appropriate group size. Most sources advocate groups between five and twelve people. With skilled leadership, however, effective sessions can be conducted with larger or smaller groups.

5 Use a location that is different from the normal working environment. Such a setting can be more conducive to creativity. Aim for comfortable seating, room, lighting, and temperature. Be sure there is room for the people who like to pace while they think.

6 Share responsibility to help enforce the following guidelines: suspend judgment, accept and record every idea presented, and encourage people to build on the ideas of others (piggy-back on others' ideas).

Figure 7.5   Guides for Brainstorming

1 Try to define what something is not.

2 What is everybody else **NOT** doing?

3 What if we _____?

4 What could we adopt and/or adapt from other places? What else is like this?

5 Plug in a variety of opposites. For example what if we …

Magnify/Minify:
What to add? Greater frequency? Stronger? Larger? What to subtract? Eliminate? Split up? Less frequent?

Substitute/Combine:
Who else instead? What else instead? Other place or time? How about a blend, an assortment? Combined purposes or ideas?

6 How can we modify our programs? We can change meaning, participants, motion, degree of difficulty, equipment, sound, odor, taste, form, and/or shape.

7 How can we put the program to other uses? New ways to use it? Other uses if modified?

8 How can we rearrange: the layout? the sequence? the pace?

9 How can we reverse? Opposites? Turn it backward? Turn it upside down? Turn it inside out?

10 What are the assumptions of the problem? What happens as we drop some of these assumptions either individually or in combination?

Figure 7.6   Idea Generating Questions for Brainstorming
(Adapted from Russell, 1982)

the greatest stimulus to our thinking do so because they force us to make new connections in order to understand the situation. Van Oech (1983) calls this a "Whack on the Side of the Head." Thus, to enhance our creativity we should insert programming interruptions into our day. We could change our working hours, get to work a different way, listen to an unfamiliar radio station, read a magazine we wouldn't normally read, try a new recipe, or watch a television program or film we wouldn't normally watch. Provocative ideas are often stepping stones that get us thinking about other ideas. Butting ideas against each other can cause friction that creates new thought-paths.

Forced Analogy

Forced analogy is a very useful and fun-filled method of generating ideas. The idea is to compare the problem with something else that has little or nothing in common and gain new insights as a result. We can force a relationship between almost anything, and arrive at new insights. Think about similarities between companies and whales, management systems and telephone networks, or our relationship with a supervisor and a pencil. Forcing relationships is one of the most powerful (and fun) ways to develop new insights and new solutions. A useful way of developing the relationships is to have a selection of objects or cards with pictures to help generate ideas. Choose an object or card at random and see what relationships we can force with the topic at hand. For example, imagine a leisure service organization as a matchbox (see Table 7.1). This type of exercise can be insightful in realizing the importance of flexibility or that the organizational structure should be adaptable if the need arises to change and try a new direction. For recreation programmers, a possible analogy might be to compare recreation programming to a three-ring circus—lots of things go on at once.

Mental Imagery/Visualization

Mental imagery has been used in sports psychology for a long time. Athletes are asked to visualize themselves winning or performing their best. This type of mental imagery can also be used to design programs. Mental imagery provides a unique access to the unfolding of a program or event and can be used to experience the program from a participant's

Table 7.1	Forced Analogy: Comparing a Recreation Organization to a Matchbox
Matchbox Attributes	**Organization Attributes**
Striking surface on two sides	Organizations need protection from unexpected risks.
Sliding center section	The organization should be flexible in order to respond to changing situations. The core of the organization is protected by its cover.
Made of cardboard	Inexpensive method of structure. The structure is not important; it is built to protect what is inside.

point of view, to anticipate and/or solve problems, to identify critical moments of interaction with participants, and to experience the entire operation of a program (Rossman, 1996). For example, in experiencing the entire program or event, mental imagery involves visualizing the event or program as we would expect it to unfold and then identifying the necessary steps to making all those elements happen.

Mental imagery and visualization can also be used to improve the quality of programs and events by visualizing all the thousands of specific moments that combine to create the total customer experience. These moments may be thought of as "moments of truth" in which staff have opportunities to impact the quality of the experience for participants. These "moments of truth" may be visualized in terms of a cycle of service. According to Albrecht and Zemke (1985) a cycle of service is *a repeatable sequence of events in which various people try to meet the customer's needs and expectations at each point.* The cycle begins at the very first point of contact between the customer and an organization. It ends, only temporarily, when the customer considers the service complete, and it begins anew when that person decides to come back for more.

By visualizing a cycle of service chart staff can identify potential moments of truth for the customer (see Figure 7.1, page 114). In many ways the chart forces us to see things as the customer sees them, without contaminating our perceptions with our own knowledge of what's *supposed* to happen behind the scenes. According to Albrecht (1992) this tool works best when we want to focus staff attention on the customer's chain of experience and how the succession of "truth moments" builds to a complete perception of quality by the completion of the cycle. Thus, this cycle allows staff to realize that the customer experience is cumulative and should be managed as such.

Mind Mapping

In addition to visually anticipating all aspects of a program we can also use our cognitive abilities to map out the program. In some ways our brains are very much like computers; in other ways we are quite different from a computer. Whereas a computer works in a linear fashion, the brain works associatively as well as linearly—comparing, integrating, and synthesizing as it goes. Association plays a dominant role in nearly every mental function, and words themselves are no exception. Every single word and idea has numerous links attaching it to other ideas and concepts in our minds. Mind maps are an effective method of taking notes, and useful for the generation of ideas by association. To make a mind map, individuals begin by writing a word representing the main idea in the center of the page and work outward in all directions with additional words, producing a growing and organized structure composed of key words and key images. Key features of mind maps include clustering of ideas through association and the visual memory it creates for individuals (see Figure 7.7, page 120).

Mind maps help organize information. Because of the large amount of association involved, they can be very creative, tending to generate new ideas and associations that have not been thought of before. Every item in a map is, in effect, the center of another map. The creative potential of a mind map is useful in brainstorming sessions. We only need to start with the basic problem at the center, and generate associations and ideas from it to arrive at a large number of different possible approaches. By presenting our perceptions in a spatial manner and using color and pictures, a better overview is gained and new connections can be made visible.

Mind maps are also very individual and original. For example, if we were to compare the mind maps of two different individuals around one central theme they would be vastly different. Research has shown that even simplified mind maps (with as few as seven related words) of any two individuals would average only one word in common, and anything above two is very unusual (Buzan & Buzan, 1996). An example of a mind map (Figure 7.7) along with the instructions for using mind maps is presented in Figure 7.8 (page 120).

Unconscious Problem Solving

This method relies on the unconscious mind to continually process the various sensory inputs stored in short-term and long-term memory. It entails using our unconscious to solve problems. It is a process of listening and a readiness to record ideas as they percolate into our conscious mind. Some of the greatest thinkers were great relaxers. Albert Einstein was a daydreamer and spent much of his relaxation time sailing on a lake. Ralph Waldo Emerson enjoyed fishing. It's all very well to work hard on a problem under the stressful pressure of deadlines; the opposite condition of relaxation and not working on a problem is also very valuable.

A practical application of this technique is to saturate ourselves in the problem and then take a break. For instance, some people write down the problem on a writing pad and leave it by their bedside. When they wake up, they lie in bed, think some more about the problem, and write down their thoughts—even in the dark. This process is particularly helpful when planning special events. Often, thoughts wake us from sleep; particularly related to things we need to attend to the next day (e.g., security, ticketing, trash recycling) and it's very difficult to remember them in the morning. By writing them down at night, we can be sure to tend to our tasks, and get a good night's sleep.

Factors to Consider in Program Design

We have already examined the role of an organization's philosophy and needs assessment in the program planning cycle. In designing programs these serve as the building blocks or foundation for goals and objectives upon which specific programs should be developed. Within the actual design phase of programming the programmer has to make a myriad of decisions related to a variety of factors. These factors include program areas, program formats,

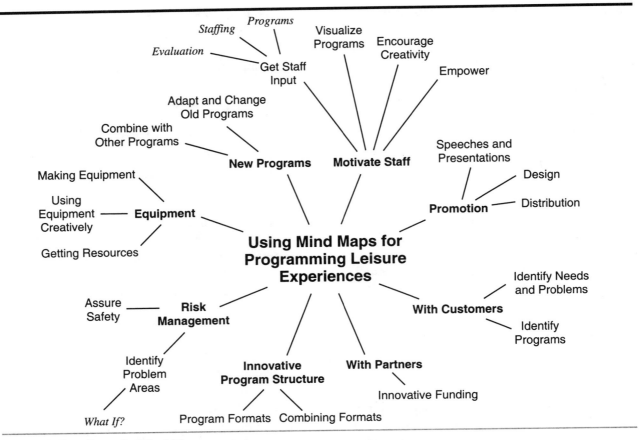

Figure 7.7   Sample Mind Map

Step One   Lighten Up

Let go of finding the perfect program, solving all the problems of the organization, or writing the perfect program evaluation. Mind mapping is simply a brain dumping process that helps stimulate new ideas and connections. Start with a playful attitude—you can always evaluate later.

Step Two   Think Fast

Our brains work best in 5 to 7 minute bursts so capture that explosion of ideas as rapidly as possible. Key words, symbols and images provide a mental shorthand to help us record ideas as quickly as possible.

Step Three   Judge Not

Similar to brainstorming, this phase of mind mapping asks us not to evaluate, but rather to record everything that comes to mind even if it seems to be totally unrelated.

Step Four   Break Boundaries

Break through the idea that we have to write on white, letter-size paper with black or blue ink. Use ledger paper or easel paper or cover an entire wall with butcher paper...the bigger the paper, the more ideas we will have. Use wild colors, fat colored markers, crayons, skinny felt-tip pens, or anything else you can find.

Step Five   Center First

Our linear, left-brain education system has taught us to start in the upper left hand corner of a page. However, our mind focuses on the center...so mind mapping begins with a word or image placed in the middle of the page that symbolizes what we want to think about.

Step Six   Free Associate

As ideas emerge, print one or two word descriptions of the ideas and connect them to the thought that generated the idea. Allow the ideas to expand outward from thoughts as they emerge.

Step Seven   Keep Moving

Keep moving. Avoid getting stuck on one idea. The more ideas generated, the better.

Step Eight   Allow Time for Organization

Compare your individual mind map to the maps of other people who are working on the same problem. Begin to look for linkages, that is, pieces of information that can be linked together in some way. Sometimes we will see relationships and connections right away, while other times it may take some time. Just remember the main purpose of mind mapping is to get ideas out and on paper.

Figure 7.8   Mind Mapping—Basic Rules (Adapted from Wycoff, 1991)

equipment, physical environments, policies and procedures, risk management, staff, staff/customer interactions, scheduling, and the program life cycle (see Figure 7.9). The remainder of this chapter will address each one of these factors individually, while the next chapter will examine how these factors interact to create the overall programs and services of an organization.

Program Areas

In Chapter One we acknowledged that there is no universal definition for leisure that explains what leisure is in every society and every situation. We also indicated that there are a great variety of activities and endeavors that could be referred to as recreation. Parks, recreation, and leisure service organizations, as a result of this variety, have traditionally found it necessary and desirable to catalog recreation behavior into program areas. An abbreviated list of possible activities organized by program area is presented in Table 7.2 (page 122).

Classifying the experiences that offer satisfying leisure and recreation experiences can be a difficult task. The possible categories are limitless and the means of classification are often arbitrary (Russell, 1982). Leisure activities can be classified based on the type of activities, involvement of customers (passive or active), indoor/outdoor, skill level, cost, season of the year, benefit outcomes, age, gender, level of risk, facility or setting, goal structure, and so forth. Furthermore, any one activity could be classified in a number of different ways. For example, in Table 7.2 scuba diving is commonly classified under aquatics although it could also fit under adventure recreation, outdoor activities, or even environmental activities. Despite the problem of overlap, these classification systems are designed to facilitate generalizations about leisure activities and programs and to contribute to the development of theory in program development (Edginton, Hanson, Edginton & Hudson, 1998).

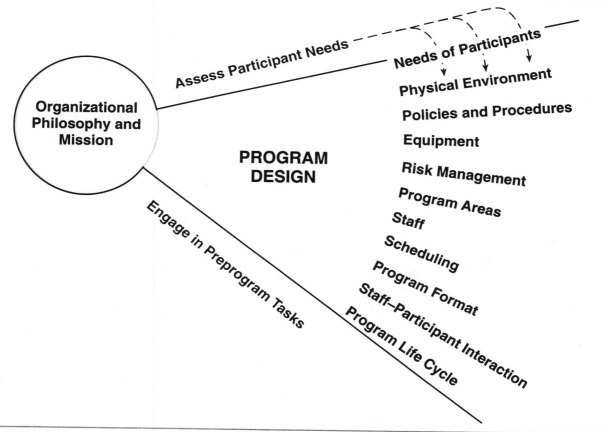

Figure 7.9   Decision Factors in Programming Design

Table 7.2   Program Areas and Sample Programs

Sports and Games
Competitive athletics (e.g., softball
    league, soccer league)
Individual sports and games (e.g., golf)
Dual sports and games (e.g., tennis)
Team sports and games (e.g., volleyball)

Fitness/Wellness Activities
Fitness activities
Nutrition education
Aerobic activities
Weightlifting

Aquatics
Swimming
Water polo
Scuba diving
Lessons
Pool parties
Aquacize

Service/Volunteer Opportunities
Service learning
Serving on boards
Direct service
Coaching
Fund raising
Interpretive guide

Dance
Folk
Modern
Social/Ballroom
Tap
Square
Ballet
Hip-hop
Stepping

Drama
Films/movies
Plays
Storytelling/Dramatic readings
Puppetry
Reenactments

Music
Instrumental (individual or group)
Performance
Listening
Instruction
Composition
Study/Practice
Children's rhythms
Vocal (individual or group)

Arts and Crafts
Ceramics
Photography
Weaving
Paper making
Painting
Jewelry making
Leathercraft
Sculpture

Environmental Activities
Environmental education
Camping
Nature crafts
Outdoor living skills
Birdwatching

Adventure Education
Backcountry travel
Ropes courses
Initiative activities
Team building
Rock climbing

Extreme Sports
Bungee jumping
Snowboarding
In-line skate competitions
Motocross

Travel and Tourism
Trips and tours
Travelogues
Adventure tourism
Field trips

Social Recreation
Parties
Board games
Social integration games
Mixers
Picnics

Hobbies
Collecting
Creative work
Education
Gardening

Cognitive and Literary
Creative writing
Debates
Book clubs
Visiting museums

Self-Improvement/Education
Retreats
Conferences
Advocacy groups
Genealogy research
Stress management
Leisure education

Within each of these program areas, unique program design features may come into play. Due to the sheer numbers of possible program areas we do not try to present the design features of all possible activity types that could be offered to participants. Rather we attempt to present some overall design considerations for all activities throughout this chapter.

Program Formats

Within each program area a variety of different program formats may be used to conduct each activity. Program formats may be viewed as the way in which an activity is organized and structured for delivery to the customer. More specifically, program formats may be viewed as the configuration or "way in which

experiences are sequenced and linked to one another to increase the likelihood that customers will achieve desired benefits" (Edginton Hanson, Edginton & Hudson, 1998, p. 257). Different benefit outcomes are emphasized in different program formats for the same event. As a result, it is important to match the appropriate program format with the needs and wants of constituents.

A list of possible program formats identified by a variety of authors is presented in Table 7.3. For the purpose of this book we will explore the following formats: competitive, drop-in (including opportunities to promote self-directed opportunities), special events, clubs (including special interest groups), instructional (including classes, workshops, and

Table 7.3   Program Formats

Russell (1982)	Kraus (1985)	Farrell and Lundegren (1991)	Rossman (1995)	Edginton, Hanson, Edginton and Hudson (1998)	DeGraaf, Jordan and DeGraaf (1999)
Competition	Organized Competition	Competition	Competition/ League Tournaments	Competition	Competition
		Participant Spectator			
		Self-Directed	Self-Directed, Noncompetitive		
Open Facility	Unstructured Participation		Drop-In	Drop-In/ Open Facility	Drop-In
Special Events	Special Events		Special Events	Special Events	Special Events
Club	Special Interest Groups		Clubs/Groups	Club and Interest Groups	Clubs
Class	Instruction	Self-Improvement		Class	Instructional
	Leadership Training		Skill Development		
Workshops/ Seminars				Workshops/ Seminars	
	Performances, Demos, Exhibits				
Trips/Outings	Trips/Outings				Trips
				Outreach	Outreach
Voluntary Service		Social			Service Opportunities

seminars), trips, outreach, and service opportunities. As with program areas there does seem to be some overlap between these format areas. For example, a special event may include a competitive tournament, opportunities for service, resource information (drop-in format), and the chance for a specific club to display some of its products (i.e., art display). Despite this overlap, we feel there is enough difference to warrant individual consideration of the program formats depicted in Figure 7.10 (page 124).

Competition

Within a competitive format, performance of an individual or a team of individuals is compared to the performance of another individual or team, or an established criteria or standard. Thus, individuals or teams may compete against themselves, the

environment, or other individuals or teams. Within leisure service organizations, competition may take many different forms such as:

- A one-day tournament or meet where teams or individuals play one another (e.g., softball tournament, track meet, chess tournament, golf tournament);

- A contest where individuals compare ability through parallel performances, with a set standard determining the winner (e.g., gymnastic or ice skating competition, cook off, baking contest, voice competition, spelling bee); and

- League play where teams or individuals play one another over an extended period of time (e.g., bowling league, Little League Baseball, volleyball league).

Although the competition format has traditionally been dominated by sports there are a variety of other program areas that lend themselves to competition such as board games, music, and drama. Several tournament designs such as single elimination and double elimination tournaments, ladder tournaments, and round robin tournaments are presented in Appendix A.

Competition is a popular and important format for many leisure service organizations. We should, however, be very aware of its limitations and try to avoid the "win at all costs" mentality that cause many people to not participate because they feel they are not skilled enough to compete. Participants, particularly in youth leagues, need to feel that their efforts are respected by coaches or leaders as well as parents. Skill development and dignity in play should serve as a foundation to competitive activities. To this end, programmers should strive to remember the following two principles.

- Provide participants opportunities to compete with others of similar skills and abilities, or have mechanisms to equalize the competition between individuals. For instance, in golf and bowling less skilled participants are often given a handicap in an effort to create opportunities for players of all abilities to compete evenly with each other. In other circumstances, programmers can be creative in adapting activities or equipment so individuals of varying abilities can play together. For example, in an intergenerational game of softball the size of the ball and bat could be changed to accommodate differing skill levels. Less skilled, younger players could use a bigger bat and try to hit a bigger ball while players with better skills would use a regulation size ball and bat.

- Participants should always feel they are competing in a safe and fair environment. Safety (physical *and* emotional) is always a high priority in all programming efforts, and these efforts should be easily discernible by those involved. Furthermore,

Figure 7.10   Program Formats

participants feel more in control of their own circumstances if they can be a part of the development of rules and guidelines to keep things fair and equitable.

Drop-In

Casual or drop-in participation is used to encourage spontaneous involvement by participants. This format usually involves setting aside a specific amount of time for unstructured play. For example, a recreation center may schedule open gymnasium time when individuals can drop-in and play pick-up basketball. Other program facilities that may lend themselves to drop-in time include ice rinks, swimming pools, tennis courts, driving ranges, bowling lanes, craft facilities, and music rooms.

Drop-in activities do not require any advance commitment from the participant (e.g., they do not need to register for a class). For example, the city of Cedar Falls, Iowa, offers an indoor park experience for young children from October to April each year. Parents and their preschool children can drop into the gym on Tuesday or Thursday morning from 9:00 a.m. to 11:00 a.m. During this time a variety of equipment, mats, and toys are provided for children to play with in an indoor setting.

Another form of drop-in programming is that of a resource center which empowers individuals to be self-directed in planning their own leisure experiences. Creating resources such as providing information, creating connections between people, and offering equipment rental can be all that some people need to be self-directed in terms of their leisure needs. Consider IMU Outfitters at Indiana University which provides students with an area to study books, maps, and other resources to plan outdoor trips in the surrounding area. In addition, IMU Outfitters offers students a shared adventure board so they can connect with other students with similar interests. Other services include environmental information, a bulletin board to sell used equipment, and an equipment rental program.

Very little is needed from the organization in preparing for drop-in activities. Equipment may or may not be provided. Staffing is usually minimal and limited to general supervision of the area or facility. Programmers do need to be aware of several issues however. For example, programmers need to be alert to the situation where parents drop off young children, and then leave. In essence, drop-in programs can be used as a childcare. Some drop-in programs are designed this way, while leaders of other programs may be faced with unique problems because of absent parents. Programmers also need to be aware of other issues such as violence and other social ills which contribute to supervision issues. Some programmers must now be prepared to deal with between-participant altercations, unwanted (troublesome) participants, and gang infiltration. In addition, in urban areas the numbers of homeless individuals who enter drop-in programs for protection from the elements are increasing. Organizational policies related to addressing these types of situations are necessary.

A programmatic concern related to providing drop-in opportunities is scheduling. Russell (1982) notes that the drop-in approach is often overlooked or underplanned for, and time is usually limited to what is left over before or after structured and scheduled programs. Programmers are thus encouraged to not forget this program format in developing the overall program plan for a facility. Careful attention must be paid to understanding when people want to be able to drop-in and then program accordingly.

Special Events

Special events describe programs that deviate from the norm such as festivals, playdays, carnivals, banquets, celebrations, shows, pageants, exhibitions, fairs, and other activities or combination of activities that do not fall within the other forms of leisure program formats. Jackson (1997) has noted that special events are

> extraordinary, nonspontaneous, planned occurrences designed to entertain, inform, or provide enjoyment and/or inspiration to audiences and/or spectators. (p. xii)

Jackson goes on to note two additional characteristics of special events, the use of volunteers and the use of sponsors to provide financial support of some kind.

The use of special events as a means to deliver services is continuing to grow. For example, there are over 20,000 recurring community festivals alone in the United States each year; this figure is growing at approximately 5% each year (Janiskee, 1996). The use of other types of special events also continues to grow as programmers begin to understand the potential of special events to draw specific attention and/or advocate for a specific product, program, service, philosophy, message, or group. Figure 7.11 (page 126) presents a few possible goals of special events for various types of organizations.

Jackson has categorized special events into eight groupings depending on the scope of the event (see Figure 7.12, page 126). In terms of special events, many programmers feel that the larger the event the better. However, this is not always the case. As with most programs the most important consideration is whether or not the event meets the goals and objectives put forward for the program.

Using this as a barometer for success small special events can be very successful if they are well-planned and meet their goals and objectives. For example, one nursing home sponsors an "over 80" party each year in May to commemorate Older Americans Month. The goal of this event is to celebrate the lives of residents who have lived 80+ years with their family and friends in the community. A variety of special events are included such as living histories, photo displays, biographical information,

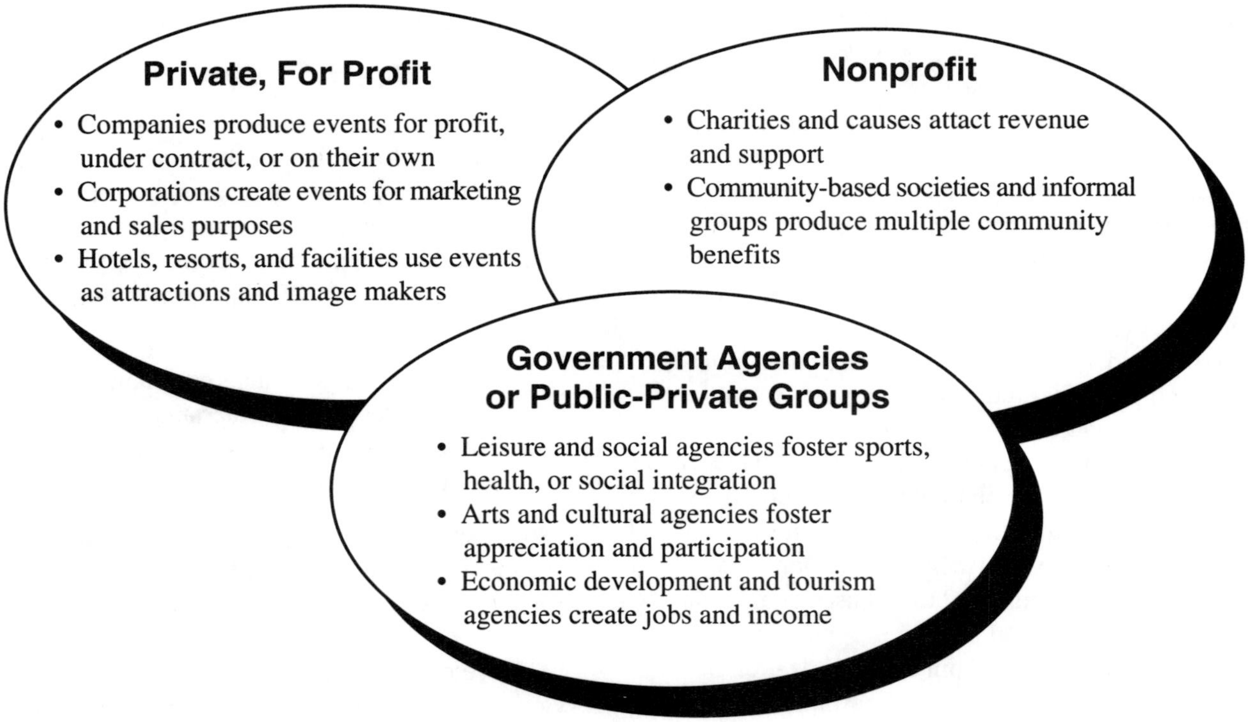

Private, For Profit
- Companies produce events for profit, under contract, or on their own
- Corporations create events for marketing and sales purposes
- Hotels, resorts, and facilities use events as attractions and image makers

Nonprofit
- Charities and causes attact revenue and support
- Community-based societies and informal groups produce multiple community benefits

Government Agencies or Public-Private Groups
- Leisure and social agencies foster sports, health, or social integration
- Arts and cultural agencies foster appreciation and participation
- Economic development and tourism agencies create jobs and income

Figure 7.11   Possible Goals for Special Events (Getz, 1997)

- **Neighborhood Events.** A gathering or program put on by homeowners, associations, local merchant groups, perhaps a church or school.

- **Community Events.** These events expand to several neighborhoods, up to and including suburban satellite cities or quasicities. These may include festivals named after food and flowers (e.g., the Strawberry Festival of Poteet, TX, and the Lilac Festival of Rochester, NY), commemoration of historic events (Tom Mix Film Festival in Guthrie, OK), amateur athletic competitions, and other similar festivals.

- **Metro Area Events.** Those whose operations and appeal encompasses several contiguous cities, communities, and neighborhoods. Most often, these events include large family-oriented festivals, musical offerings, major athletic competitions, historically or geographically themed happenings, and so on.

- **Statewide Events.** Obviously those aimed at involving the entire state. A primary example is the celebration of a state's 100th anniversary of statehood, but there are others which are primarily political, social, educational, and professional in nature.

- **Regional Events.** Ordinarily, statewide events broadened and clustered by contiguous states; often the link between state and national events. Often these are seasonal and relate to natural events (e.g., Buzzard Weekend in Hinkley, OH—one weekend each spring when the buzzards return from their migration to roost in the rocky cliffs of the area).

- **National Events.** Large scale events that include such things as political party conventions and other conventions that are national in scope (e.g., NRPA, AAHPERD).

- **International Events.** Events that draw an international audience including such events as sporting competitions (e.g., the Olympics). Other important events focus on issues dealing with global health, social, political, religious, and economic issues. The International Women's Conference in Beijing in 1996 was an example of this.

- **Promotional Events.** Can be any of the above mentioned events that includes a promotion of a product or service. An example of this is the MacWorld Expo.

Figure 7.12   Special Event Groupings

and intergenerational activities (Schlis, 1996). The success of the event is founded in the collaboration of area social services and families to celebrate the gift of life. It is not a huge event, yet it is extremely popular with those who are involved.

As special events get larger the tasks unique to planning and implementing them become more complex. Crowd control, parking, sanitation, scheduling, Porta-Potties, concessions, a wide variety of events, and extra clean-up are all examples of the extra details that may accompany a larger special event. As a result, special events are often the result of a variety of partnerships with a wide range of organizations. This allows for one organization to take the lead while delegating a variety of additional tasks to others. Thus, programmers should allow plenty of lead time for planning and organizing.

Consider the world's largest barbecue, an annual community event held in Abilene, Texas. The event has been jointly sponsored by the city of Abilene and the Dyess Air Force Base Morale, Welfare, and Recreation (MWR) department since 1965. By 1995 the event had grown to include over 225 volunteers, one thousand pounds of Texas beef, a truck load of coleslaw, baked beans, and more than 10,000 hungry people (Bailey, 1995). This cooperative event has won the Air Combat Command Community Relations Award as an event that displays the best relationship between a military base and a community.

National and international special events continue to compound the issues that events programmers have to manage. Large-scale events are often viewed as major catalysts for tourism and economic development. For example, the annual Taste of Chicago festival held on the lakefront in Chicago each year is a major festival. In 1995 over three million visitors enjoyed food and entertainment during the eleven days of the event. As reported in a 1995 visitor's survey over 35% of the visitors to the Taste of Chicago were from Chicago suburbs, while 19% came from the midwestern United States or beyond. Over 85% of these visitors reported that the Taste of Chicago was their primary motive for visiting the city, and a majority stayed one or more nights in a downtown hotel or motel. Experts estimated that in 1995 the Taste of Chicago generated over 29 million dollars in direct spending in food and lodging expenditures (Getz, 1997).

Clubs

Clubs, or special interest groups, are groups of individuals organized around the enjoyment or practice of a particular activity or purpose (Russell, 1982), usually for an extended period of time. Clubs in leisure service settings are normally organized around an activity interest, but they also can be organized around some unifying factor such as age group, the exchange of information or ideas, or a specific issue. The club format offers both socialization and continuous opportunity and support for participation in a specific activity or event.

Clubs typically sustain themselves through dues they collect from members, and sometimes, through the sale of club goods (e.g., crafts, food). In addition, most clubs have officers and some type of bylaws to govern the group. This helps the club to respond to member needs and desires. Furthermore, clubs often program their own events for both club and nonclub members. Club members often receive discounts on goods and services from within a community. The possibilities for various clubs are endless. Examples of clubs include gourmet cooking, model airplanes, civil war reenactment, ham radio, runners, rugby, bird-watching, book-of-the-month, current events, the Magic School Bus explorers club, ultimate Frisbee, hiking, and computer user groups.

The club format requires little involvement of the leisure service organization once they have been established. Clubs exist for their members and, as a result, it is the members of the club who take on the leadership role of directing the activities of the club. This involvement can be very empowering for members as they work together to develop their own internal organization which may be formal or informal. Formal clubs typically develop a constitution and bylaws. A constitution states the intended purpose of the club and the fundamental principles by which the club operates. The bylaws establish the rules by which the club is to function.

Beyond sometimes providing club leadership, parks, recreation, and leisure service organizations often provide meeting space and help to ensure that club membership is open to all interested parties. In addition to encouraging open membership, leisure service organizations also make sure that all aspects of the club are conducted within the spirit and philosophy of the sponsoring organization. A golf or country club is one example of a club format. It primarily is focused on providing grounds and facilities for potential participants, yet it also offers other amenities (e.g., a pro shop, sandwich shop, rental equipment). On occasion, a country club will sponsor either educational or competitive events for its membership (see Figure 7.13).

Instructional

Instructional formats are very common within a variety of program areas. Instructional formats include classes, seminars, workshops, and clinics. The goal of each of these formats is to teach and further develop skill levels of participants. The difference between each of these formats lies in the length of time devoted to instruction. Classes are usually offered over an extended period of time (e.g., several weeks or months) while seminars, workshops, and clinics are conducted over a short period of time (e.g., several hours or a day).

The instructional format is usually highly structured, has a high degree of leader control, and a limited number of participants. There are several techniques for presenting information in an instructional setting including lecture, video and other visual aids, video feedback, demonstration, guest speakers, class member experimentation, and practice. It is the leader's responsibility to choose the most appropriate means of instruction considering the activity, participants, size of the group, location, and equipment available.

Considerations for developing instructional formats include keeping a class or workshop size small. Although it may vary according to the technique and information being presented, a reasonable class size is between 10 to 20 participants per leader. Scheduling should also be considered. For example, scheduling of classes should allow for enough time for participants to practice each skill presented. Skills should also build on each other as participants move through the class, workshop, seminar, or clinic. Furthermore, sessions need to be scheduled at times when the potential participants are available (see Figure 7.14).

Outreach

In many situations, customers cannot go to the parks, recreation, and leisure service organizations for services and programs due to a variety of factors. Poor health, lack of resources, lack of time, and psychological reasons (e.g., people think they don't

The Bike Club is Back!

Last summer The Bicycle Shop of Chaska initiated the first Bike Club for the community of Chaska. We met each Wednesday and Friday evening at the Bicycle Shop and explored the various trails in and around Chaska.

Starting May 3rd

This year we are setting things up a little different and offering some educational maintenance classes as well. Wednesday nights will still be devoted to the recreational rider, but in addition we will spend approximately 30 minutes after the ride going over various routine maintenance schedules on your bike. These will include changing a tire, adjusting derailleurs, truing wheels, etc. There is a group of riders that ride Tuesday and Thursday evenings off road. We will be coordinating with them for the rider who is looking for more bumps and stumps. The group we have not yet been able to satisfy is the roadies. We would like to support their sport and would be more than interested in cooperating with any individual or group that would like to start a road club.

The Benefits of the Club

To encourage people to participate in the Club and learn more about the area trails, new and changing bikes and equipment, not to mention the opportunity to meet new and exciting people (as if this were not enough!) we are offering 10% off any accessories purchased on that day.

Family First

Again, our emphasis is on the family and to encourage community involvement; so don't be afraid to bring your family down for a ride and encourage your friends and neighbors to come too. We will be setting up a Family Bike Ride this summer with the City of Chaska as a part of River City Days. Look for more information to come. In addition to the Family Bike Ride we will be conducting another Bicycle Rodeo with the Chaska Police Department to encourage and teach proper bike safety and maintenance to children.

Figure 7.13   Sample of a Club Program Format
(Complement of Chaska, MN)

Winter Mass Registration

A registration flyer with specific skills for each level and class times is available at the front desk of the CCC. Registration will continue to be taken after mass registration at the front desk of the CCC. Please be prepared to show proper ID. For more information, call Lori at 555–5633 ext.106.

Date Saturday, December 20, 1997
Time 9–11 a.m. Residents and Members
11 a.m.–12 noon Non-Res.
Place Community Room in the CCC

Learn to Swim Program

Winter Swimming Lessons
Swimming lessons are offered on Tuesday and Thursday evenings and Saturday mornings. All classes are taught by American Red Cross trained instructors and lifeguards. Each session is eight weeks and meets one day a week. Various levels of swimming are offered for each hour listed below. For specific skills and levels offerings, please pick up a flyer at the CCC Front Desk.

Tuesday Evening
Dates Session I January 13 – March 3
Session II March 17–May 5
Times 4:45–5:25 p.m., Levels 1–3
5:30–6:10 p.m., Levels 2a–4
6:15–6:55 p.m., Levels 1–3

Thursday Evening
Dates Session I January 15 – March 5
Session II March 19–May 7
Times 4:45–5:25 p.m., Levels 2a–5
5:30–6:10 p.m., Levels 1–4
6:15–6:55 p.m., Levels 1–2b, 6, 7

Saturday Morning
Dates Session I January 10 – Feb. 28
Session II March 21–May 10
Times 9:00–9:40 a.m., Levels 1–4
9:45–10:25 a.m., Levels 1–4
10:30–11:10 a.m., Lvls 1–3, 6, 7
11:15–11:55 a.m., Levels 2a–5

Leisure Pool Schedule

January 5 – May 31, 1998

Schedule is subject to change depending on swimming lessons.

	Sun.	Mon.	Tues.	Wed.	Thurs.	Fri.	Sat.
9 a.m.							Swim Lessons 9 am – 12:50 pm
10 a.m.		Tot Time 10:15 am – 12:15 pm				Tot Time 10:15 am – 12:15 pm	
11 a.m.							
noon							
1 p.m.	Open Swim 1 – 5 pm	Leisure Swim 1 pm – 3 pm	Leisure Swim 1 pm – 3 pm	Leisure Swim 1 pm – 3 pm	Leisure Swim 1 pm – 3 pm	Leisure Swim 1 pm – 3 pm	Open Swim 1 – 5 pm
2 p.m.							
3 p.m.		Water-Slide Open Swim 3–4:55 pm	Water-Slide Open Swim 3–4:30 pm	Water-Slide Open Swim 3–4:55 pm	Water-Slide Open Swim 3–4:30 pm	Water-Slide Open Swim 3–4:55 pm	
4 p.m.							
5 p.m.			Swim Lessons 4:45 – 6:55 pm		Swim Lessons 4:45 – 6:55 pm		
6 p.m.	Open Swim 6 pm – 8:30 pm	Open Swim 7–8:30 pm	Open Swim 7–8:30 pm	Open Swim 7–8:30 pm	Open Swim 7–8:30 pm	Open Swim 6 – 9 pm	Open Swim 6 – 9 pm
7 p.m.							
8 p.m.							
9 p.m.							

Introducing a New Water Tot Program

To better meet the needs of parents and children of the preschool age, a new format for preschool age swim lesson is being introduced. Each class is 30 minutes.

Monday Evening
Dates March 17–May 4
Times 6 to 18 months
5:00–5:30 p.m.

18 to 36 months
5:35–6:05 p.m.

3 to 4 years
6:15–6:45 p.m.

Adaptive Swim Lessons

Preregistratioin is required so that ample instructors are available to provide quality lessons. Contact Lori at 555–5633 ext. 106 for more information.

Dates Session I January 10 – Feb. 28
Session II March 21–May 10
Times Saturdays 12:00–12:45 p.m.

Semi-Private and Private Lessons

Available for ages 6 and older, and all skill levels. Lessons will be structured and based on needs of each student, and time available in the pool area. The intent for these lessons is to progress children through a level they may have difficulties with. Contact Lori at 555–5633 ext. 106 for more information.

Figure 7.14 **Sample of an Instructional Program Format** (Complement of Chaska, MN)

know how to do an activity) are a few examples of possible barriers preventing customers from going to parks, recreation, and leisure service sites. To overcome these barriers many leisure service organizations reach out to people where they reside through outreach programs. In this format we can reach out to individuals who are alienated or excluded from services, or who are simply not aware of services (Bannon, 1973).

According to Edginton and Edginton (1996) outreach does not simply involve the provision of a set of activities. Rather, outreach involves a myriad of programs, services, and personal interactions which respond to situation specific, site-specific, and individual specific needs. Outreach programs can be used to provide needed programs such as mobile libraries or art-in-the park activities. Outreach programs can also be used as intervention techniques which address specific social problems. An example of this is using family recreation activities to teach parenting skills.

Edginton and Edginton (1996) further identified outreach as a technique to maintain a leadership presence with a specific group or neighborhood. Within this orientation the leader does not directly suggest options to participants, but rather serves as a role model who "is around" to serve as a resource to the community, neighborhood, or individual. The ability of staff to assimilate to the environment and relate to participants impacts the success of the outreach program.

Examples of outreach programs are extensive. Public recreation departments have mobile recreation programs which travel to different parks throughout the summer. Nonprofit organizations also reach out to their constituents through a variety of programs. For example, both Girl Scouts and Boy Scouts offer scouting programs at schools during lunch hours in an attempt to meet students at times and places that are convenient to members. Nonprofit and commercial healthcare providers reach out to individuals who are home-bound through recreation-based programs. For many involved in home healthcare the contact with people may be of equal or greater value than the activities themselves.

One growing opportunity for outreach programs may be found in therapeutic recreation where home healthcare is growing. Programs delivered to participants in their homes can be thought of as outreach programs. There has already been some precedent set for including recreation services in home healthcare. An aging conference sponsored by the White House in 1981 recommended that recreation, leisure, and fitness services be included in home help care programs. Further attempts need to be made to develop home-based recreation. An example of one successful initiative is the REACH program (Recreation and Exercise Activities Conducted at Home) which was conceived and piloted in Ames, Iowa. The major purpose of REACH was to develop, field test, revise, and prepare for national dissemination an exemplary program for delivering in-home recreation and exercise activities to frail elderly (Wilhite, 1987). The REACH model is being used by many recreation therapists today.

Other opportunities for in-home care include respite programs for children with various disabilities. Respite programs offer to care for children with special needs while parents or caregivers take a needed break to accomplish other tasks or just to relax. One in-home recreational therapist indicated that her recreation background allowed her to interact with children in meaningful way and to work on specific goals identified through other outpatient programs (Commack, 1996). The area of respite care combined with goal directed activities may be a growth area for therapeutic recreation professionals in the future.

Trips

Trips are closely identified with the program area of travel and tourism, yet they may be viewed as a specific format for delivering desired benefits in a wide range of program areas. For example, a Little League baseball team might take a trip to see a professional baseball team play, or a painting class might hold a session in a nearby wooded area rather than a typical classroom. Trips can add value to many traditional programs as most people seem to respond to going someplace new and exciting.

Taking trips adds responsibilities to programmers—making necessary arrangements to ensure the trip runs smoothly is a must. Direct leaders also have additional responsibilities to make sure the group stays together and everyone's needs are met. Oftentimes additional supervision is needed for trips, especially with children. Volunteers are often enlisted to provide this additional supervision, but it is still up to the leader to organize and provide the needed information for success. It is the programmer's responsibility to see that volunteers are screened. In fact, many organizations can only "hire" volunteers who have passed a federal and state background check—especially if they are to work with or around children.

Service Opportunities

Although various authors differ in classifying whether service opportunities are a program area (Edginton, Hanson, Edginton & Hudson, 1998) or a program format (Russell, 1982), the importance of this topic cannot be overlooked. We have chosen to discuss it as a program format because programmers can develop formats in which to use volunteers in a variety of program areas.

Volunteers perform a wide range of services within programs without financial reward. Thus, volunteers perform valuable services to organizations. In addition, successful volunteer programs commonly provide a great deal of satisfaction to the volunteer. Volunteering skills and energy to coach youth sports, serve as a Big Sister/Brother, referee youth basketball games, play a game with a hospital patient, take a Girl Scout troop camping, or establish fishing habitat often provides the same satisfaction that others receive from being participants in these activities. It also provides the additional satisfaction of contributing to the development and pleasure of others (Russell, 1982).

Most parks, recreation, and leisure service organizations have volunteer programs—especially those within the public and nonprofit settings. An example of a comprehensive volunteer program is Special Olympics.

> Special Olympics is an international movement, which through year-round sport training and competition in the Olympic tradition, gives people with mental retardation the chance to strengthen their character, develop their physical skills, display their talents and fulfill their human potential. (Staff, 1990, p. 24)

More than a million children and adults with mental retardation have participated in Special Olympics programs worldwide since its founding in 1968.

Special Olympics in the United States is organized into 53 chapters (states and territories). Internationally, Special Olympics programs are established in nearly 80 countries. Beyond a core of paid staff

on the national and state levels, volunteers organize and run local Special Olympics activities. Over 500,000 volunteers of all ages are involved in Special Olympics. By varying the time commitment and skill level needed to be a volunteer Special Olympics reaches out and provides a wide range of volunteer opportunities. Individuals can make a one-day commitment to serve as a volunteer buddy, driver, or game official, or make a longer term commitment to serve as a coach or board member on the local, state, or national level.

Program areas and formats may be combined in any number of ways. Consider the program area of

Cheers for Volunteers!

Special Olympics volunteers are vital to the success of all of our programs! Coaches and workers at athletic events, lunch makers, fund raising committee members, special event "worker bees," volunteer coordinators, games committee members, gift wrappers, envelope stuffers and more. . . . . .Special Olympics wouldn't happen without you!

In future issues, we will endeavor to list all of the volunteers who make Special Olympics happen. For now, we would like to thank all of you, over the past many years, who have contributed so much time and energy.

Figure 7.15   Cheers for Volunteers

arts and crafts. Table 7.4 presents the many different formats that can be used to provide arts and crafts programs. Within the program design step of the program planning cycle, one aspect of decision making entails selecting the best format for the activity which meets the needs of participants.

Creativity is needed in all aspects of programming and decisions about program areas and program formats. In addition to considerations in those areas, programmers also need to plan for equipment and supplies, the physical environment, budgeting, and risk management. These areas will be addressed in this next section of this chapter.

Table 7.4	Adapting Program Formats to Specific Program Areas— An Arts and Crafts Program
Format	**Example**
Competitive	Best of show painting contest
Drop-in	The arts zone in a facility
Special Event	Neighborhood Arts Faire
Club	Local artist guild
Instructional	Painting class
Outreach	Art in the park (rotating art program during the summer)
Trip	Trip to an art museum in a nearby city
Service Opportunities	Teaching a painting workshop

Equipment and Supplies

Equipment and supplies are critical components of implementing programs and can influence when and where programs can be offered, as well as the costs associated with specific programs. As a result, it is important for programmers to consider the need for equipment and supplies in the design of programs. For our discussion we will refer to equipment as permanent and reusable items (e.g., balls) while supplies are materials that are consumed during an activity and not reusable (e.g., clay, paint).

In designing programs, programmers must know what type of equipment is needed, what equipment is available through the organization, and where needed equipment can be obtained. In many situations, equipment is shared between different programs and organizations. To ensure equipment

availability, then, programmers need to pay specific attention to scheduling programs and events across programs (within one organization) and organizations (between two or more organizations). For instance, a kiln and pottery wheels may be shared between two organizations. Each will have to work with the other when scheduling so as to avoid double-booking the equipment.

Equipment may also be manipulated through the program design process to achieve desired outcomes. For example, programmers can purposely use objects that are unfamiliar to participants (e.g., paint with sponges, play tag with rubber snakes). Changing the equipment used in a game can alter the activity level, the degree of challenge, and potentially alter the experience of the whole game (Rohnke & Butler, 1995).

For many people equipment is an invitation to play. Something novel and unusual arouses our curiosity as well as desire to participate. Likewise, the "same old" equipment can be a demotivator for people. For example, if someone brings out a basketball for a basketball game there are a number of expectations that go along with this piece of equipment and game (e.g., this activity is only for tall people). When we use equipment that is unfamiliar, participants have fewer expectations and as a result may be more open to trying new activities (i.e., using a beachball to play basketball). Developing new equipment or simply modifying existing equipment can also be very cost effective for organizations and will be discussed in Chapter Fourteen.

Physical Environments

Identifying where a program or service will be offered is an important element of program design which encompasses the variables of location and atmosphere. Location refers to such issues as accessibility, usability, and safety of the location. Accessibility may refer to a number of components such as ease of access as it relates to travel time or actual distance, parking, and accessibility of the facility for people with disabilities.

The types of areas and facilities used to deliver recreation programs are almost endless. Grassy fields, lakes and their waterfront, urban open spaces, virtual reality machines, and multipurpose rooms are all different types of physical environments in which programming occurs. When designing programs we must bear in mind that the suitability (for the activity) and customer perceptions of an area or facility are important. We must determine if the area or facility offers all the necessary amenities to deliver the program (e.g., adequate space, lighting, privacy, toilets). The actual atmosphere portrayed by the area or facility is also important: Is it warm and inviting? Other issues for consideration include participant comfort and safety.

When designing a service, programmers need to ask key questions regarding the physical environment of the program or service.

> Is the proposed area convenient and easily accessible for your target audience? Will the participants perceive the location as safe, attractive, and appropriate for them? Does the area or facility have a look that makes the proposed program look suitable for it." (O'Sullivan, 1991, p. 91)

Budget

Budget concerns include all aspects of potential income and expenditure for programs, both individually and collectively. Both the income and expenditures for programs are influenced by many of the factors listed in Figure 7.9 (page 121), which ultimately dictate the price charged for programs and services. Budgeting and considerations in setting fees and charges are examined in greater detail in Chapter Ten. It is mentioned here to encourage programmers to begin to be aware of costs throughout the program design phase of the programming cycle.

Policies, Procedures, and Rules

Policies, procedures, and rules are the boundaries in which programs are developed and implemented. Policies should flow from the goals and objectives of an organization and give direction to the operation of an agency. They direct the behavior and actions of employees so behaviors are consistent with the philosophy, values, goals, and objectives of an organization.

Policies tend to be broad in their scope and application, whereas procedures are the specific actions or approved steps required to carry them out (Kraus & Curtis, 1990). Unlike policies, which many times involve the whole organization, procedures tend to be applied to departmental or interdepartmental activities (Szilagyi, 1988). Examples include how customer registrations are to be handled, how staff are hired, how fees and charges are calculated, and how environmentally friendly purchasing can be achieved.

Rules are the narrowest boundaries, in that they deal with specific activities or behaviors. In general, rules guide the behavior of individual staff and participants during specific programs or events. Although rules are necessary for the managed presentation of recreation activities, rules do not have to be overtly constraining or ruin the fun (Jordan, 1996). General guidelines for rules are presented in Figure 7.16.

In designing programs, programmers must understand and follow the policies and procedures of the organization. For example, if the organization believes it must serve as a model of environmental responsibility and promote an outdoor ethic in participants, then the programmer would be well-advised to design a program that is environmentally friendly. Likewise, as programs are designed programmers should give some thought to how rules and guidelines will be developed and implemented, and how they augment the organizational mission.

Rules should:
- Have reasons
- Be equitable
- Define responsible behaviors
- Be appropriate for participants

Rules must be:
- Enforceable
- Clear and succinct

When using rules, you should:
- Design rules in conjunction with participants whenever possible
- State rules in positive terms
- Clarify, practice, and monitor rules continuously
- Follow through with enforcement
- Give a warning when rules are broken
- Have only a few rules

Figure 7.16   General Guidelines for Rules
(Jordan, 1996)

Risk Management

Risk management is an extension of organizational policies and procedures. We believe in managing risks to maintain high-quality programs, rather than from a perspective of minimizing lawsuits. Presenting high-quality programs is a very proactive position, while operating from a mindset to minimize lawsuits is a defensive (and often ineffective) approach.

Risk management describes the steps we take to minimize the undesirable risks found in the conduct of parks, recreation, and leisure services. There are risks inherent in everything we do—we might slip in the bathtub, burn ourselves while cooking, or trip over our own feet as we walk down our front walk. These types of risks we accept as integral to living and if they occur, we consider them to be accidents.

There are risks we do not accept (or expect), however, which might include the following: slipping in the shower at the recreation center because the cleaning crew did not rinse a slippery film off the floor; burning ourselves while at a park-sponsored cookout because gasoline was used to light the charcoal; and tripping on the sidewalk at a golf course where the concrete had buckled and not been repaired (or cordoned off). In one set of instances, the injury was due to expected and accepted hazards of daily living. In the second set of examples, the injuries were due to hazards that could have (and should have) been addressed and "fixed."

How are unexpected and unacceptable risks addressed in parks, recreation, and leisure services? Risks are typically managed in four ways—eliminating the risk, accepting the risk, transferring the risk to another (through insurance), and reducing the risk (van der Smissen, 1990). In parks, recreation, and leisure services, we utilize all four strategies. We eliminate risks by choosing *not* to offer something (e.g., in many states gymnastics programs were eliminated because of the concern for participant injury). We accept the risks inherent in many programs—there is a risk, for instance, of spraining an ankle in many sports; yet we still offer and engage in these activities. Risks are transferred through insurance policies which are commonly decided upon and purchased by agency administrators. For instance, many agencies carry million dollar policies to cover personnel in the event of a negligence lawsuit. Risk reduction describes those actions we

Eliminate the Risk

Transfer the Risk

Reduce the Risk

Accept the Risk

Figure 7.17 Four methods of managing risks in recreation programming.

take to limit the negative risks inherent in an activity. For example, we know that in bicycle riding there is a risk of falling off the bike and sustaining head injuries. In parks, recreation, or leisure service sponsored bicycle events, then, we require the wearing of helmets to reduce this risk.

Relative to recreation programmers, we are responsible for managing the risks associated with the process of programming. This entails managing risks related to the planning process, through implementation, evaluation, and follow-up. It also involves staff, participants, areas and facilities, and policies and procedures related to the programming process. Risks usually are addressed through the development and utilization of a risk management plan, through proper activity selection, appropriate staff and supervision, periodic facility checks, and a thorough preprogram safety check. Before we get into some of the details of risk management, we should discuss the meanings of several related terms.

Negligence

Negligence is a term that describes an act which results in personal injury to another person, or their property (Baley & Matthews, 1989; Hronek & Spengler, 1998; Kaiser, 1986; Peterson & Hronek, 1997; van der Smissen, 1990). As a legal term it refers to a situation where an individual was careless in the course of her or his duties resulting in injury to another party. For negligence to exist four elements must be present: *duty, an act or standard of care, proximate cause,* and *injury/damage.* If any one of these four elements is not found, there is no negligence (and no standing for a lawsuit).

Duty. The term *duty* refers to an obligation one person owes to another individual based on a legal relationship between that individual and the other (Baley & Matthews, 1989; Kaiser, 1986; van der Smissen, 1990). Typically, in parks, recreation, and leisure service settings a programmer and participants are engaged in the conduct of a leisure or recreational pursuit. In this case there is a legal relationship (duty) between the leisure services professional and the participant. The programmer has a duty, or obligation, to provide reasonably hazard-free activities and facilities to all participants and staff.

In leisure services programming the duty owed to participants includes a responsibility to plan and implement programs in a safe and prudent manner, to warn of hidden and visible hazards (e.g., wet floor), to provide staff who are skilled and competent in their job duties, and maintain a safe environment through appropriate policies and procedures—this duty is owed when participants are using leisure facilities, in the conduct of activities, and in the general provision of leisure services.

Act/Standard of Care. The second element of negligence is the *act.* This refers to the actions (or omissions) of a person (leisure services programmer)

in light of the duty owed to participants. A certain *standard of care* is required to maintain a hazard-free environment for all participants. When a person claims negligence, a programmer will be held to a standard of care which

> *would be measured by the moral qualities, judgment, knowledge, experience, perception of risk and skill that a person in the capacity of a professional would have.*
> (van der Smissen, 1990, p. 43)

In other words, a leisure services programmer must act in the same way that another person competent for a similar position would (also true for an intern or volunteer). There are three ways we can breach our standard of care: *malfeasance, nonfeasance,* and *misfeasance.*

Malfeasance. Doing something that one ought not to have done (which may also be illegal) is considered malfeasance. For instance, malfeasance would have occurred if a programmer scheduled a soccer team for five year olds to play against a team of 13 year olds. The potential for injuries due to physical mismatches is extremely high and this scheduling match should not have been made.

Nonfeasance. Nonfeasance is the neglect of duty; it is often thought of as passive negligence because it results out of uninvolvement (van der Smissen, 1990). An example of nonfeasance would be failing to maintain a facility by passively allowing it to age without regular maintenance or upkeep. If, due to this neglect of duty an individual were to become injured (by a swingset chain breaking, for example), nonfeasance might be the claim and negligence the result.

Misfeasance. Those acts whereby a programmer did not exercise the appropriate level of care for the rights of the participants are termed misfeasance (van der Smissen, 1990). This type of breach of

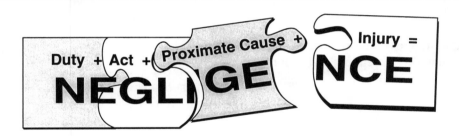

Figure 7.18   For negligence to exist, all four elements must be found.

duty includes both a failure to act as well as the improper conduct of an act. An example of misfeasance in an act of omission, for instance, might include the following: a festival was held in a recently mowed field where poison ivy was known to grow. No attempt was made to check for poison ivy, nor was the area sprayed to kill the plant. Festival-goers were exposed to the plant, and came down with severe cases of poison ivy which caused health problems for some.

As an example of improper conduct consider the following hypothetical situation: an amusement ride attendant was strapping in a rider to a Ferris wheel ride. The attendant wasn't paying attention and incorrectly connected the straps. During the course of the ride the rider fell out and was injured. The act (strapping in) was appropriate, but it was done incorrectly. This is an example of misfeasance during an act of commission.

Proximate Cause. In addition to duty and a breach of that duty the third element that must exist for negligence to be proven is *proximate cause*. For negligence to be attributed to an action, it must be shown that the injury was the direct result of the action—this is proximate cause (Hronek & Spengler, 1998). For example, if the festival-goers who were exposed to poison ivy were exposed not at the festival location, but earlier in the day while they were fishing in the local river, the earlier exposure would be the proximate cause, not the festival incident.

Injury/Damage. The fourth element that must exist for negligence to be found is actual injury (to a person) or damage (to physical property) (van der Smissen, 1990). The injuries might be physical (e.g., fracture, sprain, head injury), emotional or mental (e.g., anguish, humiliation and embarrassment, emotional trauma, psychogenic shock), or economic (e.g., replacement cost for equipment, loss of one's job, future medical bills).

Understanding the four necessary elements of negligence is critical to beginning the process of reducing and minimizing risks and hazards. To provide high-quality programs and minimize risks, the area in which parks, recreation, and leisure professionals might choose to focus throughout the programming process is on the act/standard of care.

Program Planning

Planning is a necessity in risk management; plans must be reasonable, well-thought-out, and based on our knowledge of the activities, participants, and the environment (Baley & Matthews, 1989). Plans should be continuously updated and documented (written down) so that we have a record of the plans and a solid knowledge-base. It becomes important, then, to attend to and follow the program plan, and to document changes as they occur. In this way, we will protect ourselves from some assertions of negligence related to planning, particularly if the plan was well done and approved by supervisors. The planning process should include a thorough consideration of the risks involved in the program and how they will be addressed. Furthermore, the program plan is the document where we indicate our understanding of the agency risk management plan, potential participants, the activity, and the areas, structures, and facilities.

Activity Selection. In the process of program planning, an activity of some sort is selected and offered—even if we only provide facilities for others' use. It might be a special event, something focused on skill development, a sport league, an activity related to the arts, or one of many other recreation or leisure activities. In selecting an activity or event, we must try to foresee every possible negative risk and address that risk. Obviously, there are times when we will not be able to foresee everything, but by asking several people to participate in this process, we can address a good number of the potential undesirable risks. Certainly, the activity must be a fit for the anticipated participants as well as the available areas and facilities.

In addition, there are some activities that have more inherent dangers or risks attached to them than others. For instance, all water-based activities have high amounts of inherent risks; board games have very low inherent risks. Highly active activities have the potential for more injuries than do low active events. We do not advocate removing all risks from every event, but the risks must be known to and accepted by participants. In addition, the risks must be manageable and should enhance or be integral to the nature of the leisure pursuit. For instance, risks abound in alpine (downhill) skiing—indeed, that is the draw and thrill of the activity for many participants. The risks are known to and accepted by participants (in fact, ski lift tickets are contracts that stipulate this), are managed (by clearly identifying slope difficulty, providing monitoring by ski patrol members), and without which, skiing would not be skiing.

To wisely choose appropriate activities in our programming efforts we must have a solid knowledge and understanding of the activity itself; how it impacts on participants (and how participants impact on it); how it interacts with the environment; and how, in the course of the activity, participants interact with one another as well as staff. In addition, we must continually learn about changes in activities and events as technology and our collective professional understanding increases. Technological advances may necessitate changes in our approaches to programming and activity selection, and as professionals we are expected to be aware of these changes.

As programmers, we should also be concerned with the sequencing and progression of activities we offer. It is important to offer activities in such a way that the skill development of participants matches the skills required by the activities. We might sequence events from easiest to most difficult (in terms of physical skills), from low activity to high and back again, or from simplest to most complex (in terms of rules and intellectual involvement). Choices related to sequencing and progression are impacted by the goals of the program, needs of the participants, staffing and equipment issues, and external factors such as time of day and weather conditions.

Being Facility and Equipment Aware. Another aspect of risk management that is extremely helpful in the programming process is being aware of the areas and facilities to be used for the planned events. Legal concerns about leisure services facilities and environment fall into two general categories— agency liability for maintenance of facilities, and leader liability for

conducting an activity on unsafe premises. Programmers should be concerned about both of these issues.

Equipment can cause risk management problems in several ways—through improper use of equipment, inadequate maintenance of equipment, and improper substitution of equipment (Hronek & Spengler, 1998; Peterson & Hronek, 1997; van der Smissen, 1990). Programmers need to be well-aware of equipment limitations, maintenance, and availability in planning parks, recreation, and leisure programs. Improper use of equipment includes such things as attempting to stand on a six-foot-diameter earth ball, using a badminton racket for tennis, and using a water ski for snowboarding. Examples of inadequate maintenance include failure to maintain bases on softball and baseball fields and failing to keep a pool filtration system in working order.

PRE-TRIP STAFF CHECKLIST

Date _____

Trip _____

Checked Bus Schedule _____

Divide Campers into Groups _____

Written List of Groups to: Camp Director _____

Camp Leaders _____

Checked Supplies for Trip Pack _____

Counted Campers ____ How many campers? _____

Advised Staff of Absentees

_____

_____

Informed Campers of:
- What to do if separated from the group _____
- How to deal with the public _____
- What to do if emergency help is needed and where it is located at this facility _____
- What to do if approached by a stranger _____
- Where to report in case of threatening weather _____
- What to do in case of fire _____
- Staff person in charge of trip _____
- Staff person with first aid and CPR _____
- Parents or additional help on trip _____
- Review and questions for campers _____

Figure 7.19   Pre-Trip Staff Checklist

Improper substitution of equipment might include using a carpet cutter (which utilizes an unprotected razor blade) instead of scissors in a crafts project and substituting folded blankets for mats under gymnastics equipment.

Forms, Forms, Forms. Program planning involves many steps including an attempt to anticipate all types of risks associated with a program. Unfortunately, we cannot anticipate all risks and must also address that concern. One way to address these unknown and unanticipated risks is to encourage the use of risk management forms as part of the program process. You probably recognize the names of various risk management forms—waivers, assumption of risk forms, releases, incident/accident report forms, and medical information forms (see Figure 7.20). Each of these forms has a particular purpose in an overall risk management plan.

The purpose of using forms in risk management is to limit the liability of individual employees and that of a particular agency. There have been many questions about the effectiveness of waivers and release forms; the courts have found them to be useful in determining participant understanding of the risks involved in an activity (Baley & Matthews, 1989; Kaiser, 1986; Niepoth, 1983; van der Smissen, 1990). In other words, risk management forms *are* useful and do serve a purpose. As a program is developed planners should consider the potential as well

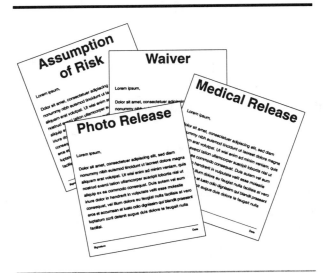

Figure 7.20 Program planning includes an attempt to anticipate all types of risks associated with a program.

as unanticipated risks involved and decide which forms, if any, would be appropriate to aid in minimizing liability risks to the agency and personnel.

In addition to the concerns related to equipment and supplies, the physical environment, and risk management, other components of program design must also be considered. The following section will address the issues of staffing, scheduling, staff/customer interactions, and program life cycle.

Staff

Staffing leisure programs is a comprehensive task and includes the recruiting, selecting, training, supervising, evaluating, and compensating of individuals. Management of staff is beyond the scope of this chapter. There are several concerns about staff relative to program design, however. In designing programs, supervisors need to be aware of interests and skills of their staff, as well as understanding what they are passionate about. As Wilson (1981) has noted, the world has plenty of talent (creativity), but lacks passion; "the best creative work represents passion fulfilled, whereas a neurosis may be thought of as passion thwarted. Enthusiasm is the elixir that pervades creativity, inspires it, frees it so that anything seems possible, and enlists others in the cause" (p. 19). It seems that a love of something sparks creativity.

Appropriate staffing relates to designing and delivering programs because we find that passionate leaders are willing to put extra time into an activity or event to make it special. They love what they do. They believe in what they are doing. They are growing, learning, and improving themselves. They are also able to incorporate the ideas, hobbies, and interests about which they are passionate into programs. Understanding the passions of staff allows supervisors to develop creative programs built on these passions (DeGraaf, 1997).

In addition to passion, part of the program planning process includes matching staff with activity leadership. Some activities are highly staff intensive (i.e., aquatic activities, activities with participants who have severely disabling conditions) while others require very little staff supervision (i.e., open gym at the center, video arcades). Matching appropriate staff and the appropriate numbers of staff with an event is important to managing risks. Staff should be knowledgeable about the activity, participants, facility, and policies and procedures related to the program and the agency. Just as we would never think to place a noncertified person in a lifeguard stand, so too we should avoid placing staff who have few skills or knowledge about a particular program in a similar position of responsibility.

Not every staff member is equally suited to all activities in terms of temperament and knowledge/experience. A job description is a first step to learning about which staff are best suited to leading and supervising which programs. It also is important to learn about each staff member in terms of their interpersonal skills and previous experience in similar situations. In this way, the best staff and combination of staff can be selected and assigned to particular programs.

Staff-Customer Interaction

The staff-customer interaction is what creates many of the benefits we provide as parks, recreation, and leisure service organizations; staff and customers are so intertwined it is difficult to separate one from the other (DeGraaf, 1994). Many organizations fail to produce benefits to the customer because they have failed to realize the importance of this interaction. Regardless of cutting-edge facilities or an organization's well-grounded program philosophy, the interaction among staff, among participants, and among staff and participants is paramount to delivering quality programs. It is important to recognize that none of these relationships is formed or maintained in a vacuum and has the potential to greatly influence all other relationships. The interaction among participants, staff, equipment, and physical environment will be examined in greater detail in Chapter Eleven. It is mentioned here to encourage programmers to begin to think about how to encourage positive interactions through the design of the program.

Scheduling

The issue of scheduling is twofold. First, scheduling is concerned with offering programs that fit with the timing needs of customers. Timing may refer to a multitude of variables including: time of day, day of the week, season of the year, length of time, and frequency of offerings (O'Sullivan, 1991). With increased demands being placed on people's time it

is critical for programmers to identify the best time of day, week, month, or year, as well as the amount of time that people are either willing or able to spend on a specific program or activity. For example, some people might be able to commit to a weekend volleyball tournament, but not be able to commit to a volleyball league that stretches over a long period of time.

The issue of timing also includes identifying which types of programs should be offered at the same time. This concept is often referred to as packaging or bundling services. This concept suggests that as time constraints continue to grow there will be a need to cluster services that allow individuals and families to have a quality leisure experience under the same roof at the same time (Edginton, Hanson, Edginton & Hudson, 1998). For example, a fitness center might offer childcare, instructional leagues for children, aerobic classes, and open weight room hours in an attempt to meet the needs of the whole family at the same time. This concept has been applied successfully at many large commercial malls in which group childcare, food concessions, shopping, and entertainment opportunities are offered at one convenient location during the same hours.

The second issue of scheduling is making the best use of the areas, facilities, and equipment which an organization controls. The scheduling of parks, recreation, and leisure programs should also complement the selected program area and program format discussed earlier in this chapter. This often involves creative thinking as recreation facilities and programs usually experience peak times when space is hard to find, as well as down time when demand is relatively low.

With these two issues in mind, scheduling may be thought of in at least three different patterns (Farrell & Lundegren, 1991). The first involves the seasons or natural block periods in the year (e.g., holidays). This approach may be most convenient for organizations located in regions of the country that experience seasonal change (i.e., winter, spring, summer, and fall). Promotional efforts can be easily coordinated within this scheduling pattern. Pamphlets, flyers, and brochures can be coordinated to focus on each program that is being offered during a specific season (see Figure 7.21).

The second scheduling pattern is based on a shorter duration such as a monthly or weekly focus.

This pattern is most appropriate for facility-centered programs (e.g., swimming pools or ice rinks) where the traffic flow of participants is constant and where program activities occur the same day each week indefinitely (Russell, 1982). Communicating the program schedule by the week or month helps to keep regular users informed and reminded of upcoming programs.

The third, and perhaps most critical pattern for consideration in scheduling, is the daily time frame

WINTER in Cedar Falls

December 1997 - February 1998 Calendar of Events

Tuesdays Hearst Film Series ~ Each Tuesday evening beginning at 7:00. Call 273-8641 for more information. Donations are accepted at the door.

Dec

1 **UNI Men's Basketball vs Missouri-Kansas City**, Young Arena, Waterloo, 7:05 p.m. Call 273-DOME.

2 **A Visit to Christmas Past and Present at the University Museum, UNI.** Kick off the holiday season with storytelling and carols in the one-room school house on UNI's campus. Hot cocoa and cookies served before strolling through campus to the tree-lighting ceremony. 6:00 - 7:00 p.m. 273-2188.

4 **Winter Welcome** ~ presented by the Grout Museum District, Waterloo. This has become a tradition for the holiday season. It's an evening of entertainment and activities throughout the Museum District with each site featuring its own style of holiday celebration. 6:30 - 8:30 p.m. 234-6357.

5 - 14 **Cedar Falls Community Theatre presents** *The Man Who Came to Dinner* (A Classic Comedy) at the Oster Regent Theatre. Sheridan Whiteside, having dined at the home of the Stanley's slips on their doorstep, breaking his hip. A tumultuous six weeks of confinement follow. For ticket information call A-P-P-L-A-U-D.

5 **The Ray Boltz Christmas Show**, is a Christian music concert at McElroy Auditorium, National Cattle Congress Grounds, Waterloo. 7:30 p.m. Call 234-7515 for ticket information.

7 **Cedar Falls Historical Society Christmas Walk.** An old fashioned Christmas celebration with music, refreshments, horsedrawn trolly rides and a tree lighting at Overman Park. Includes tours of the Victorian Home Museum, George Wyth House, Little Red School House, Cedar Falls Women's Club and Odd Fellows Hall. Call 266-5149 for more information.

7 **The Les Hale Chorale** will present a Holiday Concert and Dessert Buffet. Desserts will be served at 2:00 and the concert begins at 3:00. This is a holiday tradition you won't want to miss! Call 266-8331 for tickets.

7 **Northeast Iowa Figure Skating Club presents Winter Wonderland on Ice.** This benefit event for Cedar Valley Hospice will feature the KWWL news team of Bobbie Earles, Ron Steele, and Craig Johnson as well as Katie and Quincy Koala. The show begins at 3:30 p.m. and hot chocolate and homemade cookies will be served. Call 272-2002 for tickets.

7 & 8 **UNI School of Music Spotlight Series:** UNI Concert Chorale and Northern Iowa Symphony Orchestra Concert. Bruce Chamberlain, conductor - St. Edward's Catholic Church, Waterloo. Performances begin at 3:00 p.m. on the 7th and 8:00 p.m. on the 8th. Adm. 273-2024.

8 **UNI Women's Basketball vs Chicago State**, 7:05 p.m., West Gym.

9 **UNI Men's Basketball vs Iowa**, 7:05 p.m., UNI-Dome.

11 **UNI Artists Series:** La Negra Karin y Los Llaneros, Lang Hall Auditorium. 8:00 p.m. Adm. 273-2725.

11 **Jazz n' Joe** at the Waterloo Recreation and Arts Center. 8:00 - 10:00 p.m. Enjoy an informal coffee house setting and the hot sounds of great jazz on a chilly fall evening! As an added treat, Cup of Joe will be offering coffee and delicious desserts for sale throughout the evening. The public is invited to bring instruments and join in the fun or just come to listen. Call 291-4491.

12 & 13 **Waterloo/Cedar Falls Symphony Orchestra presents "A Swingin', Singin' Yuletide"** with the Waterloo/Cedar Falls Symphony Orchestra. Guest conductor Jeffrey Tyzik joins the symphony in their annual holiday concert. Members from six area high school choirs will also be on hand performing both traditional and contemporary seasonal favorites. 8:00 p.m. Young Arena, 235-6331.

14 **UNI Men's Basketball vs Tennessee State** at Young Arena. 1:05 p.m. 273-DOME.

14 **UNI Women's Basketball vs Northeastern Illinois** at Young Arena. 3:35 p.m. 273-DOME.

20 **UNI Commencement**, 11:00 a.m., UNI-Dome.

20 **Shaver Motorsports presents Indoor Racing** at McElroy Auditorium, National Cattle Congress Grounds, Waterloo. Motorcycles, go-carts and quads competition. Call 234-7515.

21 **Community Christmas** is a Christmas Variety Show with local talent held at Oster Regent Theatre. This event, which is hosted by Community Main Street, is for the whole family.

21 **UNI Men's Basketball vs Chicago State**, 3:05 p.m., UNI-DOME.

26 - 31 **Holiday Fun:** Trinkets, Toys and Tokens at the Grout Museum of History & Science. Tues. - Fri. and Sun. 1:00-4:30 p.m., Sat. 10:00 a.m. - 4:30 p.m. Adm. 234-6357.

29 - 30 **African Adventure** at the UNI Museum, 1:00 - 4:00 p.m. There will be activities to do and things to make. 273-2188.

30 **UNI Men's Basketball vs Creighton**, 7:05 p.m., UNI-DOME.

31 **Firstar Eve.** For the fifth consecutive year, Firstar bank invites people of all ages to ring in the New Year at Holmes Junior High School in Cedar Falls and the Boys & Girls Club and Family YMCA in Waterloo. Festivities begin with a fireworks extravaganza at 6:00 p.m. at Holmes Football Field followed by magic, comedy, singing, dancing, bingo,

Figure 7.21   Example of a Seasonal Schedule

for activities. This approach requires programmers to understand the lifestyle patterns of participants. Traditionally this approach has focused on morning sessions, early afternoon sessions, late afternoon sessions, early evening sessions, and late evening sessions (Russell, 1982; Farrell & Lundegren, 1991). See Figure 7.22. However, with the increased complexity of individual schedules and the changing lifestyle patterns of participants, programmers need to focus on all possible time periods (e.g. midnight

basketball, teen lock-in overnights) for providing programs which meet the needs of customers.

Program Life Cycle

The program life cycle concept is drawn from the discipline of marketing. The concept is derived from an analogy with human biological development and suggests that parks, recreation, and leisure programs have a definable life span. Following this human development model, the program life cycle has been

	Monday	Tuesday	Wednesday	Thursday	Friday
9:00	**Daily Welcome** • Songs • Drama • Announcements	**Daily Welcome** • Songs • Drama • Announcements	**Daily Welcome** • Songs • Drama • Announcements	**Daily Welcome** • Songs • Drama • Announcements	**Daily Welcome** • Songs • Drama • Announcements
10:00	**Small Group Time** • Name Games Make sure everyone knows one another • Initiatives Help the group work together	**Clubs** • Drama • Arts & Crafts • Nature Activities • Sports & Games	**Field Trip** Make sure field trips are checked out in advance. Create a number of bus activities for campers to do en route. Count number of campers both on and off the bus to Ensure everyone gets back to camp safely.	**Clubs** Encourage a good selection of clubs each week to give campers a variety of choices.	**Small Group Time** • Special Event Preparation
11:00	**All Camp Activities** • Active Games	**Small Group Time** • Low Organized Games		**All Camp Activities** • Sports	**All Camp Activities** • Special Event (e.g., carnivals, parades, treasure hunts, parties)
12:00	**Lunch and Quiet Time** • Low Organized Games	**Lunch and Quiet Time** • Story Time Read stories to campers. Use the library		**Lunch and Quiet Time** • Board Games	**Lunch and Quiet Time** Make a special meal to go with the special event
1:30	**Clubs** Have counselors do commercials to promote clubs	**Rotating Activities** • Swimming • Arts & Crafts • Sports & Games		**Rotating Activities** Use resources in the community • Bowling • Rollerskating • Swimming	**All Camp Swimming**
2:30	**All Camp Swimming**		**All Camp Swimming**		**The Big Show** Have clubs or small groups present skits, songs or other presentations
3:30	**Camper's Choice**	**Camper's Choice**	**Camper's Choice**	**Camper's Choice**	
4:00	**Closing Activities** • Songs	**Closing Activities** • Announcements	**Closing Activities** • Drama	**Closing Activities** • Stories	**Closing Activities** • Spirit Stick

Figure 7.22   Sample of a Generic Weekly/Daily Program Grid

adopted as a way to trace the evolution of programs and services. The life cycle presented in Figure 7.23 includes the following stages: introduction, take-off, maturation, saturation, and decline or extension.

During the introduction stage, potential customers are slow to accept the program. This reluctance is overcome during the take-off stage as participation in the program grows rapidly. The take-off stage continues until the rate of participation begins to slow down and the program reaches maturity and moves into the saturation stage. During the saturation stage the program relies on repeat involvement for its survival. Very few new participants seek out the service. Typically, the saturation stage is longer than previous stages as program involvement peaks and begins to decline slightly. At that time existing participants drop out, and there are very few new participants to take their place.

In the last stage the program begins to decline. At this point programmers can consider various strategies for extending or stretching the program life cycle. There are a number of critical questions to examine at this point of the program life cycle. Could the program be revitalized by assigning new staff, adopting a fresh approach, using a different facility, or developing an alternative structure or format? Can new customers be developed? Can the program be adapted to meet the particular benefits sought by different target audiences? It is also important to remember that not all programs can be revitalized; in this case we need to acknowledge this, reduce the time and money invested in the program, and let it end.

The program life cycle is important to program design in a number of ways. First, the program life cycle allows for preplanning; the programmer can be proactive in program implementation instead of being forced to react to what has already happened. By utilizing the life cycle concept, program design and development can be planned more systematically. This is because a life cycle suggests a pattern that new programs are likely to follow (Russell, 1982). Understanding the program life cycle also assists the programmer in making decisions about promotion, program duration, resource allocation, and when to cancel programs. Perhaps the greatest benefit of understanding the program life cycle is that it reminds the programmer of the importance of constantly developing and designing new programs and services to replace programs on the decline.

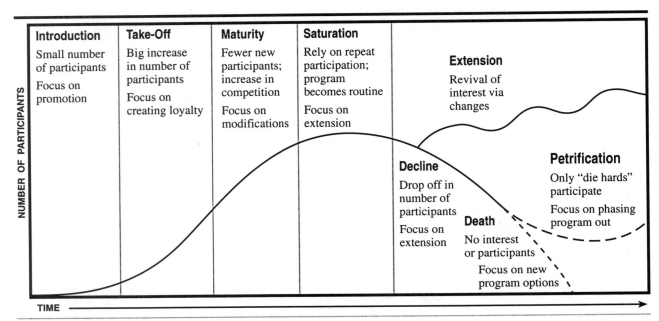

Figure 7.23 Program Life Cycle (O'Sullivan, 1991)

A Servant Leadership Approach: Empowering Participants in the Program Design Stage

In previous chapters we have indicated that parks, recreation, and leisure professionals need to be servant leaders and work to empower participants to meet their own leisure needs whenever possible. Within the program design phase this means assisting participants to design their own programs. However, it should be noted that some participants simply do not have the inclination, time, or skills to take control of their own destiny (Hutchison & Nogradi, 1996). As a result, programmers often take the responsibility for designing programs and events that meet the needs of specific target audiences. In this process, programmers can still work to empower participants and foster creativity through program design. Both empowerment and creativity may be fostered by listening to participants, providing choices in programs, and letting participants make their own decisions within the program once it has begun.

Summary

Parks, recreation, and leisure programs should flow from the needs of customers as well as the values and philosophy of the organization. Once needs have been identified and the goals and objectives of the program established in line with the philosophical foundation of the organization it is time to design the actual program. Designing programs demands both divergent and convergent thinking. Divergent thinking involves being creative to generate as many original, diverse, and elaborate ideas as possible. Convergent thinking demands looking at all these ideas and selecting the best ideas in conjunction to a number of factors.

The factors impacting program design addressed in this chapter include program areas, program formats, equipment, physical environments, policies and procedures, risk management, staff, the interaction between staff and participants, scheduling, the program life cycle, and other considerations. The next chapter will examine how to integrate these factors in program design decisions to assure programs (both individual and collective) that serve the customers of park, recreation, and leisure organizations.

References

Albrecht, K. (1992). *The only thing that matters.* New York, NY: Harper Business.

Albrecht, K. and Zemke, R. (1985). *Service America.* Homewood, IL: Dow Jones-Irwin.

Bailey, S. (1995, December). The world's largest barbecue. *Parks and Recreation, 30*(1), 50–51.

Baley, J. and Matthews, D. (1989). *Law and liability in athletics, physical education and recreation, 2nd ed.* Dubuque, IA: Wm. C. Brown.

Bannon, J. (1973). *Outreach: Extending community services in urban areas.* Springfield, IL: Charles C. Thomas.

Bannon, J. and Busser, J. (1992). *Problem solving in recreation and parks, 3rd ed.* Champaign, IL: Sagamore.

Blohowiak, D. (1992). *Mavericks.* Homewood, IL: Business One Irwin

Buzan, T. and Buzan, B. (1996). *The mind map book: How to use radiant thinking to maximize your brain's untapped potential.* New York, NY: Plume.

Commack, E. (1996). In-home recreation therapy care: A case study of Dillon. *Parks and Recreation, 31*(5), 66–67.

DeGraaf, D. (1997). Adapting equipment and activities for creative programming. In G. Hitzhusen and L. Thomas (Eds.), *Expanding horizons in therapeutic recreation* (pp. 183–192). Columbia, MO: University of Missouri.

DeGraaf, D. (1994). What do we really have to offer: The million dollar question. *Humanics: The Journal of Leadership for Youth and Human Service, 4*(1), 9–12.

Edginton, S. and Edginton, C. (1996). *Youth outreach and service excellence.* Washington, DC: U.S. Army Child and Youth Services.

Edginton, C., Hanson, C., Edginton, S. and Hudson, S. (1998). *Leisure programming: A service centered and benefits approach.* Boston, MA: WCB, McGraw-Hill.

Farrell, P. and Lundegren, H. (1991). *The process of recreation programming: Theory and technique.* State College, PA: Venture Publishing, Inc.

Getz, D. (1997). *Event management and event tourism.* Elmsford, NY: Cognizant Communication.

Hronek, B. and Spengler, (1998). *Legal liability in recreation and sports.* Champaign, IL: Sagamore Publishing.

Hutchison P. and Nogradi, G. (1996). The concept and nature of community development in recreation and leisure services. *Journal of Applied Recreation Research, 21*(2), 93–130.

Jackson, R. (1997). *Making special events fit in the 21st Century.* Champaign, IL: Sagamore Publishing.

Janiskee, R. (1996). The temporal distribution of America's community festivals. *Festival Management and Event Tourism, 2*(1), 10–14.

Jordan, D. (1996). *Leadership in leisure services: Making a difference.* State College, PA: Venture Publishing, Inc.

Kaiser, R. (1986). *Liability and law in recreation, parks, and sports.* Englewood Cliffs, NJ: Prentice Hall.

Kraus, R. (1985). *Recreation program planning today.* Glenview, IL: Scott, Foresman & Company.

Kraus, R. and Curtis, J. (1990). *Creative management in recreation, parks and leisure services.* St. Louis, MO: Times Mirror/Mosby.

Niepoth, E. W. (1983). *Leisure leadership.* Englewood Cliffs: Prentice Hall.

O'Sullivan, E. (1991). *Marketing for parks, recreation and leisure.* State College, PA: Venture Publishing, Inc.

Peterson, J. and Hronek, B. (1997). *Risk management for park, recreation, and leisure services, 3rd ed.* Champaign, IL: Sagamore Publishing.

Rohnke, K. and Butler, S. (1995). *Quicksilver.* Dubuque, IA: Kendall Hunt.

Rossman, R. (1996, July 17). The use of mental imagery in leisure program design. Presented at the *World Leisure and Recreation Association, 4th International Congress*. Cardiff, Wales, United Kingdom.

Rossman, R. (1995). *Recreation programming: Designing leisure experiences*. Champaign, IL: Sagamore Publishing.

Russell, R. (1982). *Planning programs in recreation*. St. Louis, MO: C.V. Mosby Company.

Schlis, P. (1996, May). May is older Americans month. *Creative Forecasting, 8*(5), 36.

Shrieves, L. (1996, February 4). Kindle your creativity. *Des Moines Register*.

Staff. (1990, March). *Exceptional Parent, 20*, 24–25.

Szilagyi, A. (1988). *Management and performance, 3rd ed.* Glenview, IL: Scott, Foresman & Company.

Thompson, C. (1992). *What a great idea*. New York, NY: Harper Perennial.

van der Smissen, B. (1990). *Legal liability and risk management for public and private entities*. Cincinnati, OH: Anderson.

Vance, M. and Deacon, D. (1995). *Think out of the box*. Franklin Lanes, NJ: Career Press.

von Oech, R. (1983). *A whack on the side of the head*. New York, NY: Warner Books.

Wilhite, B. (1987). REACH out through home delivered recreation services, *Therapeutic Recreation Journal, 21*(2), 29-38.

Wilson, M. (1981). *Survival skills for managers*. Boulder, CO: Volunteer Management Associates.

Wycoff, J. (1991). *Mindmapping: Your personal guide to exploring creativity and problem solving*. Berkley, CA: Berkley Publishing Group.

Chapter Eight

Program Promotion

In this and like communities, public sentiment is everything. With public sentiment, nothing can fail, without it nothing can succeed.

Abraham Lincoln

Effective communication with customers is a vital ingredient of success for all organizations. Without the ability to "get the word out" about our organizations and programs we would have no staff, volunteers, or customers to serve. This has been substantiated by over a dozen studies which have examined constraints to recreation participation in public parks and recreation. Respondents in these studies have identified lack of knowledge as one of the leading barriers to their participating in recreation programs (Lankford, DeGraaf & Neal, 1996).

Every parks, recreation, and leisure service organization faces the task of finding ways to effectively communicate with its various publics and constituents. As a result, program promotion is an important component for leisure service managers to both understand and to know how to use it effectively. In this chapter we present material about the promotion process, tools, and techniques used in promoting organizations and programs, and information about how to develop an effective promotional mix.

Definitions

In examining the topic of promotion there is often a lot of confusion surrounding definitions of related terms such as marketing, advertising, publicity, and selling. It can make discussions about program promotion confusing. As a result, we believe it is important that everyone starts on the "same page" by defining many of these terms and demonstrating how they relate to one another within the context of an organization's promotional mix.

Marketing

Although marketing often is confused with terms like promotion, advertising, and publicity, it is a much broader concept. As presented in Chapter Two, marketing is *the umbrella for all management functions that foster desired exchanges*. It is a customer-oriented approach to delivering services and requires extensive knowledge of who we are going to serve in our programs. The real contribution of marketing is that it leads institutions to search for meaningful positions in the larger market. Instead of all parks, recreation, and leisure service organizations offering the same services, marketing leads each organization to shape distinct service mixes to serve specific market segments. This is done by managing such variables as price, place (location of service), and promotion. Thus, marketing at its best creates a pattern of varied institutions, each clear in its mission, market coverage, specialization area, and services and programs provided.

Public Relations

Public relations is similar to marketing in that it is a broad management function that includes promotion. Specifically, public relations is

> *any process that evaluates public attitudes, identifies the policies and procedures of an organization with the public interest, and plans and executes a program of action to earn public understanding and acceptance.* (Berkman & Gilson, 1987, p. 501)

Thus, promotion is only one of the many functions that fit within a public relation strategy (see Figure 8.1). Within the promotion context public relations is both mass and personal communication which is image directed. Inherent in public relations is the presentation and dissemination of information which casts an organization in a positive light.

Promotion

For leisure service organizations promotion is *any form of communication used to inform, persuade, remind, and/or educate people regarding the benefits offered through an organization's programs and services* (Crompton & Lamb, 1986). Effective communication communicates *with* the potential customer rather than *to* the potential customer. The communication process is not complete until the

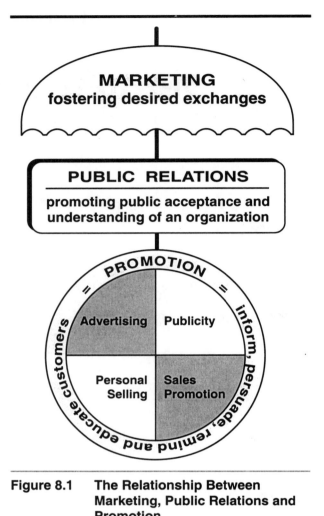

Figure 8.1   The Relationship Between Marketing, Public Relations and Promotion

potential participant acts upon the message she or he has received. In their communication programs, organizations may be involved with one or more of the four basic types of promotion: advertising, publicity, personal selling, and sales promotion (Evans & Berman, 1990).

Advertising

Advertising is *paid, nonpersonal communication regarding programs, events, goods, services, organizations, and ideas*. This communication is transmitted through various media by business firms, nonprofit organizations, and/or government agencies, which are in some way identified in the advertising message as the sponsor (Evans & Berman, 1990). Advertising includes such varied media as magazines, newspapers, radio, television, outdoor media (e.g., billboards, signs, skywriting), novelties, cards, catalogs, directories, and direct mail. Advertising is a huge business. In 1993, total advertising in the United States was estimated to be $138 billion. Worldwide advertising expenditures were $301 billion (Kotler & Andreasen, 1996).

Publicity

Publicity is *nonpersonal communication regarding programs, events, goods, services, organizations, and ideas which is transmitted through various media, but not paid for by an identified sponsor.* As a result, the message is generally controlled by the media rather than an organization or agency (Evans & Berman, 1990). Publicity may be found in a wide variety of media. For example, a newspaper may offer to run a feature article on a program, or public service announcements may appear on television and radio. The relationship between public relations, advertising, and publicity is presented in Table 8.1.

Personal Selling

According to Kotler and Andreasen (1996) personal selling refers to

> *attempts by an organization, staff member, or volunteer by using personal influence to affect target audience behavior.* (p. 573)

This means personal selling promotes one-on-one contact and is used most often in the commercial sector. Public and nonprofit organizations have often been reluctant to employ this method of promotion for two reasons. First, public and nonprofit organizations often perceive their programs or services as inherently good and as a result they should be automatically accepted by the general public. Second, organizations often view personal selling as synonymous with manipulation, thereby finding it unethical (Kotler & Andreasen, 1996). It is interesting to note, however, that word-of-mouth (i.e., personal selling) is often cited by participants as one of the best ways to communicate opportunities for participation in programs (Edginton, Hanson, Edginton & Hudson, 1998). It is important to remember that every time a member of an organization and a member of the public interact there is an opportunity to inform, persuade, remind, and/or educate about the organization and its programs.

Table 8.1 **The Relationship Between Advertising, Public Relations, and Publicity** (Adapted from Evans & Berman, 1990)

Concept	Examples
Advertising	An ad for XYZ Cruise Lines (paid, demand-directed). An ad showing XYZ Cruise Lines as an environmentally friendly vacation choice (paid, image-directed).
Public Relations	An ad showing XYZ Cruise Lines as an environmentally friendly vacation choice (paid, image-directed). A speech at a local college or university by a representative of XYZ Cruise Line (personal contact, image directed). A report on the local/national news about the success of XYZ Cruise line partnership with a local craft cooperative to sell souvenirs on their cruises (nonpaid, image-directed).
Publicity	A report on the local/national news about the success of XYZ Cruise line partnership with a local craft cooperative to sell souvenirs on their cruises (nonpaid, image directed) A newspaper article showing the economic value of an XYZ cruise (nonpaid, demand directed).

Sales Promotion

Sales promotion *involves paid communication activities (other than advertising) that stimulate consumer behavior* (Evans & Berman, 1990). Sales promotion for parks, recreation, and leisure programs includes incentives (coupons), giveaways, demonstrations, and various other limited time efforts not in the ordinary promotion routine.

As presented in Chapter Two there are a wide variety of philosophical orientations (e.g., social advocacy, social planning, social marketing, marketing and individual/community empowerment) which an organization can adopt. Whatever an organization's philosophical framework, it still must promote its programs in some way. As a result, the focus of the remainder of this chapter will be on identifying promotional strategies (using a mix of advertising, publicity, personal selling, and sales promotion) to promote a parks, recreation, and leisure organization, as well as promoting specific events and programs.

Promotional Tools and Techniques

Promotional tools and techniques are like ambassadors for an organization and the programs it offers. Through various promotional tools and techniques organizations are able to compete for the attention of customers. This is important because in today's fast-paced world, we are bombarded by 580–1,800 promotional messages daily (Stern, 1992). With such tremendous competition for attention and so little time to make an impact, a promotion

> has to say something, say it well and say it fast. It has to create an initial reaction that draws people in, that says, 'This is good. This could be for me'. (Stern, 1992, p. 73)

To be effective there must be a good fit between the program, the promotional tool and/or technique, and the target group we are trying to reach. In beginning to examine how to fit these factors together, it becomes imperative that programmers understand the wide variety of tools and techniques available, as well as the strengths and weakness of each approach. What follows is a discussion of a wide variety of tools and techniques used in promoting parks, recreation, and leisure programs.

Broadcast Media

Radio and television are often considered to be the broadcast media. Both radio and television are organized by networks at national and regional levels. CBS television and radio are examples of such networks. Other radio and television networks are operated by local independent stations. Distinguishing characteristics of broadcast media include passive audience involvement, immediacy, and public control (Berkman & Gilson, 1987). This means that while it requires some active involvement to read a newspaper or magazine, radio and television can "just be there." In addition, television and radio are on the air 24 hours a day. As a result they tend to be regarded as having the most up-to-date stories with the greatest potential to offer late-breaking news and events.

The last distinguishing characteristic, being under public control, means that the air waves are viewed as public resources which are managed by the government through the Federal Communication Commission (FCC). Station managers must apply for licenses to operate, and must prove to the FCC that they are serving the public through such things as public service broadcasting and public service advertising. Cable and pay-per-view television are somewhat different in that viewers pay for these services directly. To operate, these stations still need FCC approval, however.

Berkman and Gilson (1987) have noted that broadcast media have a far more pervasive influence on most Americans' lives than newspapers and magazines due to the sheer volume of exposure most Americans have with radio and television. Consider the average American who wakes to the sound of a radio alarm, eats breakfast watching a morning news show, and rides to work listening to the radio. While on the job there maybe a radio playing in the background; then it is back home in the car listening to the radio. Following dinner, the television is often turned on for the remainder of the evening. While this scenario may not represent all Americans, it is difficult to argue with the fact that 97 percent of American homes have a television and over 98 percent have radios (Berkman & Gilson, 1987).

Beyond advertising (which will be discussed later) radio and television also offer other potential opportunities for park, recreation, and leisure service programmers to promote their programs. For example, talk shows are becoming an increasingly popular format for both radio and television and offer an opportunity for more lengthy promotion of an idea or service than a traditional commercial would allow (Edginton, Hanson, Edginton & Hudson, 1998). The format for talk shows is usually question and answer, giving the programmer an opportunity to make specific points concerning her or his organization, program or event. Opportunities for being invited on talk shows may be enhanced by developing a long-term relationship with broadcast media—both television and radio—in one's local area.

Radio

Radio is enjoying a healthy revival after its popularity dipped during the 1950s, 1960s, and 1970s when television became popular. One reason for the rebirth of radio is the fact that television has become

Figure 8.2   Examples of Broadcast Media

too expensive for many advertisers. Because of the great competition among radio stations for advertiser dollars, advertising time slots are rarely sold out. Thus, costs are negotiable. Radio also allows organizations to target specific groups as radio stations keep extensive data on their listeners. A third advantage of radio advertising is the portability of the medium. Radios are everywhere—in cars, on the beach, and on bike paths. Anywhere potential customers go, radios can be taken along. Disadvantages of radio include the need to help listeners visualize programs and services as well as the fact that people often listen to the radio in conjunction with other activities. This tendency to become involved in a variety of activities is referred to as "clutter" by advertisers. The more clutter that exists, the more difficult it is to focus listeners on specific advertisements. As a result, organizations that use radio often run ads frequently to increase exposure. It helps that radio offers high frequency at a low cost.

Radio offers an additional opportunity to organizations planning programs and events in the community. Oftentimes radio stations broadcast live from community events. These appearances can either be paid or public service opportunities and provide invaluable exposure for organizations and their specific events and programs.

Television

The figures on television usage are staggering as television viewing surpasses all other uses of free time, accounting for about 40 percent of all free time of Americans (Godbey, 1997). As a result, the major advantage of using television to promote parks,

recreation, and leisure programs and services is that it reaches a large number of potential customers. Other advantages of television include frequency and visual representation. Television offers great frequency potential as one commercial can be run over and over again for a long period of time. Television also offers the ability to offer a visual representation of the benefits of participating in a specific program or service from the comfort of one's own living room.

Disadvantages of using television include cost as well as clutter. Producing and airing television commercials is expensive. Simply producing television commercials can run anywhere from $1,000 to several hundred thousand dollars. A similar range exists in buying air time; a 30-second spot during the Super Bowl can run into millions of dollars while the same length spot on a local news show can cost under $1,000.

Advertising on television also suffers from a lot of noise and clutter meaning that commercials offer individuals the opportunity to channel surf, to get another drink, or take a break before returning to continue watching their program. Likewise, television viewing is often a secondary activity, meaning that people are doing other things while watching a show.

Television should be considered an effective marketing tool, but it has to be used wisely. Many large commercial organizations (e.g., Disney World, Carnival Cruise Lines) can make the commitment to national television campaigns while smaller regional or local organizations might choose to use television sparingly during specific time slots. For many public and nonprofit organizations television is out of reach except through the use of public service announcements. However, one emerging trend in the television industry may make television exposure more affordable and available, especially to public and nonprofit organizations. This trend is the expansion of cable and direct television giving consumers increased options. Included in this expansion are additional channels for community access programs. These channels may offer additional outlets to promote specific programs and events.

Emerging Technology

It is hard to predict what the future holds concerning technology, but we do know that we need to stay current and understand the potential of emerging technology in delivering and promoting programs and services. A majority of the new technology today is interactive in nature, making it possible for viewers to interact with and through the media. Leading the way in a new wave of emerging technology is the computer, which is taking American homes by storm. In 1990, less than 10 percent of all American homes included a computer, by the end of 1995 this had risen to nearly 40 percent (Godbey, 1997). One of the major factors behind this surge is the diffusion of on-line services (e.g., America Online, Prodigy, Compuserve) which has more than doubled from 1994 to 1995 to include almost one in ten American subscribers (Robinson & Godbey, 1997). On-line advertising through the World Wide Web offers a tremendous opportunity to businesses—large and small. In addition, computers have also made such opportunities as CD-ROMs and information kiosks available to the general public.

Leisure service organizations must look to maximize the opportunities offered by computer-related technologies. At the same time, they must also remember the limitations of emerging technologies, especially in terms of access. We have to wonder if the future will see an increasing gap between the information rich and the information poor in our society. In choosing to use new computer technologies exclusively we may shut out many people from our services and programs. Thus, we must move forward cautiously and look for ways to overcome concerns about access (Reinhold, 1993).

CD-ROMs

As new computers come equipped with CD-ROM drives, organizations have the opportunity to produce CD-ROM disks that promote their image, services, and programs. Figure 8.3 displays the CD cover from the "Inside Guide to Park City." The CD was produced by a real estate company and provides a variety of information about Park City, Utah (e.g., real estate, dining, shopping, night life, recreation, leisure). "Simply place our CD-ROM into your computer and enjoy the special lifestyle of the West's most exciting destination—Park City, Utah…site of the 2002 Winter Olympics."

Electronic Kiosks

Interactive computers operating from small kiosks are being placed in a wide range of locations. For example, the city of Salt Lake City, Utah, has kiosks placed in malls to provide information about local attractions. Some states have placed kiosks at rest

Figure 8.3   An Example of a Promotional CD-ROM from Park City, Utah

stops on major interstates to inform travelers about events and opportunities in nearby regions. Many visitor centers, hotels, and tourist attractions also have electronic kiosks. These "new age bulletin boards" provide individuals with 24-hour-a-day access to information about many services and programs offered by local, state, and federal government; nonprofit agencies; and commercial organizations in the local area.

The Commonwealth of Kentucky is a fine case study in the use of electronic kiosks for promoting parks and recreation. Interactive multimedia kiosks have been placed in locations ranging from park headquarters to remote, interstate highway visitor centers. The kiosks offer a wide variety of information which individuals can use in planning their own recreation experiences. Data collected from five such kiosks (located at highway rest areas) indicate that more than 35,487 individuals used the kiosks over a 109-day period (Estes, 1994).

According to Estes (1994) the most significant factors determining use and public acceptance of an electronic information system were the content of the system, user-friendliness, interactivity, and intelligence of the user. In the future, computer hardware and software will continue to evolve offering parks, recreation, and leisure programmers greater opportunities to improve customers' access to needed information quickly and easily.

Internet

The Internet is a collection of millions of interconnected computers located in countries throughout the world—all linked by phone lines and high-speed cables to form a gigantic computer network system (Gonyea & Gonyea, 1996). The Internet is the largest network of computers in the world today with some experts estimating that over 50 million computers are currently connected to the Internet with thousands of new computers being plugged into it daily. The Internet is quickly becoming the preferred means of communication and information retrieval by millions of people worldwide, especially by organizations interested in a fast, global and inexpensive means of reaching customers. To "travel" on the Internet, we can use a variety of communication options. Two of the more popular mediums are e-mail and the World Wide Web (WWW).

E-mail. E-mail, an abbreviation for electronic mail, enables individuals to send text and some graphic messages back and forth to each other quickly over telephone lines. E-mail has quickly become one of the preferred methods of communication between individuals, whether they are in close proximity (such as the same building), across town, or on opposite sides of the world. It is projected that the 44 million e-mail boxes in use at the end of 1995 will escalate to 216 million by the of the year 2000 (Marlow, 1997). Using e-mail, organizations can set up distribution lists of specific target groups or ask users to sign up for specific lists. Such lists provide an easy way to communicate with groups of people about specific programs or upcoming events. Mailing lists are also a means by which individuals can keep up-to-date with a specific topic. We believe electronic mailing lists should not be created for the sole purpose of advertising; such a practice can quickly degenerate into electronic junk mail. Organizations can indirectly benefit from these lists, however, as more and more people learn about parks, recreation, and leisure service organizations within the context of a specific mailing list topic (Gonyea & Gonyea, 1996).

World Wide Web. If any function on the Internet is exciting, intoxicating, and habit forming it is the World Wide Web (WWW); commonly referred to as the Web. The Web may be thought of as a superhighway on which a computer user who is "on-line" can travel throughout the world to specific Web sites of individuals, organizations, and agencies who constantly add and update their sites. Web sites may include photographs, text, audio, and video, all packaged in such a way as to provide organizations with a visually attractive means to provide accurate up-to-date information. The Internet, including the Web, gives customers an opportunity to receive information, and even purchase programs and services without ever leaving their homes.

The Web offers parks, recreation, and leisure service programmers a variety of options for promoting programs and services. Web sites, or homepages, can be used by organizations to inform and educate about their overall program or specific special events (see Figure 8.4, page 154). Some organizations allow participants to register for a specific program, reserve hotel rooms and airline tickets, and purchase products via the Web and the Internet. Other organizations encourage staff to

A SUMMER CAMP FOR YOUNGER GIRLS & BOYS AGES 5 to 12

Gwynn Valley has been in continuous operation since 1935 as a residential camp for younger children. From its beginning, Gwynn Valley has offered a special community of learning and sharing in a pristine mountain setting. Away from competition, worldly expectations and pressures, a child has the freedom to discover and become his or her best. Realizing new talents and personal strengths, a child can venture into the world with new self-confidence. Through working and playing together with people from diverse backgrounds, children are empowered to believe they can make a difference in the world around them.

The staff is carefully chosen for maturity, experience and love of children. One third come from international countries, and each member has his or her own special skill, in addition to being able to relate well to children and set a good example. The unusually large staff (one staff member for every three children) results in thorough care of safety and developmental needs. Gwynn Valley has its own physician in residence, and is accredited by the American Camping Association.

Children are placed in cabin groups according to their grade completed in school. We offer a Main Camp Program for K-5th graders and a Mountainside Program for 5th-6th graders. We welcome you to learn more about our 1998 program.

Gwynn Valley Program Areas:

The Farm
Animal Care, Gardening, Veterinary Science

Texture + Pioneer Crafts
Weaving, Enameling, Papermaking, Tye-Dye, Pottery, Broom-making, Candles

The Grist Mill
Grinding, Fishing, Cornbread, Ice Cream

Horseback Riding
Ring & Trail Riding, Barn Lessons, Crafts

Waterfront
Swimming, Canoeing, River Trips, Creek Hikes

Rainbow Sports
Individual and International Team Sports Archery, Soccer, Mountain Biking, Cricket

Fine Arts
Creative Writing, Drama, Music, Folk Dance

Web of Life + OLS
Hiking, Nature Study, Aqua Biology , Camp-outs, Cook-outs, Fire-building

**Would like us to send you camper materials?   Are you a long lost Alumni? (Newsletter, email)
Are you interested in summer staff positions?**

Figure 8.4   Gywnn Valley Homepage

apply for positions via the Web. Commercial organizations also include advertising in on-line magazines and newspapers which are updated on a continuous basis.

Advertising on the Web is not simply an electronic version of a print, radio, or television advertisements. The Web offers the opportunity to actually interact with potential customers. Thus, the use of the Web for marketing and promoting organizations, products, and services will continue to rise. ActivMedia, Inc. estimated that sales generated by the Web was going to reach $2.9 billion by the end of 1996. In 1997, sales were expected to reach $13 billion and by 1998, over $45 billion (Marlow, 1997). With numbers such as these it is not a matter of whether the Internet will become a significant venue for marketing, public relations, and promotion; it is a matter of when. As Marlow reminds us,

> when videotape first came onto the scene commercially in 1956, most people thought it was a medium to help with broadcast time zone delays. Instead it spawned the home video industry.... Videotape also helped lead to the development of the videodisc, in turn the CD-ROM. There are

some who presume to know what the Internet will evolve into. Take your own guess. At the very least, the medium is fast becoming a viable and primary strategic communication tool. (p. 16)

Display Media

Display media is a broad category of tools which includes billboards, bulletin boards, exhibits, point-of-purchase advertising, posters and signs. As is evident from this list, display media may be found in both indoor and outdoor environments and includes both two- and three-dimensional objects. Parks, recreation and leisure service organizations may use such display media to highlight program services and organizational efforts, or for purposes of interpretation. Displays may be used as part of an actual program (e.g., a display in a museum) or as a vehicle to facilitate promotional efforts aimed at public involvement or support of a program (e.g., to promote a special event) (Edginton, Hanson, Edginton & Hudson, 1998).

Figure 8.5   An Example of Display Media

Billboards

Billboards, often referred to as part of the outdoor advertising industry, offer an excellent and affordable way to catch the customer on the move, whether traveling by foot, in a car, or via public transportation. Billboards may be found on the side of a building, within stadiums or arenas, on the sides of buses and taxis, and along roadways. The key to using billboards is "location, location, location." Kaatz (1995) has identified the following characteristics of effective outdoor advertising. It is:

- Easy to see and read at a high speed;
- Visually striking and grabbing; billboards make use of a unique size or shape whenever possible;
- An opportunity to reinforce a message the customer has received via another medium; and
- Uses seven words or less.

The price for billboard advertising varies considerably depending on location, but overall it is an effective and relatively inexpensive means of promotion. For public and nonprofit organizations billboard space may be even more affordable through public service programs in many areas.

Bulletin Boards

A bulletin board is generally a two-dimensional display prepared on a wall surface that can be used to present information about a specific organization, program, staff member, or service or as a means to promote an upcoming event. A bulletin board may be fixed or portable. Location of the bulletin board is a very important determinant of the effectiveness of the display. Using attention getting devices like an unusual design, striking color combinations, or leading statements to catch people's attention is a good idea. Whenever possible try to involve participants in the creation of bulletin boards. For instance, using children's arts and crafts projects can be a creative way to encourage parents to read about upcoming classes and events. Themes can be used to highlight upcoming programs during a specific time of year. We should remember that bulletin boards are intended to be temporary and should be changed periodically to remain current and stimulating.

Figure 8.6   An Example of a Billboard

Exhibits

An exhibit is often three-dimensional and may be used as an interpretation tool to educate the public about an issue or event. For example, the Cook County Forest Preserve outside Chicago use exhibits to educate the general public about the use of prescribed burning in specific areas of the forest preserve. Other types of exhibits include display boards that promote the overall organization and/or specific programs and events. Such displays are often portable allowing them to be set up in a variety of different locations. One ingenious public recreation director asked a bank for a permanent display table. Every month, a new display is set up, promoting upcoming events (Clark, 1993).

Point-of-Purchase Advertising

An organization's last chance to promote its programs and services to potential customers is at the point-of-purchase (P-O-P). Point-of-purchase advertising serves either as a reminder to buyers, when a program or service is heavily advertised in another medium, or as a stimulus to impulse buying (Nelson, 1989). Point-of-purchase advertising comes in an infinite variety of forms, including posters, banners, floor stands, signs, and display racks. These P-O-P units may be temporary or permanent and be located inside or outside of an organization. For example, many youth centers on military bases use banners at the youth center to remind parents and youth when it is time to register for sports leagues or specific special events.

Posters

Posters offer an alternative to large stationary billboards. They can be professionally produced (and mass produced) or created by staff or customers on-site. As a result, posters are a very versatile form of promotion. Posters may also be given (or even sold) to the general public. A secondary benefit to attractive posters is their staying power. If suitable for framing, they have the potential to be around for years (see Figure 8.7).

In developing posters it is important to pay close attention to image; the message must be both eye-catching and worthwhile. Use various shapes whenever possible. For example, when advertising the world's largest banana split we might create the poster in the shape of a banana split.

Figure 8.7   Example of an Eye-Catching Poster

As with other display media, success with the use of posters is based on location. For example, a poster promoting a youth program sponsored by a nonprofit organization should not be hung in a bar. Posters can, however, be placed in a variety of locations such as buses, bus shelters, airports, city benches, and so on. Ultimately, the flexibility in displaying posters makes them an effective and inexpensive means of promotion.

Presentations

Presentations include any opportunity to present information concerning an organization, programs, or services to a group of people. Examples of presentations are public speaking at local civic clubs, schools, churches or synagogues, and conferences. Such public speaking opportunities may include slide shows and videos. Computer software (e.g., Microsoft's Powerpoint) enables individuals to create their own slide shows that can be informative, entertaining, and aesthetically appealing.

When well done and geared to their audience, videos can be an excellent promotional tool. We should, however, consider a video as a part of an overall promotional strategy, never in place of one (Stern, 1992). For example, many private independent camps produce videos which can be sent to potential customers to give them a visual impression of the benefits of attending their specific camps. Such videos are followed up with other promotional methods such as a personal phone call or a camp brochure. Fitness clubs and resort areas also use videos as promotional tools. For example, Walt Disney World sends a free video to potential customers so that they can "tour" the park, decide what they would like to do when visiting, and where to make reservations that best suit their needs. If we choose this method as an element of promotion we should remember to ensure that the videos depict up-to-date scenes (including the way people are dressed). In addition, if used as a part of presentation, videos should be kept short and complement other elements of the presentation.

Printed Media

The print media offers a wide range of options in terms of promoting and advertising an organization's programs and services. Despite the emerging potential of television and computer technologies, print is still the most important worldwide advertising medium; it accounts for nearly 45 percent of all media expenditures (Berkman & Gilson, 1987). Generally, print media includes newspapers and magazines; however, we include several other mediums in this category (e.g., annual reports, brochures, fliers, newsletters, and the yellow pages).

A major consideration concerning printed media (beyond newspapers, magazines, and the yellow pages) is how the brochure, flier, or other printed material is distributed. Before the time and expense of developing printed material is committed, organizations need to identify strategies to reach their intended audience. Creativity is an important element of this decision. Consider the city of Des Moines, Iowa, where the Convention and Visitor's bureau identified taxi drivers as city ambassadors and created a brochure rack for the backside of the drivers seat. This rack contains brochures of a wide range of recreation opportunities offered by commercial,

nonprofit, and public parks, recreation, and leisure service organizations throughout the area.

Annual Reports

Annual reports are comprehensive summaries detailing the financial status, program services, physical developments, and prospective changes in a parks, recreation, or leisure service organization. Considered a "must" by many nonprofit organizations, an annual report is also submitted to a governing body or board of directors (of the organization) and is available to the general public. In some organizations the annual report can replace a brochure, especially in organizations that change a good deal from year to year (Stern, 1992). Important points to remember with annual reports are to pay close attention to the overall image of the report and think through and select appropriate distribution channels. In this way the potential of the annual report to promote the overall organization is maximized.

Brochures

A brochure may be seen as an organization's business card. As a result, brochures are often created for the organization as a whole, or for major components of the overall program as well as for specific one-time events. Brochures come in a variety of sizes and shapes and may include different types of information—see Figures 8.8 and 8.9 (pages 159 and 160). For example, a brochure promoting a specific event will include a description of the event, when and where the event will be held, as well as a registration form or a phone number and address to get additional information. A brochure promoting a specific organization might include a brief history of the organization, its mission, and an overview of its programs; a brochure promoting a facility or location might include pictures and descriptions of the equipment and facilities.

When developing a brochure it is important to remember the final use of the brochure. Will customers put it in their pocket and use it as a guide? Will office staff be mailing the brochure (will it fit in an envelope or stand alone)? Understanding the intended use of the brochure, the audience, and the image we want to portray are important early steps to creating effective brochures. Additional factors impacting the development of brochures include content (see Figure 8.10, page 161), layout and design (see Figure 8.11, page 161), timing (to ensure

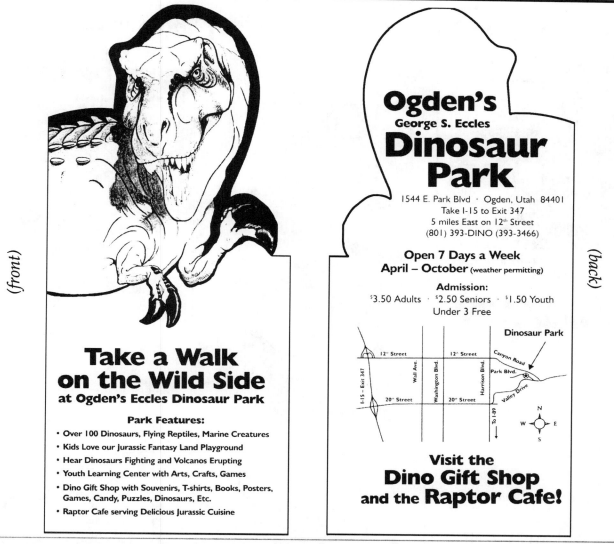

Figure 8.8   An Example of a Brochure from Ogden's Dinosaur Park

maximum visibility and impact), means of distribution, and costs (e.g., paper, printing, number of photographs, color or black-and-white, staff time, and distribution method).

Fliers

One of the most widely used forms of promotion in parks, recreation, and leisure service organizations is the flier. A flier is a short written message that is usually printed on one side of a sheet of paper and handed out, posted on a bulletin board or in a hallway, or sent through the mail. As a result, fliers must be able to catch the attention of people quickly and deliver a short, understandable message upon which an individual can then act. Fliers may be used as

fact sheets or as educational tools to provide vital details about upcoming programs and events.

Costs for producing fliers vary. Fliers created in-house may be inexpensive and easy to produce, while elaborate fliers produced by professional printers can be quite expensive. Regardless of cost, effective fliers are kept simple and constructed around a central theme or idea. For instance, fliers promoting specific programs or events should include the name of the program/event, at whom the program/event is targeted, location, date and time, the sponsoring agency, and a point of content if additional information is needed (see Figure 8.12, page 162).

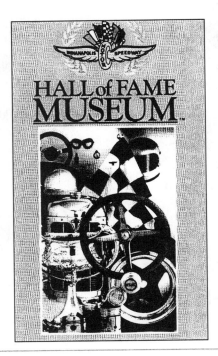

front cover   *inside*

Figure 8.9   Examples of Mini Brochures (shown in actual size)

How to Write Effective Copy for Brochures

- Find examples of promotional materials that you admire and analyze what could work for your organization.

- Write in language that sells. The first goal is to get people to stop and read the text. The copy on brochures should be benefit-oriented and motivating. Remember, customers buy benefits rather than programs. Use the brochure to create a relationship with the prospective customer.

- Use headlines to convey the essentials and make sure your headlines stick out. Your headlines should be simple and catch the readers' attention. Four out of five people will never read beyond the headline; thus, you must write a headline that appeals to readers' self-interest. Use benefit words that have impact. Recent research has reported that headlines with a benefit are read by an average of four times more people than headlines that don't.

- Under each headline you must elaborate on the benefits you have promised in the headline. Be specific and offer proof of the headline's claims. Vary sentence length and structure in your writing. Limit sentence length to seventeen words. Readership studies show comprehension drops like a rock at word 18. Strive to achieve a rhythm and variety in your writing.

- Include testimonials when possible. Coupling the testimonial with a photo of the participant creates a highly motivational piece.

- Give your copy closure by asking for an action. Call readers to action by asking them to register, make a phone call, a visit, or request they get more information. Give readers time constraints or limits within which they must act. Include a registration form or questionnaire with the brochure.

- Include a graphic or photo on the cover that will draw the reader in. Continue to use visuals throughout the brochure whenever possible. Captions should be included with all photos and other visuals.

- Reference materials. Let prospects know how to reach you. Registration information, pages, and forms should be geared for convenience, speed, and even fun. While registration information is often moved to the back of the brochure, the reader should be able to find the registration phone number in 10 seconds. Other important information includes location (a map), hours of operation, address, phone numbers, and Web sites.

- Show what you write to a number of people and ask them to give you feedback.

Figure 8.10 **Writing Effective Copy for Brochures** (Adapted from Stern, 1992; Learning Resources Network, 1997; Kerstetter, 1991)

How to Design Effective Brochures

- Find examples and be aware of current design trends.

- Use the front and back covers of brochures. Front and back covers are being recognized as prime space to promote classes, special activities, or the program in general. The use of photos, clip art, color, and humor have reached new heights on front and back covers.

- Increase the amount of white space, especially at the top and sides of the margin. More white space makes the brochure or flyer more readable and helps call the reader's attention to what is most important. Throughout the brochure and flyer use restraint to avoid a cluttered look.

- Use clip art, photos, and graphics wisely. An unbelievable array of line drawings are available. Use visuals that relate to the copy; never use it simply as a filler.

- Use typefaces carefully—and creatively. Using a variety of styles and sizes help direct the reader's eye. Use fonts that complement each other. For example, use serif fonts (i.e., letters with hooks and extensions) for body copy and sans serif (i.e., letters without hooks and extensions) for headlines.

- Pay attention to the leading (i.e., space between lines) of text copy. Keep columns ragged right (rather than justified) and less than 50 characters wide.

- Use accents with care. Accents are italics, bolds, boxes, rules, screens, and colors. These are used to highlight certain works or passages. Used sparingly they do the job. Overused, they lose their punch.

- When the brochure is in final draft form, step back and pretend you are looking at it for the very first time. See how all the elements work together.

- Get additional training. Work with printers, go to workshops, and look into design courses.

Figure 8.11 **Design Tips for Brochures and Fliers** (Adapted from Stern, 1992; Learning Resources Network, 1997)

At Calvin College

What   Food, Fun, & Games with other Families & Churches

Who   All Students & Families Participating in the *Pathways to Possibilities* Program

When   Friday, December 4, 1998 6:30-9:30pm

Where   Calvin College Field House

For more information contact Rhae Ann Booker, 555-6161

Sponsored by Pathway to Possibilities Program & Calvin College's Recreation 305 class

Figure 8.12   An Example of a Flier

Magazines

The major advantage of using magazine advertising is the ability to target a specific group of potential customers (see Figure 8.13). This is because magazines offer organizations an opportunity to access individuals who share common lifestyles or special interests. Other advantages include a good deal of flexibility in reproduction quality (i.e., magazines offer much greater quality than newspapers while still offering a wide range of options in terms of costs, size, and quality of the ad), and long life, which means the magazine will reach an audience over a long period of time.

Disadvantages of magazines include early closing dates, a slower pace of reading, and clutter (Berkman & Gilson, 1987). Magazine layout takes time so ads must be submitted a long time before publication. In addition, because some magazines are read slowly, it may take a long time for a reader to actually act on an advertisement. Clutter refers to the number of advertisements included in each issue of the magazine. Some magazines have over 50 pages of ads.

An additional promotion opportunity offered by magazines is feature articles. These articles may be written about an organization as a whole, promote an upcoming event, or describe a past program. Articles may also be developed along specific themes (e.g., developing your leisure repertoire, how to solve the summertime blues, fun, family travel tips). Although such an article may not be directly related to a specific organization it can offer an indirect promotional boost.

Newsletters

A newsletter is a means of communicating with an organization's membership and/or constituents. Newsletters let people know your organization is alive and well, and when well-written, can produce loyal readers and a good response. Beach (1993) has identified three main newsletter categories: promotional newsletters for marketing programs and services (readers receive the newsletter at no cost); informational newsletters for employees or members which are about people, places, and ideas (readers receive the newsletter as part of membership in an organization); and subscription newsletters that try to make readers richer, smarter, or healthier (readers pay for the newsletter). The

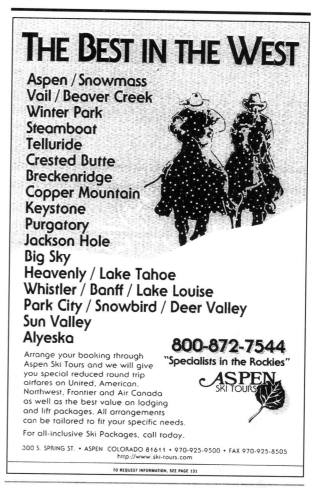

Figure 8.13   An Example of an Advertisement from *Outside* magazine

majority of newsletters in the parks, recreation, and leisure field are either promotional or informational.

In developing newsletters it is important to remember the purpose of the newsletter—this will guide design decisions. Consistency is also important. A well-designed newsletter has its own look (Brigham, 1991)—see Figure 8.14 (page 164). Rather than appearing like a collection of different sections and articles, everything in the newsletter should flow together. The paper's style and appearance should assist readers in recognizing the newsletter immediately when it arrives.

Setting up a consistent style enables an agency to establish a visual language to which people respond, often without knowing it. For example, placing a list of articles in a specific shaded box in the same location every issue, readers quickly learn just where to look and what to look for, so it's easy to find

SPRE *Newsletter*

Summer, 1998
Volume 22,
Number 3

Society of Park and Recreation Educators

**The National Recreation
and Park Association**

**RECREATION
AND PARK EDUCATION**

What's Inside?

PRESIDENT'S MESSAGE

Tom Goodale

At the department heads meeting last February in Tempe, AZ, the University of Phoenix often entered the discussion. Phoenix was just next door, of course, and James Traub featured the University of Phoenix in his October 20 & 27, 1997 *New Yorker* article, "The Next University — Drive-Thru U." Most of those in attendance had read Traub's article, and others of a similar nature, about how higher education was changing. In their own universities and programs, most were wrestling with those changes, often with some ambivalence.

My small contribution to the meeting was distributing copies of the most recent letter Dr. Tim Sullivan, President of the College of William and Mary in Virginia, periodically sends to several thousand alumni and friends of the college. As I could not hope to match the substance and tone of President Sullivan's letter, and with his leave, I decided to share it, verbatim and in its entirety, with you.

November 1997

Dear Friends of William and Mary:

Just a few weeks ago, some 8,000 of you arrived in Williamsburg to celebrate Homecoming. You came to renew friendships and to recall a very special time in your lives. But it was quite clear to me, as I spoke with you at the Ball, or before the parade, or during the football game, that you were not here simply to relive the past. You asked me some serious questions about the present and future of William and Mary. And you wanted reassurance that it has not become the kind of place you read about in the popular media.

You might well be concerned: you read that liberal arts education is outmoded, that standards have declined, that curricula are incoherent, that esoteric research has eclipsed effective teaching, that students are listless and disaffected, that universities are unresponsive to the needs of students and their families, that values no longer matter. In short, you read that American universities are at best anachronisms and at worst money-pits.

This letter, then, will be a little different than others I have written. I will speak less than usual about what we do and more about why we do it, in order to counter some of those charges levied against higher education. Of course, I cannot speak for all institutions, only for my own. But in so doing, I hope I am able to convince you that, far from being an anachronism, William and Mary stands as what ought to be the standard for education in this country at this time.

Let me begin by saying a little about what William and Mary is not. Around the same time that you were celebrating Homecoming, I happened to read an article in the *New Yorker* entitled "The Next University," about a university designed in response to those charges I just mentioned. There is no debate at the "next university" about the

(Continued pg. 2)

Figure 8.14   An Example of a Newsletter from the Society of Park and Recreation Educators (SPRE)

what interests them (Brigham, 1991). It is also important to remember that many people only scan newsletters, so pictures, headlines, subheadings, pull-out quotes, and white space are important to use. Such techniques allow readers to get a quick handle on what is being presented.

Newspapers

Newspapers are usually local except for a few, such as *USA Today*, the *Wall Street Journal*, and the *New York Times,* and *Chicago Tribune* all of which have many subscribers outside their areas of origin. On average, most newspapers come out daily although some small town papers or neighborhood papers come out less frequently (e.g., semiweekly, weekly, biweekly).

The advantages of using newspaper for promotion are its geographic sensitivity, the fact that it fosters immediate customer response, and offers a fast production turnaround. In addition, 60 percent of readers actually say they look forward to newspaper ads as compared with only 7 percent of television viewers. On television and radio, commercials are often perceived as an intrusion into entertainment time, whereas in newspapers they seem to be regarded as part of the overall entertainment value. This often prompts readers to act in a timely manner (Berkman & Gilson, 1987). Disadvantages of using newspapers are poor demographic selectivity (i.e., we have no idea who the readers are; there is no way to target consumers), poor production quality, a short life span, and clutter on certain days. Newspapers offer organizations a variety of opportunities for promotion including ads, classified ads, editorials and letters to the editor, feature articles, and sports and athletic news.

Newspaper Advertising and Classifieds. Both advertising and classified ads are initiated by the organization and are forms of paid promotion. Advertising space may be found throughout the paper while classifieds are organized under categories in a specific section. Rates for both advertising space and classifieds are quoted either by the line or by the column inch. Although there is usually a flat rate per line, newspapers will often offer discounts for local advertisers as well as for increased volume (i.e., the more space you buy during the year, the lower the line or column inch rate will be).

Newspaper advertising is a mainstay for many commercial recreation and leisure service organizations (especially small, local operators—see Figure 8.15). Organizations such as bowling centers, roller skating rinks, movie theaters, and community theaters rely extensively on newspaper advertising. Public and nonprofit leisure service organizations tend to rely on newspaper advertising more for special events rather than the day-to-day operation of the organization.

Editorials and Letters to the Editor. Newspaper editors are often accessible to the general public and will consider and encourage thoughtful, well-documented points of views on issues that

TOURING FAMILY MUSIC FESTIVAL
FEATURING THE COUNTRY'S BEST CHILDREN'S RECORDING ARTISTS

WHERE: NAVY PIER
700 EAST GRAND AVENUE
CHICAGO, ILLINOIS
WHEN: SUNDAY, FEBRUARY 1, 1998
TIME: 11:00 A.M. – 4:00 P.M.
ADMISSION: $5.00 (ADULTS & CHILDREN)
MUSEUM ADMISSION INCLUDES SHOW

 FOR INFORMATION CALL:
1-888-889-2408
DREAM TEAM MARKETING, INC.

 CHICAGOPARENT

Figure 8.15   Sample Newspaper Ad

concern their readership. Editorials offer recreation programmers the opportunity to comment on such issues by offering individual viewpoints or an organizations view the subject. Quick response time is important as one becomes aware of local issues which involve the organization. Editorials offer high visibility for the organization and make a contribution to public debate on important issues.

Letters to the editor also offer individuals an opportunity to contribute to the public debate. Such letters, when timely, well-thought-out and well-written, are very often published. If an individual or organization has a strong position on an issue within the community, letters to the editor may be used to educate others about their position. Other uses for letters to the editor include thanking others in the community for their support, or responding to earlier positive or negative letters to the editor written by parties outside the organization. Organizations should be on the lookout for such letters and respond accordingly with the individual as well as following up with the newspaper (often in the form of a letter) either acknowledging positive publicity or responding to negative publicity in a constructive manner.

Features. Reporters are always looking for news in their communities. If an organization has an event or program that is timely, unique, interesting or new, it should contact the newspaper for possible coverage. A news release or a personal call could be used to inform the paper of noteworthy items. When dealing with newspaper reporters, staff should be careful to avoid saying anything they would not want to read in print in the morning. Feature stories offer high volume, but short-lived coverage for the organization. Encourage the use of photographs with all articles to help bring to life the written word.

Sports and Athletic News. Sports editors are often open to including a wide variety of information about community sports leagues (including hunting and fishing contests). Feature articles prior to the start up of a league or following league play are possibilities while ongoing opportunities to inform the public may be found in game announcements, game summaries, and box scores. Some newspapers expect such information to be submitted in writing while others allow scores and other pertinent information to be phoned into the paper. Whatever the method, it is important for the programmer to build a relationship with her or his contact at the paper.

Yellow Pages

The Yellow Pages are the lifeline that ties a company to its customers and potential customers—especially for commercial organizations. As the nation's fourth largest advertising medium, it is the place customers go when they want to buy and need to know where to buy something (Kaatz, 1995). To be effective, organizations should incorporate the following principles into their yellow page advertisements (Kaatz, 1995).

- The headline should focus on what the business offers as well as its name, and the ad itself should be uncomplicated and avoid wordiness.
- The ad should be placed under the heading or headings where consumers might go for the product or service.
- Location and phone number need to be large and clear.
- For hard-to-find locations, the ad should show how to get there by including a map.
- The ad should include those special features of the organization that might attract the consumer. (See Figure 8.16)

Other Promotional Tools

The techniques and tools used to promote organizations, programs, and events are endless. With a little creativity and hard work, individuals can constantly create new promotion techniques. Consider one park and recreation organization that printed pertinent information concerning an activity on narrow slips of paper and inserted them in a batch of homemade fortune cookies (Clark, 1993). With this in mind the following is not an exhaustive list, but rather one which we hope will generate additional ideas about potential promotional tools.

Awards and Citations

Agencies constantly look for ways to recognize staff, customers, community organizations, and groups for their contributions to the success of the agency. Awards are thought of as publicity and a public relations tool. Remember, awards can be meaningless if given too freely, but should be presented when deserved. Examples of awards include: certifications for the completion of classes, volunteer appreciation certificates, outstanding service awards for staff, and

Figure 8.16   Example of a Yellow Pages Ad

recognizing the efforts of community groups who have assisted in programs or done other noteworthy service (see Figure 8.17). The process of giving awards can itself become a new promotional tool. When giving awards, if it is appropriate to inform local newspapers, radio, and television through a press release about it, do so. A picture and a short article in a community paper can promote a positive image for an organization and spark additional interest in the organization's programs and services.

Celebrities/Spokespeople

Using celebrities to promote an organization and/or a specific program or event can be fun and worthwhile. Celebrities serve as attention getters, but seldom in and of themselves make the sale. Organizations look to both local and national celebrities to promote their programs. National organizations are often more suited to attracting big time stars, but local affiliates and local organizations can look for local radio and television personalities in promoting events. We offer one note of caution in selecting a spokesperson—make sure the person embodies the values of your organization. One example of use of a celebrity spokesperson is the use of World Wrestling Federation (WWF) wrestlers at grand openings of various stores and malls. The characters draw huge crowds for pictures and autographs, and visitors often buy goods while there for autographs.

Contests

Contests can bring attention to an organization or to a specific event or program. Contests often serve as a lead-in to a specific event, priming individuals or groups for the main event. Contests can range from coloring contests for children to design competitions

for posters to fund-raising drives. Contests can also often be included in an actual event (e.g., hospital bed races, cooking contests) or may be the main event (e.g., dragon boat races, pet shows). Prizes are often given to winners; examples of prizes include cash awards, trips, donated merchandise, or a variety of novelty items with the organization logo on them.

Coupons

Coupons such as "Buy One Registration, Get a Second Registration for Half Price" are effective means to encourage individuals to try new programs or services, thereby creating a returning customer base. Coupons may also be incorporated into other types of promotion such as fliers and brochures. Berkman and Gilson (1987) have documented the increasing use of coupons for retail products and believe this use will continue, thus making coupons an effective approach in persuading customers to save money and try new programs and services. For example, coupons have been used very effectively in leisure services for senior citizen participation. Many organizations provide reduced rates for seniors (often during a specific time of day or day of the week) providing they have a special senior's discount card.

Direct Mail

Direct mail is carried out by an organization that wants to get a complex message across at a reasonable cost. This form of communication involves mailing a brochure, letter, or other piece of promotion directly to an individual whom the organization has targeted as a potential customer, donor, or stakeholder in the organization (Espy, 1993). Mailing lists may be generated from past participants, new residents, people in a specific geographic area, or individuals who have expressed an interest in a particular program area. Unfortunately, many people feel bombarded by "junk mail" which has lessened the effectiveness of direct-mail techniques. Another consideration that might lessen our enthusiasm for direct mailing is the environmental cost. Direct mailing can consume a great deal of resources (mainly paper) which may give our organization an unfavorable image. Despite these concerns, with careful targeting and message development, direct mail can be an effective means of communication.

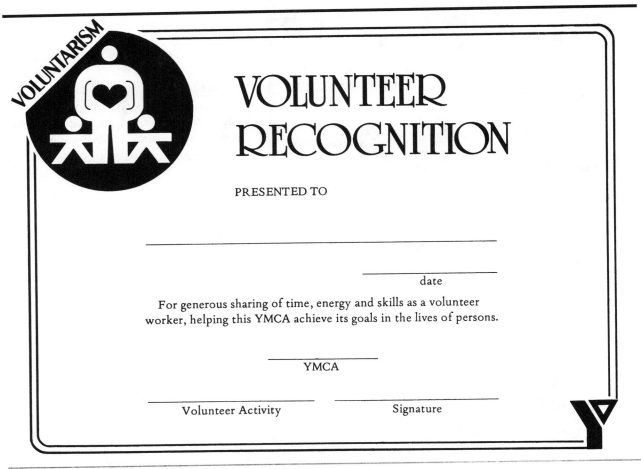

Figure 8.17   An Example of an Award for Exceptional Volunteers

Involvement in Special Events

Neighborhood festivals, art fairs, and other special events take place throughout the year. Having a presence at these types of community events is important to promote an organization's involvement in the community and/or increase name recognition for an organization with the general public. An organization's involvement could take on a variety of forms such as a game booth, entertainment, hands-on projects for children, or simply an information booth which disseminates brochures, fliers, and other promotional materials about programs and services. Organizations can also sponsor specific special events of their own as a way to promote a cause, celebrate a holiday, and/or promote a specific service or program. Such special events are hard work, but are a good way to renew or maintain personal contact with other organizations and individuals in the community on a large scale.

Logos, Emblems, and Trademarks

Logos, emblems, and trademarks are visual symbols that represent an organization. Logos and emblems have an important advantage over other forms of communication—the advantage of speed. If a logo is well-designed, it will catch the eye, generate interest, and be recognized instantaneously. Logos, emblems, and trademarks can be used in a variety of ways. Good trademarks and logos can stand alone as well as be used on stationary, envelopes, decals, T-shirts, and organization vehicles; almost anything an organization develops can include their logo or trademark signature.

From a design standpoint, logos and trademarks may take the form of a symbol, type (or lettering) or a combination of the two (see Figure 8.18). The most successful logos and trademarks are original, legible, stimulating, appropriate to the product, and easy to remember (Nelson, 1989).

Figure 8.18   Examples of Logos

News Conferences

A news conference is an event to which the media or the general public is invited during which a specific issue is addressed. News conferences may be effective for dealing with an issue that is very big, controversial, or out of the ordinary; however, it is important not to overuse them. According to Kaatz (1995) the media generally avoid news conferences if they can obtain the news another way. They will attend only if a major personality is announcing something or if a major issue is to be discussed.

Photographs

"A picture is worth a thousand words" is an adage which runs true for promoting the benefits of recreation programs. Thus, photographs should not be overlooked in the overall promotional mix. Although photographs are usually used in conjunction with

other promotional tools (e.g., newspaper articles, brochures, newsletters) there are several specific considerations to keep in mind. First and foremost, organizations should build a photo file so they have quality pictures available when they are needed. Such a file should be continually updated and expanded, and captions should be kept with all pictures. A wide range of pictures should be kept including pictures of staff members, facilities, group shots, and perhaps most important—pictures of participants in action.

Although photographs may be rented from ad agencies, it is best for pictures to be taken from actual programs and events sponsored by the parks, recreation, or leisure service organization. Oftentimes organizations hire photographers or use in-house staff to take photos. A third option may be to involve local newspapers and let them know of opportunities for a good photo shoot. If a photographer does take some pictures she or he is often willing to share them. For example, a parks and recreation supervisor contacted a local paper before a "mud bowl" special event for adults. The paper sent a photographer who took several pictures which were then picked up by the Associated Press and published in newspapers across the country (Clark, 1993).

One important consideration when shooting pictures during a program is to have participants sign photo releases. Permission must be gained prior to publishing any customer photographs where individuals might be identifiable, especially if a monetary gain is experienced, if the subjects are minors, or have special needs. Failure to do so could result in a lawsuit based on invasion of privacy (Jordan, 1996).

Press and/or Information Kits

To take advantage of unexpected opportunities to promote an organization a press kit can be developed. Such a tool can be distributed on a moment's notice to program visitors, dignitaries, potential customers, and/or media representatives. A press or information kit might include items such as a brief history of the organization, an organizational chart, biographical information of specific staff, brochures, the annual report, a list of major accomplishments or programs offered, photographs, unique products from past programs (i.e., a child's arts and crafts program), a list of major supporters or customers of the agency or organization, as well as reprints of articles about the organization, and letters of support from customers and community figures (Espy, 1993). By keeping this type of information on file within the organization it can be quickly accessed to create a customized press or information kit to meet the needs of a variety of situations. A press kit may be assembled in a binder or folder for easy access to recipients. It is important to keep information used for such press or information packets current.

Press Releases

A press release serves to make a specific statement that the organization hopes will be picked up to receive free publicity in the media. Press releases may publicize an event, provide information about the organization, or announce the opening of a new program. In many cases organizations develop relationships with the media that will facilitate the publication of press releases (Espy, 1993). One type of press release is a news release.

A well-written news release may result in a feature story or other free publicity. To be successful and present a professional looking release, we suggest the following standard format developed by Clark (1993). Editors prefer a one-page news release, double-spaced with wide margins which allows space for them to add notes. By typing the words NEWS RELEASE across the top of the page, editors are able to quickly identify what it is. Include succinct information about the five Ws in the first paragraph (i.e., who, what, why, when, and where). Editors often call for additional information, so be sure to include a contact person and phone numbers. In addition, stress the benefits of the event and emphasize its community appeal (see Figure 8.19).

News releases can be sent to a variety of sources beyond newspapers. For example, consider sending news releases to churches for inclusion in their church bulletin. One YMCA had an intern personally call every pastor in their city, asking if they wanted occasional information about community events. Over 70 percent were happy to receive the material and said they would include it in the weekly church bulletin (Clark, 1993). When sending out news releases address them to specific individuals whenever possible. Allow two to three weeks notice for sending out news releases. Editors' most frequent complaint involves news releases scribbled on postcards, two days prior to the event (Clark, 1993).

Promotional Merchandise (Novelty Items) and Prizes

Organizations can use a variety of promotional merchandise to promote their organization or specific program or event. Novelty items (imprinted in some way with the name of the organization or program) include bumper stickers, pins, pens, pencils, mugs, clothing (e.g., T-shirts and sweatshirts), calendars, banners, flags, small toys, matchbooks, postcards, patches, magnets, and other merchandise. For example, T-shirts can be printed and handed out to volunteers during a special event. In such a capacity the T-shirt may be viewed as a sign of appreciation to the volunteer as well as a way to designate who can help participants during the event. T-shirts may also be sold to the general public during an event as a means to generate funds and to promote the organization or event for the future (see Figure 8.20, page 172).

Promotional items also are used as prizes leading up to specific events or during the actual program or event. For example, tickets for special events may be given to radio stations or other commercial organizations for giveaways prior to the event. Prize and giveaways of novelty items can create a sense of goodwill between organizations and customers, if used wisely.

Public Service Announcements

Public service announcements (PSAs) are announcements aired on the radio or television intended to educate or benefit the consumer audience in some way (Kaatz, 1995). There was a time when radio and television stations were required by the Federal Communications Commission to run public service announcements. Although this law is no longer in effect most radio and television stations still include PSAs as part of their programming. This is in part because they need to fill otherwise empty air time with interesting material, but more so because the stations want to be good citizens (especially when license renewal time comes around) (Kotler & Andreasen, 1996). Public and nonprofit leisure service organizations can take advantage of this opportunity by creating their own PSAs. The organization can advance an idea (e.g., Parks and Recreation—The Benefits Are Endless) or provide information about its programs or services (e.g., promote a specific upcoming event). A 1985 survey indicated

---

News Release

For Immediate Release   **July 6, 1998**

<u>Join Us for Goofy's Birthday Party</u>

Who	Madiera Beach Parks & Recreation Department in partnership with Ben & Jerry's Ice Cream
Contact	Winnie Wong
	(813) 555–6966
What	Goofy's Birthday Party, complete with a critter parade and prizes for the four-legged critters and ice cream for the two-legged critters.
Why	To celebrate two exciting occasions—Goofy's Birthday and Creative Flavor Ice Cream Day
When	Monday, July 20, 1998
	6:30 to 8:30 PM
Where	Beachfront Park Community Center
	1300 West 3rd Street
Cost	Critter Parade Free
	Make your own creative ice cream flavor for $1.00

Celebrate Goofy's Birthday with us by joining the family critter parade and ice cream social from 6:30 to 8:30 PM at Beachfront Park Community Center. Children and their parents can enter their pet in a variety of contests and participate in over 15 different booths and activities relating to pet care. The Boys' and Girls' Club will sponsor a "create your own creative ice cream flavor" as a fundraiser for the Humane Society of Pinellas Park. Donations by local merchants ensure prizes for everyone.

Figure 8.19   Example of a Press Release

Figure 8.20 Examples of Promotional Items

that TV stations were most apt to use PSAs under the following conditions (*Marketing News*, 1985):

- PSAs of differing length were offered (15, 30, 45, 60 seconds).

- One of the following subjects is dealt with: health, safety, alcohol and drug abuse, child abuse and molestation, family and social relations, education, crime prevention, and drunk driving.

- There is a possibility for a local connection (respondents said they broadcast 56 percent of PSAs for local organizations and 44 percent for national issues).

- The target audience is children, the elderly, minorities, or people with disabilities.

Many recreation organizations include many of these conditions and would be well-suited for PSAs. Additional help from The Advertising Council may be available to public and nonprofit organizations in developing PSAs. The Ad Council operates through donations from advertising firms. The public or nonprofit organization pays for material costs, but receives creative and media support free (Kotler & Andreasen, 1996). Over the years The Ad Council has been deeply involved in American life, creating over 1,000 campaigns, bringing us many memorable characters (e.g., Smokey Bear, McGruff the Crime Dog, and Vince and Larry—The Crash Dummies), and producing some of the following familiar slogans:

- Only you can prevent forest fires;

- A mind is a terrible thing to waste;

- Help take a bite out of crime; and

- Pollution: It's a crying shame.

Word of Mouth and Testimonials

Last, but certainly not least, the essence and image of our organization is communicated daily through word of mouth by customers, staff, and a variety of other people both within and outside an organization (Espy, 1993). Such word-of-mouth publicity contributes to the overall image of the organization. Stern (1992) identifies the following three ways an organization can foster word-of-mouth publicity. First, by doing what we do so well that people are excited and want to talk about it. Second, by making sure everyone associated with the organization is informed, enthusiastic, and pleased to tell anyone and everyone about who we are and what we do. Third, by asking everyone we know to pass along a good word. In addition, organizations use testimonials to record positive impressions that people have with their programs and services. Testimonials can then be used in a variety of promotional formats.

Factors to Consider When Promoting Programs

Given tight budgets and time constraints, practitioners will probably not be able to do everything they want to promote their program, service, or idea. As a result, organizations must give concerted thought to making decisions which will maximize the effectiveness of a promotional campaign as well as make the best use of time and money. These decisions are dependent on many factors. The following questions serve as a guide to assist programmers in making these decisions.

What Are the Promotion Objectives?

The overall goal of promotion efforts is to encourage the public to derive full benefit from the program and services that an organization provides. Within this broad goal, however, the objectives of specific promotional efforts should be clearly established as to whether the promotional effort is intended to inform, educate, persuade, or remind (Crompton & Lamb, 1986).

For example, if an organization's objective is to inform, then it may attempt to create mass awareness of a new program or service by emphasizing advertising and publicity. For example, Crompton and Lamb (1986) cite a promotional campaign in Seattle, Washington, that created awareness of a special bus service running through the city's major parks. Promotional techniques included publicity in daily and community newspapers; PSAs on local radio stations; wide distribution of the bus schedule through city centers, public agencies, and tourist accommodations; posters in libraries, restaurants, community centers, and other public locations; and a feature article in *Sunset Magazine*, a regional magazine.

Who Is the Target Audience?

It is important for an organization to understand the target audience for the overall organization as well as for specific programs and services. Organizations need to gear the promotional tool to the audience—programmers need to think about how the audience lives, where they go, what they are most likely to look at, listen to, or read. Then programmers need to think about the tool that fits into that picture.

For example, a staff member could develop the best newspaper ad in the world, but it probably would not reach teenagers, because teenagers do not read newspapers. The staff would be better off developing a public service announcement for MTV. Likewise, a great Web page might be very ineffective if we are trying to reach customers who do not have access to a computer.

What Is the Budget?

Clearly, the amount of money an organization has available for promotional activities has a substantial influence on the number of promotional tools and techniques that are used, as well as the frequency with which they can be used. As a result, programmers should be sure to utilize as many free and low-cost techniques as possible, but should not overlook the hidden cost in terms of staff time needed for creating effective promotional techniques. Many publicity tools are dollar free, but staff intensive. Consider the amount of time it may take to develop relationships with a magazine editor in getting a feature article published or in creating in-house promotional items. Programmers need this information before decisions are made concerning the promotional tools and techniques used to promote an organization or program.

What Is the Program?

The actual program may dictate the most appropriate promotional technique. Different events have different potential for using various promotional techniques. For example, television is a much better medium to promote active events; media categories have different potential for demonstration, visualization, explanation, believability, and color.

At What Stage Is the Program Within the Product Life Cycle?

In Chapter Seven we observed that programs go through a life cycle beginning with introduction and ending with decline. According to Crompton and Lamb (1986) in the introduction stage the promotional objective is normally to inform and educate prospective customers. In the middle stages of the program life cycle, advertising is often used to persuade and remind clients of the availability of the program or service. During the final stage of the program life cycle, promotional activities are normally reduced and phased out as fewer and fewer people are interested in the program.

What Is the Time Frame?

The issue of time is relevant on many different levels. First and foremost, is the timing of the promotional technique in conjunction to what is being promoted? For example, if we have a short time span until an actual event or program is to take place radio, newspaper advertisements or fliers may be the best choice as such mediums can be created quickly and can prompt potential customers to move quickly. A second related issue of time revolves around the amount of lead time needed to create the promotional piece. For example, brochures and magazines take a long time to produce, but they do have a much longer life than fliers and newspaper advertisements.

Coordinating the Promotion Mix

In answering the questions described in Figure 8.21, programmers should be able to identify the promotional tools and techniques that are most appropriate for specific programs or events. Yet, it is also important to remember the overall promotional mix of the organization. Thus, programmers should examine the overall promotion strategy of the organization using the same questions listed in the preceding sections. Ultimately it is important to pick the right mix of techniques within our budget to promote individual programs and which promote the organization as a whole. Ideally, the promotion mix for the organization as a whole will include some combination of all four components of promotion

(i.e., advertising, publicity, personal selling, and sales promotions) discussed earlier in this chapter.

The key to a successful promotion mix is integrating a wide variety of techniques. Each element must dovetail with others. Using a variety of approaches generally ensures a greater target audience. It is important, however, that all efforts be coordinated to ensure that each impression the customer or potential customer receives will fit with what he or she knows or believes about the program and the organization behind it.

Developing a Promotion Strategy—TREATS

In examining the importance of promotion to an organization, consider the communication tasks facing TREATS. The organization TREATS is a nonprofit organization operating in Hong Kong. The mission of TREATS is to integrate children and youth of different backgrounds and ability through recreation and play. Although services are primarily offered to children and youth, TREATS focuses its promotion efforts on parents, teachers, school administrators, and potential funders for the program, as well as children and youth. Within this context, consider the promotional needs of TREATS in terms of informing, educating, persuading, and reminding the community of its services.

Informing

In order to make decisions about whether or not to attend TREATS programs, school administrators, teachers, parents, children and youth need basic information about TREATS, the programs it offers, and how they can get involved. Promotion is needed to inform target audiences about the possibilities.

TREATS informs their many target audiences in a variety of ways. Word of mouth is their most effective promotional tool. After participating in a program, teachers, school administrators, and parents often encourage other schools to become involved in the program. A community service officer also works to develop new contacts through the Education Department. In addition, direct mailings, presentations, and personal contacts are used to inform groups about programs and services.

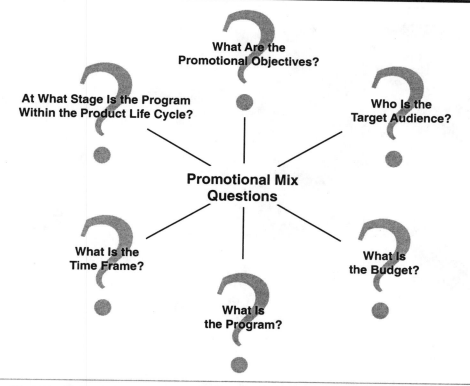

Figure 8.21   Questions Pertaining to the Promotional Mix

Educating

For most people, an appreciation of the concept of integration of people with and without disabilities is learned or acquired over time. This means that expansion of the target audiences (e.g., participants, funders, volunteers) requires developing a level of understanding about integration and the benefits it provides to arouse a desire to get involved on some level with TREATS. This objective is distinguished from informing or persuading because only through education can an individual begin to recognize the value of integration.

TREATS must continue to educate participants, funders, and volunteers regarding the inherent value of participating in their programs. This means educating about the potential benefits of integration. This includes helping all aspects of the community recognize the equal rights of children and adults from different backgrounds and abilities to take part in life's activities and to become accepted members of the community.

TREATS believes that everything it does should have an educational component. Promotional materials (i.e., brochures—see Figure 8.22, page 176), newsletters, feature articles in magazines and newspapers) as well as presentations are designed to educate about integration as well as promote TREATS and its programs.

Persuading

In addition to being given information, participants, funders, and volunteers may need to be persuaded to become involved in a TREATS program. There are many possible persuaders including the quality of the experience, the unique nature of the program, opportunity for personal enrichment, location of the program, social interaction, assistance with transportation to and from events, reduced rates, and so on. The importance of each of these persuaders will vary according to the type of event and target audience. TREATS's promotional efforts communicate this benefit information (usually through personal contacts like school meetings) in an effort to persuade school administrators, teachers, and students to participate in programs.

Outside Cover

「親切」匯聚不同能力的兒童及青少年，以提倡共融的理念，並促進其個人及群育的發展。

TREATS —
brings together young
people, with and without
disabilities, to promote
integration and develop
personal and social skills.

What is the aim of TREATS?
To provide co-operative and team-based learning opportunities for young people of all abilities to participate as equals and develop life skills.

What does TREATS offer?
A role model for integration and personal growth. Integrated day and overnight recreation activities, youth development programmes, community projects, professional and volunteer training.

Through the process of experiential learning, co-operative games and creative workshops, the young people can
- expand horizons and break through barriers
- increase confidence and self esteem
- learn to co-operate and trust
- make new friends
- have some fun!

Who benefits from TREATS?
All young people, particularly those with physical, mental, emotional and behavioural problems; those living in care,

temporary housing, crowded public housing, new arrivals from other regions of China and those on public assistance.

TREATS — 19A, Block F
5 Lok Man Road, Chai Wan
Hong Kong
Tel: 2889 1332 Fax: 2898 3385
E mail: treats@netvigator.com

TREATS is a member of the Community Chest and The Hong Kong Council of Social Service

Acknowledgements —
Photos: Piers Marson, Bobby Lee;
Design: Format Ltd.
Translation: Eleanor Hui &
Associates Ltd.

「親切」的服務目標
提供合作及國際形式的學習機會予不同能力的兒童及青少年了解參與，並發展其生活技能。

「親切」提供的服務
為其理念及個人發展提供一個典範模式：籌辦綜合性的康樂日營及宿營；推行青少年發展計劃；舉辦及參與社區活動；以及提供專業和義工訓練。

透過合作性遊戲與創意工作坊，讓兒童及青少年從體驗中學習，並：
- 從垃圾中擴闊個人領域、衝破人際隔膜
- 增強自信和自尊
- 學習與別人合作和信任別人
- 結識新朋友
- 享受樂趣！

「親切」的服務對象
所有兒童及青少年，特別是那些傷殘、弱智、在結諸和行為上需要較多關心的；居住在安置中心、臨時房屋及擠迫的公共屋邨、剛從國內來港定居或接受公共援助的兒童及青少年。

親切　香港柴灣樂民道4號
F座19樓A室
電話：2889 1332 傳真：2898 3385
電子郵件：treats@netvigator.com

親切　乃公益金及香港社會服務聯會會員機構

誠蒙 Piers Marson 及李民權借出照片，化美有限公司提供設計服務及Eleanor Hui & Associates Ltd 協助翻譯，特此鳴謝。

Inside

Figure 8.22   Example of Promotion Strategy: TREATS Brochure

Reminding

Individuals and organizations have many alternatives on which to expend their time and money other than supporting TREATS. Therefore, it is necessary to constantly remind them of the personal and community benefits that accrue from their support while also demonstrating appreciation for their patronage. This approach is crucial for confirming and reinforcing future support. TREATS continues to develop its relationship with various audiences in a variety of ways including an annual newsletter (see Figure 3.3, page 45), a bimonthly volunteer newsletter, brochures (see Figure 8.22), and personal contact between schools and TREATS staff.

Promoting Programs: A Servant Leadership Approach

Some people believe promotion is wasteful, an opinion that is reflected in the following quote attributed to Ralph Waldo Emerson.

> If a man [*sic*] can write a better book, preach a better sermon, or make a better mousetrap than his neighbors, though he builds his house in the woods, the world will make a beaten path to his door. (Fern, 1985, p. 69)

This suggests that promotional efforts are not needed if the product, program, or service is of high quality. This view would seem to fit with servant leadership which we have proposed as a framework for delivering recreation programs and services. As servant leaders, programmers follow the needs of their constituencies rather than creating interest in programs through promotion.

In dealing with this criticism, let's go back to the quote from Ralph Waldo Emerson. In many instances better books, sermons, and mousetraps have been produced. Yet

> many have remained unread, unheard, and unused. Unless the world knows that organizations, programs and services exist, as well as believing that they offer 'want

satisfying' benefits, these offerings will remain unsuccessful. (Crompton & Lamb, 1986, 379–380)

Without promotion an organization and its programs and services literally do not exist in the public consciousness.

Effective promotion increases the net benefits provided by an organization in many ways. First, it increases the number of people who are aware of an organization's services, thus overcoming an identified barrier to recreation participation. Second, it can decrease the cost of services by increasing the number of people participating and thus paying for services. When promotion decreases net cost to participants and increases individual and community benefits, it may be viewed as an investment (Crompton & Lamb, 1986).

As a result, we believe servant leaders should invest in promoting their organizations, programs, and services within the following ethical principles. First and foremost, promotion should not be misleading. An organization seeking the lasting patronage of its customers will succeed only if it provides accurate and honest information about its programs and services (Crompton & Lamb, 1986). Thus, servant leaders should resist the tendency to overpromise. If an organization promises more from a program

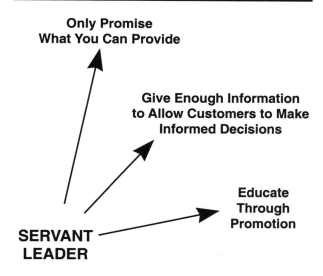

Figure 8.23 Program Promotion: A Servant Leadership Approach

than it is able to deliver, its credibility can be damaged, and it will not be serving the customer.

A related issue to overpromising is not giving customers enough information to make good decisions. Servant leaders will provide customers with the information they need to make informed decisions. Thus, the education aspect of promotion is especially important to servant leaders. Promotion is an opportunity to serve through education. Servant leaders seek to convince others, rather than coerce compliance. This aspect of servant leadership also ties into the issue of stewardship described in Chapter One. Servant leadership, like stewardship, assumes a commitment to serving the needs of others. It also emphasizes the use of openness and persuasion, rather than control.

Summary

Promotion is primarily communication that seeks to inform, educate, persuade, or remind various target groups about an organization's programs and services. Organizations that have a successful promotion strategy include a well-thought-out promotion mix. The promotion mix is a set of four communication tools available for an organization's use. These tools are advertising, publicity, personal selling, and sales promotions. Within these four components are a wide variety of techniques and tools that programmers can use in promoting their programs and services. To identify the most appropriate techniques for specific programs and events, the programmer must consider a variety of factors. These factors are discussed in question format and include the following:

- What are the promotion objectives?
- Who is the target audience? What is the budget?
- What is the program?
- What stage is the program within the product life cycle?
- What is the time frame? and
- Where do the promotional efforts for this specific program fit within the overall promotional mix of the organization?

It is also important to remember to coordinate the overall promotion mix of the organization. As a result, programmers should examine the overall promotion strategy of the organization using the same questions listed above. Ultimately it is important to pick the right mix of techniques within one's budget which promote individual programs and that promote the organization as a whole. Ideally the promotion mix for the organization will include some combination of all four components of promotion (i.e., advertising, publicity, personal selling, and sales promotion).

A servant leadership approach to promotion means seeing promotion as an investment rather than a wasteful activity. Servant leaders resist the tendency to overpromise in their promotional efforts. Another consideration for servant leaders is giving customers enough information to make informed decisions, and using promotion as a tool for education.

References

Beach, M. (1993). *Newsletter sourcebook.* Cincinnati, OH: North Lights Books.

Berkman, H. and Gilson, C. (1987) *Advertising concepts and strategies, 2nd ed.* New York, NY: Random House.

Brigham, N. (1991). *How to do leaflets, newsletters, and newspapers.* Cincinnati, OH: North Lights Books.

Clark, S. (1993). *Taming the recreation jungle: 100 ways to improve the quality of recreation programs.* Seattle, WA: Book Partners.

Crompton, J. & Lamb, C. (1986). *Marketing government an social services.* New York, NY: John Wiley & Sons.

Edginton, C., Hanson, C., Edginton, S. and Hudson, S. (1998). *Leisure programming: A service centered and benefits approach.* Boston, MA: McGraw-Hill.

Espy, S. (1993). *Marketing strategies for nonprofit organizations.* Chicago, IL: Lyceum Books.

Estes, G. (1994). Once upon a time...when the fantasy is real. *Parks and Recreation, 8*(6), 44–47.

Evans, J. and Berman, B. (1990). *Marketing, 4th ed.* New York, NY: Macmillan.

Fern, D. (1985). A better mousetrap. *Inc., 7*(3).

Godbey, G. (1997). *Leisure and leisure services in the 21st century.* State College, PA: Venture Publishing, Inc.

Gonyea, J. and Gonyea, W. (1996). *Selling on the Internet.* New York, NY: McGraw-Hill.

Jordan, D. (1996). *Leadership in leisure services: Making a difference.* State College, PA: Venture Publishing, Inc.

Kaatz, R. (1995). *Advertising and marketing checklists.* Lincolnwood, IL: NTC Business Books.

Kerstetter, D. (1991, July). How to write effective copy for brochures and fliers. *Resort and Commercial Recreation Association*, p. 5.

Kotler, P. and Andreasen, A. (1996) *Strategic marketing for nonprofit organizations, 5th ed.* Englewood Cliffs, NJ: Prentice Hall.

Lankford, S., DeGraaf, D. and Neal, L. (1996). A comparison of barriers to leisure and sport activity participation in the United States: Implications for Hong Kong. *Hong Kong Recreation Review, 8*(1), 43–46.

Learning Resources Network. (1997, September). *The fundamentals: The ten best brochure/catalog ideas.* Manhattan, KS: Learning Resource Network.

Marlow, E. (1997). *Web visions.* New York, NY: Van Nostrand Reinhold.

Nelson, R. (1989). *The design of advertising.* Dubuque, IA: W. C. Brown.

Reinhold, H. (1993). *The virtual community: Homesteading on the electronic frontier.* New York, NY: HarperCollins.

Robinson, J. and Godbey, G. (1997). *Time for life: The surprising ways Americans use their time.* University Park, PA: Penn State Press.

Staff. (1985, August 16). Free TV abounds for public service messages. *Marketing News*, p. 7.

Stern, G. (1992). *Marketing workbook for nonprofit organizations.* St. Paul, MN: Amherst H. Wilder Foundation.

Chapter Nine

Pricing Program Services

Money is vital to how we govern because it is the universal measuring device. It does not measure everything we care about, but it is the common language we use to measure the health of our institution, as well as our promises to each other and how well we have delivered on those promises. We have created the financial function to help become fully informed and communicate about performance. Financial functions also help people, through budgets, to document and keep track of their promises. These intentions are service-oriented and a critical means for people at all levels to fulfill their stewardship responsibility.

Block, 1996, p. 135

Funding has always been and continues to be a concern for parks, recreation, and leisure service organizations. One important component of funding parks, recreation, and leisure service programs is establishing a price for a service. As a result, the pricing of leisure services has received considerable attention over the past decade (Emmett, Havitz & McCarville, 1996). This attention includes involvement by public and nonprofit organizations which are being asked to do more with less, as well as commercial organizations that struggle with increased competition for the customer dollar. A central element of these challenges is understanding how to price services (i.e., programs) in a fair and competitive manner. This chapter examines various pricing strategies as well as helps the reader understand the elements of program costs and other factors as they apply to developing pricing strategies for parks, recreation, and leisure service organizations. Figure 9.1 (page 182) presents a nine-step process to help programmers set a price for their programs and services. Inherent in this process is understanding how a servant leadership approach to programming will impact on the process of setting prices for programs and services.

Step One: Understand Trends

We live in a complex world that is constantly changing. In fact, change has become the one "constant" of our lives. This is especially true in the area of financing and pricing leisure services.

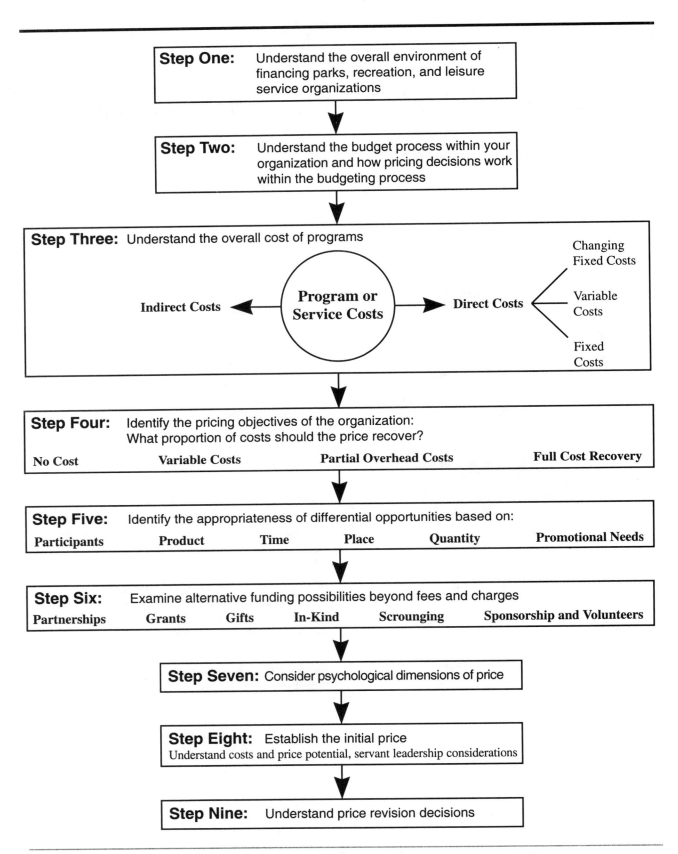

Figure 9.1   The Process of Setting a Price (Adapted from Crompton & Lamb, 1986)

The increased complexity of environments where leisure services are provided has placed greater demands on programmers to be responsive to fiscal operational concerns. Some trends that impact on fiscal and pricing decisions of programs are discussed in the following sections.

Decrease in Tax Support: Doing More with Less

Nationwide parks and recreation directors within public organizations have cited a lack of resources as the biggest detriment to parks and recreation at the local level, affecting everything from the provision of quality programs and services to the acquisition and development of land and facilities (Gladwell & Sellars, 1997). Decreases in funding from tax revenues begun in the late 1970s have combined with cutbacks in federal grant-in-aid programs, such as the Land and Water Conservation Fund, to create an environment where public parks and recreation departments have been forced to do more with less. As a result of this decrease in tax dollars, public parks and recreation organizations have turned to fees and charges as well as a variety of other sources to fund programs. Many of these additional sources of funding are discussed later in this chapter.

Contracting Services

Contracting services has gained popularity in the last twenty years as a method of utilizing the private sector to deliver services traditionally performed by government employees. Between 1981 and 1988, more than 45,700 federal jobs were contracted out to private sector firms at a savings to the U.S. taxpayer of $2.8 million dollars (Kotler & Andreasen, 1996). As a result, public agency decision makers often see contracting as a way to provide better direct-to-citizen services at lower costs.

In the 1990s contracting has continued to be popular as the private sector provides a wide variety of contracted services for public organizations (i.e., concessions and specialty services such as janitorial, maintenance, or security service); however, more recently we have begun to see public and nonprofit organizations also providing contracted services to the private sector. Consider the Jackson County Parks and Recreation Department which offers group picnics to community businesses and community organizations. The department offers complete planning, organization, and implementation of group picnics which are individually tailored to the needs of each group (Crompton, 1987). Important questions related to the use of contracting in today's competitive environment include asking what should be contracted out, and what should be done "in house." We also need to know how to make arrangements to ensure that contracting benefits all parties involved.

Expanded Definition of "Cost"

In January, 1989 *Time* magazine designated its "person of the year" to be the earth. This acknowledgment became a part of the groundswell of public support for addressing many of the environmental issues we all face (Sanction, 1989). This support for the environment has continued into the 1990s as individuals use the "power of the pocketbook" to direct companies to develop products and services that are earth-friendly. One important aspect of this commitment has been an expanded definition of "cost." Environmental costs (as well as other social costs) are now being viewed as part of the overall costs of providing programs.

In the future, stronger considerations will be given to understanding the economic, environmental, and social costs connected to programs and developing programs based on these costs. For example, an organization may identify a demand for a mountain biking program in a sensitive natural area. Economically the program maybe feasible, yet the organization may decide against providing the program due to the environmental costs connected with the program. An additional example may find the economic costs of offering a program (an educational program for teen mothers, for example) to be so high that the program is not feasible. The lack of this program, however, may produce a higher social cost than is acceptable (e.g., increased child neglect, community crimes); therefore, the organization may decide to offer the program anyway. Making these types of decisions is difficult because whereas economic costs are often relatively easy to calculate, it can be more difficult to calculate the social or environmental costs of a specific program. Despite this difficulty, parks, recreation, and leisure service organizations will be increasingly called upon to make these types of sensitive decisions.

Risk Management

In addition to environmental and social costs, programmers should always be prepared for the cost of a potential lawsuit. Highway billboards, yellow pages, and newspaper ads encourage and entice people to file lawsuits to recover costs from injury or property loss. The fear of being sued is an ever-present part of doing business in the United States, and parks, recreation, and leisure service organizations are not exempt from this trend (Hronek & Spengler, 1997). Thus, an increasing cost of providing recreation programs is protecting the organization from lawsuits. This cost is usually passed on to the consumer in some form (e.g., higher taxes, higher fees). Finding creative ways to offer safe programs while maintaining some elements of risk, an important aspect of leisure experiences for many people, will continue to be important.

Increased Competition

Within a market economy, such as in the United States, competition is good for the consumer. This is because increased competition can keep prices low and quality high. In addition, increased competition can also be good for an organization. Competition among parks, recreation, and leisure service organizations can increase the overall size of the total market as well as keep staff focused on meeting the needs of the customer (Kotler & Andreasen, 1996). As competition between parks, recreation, and leisure service organizations increases, programmers need to examine the implications on pricing leisure experiences. This might entail looking for ways to cooperate with competitors (Godbey, 1997). As Godbey notes

> there are more win-win situations than win-lose situations in the provision of leisure services. . . . The numbers of consortiums [and partnerships] which can be developed in leisure services is almost infinite. What is important is imagination, communication, and the will to do it. (p. 218)

Mission Driven and Benefits Oriented

Previously in this text, we articulated the importance of vision and mission for all organizations. This importance can be seen in motivating employees, designing programs, and evaluating the effectiveness of the overall services of an organization. This mission-driven approach has led many organizations to focus on the benefits they provide through programming (Jarvi, 1992). For public organizations

Figure 9.2   Trends Relating to Financing and Pricing

this means the development of a new paradigm where government is perceived as flexible and adaptable, responsive to customers, offers choices of services, and empowers citizens. Over time, governments will need to be viewed less as a provider of services and more as a mechanism for making sure community needs are met (Osborne & Gaebler, 1992). As a result, for many public and nonprofit organizations the budget process will become increasingly customer driven.

Step Two: Understand Budgets

Budgets may be found in all types of organizations as well as at every level of the organization. Budgets may be viewed as

> *a plan for financing and conducting a program or service for a given period of time—usually a year.* (Deppe, 1983, p. 40)

Within this definition there are a wide variety of possible functions of budgets which include some or all of the following:

1. A means of planning and forecasting;
2. A mechanism to establish and communicate program priorities;
3. A method to allocate resources;
4. An opportunity to build organizational consensus;
5. A historical record of past priorities;
6. A means to commit the organization to a course of action;
7. A reference point to monitor and control expenditures of fiscal resources;
8. A monitoring system; and
9. A process to translate the programs to reality (Edginton, Hanson, Edginton & Hudson, 1998; Murtuza, 1993).

As may be seen from this list, budgets are used in different ways. Thus, there is a great deal of variety in how budgets are developed as well as in the types of budgets used. Figure 9.3 (page 186) presents descriptions of budgets. Parks, recreation,

and leisure service organizations use different combinations of budget types and approaches. Due to this variety, discussing the various types of budgets is beyond the scope of this book. For the purpose of this chapter it is enough to recognize the importance of budgeting and to encourage programmers to understand how pricing programs impacts the overall budget process of an organization.

Step Three: Calculate the Overall Costs/Understand the Price Potential

Prior to making any pricing decisions it is important to gather effective cost information related to programs. A cost may be seen *as a monetary measurement of the amount of resources needed to create, implement, and evaluate programs* (see Figure 9.4, page 187). Knowing and understanding all aspects of these costs allows programmers to make informed decisions about the overall mix of programs offered by a specific organization. It also serves as a starting point for making pricing decisions. Before establishing the overall costs of a specific program, an organization must determine which costs are to be included. To accomplish this task one must first understand the two types of costs—indirect and direct. This will help to accurately classify and allocate the two costs to the overall cost of an individual program (Rossman, 1995).

Indirect Costs

Indirect costs are *those costs that an organization incurs regardless of whether or not it operates a specific program* (Rossman, 1995). For example, computers and other office equipment, administrative salaries, organization-wide promotion, and custodial services are indirect costs for all programs and services. The organization will have these expenses whether or not it operates any one specific program or service. Nevertheless, these costs must be absorbed by specific programs. The difficulty arises in determining how to allocate these types of costs to specific programs.

Lump Sum Budgeting

Lump sum budgeting was used primarily before 1900, and was practiced in most cities and states. For each of the departments in a city or state a lump sum of money was appropriated and no attempt was made to analyze how the money was to be spent. This gave departments freedom to use the money in any way they deemed necessary (Deppe, 1983).

Line-Item Budget

The line-item budget is a common form of budgeting in government bodies. The line-item budget appropriates specific dollar amounts to each item of expenditure listed in the budget. It lists these expenses line-by-line as they are paid out. The agency is limited to spending only the dollar amount printed on the line across from each item. Rather than listing the items of expenditure at random, the line-item budget organizes expenditures into specific categories or accounts (Howard & Crompton, 1980).

Program Budget

Program budgets present expenditures in the form of specific programs rather presenting budgets in the line-item form (e.g., salaries, maintenance, supplies), the agency expenditures are clustered into major program areas such as aquatics, golf course, day camp, or aerobics programs.

Performance Budget

Performance budgets link the amount of resources that are consumed in producing a program or service with its outputs. Actual outputs can be measured by a variety of performance indicators including workload measures, efficiency measures, and effectiveness measures. Workload measures refer to the volume of work being completed. Efficiency measures refer to how well resources of an organization are used. Effectiveness measures refer to the extent to which a program achieves its stated goals (Edginton, Hanson, Edginton & Hudson, 1998).

Planning, Programming Budgeting System (PPBS)

The PPBS budget process is a performance-based budget that focuses on the establishment of goals and objectives, long-range planning, and evaluation. Within this budget system programmers are required to identify system-wide goals and objectives and relate program and services to these goals. PPBS also requires programmers to think about costs and scope of programs over a five-year period as well as examine alternative options to determine which programs and services best meet the goals and objectives of the organization (Deppe, 1983).

Zero-Based Budget

Under the zero-based budget system a comprehensive evaluation and justification of all programs is carried out each year. Each department is then asked to build its budget from zero each year, justifying every dollar expenditure rather than relying on past expenditures to guide current appropriations.

Figure 9.3   Types of Budgets

Figure 9.5 presents several types of cost allocation methods available to programmers. In this process, programmers are faced with a number of decisions about how costs can or should be allocated. Rossman (1995) offers three principles to guide these decisions.

1. Implementing cost allocation should be an attempt to assign indirect costs to specific programs in a fair and equitable manner. The goal of cost allocation is to reflect the full cost of creating, implementing, and evaluating a program.

2. The chosen method of cost allocation should accurately reflect how much of an indirect cost a specific program actually uses or consumes. Obviously, this is a difficult task and is sometimes based on an "educated guess." In this instance, organizations have some discretion in allocating indirect costs. It should be remembered, however, that all indirect costs must be accounted for at some point. It pays for the organization to be as accurate as possible in this process.

3. In any cost allocation method there is a trade-off between accuracy and cost. Programmers need to try to achieve as much accuracy as possible within the limits of reasonable effort.

Indirect Costs	+	**Direct Fixed Costs**	+	**Direct Variable Costs**	=	**TOTAL COST**
Adminstrative Salaries		Instructor Salaries		Supplies		
Office Equipment		Facility Rent		Equipment Rental		
Organization Promotion		Program Promotion				

Figure 9.4   Total Cost of a Program

Equal Share of Indirect Expenses

In this method, each functional line or program unit receives an equal share of indirect expenses. Within this method, no effort is made to base the indirect costs to be assumed by a unit on actual costs used by the unit.

Percentage of Budget

In this method, each line unit is assigned a percentage of indirect expenses that equals its percentage of the overall budget of the organization.

Time Budget Study

With this method, the time a service unit (i.e., general administration) spends on each line item or program is studied. The percentage of time is then used to allocate indirect expenses of the service unit to line or program units. The actual allocation of expenses is similar to the percentage of budget method, except that more accurate data are being used to develop the percentage figures for allocating indirect expenses.

Space or Measurement Studies

This method of cost allocation is used in instances where one can determine the appropriate proportion of expenses to allocate to a specific line item or program by measuring the relative proportion of overall costs that are being used by each line item or program. This method is useful in situations where one can accurately determine the proportion of costs to be allocated. Allocating expenses connected to a fertilizing program in parks or maintenance in a building are examples where this method works well.

Figure 9.5   Cost Allocation Methods
(Rossman, 1995)

Direct Costs

Direct costs are *those that may be traced directly back to a specific program.* Whereas indirect costs are incurred regardless of whether or not a program is offered, direct costs are incurred only when a program is implemented. For example, hiring an aerobics instructor to teach a class may be seen as a direct cost of offering an aerobics program. Therefore, this cost may be allocated directly to this program. Direct costs include both fixed and variable costs of a program.

Fixed Costs

For our purposes, *a fixed cost item is assumed to remain constant during a specified time period* (in a program), regardless of the number of participants. An example of a fixed cost would be rental of a facility for the aerobics class mentioned previously. This cost would be directly related to the program. It would also remain constant regardless of the number of participants in the program. Whether one or twenty-five people participate, the rental fee would be the same. It is thus considered a fixed cost. We should bear in mind that fixed costs do have their limits. Consider the room where the aerobics class is being offered; it is small and thereby limits the number of participants to 25. Rossman (1989) described these types of limitations as setting the *relevant range* for the program (i.e., for the aerobics class the relevant range would be 1 to 25 participants). All fixed costs, then, are fixed within this specified relevant range.

Connected to the idea of fixed costs in specified relevant ranges is the idea of *changing fixed costs.* Rossman (1989) identified changing fixed costs as those costs that "change in the same direction, but not proportionately with change in volume or number of participants" (p. 319). These costs change within the relevant range of the program. In other words, they are costs that change after certain numbers of participants are added within the relevant range. For example, within the aerobics class an instructor would be hired to teach the class. This cost would be a direct fixed cost allocated to the program. However, let's say that the instructor would require one assistant to help with the program if the program enrollment exceeded fifteen participants. Therefore, within the relevant range of the program, the instruction cost would change after the fifteenth participant as it would be necessary to add an assistant when the sixteenth person was added to the class. From the sixteenth to the twenty-fifth participant the agency would have the additional cost of an assistant aerobic instructor. In this case, the cost of the assistant's salary would be a changing fixed cost.

Variable Costs

Variable costs are those costs that may be directly attributed to the program and vary proportionately with changes in volume (i.e., number of participants). They include such costs as supplies, equipment, and food. For example, within the aerobic class, each participant who enrolls in the class is given a fitness manual. If the manual costs $4.00, then for each participant who enrolls in the program, an additional cost of $4.00 is added to the program. Some programs have a number of variable costs. For instance, each additional camper who enrolls in a day-camp program may add the following variable costs: a T-shirt, camp bag, lunches and snacks, arts-and-craft supplies, and field trip admissions. Other programs such as our aerobics class have few variable costs.

Step Four: Determine the Proportion of Cost

Once programmers know the cost of delivering a service they can begin to decide what proportion of the cost a price should recover. It is fairly common that all program costs are NOT covered in an established price. For instance, the 50¢ to $1.00 fee commonly charged for swimming pool entry does not cover the real per-person costs of operating the pool. The program is said to be subsidized when some or all of its costs are covered by other means.

Establishing a price is an opportunity for an organization to meet its pricing objectives. Pricing objectives may differ by program or by organization. In many cases, organizations fail to realize that pricing is not only a means of accruing revenue, but also leads to a number of other outcomes. For example, public and nonprofit organizations may charge prices which may lead to:

- Income redistribution (to other programs or services);
- The promotion of efficient use of resources within the organization;
- The promotion of equity (ensuring that those who benefit from a service bear the cost of that service);
- Maximal opportunities for participation by a wide variety of constituents;
- The development of positive constituent attitudes; or
- Produce revenue (Howard & Crompton, 1980). See Figure 9.6.

For public and nonprofit organizations Crompton and Lamb (1987) have identified three categories of services—private, merit, and public. *Private services* primarily benefit those who use the service. *Merit services* are those that have tremendous societal good (i.e., the benefits are meritorious in and of themselves). Lastly, *public services* are those that benefit the local community where the services are offered. Based on which category of service we promote, different decisions about pricing are made (see Figure 9.7, page 190). A continuum of possible positions for cost recovery connected to these categories is discussed below.

No Price Charged

Programs and services are free for participants; alternative sources of funding (e.g., grants, subsidies) are required to offer the program.

Variable Costs

Programs and services are priced to cover the variable costs associated with the program. In this context, variable costs are direct operating and maintenance expenses which can be easily documented and allocated to specific programs. Within this option indirect costs and direct fixed costs are covered by other funding options. Crompton and Lamb

Efficient Use of Financial Resources
Pricing allows organizations to make efficient use of financial resources by assisting organizations in recovering costs and making a profit. Depending on the pricing philosophy of the organization prices can be set to maximize profits or recover all or part of the costs connected with a program.

Fairness or Equitableness
Pricing can be used by public and nonprofit organization to promote equity. For example, municipal governments can charge higher prices for private goods in order to subsidize both merit and public goods. Likewise, state parks can charge nonresidents more than residents to acknowledge the support provided by residents through tax dollars.

Usage Maximization
Prices can be set low to encourage participation in programs. This approach can be used to promote new programs or to expose participants to alternative programs and service provided by the organization.

Commercial Sector Encouragement
For public organizations, pricing can be used to encourage or discourage the commercial sector. By identifying prices based on the competition, public organizations can encourage potential customers to examine all options for programs and services.

Market Disincentivism
Prices can be used to reduce demand for specific programs and services. This approach to pricing can be used to reduce overcrowding or to protect a fragile resource (e.g., environmentally sensitive area).

Figure 9.6   Pricing Objectives

(1986) suggest this position for programs, services, and facilities where both participants and nonusers benefit from a program. For example, facilities and amenities offered by public and nonprofit agencies add to the quality of life of a community. As a result, nonusers receive benefits from knowing that facilities exist, and nonusers should therefore pay the indirect fixed costs required to make these programs, services, and facilities available.

Partial Overhead Costs

Programs and services are priced to cover variable costs plus some proportion of fixed costs. The remaining portion of the fixed costs represents the subsidy given to the particular program by other funding sources. Crompton and Lamb (1986) note that the amount of a subsidy is dependent on the extent to which nonusers benefit from a participant's involvement in a specific program and services. As the benefits to nonusers increase, the proportion of fixed costs met by the subsidy should increase. Benefits to nonusers could include such things as increased property values and decreased crime.

Full Cost Recovery

In this case, programs and services are priced to produce sufficient revenue to cover all the fixed and variable costs associated with the service or program as well as help the organization meet all of its indirect costs. Full cost recovery is an appropriate strategy for those programs and services that benefit only participants and offer no external benefits to the general community. There are some difficulties connected with full cost recovery. As previously noted, it can be difficult to allocate all the indirect costs of an organization. In addition, it is sometimes difficult to identify the number of participants who will be involved in a program; this has implications for the total revenue generated by a program.

For commercial organizations revenue production is the primary objective of pricing, yet pricing may also be used in other ways. For example, some programs might be underpriced in an attempt to familiarize customers with a new program or facility. Some prices might be subsidized (e.g., childcare) to encourage participation in other programs which the commercial organization offers. In addition, there is flexibility in pricing strategies as different strategies may be applied to specific programs to meet the desired objectives of the organization.

Step Five: Examine Differential Pricing

When we look at the appropriateness of differential pricing we are essentially considering charging different prices to different groups for the same service, even though there is no real difference in the costs of providing the service to each of the groups (Crompton & Lamb, 1986). There are many potential reasons for considering differential pricing such

Characteristic:	PUBLIC SERVICE	MERIT SERVICE	PRIVATE SERVICE
Who benefits?	Everyone in the community	Individuals who participate and all others in the community	Individuals who participate
Economic desirability or technical feasibility of pricing	*Not Feasible* Services cannot be priced and/or it is undesirable that they should be priced	*Feasible and Desirable* Services can be priced	*Feasible and Desirable* Services can be priced
Who pays?	*The Community* through the tax system—no user charges	*Individual Users* pay partial costs	*Individual Users* pay full costs

Figure 9.7   Differences Between Services According to Characteristics (Adapted from Crompton & Lamb, 1987)

as reaching disadvantaged participants or to stimulate demand for service during specific times. We offer several potential criteria to be considered when implementing differential pricing. They are: participants, product, place, time, quantity of use, and incentives.

Price Differentials Based on Participants

Participant price differentials are based on the perception that some groups may find it difficult to pay a recommended price while others can pay more. Three groups are frequently identified as less able to pay than most. They are children, senior citizens, and the economically disadvantaged (Crompton & Lamb, 1987). Despite the designation of these three groups, Spigner and Havitz (1992) identified a disparity of how these three groups are served by public parks, recreation, and leisure services. For example, only 17 percent of agencies charging fees offered discounts for unemployed participants as compared with 86 percent each for children and senior citizens. This has led some researchers to conclude that pricing policies in public parks, recreation, and leisure services is based on organizational financial needs rather than the actual financial needs of individual clients (Emmett, Havitz & McCarville, 1996). Commercial recreation organizations offer differential pricing base on age, rather than financial ability.

This can be contradictory in that many seniors have more discretionary income that other social groups.

While not always based on economic facts, participant price differentials are one way to address the concern about equal access to programs and services. Organizations can charge fees based on costs while making special considerations for special needs rather than charge artificially low overall fees. One technique is to offer discount tickets which may be provided to any disadvantaged group. Vouchers are often given to low-income families for program access, and in many organizations, a sliding fee schedule is developed and applied based on income.

Price Differentials Based on Product

Product price differentials are based on offering extra levels of service for additional charges. For example, many fitness organizations have a basic membership fee and, for an additional charge, members may join an executive club. The basic service provided is the same for all—the use of fitness facilities. However, executive club members receive extra benefits such as a complementary laundering of workout clothes, as well as access to a whirlpool, sauna, and a more "plush" locker room. The prices of these additional services are sometimes set to cover the incremental cost of providing them, and other times prices are set to cover the incremental costs and help subsidize other aspects of the program.

Price Differentials Based on Place

Price differentials based on place are often found at spectator events (e.g., concert, play, or sports event) where a higher price is charged for better seats (e.g., close to the performance). Another example of price differentials may be seen in public organizations charging higher prices for nonresidents and nonprofit organizations charging higher prices for nonmembers. In both of these examples if a service or program is being used to capacity, a price differential based on place may serve as an effective method to discourage use by nonresidents or nonmembers. Within nonprofit organizations, if the service or program has spare capacity, price differentials may be used to encourage individuals to become members. In commercial ventures individuals who live at a distance may be offered a price break to lure them to the organization. Many destination resort entities use this tactic—particularly during the slow season.

Price Differentials Based on Time

With differential prices set on a time basis, identical programs are offered at different times and priced differently. Typically, programs and services offered during periods of lower demand are priced lower than programs offered during peak hours. For example, bowling centers commonly offer reduced prices on bowling during weekday afternoons, usually their nonpeak time. Likewise, movie theaters offer matinee prices to encourage participation during "slow" times. Thus, differential prices set on a time basis encourage fuller and more balanced utilization of the program capacity (Crompton & Lamb, 1987).

Price Differentials Based on Quantity

Price differential based on quantity reflects the lower costs of buying in bulk. The season or multi-use discount pass for such programs and facilities as swimming pools, fitness centers, golf courses, zoos, amusement parks, and museums are all examples of

Figure 9.8   Price differentials may be based on people, product, place, time, quantity, and used as incentives.

price differentials based on quantity. The purpose of price differentials based on quantity is twofold. First, it tends to simulate additional demand for a program or service. Second, quantity price differentials reduce the costs of meeting levels of demand by helping organizations forecast the number of participants for specific programs and services.

Price Differentials as Incentives

Price discounts may be used as incentives to persuade people to try a new service or program. Incentives such as coupons (discussed in Chapter Eight) and discounts are effective in encouraging participation (especially for new users/constituents). It is important, however, that programmers emphasize to customers that such discounts are for a limited duration or restricted to a particular set of circumstances, and that after a given time or change in circumstances, the regular price will be charged. Without this caveat, new participants may feel cheated when the price increases.

Step Six: Examine Alternative Funding

As discussed in step one of this chapter there has been a decrease in tax support across the United States and public and nonprofit programmers are being asked to do more with less through self-generated revenue. Crompton and McGregor (1994) have substantiated this trend indicating that self-generated revenue increased from 14 percent of the total local public expenditures on parks and recreation in 1964 to 21.4 percent in 1990–1991. This trend of a decrease in tax support is pushing public and nonprofit organizations to continue to look for alternative funding to offer programs.

Commercial leisure organizations are also searching for alternative funding sources. Innovative funding sources allow commercial organizations to stay competitive by keeping immediate fees and charges low. Although it is impossible to identify all categories of alternative funding sources the following funding strategies are discussed below: gifts and donations, grantwriting, in-kind contributions, partnerships, scrounging, sponsorship, and volunteers.

Figure 9.9   Example of a Discount Coupon

Gifts and Donations

For many public and nonprofit organizations, gifts and other outright donations are definite possibilities for raising funds. Gifts and donations may be made for specific programs or to the overall organization. One strategy being used by an increasing number of public and nonprofit agencies is the development of a gift catalog. A gift catalog is an attractive brochure which outlines a wide variety of needed equipment, facilities, and programs that might be sponsored by individuals or organizations in the community. For each project or item, a price tag is attached so that a potential donor can choose their gift to the organization from an extensive "wish list."

Another option for stimulating gifts and donations is creating a support group for the organization. The Friends of Hartman is an example of an organization that encourages gifts and donations to Hartman Reserve, a public outdoor education center in Cedar Falls, Iowa. The "Friends" encourage donations and gifts of all types including cash, fundraising activities, memorial donations, an endowment, and volunteer efforts. "Friends" groups are common in libraries, zoos, and museums and provide opportunities for individuals to become involved in fundraising and to advocate for the goals of the organization. It is important to note that not all gifts or donations are viewed as assets (nor are they always accepted). For instance, if an organization is given a large tract of land located in another state or a building that requires major upkeep, the gift could prove detrimental rather than beneficial. Likewise, it is important to consider the message being sent by the benefactor as well as the gift. Many parks, recreation, and leisure service organizations would think twice about accepting large gifts from major tobacco companies, for instance, because of the incongruent health messages being sent.

Grantwriting

Private foundations and other philanthropic organizations are potential sources of funding for parks, recreation, and leisure service organizations. In addition to federal, state, and local government grant-in-aid programs, corporations and over 25,000 private foundations provide funds for a variety of programs and services (Hall, 1988). Federal grant-in-aid programs alone distributed over 100 billion dollars in the late 1980s (Hall, 1988). Although it is difficult to identify the specific dollar amounts awarded to parks, recreation, and leisure services, grants within the related fields of health, human services, cultural activities, and the environment have all fared well with grant-in-aid programs. Grants should not be viewed as easy money, however, as there is fierce competition among an increasing number of applicants for both public and private grants. Furthermore, grantwriting is a skill that requires a good deal of time and commitment to do well.

In-Kind Contributions

All organizations can benefit from in-kind contributions. These refer to resources made available to a program by individuals or organizations that require no financial transaction (Edginton, Hanson, Edginton & Hudson, 1998). Although in-kind contributions may include materials and supplies, within parks, recreation, and leisure service organizations, they more than likely involve the sharing of labor, facilities, and/or equipment. Consider the following example of an in-kind contribution to the Make-a-Wish Foundation. This agency arranges to bring to life the wishes of children under the age of 18 who are terminally ill. As an example, upon receiving a request from the Make-a-Wish Foundation, a New England resort donated a condominium and skiing privileges for a terminally ill child who wanted to see a white Christmas in New England (Delaney, 1991). The contribution did not involve any cash; rather it offered in-kind assistance from a profit-oriented organization to a nonprofit organization.

Partnerships

Whereas in-kind contributions are noncash donations, partnerships are a means for two or more organizations to join to further the goals and objectives of all parties. The reason partnerships are established is because each organization recognizes that it cannot achieve its vision with existing resources. By identifying a purpose for a partnership, all parties acknowledge the collaborative benefits, thus allowing partners to focus their efforts on making the partnership a success (McLean, 1993). To be successful, McLean (1993) suggests that organizations must clearly define goals, understand their partner's strengths and weaknesses, and know the real cost of their involvement and anticipated cost of future involvements. Each partner must realize that they each give up some level of control to reap the benefits of the partnership. Furthermore, they should focus on outcomes, recognize that partnerships usually require a long-term commitment, and arrange management to facilitate the process.

An example of a successful partnership that exemplifies many of these characteristics is the

PARTNERS program. PARTNERS is a partnership among Northeast Passage (a nonprofit organization and a Chapter of Disabled Sports USA), the University of New Hampshire's Recreation and Policy Department (RMP), and Granite State Independent Living Foundation (GSILF—a state-wide, consumer-controlled independent living program serving all people with disabilities in New Hampshire). The vision of PARTNERS is to provide "the transition from the rehabilitation facility to the home community through development of functional recreation skills" (Sable & Gravink, 1995, p. 36). Figure 9.10 presents a description and benefits of PARTNERS.

Scrounging

Scrounging involves locating and soliciting miscellaneous items and recycling them for short-term or long-term use (Howard & Crompton, 1980). It requires creativity and inventiveness to see the potential use for discarded materials in specific programs. With enough space dedicated for storage, a wide range of items can be scrounged and stored for later use. As many practitioners in the field can attest, leisure service programmers are legendary scroungers. We turn an old appliance box into a puppet theater, discarded tires become swings, we use old military parachutes for playground games, and so on. One example of a formalized scrounging program is seen in a children's museum in a large midwestern city. The museum collects a variety of "junk" from area businesses and places it in large bins. Items include buttons, pipe cleaners, wire, old posters, and paper, among other things. Children are encouraged to use these materials for creative art projects on-site. In addition, parents can pay a fee and fill a small, medium, or large bag with "junk" for children to use for creative projects at home.

Sponsorship

Sponsorships include in-kind contributions as well as cash and products. The purpose of sponsorships is to provide the parks, recreation, or leisure service organization with additional revenue while providing the sponsor with market recognition and promotional opportunities (Edginton, Hanson, Edginton & Hudson, 1998). The key to successful sponsorships is that both parties benefit from the relationship. An example of a sponsored activity is presented in Figure 8.7 (page 157). In this example several large corporations co-sponsor the Mid Autumn Festival organized by the Urban Council in Hong Kong. In return for their financial contributions, the corporations receive several benefits including name recognition on all promotional materials. In developing sponsors, programmers must be aware of organizational philosophies and community values. For instance, beer companies would not be appropriate sponsors for a teenage softball league, and a local casino may not be appropriate to serve as a sponsor for family night.

Volunteers

Volunteers enable many parks, recreation, and leisure service organizations to stretch their finances and provide programs and services beyond their staffing capability. Drucker (1992) estimated that an estimated 80 million Americans work as volunteers donating an average of five hours per week in nonprofit organizations. This is equivalent to 10 million full-time jobs. If volunteers were paid, their wages (even at minimum rate) would amount to $10 billion, or five percent of the Gross National Product (GNP) of the United States.

Step Seven: Consider the Psychological Dimensions of Price

In addition to considering the social and environmental issues surrounding pricing, we also need to consider the human elements in pricing. Programmers might set logical prices for programs, yet potential customers may not respond positively to these decisions. The reactions of customers to prices are often irrational. They might stem from historical perspectives, similar experiences, self-interest, and emotion—our human elements (Crompton & Lamb, 1986). Hence, in addition to economic principles, establishing a price that will be acceptable to customers requires consideration of the following psychological dimensions of pricing: protection of self-esteem, price-quality relationship, establishing a reference point, consistency of image, and odd pricing (Crompton & Lamb, 1986). We'll discuss these next.

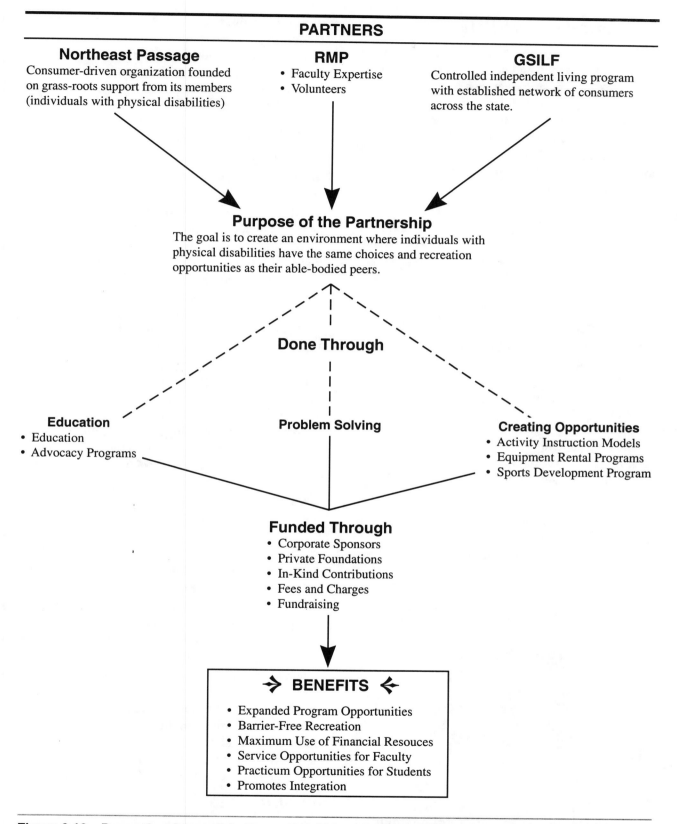

PARTNERS

Northeast Passage
Consumer-driven organization founded on grass-roots support from its members (individuals with physical disabilities)

RMP
• Faculty Expertise
• Volunteers

GSILF
Controlled independent living program with established network of consumers across the state.

Purpose of the Partnership
The goal is to create an environment where individuals with physical disabilities have the same choices and recreation opportunities as their able-bodied peers.

Done Through

Education
• Education
• Advocacy Programs

Problem Solving

Creating Opportunities
• Activity Instruction Models
• Equipment Rental Programs
• Sports Development Program

Funded Through
• Corporate Sponsors
• Private Foundations
• In-Kind Contributions
• Fees and Charges
• Fundraising

BENEFITS
• Expanded Program Opportunities
• Barrier-Free Recreation
• Maximum Use of Financial Resouces
• Service Opportunities for Faculty
• Practicum Opportunities for Students
• Promotes Integration

Figure 9.10   Promoting Accessible Recreation Through Networking, Educating, Research and Service (PARTNERS)

Protection of Self-Esteem

This psychological dimension of pricing applies specifically to public and nonprofit organizations which deal with customer groups in need of subsidized services. We have learned that is important that customers be required to pay some portion of the costs of a program or service. Through such payments (no matter how small) customers make a commitment to the program and the stigma of receiving a handout is minimized or eliminated.

Price-Quality Relationship

As most of us know from personal experience, the price of a program or service is often perceived as a reflection of the degree of quality of that program or service. Marketing studies have shown that consumers' perceptions of product quality vary directly with price (Crompton & Lamb, 1986). This means that to some degree, if program fees are high, the program is perceived to be high quality; likewise, if the program fees are low, the program may be perceived as being lower quality. As a result, a high-quality program may not be well-attended if the price of the program is perceived as low by potential customers.

Price also serves as a cue to targeted client groups that a service or program is designated for them. If a service targeted to a middle-income group is priced too low, it is possible the group may not recognize it as being intended for them. Greater involvement in some programs may follow from increasing the price rather than from reducing it. Calculating this balance point can sometimes be a bit of trial and error.

Establishing a Reference Point

Establishing a reference point refers to setting an initial price for a program or service. This first price establishes in a person's mind the "fair" price for the service. In this way it becomes the reference point against which future price changes are compared (Crompton & Lamb, 1986). Pricing experts believe that such reference points act as internal standards against which program characteristics and price information are compared (McCarville, 1996). In the mind of the consumer, this impacts on the price-quality relationship. For instance, if the initial price for a program or service is $50, that becomes THE price for that type of program. If the price is later cut (in a promotional effort), people feel like the are getting a good deal. If the price goes up, people may feel "ripped off." So, it appears that programmers have much more flexibility in pricing an initial service or program which has no reference point. Once the reference point has been set, programmers must be aware of the pricing history of programs and services as well as the "going rate" of providing the service (i.e., consistency of image).

Consistency of Image

Similar to the price-quality connection, organizations create an image in the eyes of consumers and use pricing to reflect this image. For example, state park campgrounds offer low-priced family vacation opportunities, whereas Hilton Family Resorts offer high-priced luxury family vacations. If state parks offered a product at a high price, it would be inconsistent with what customers expect. Price must be consistent with customers' perception of an organization and its offerings. Similarly, a very low price for a resort vacation would probably leave consumers wondering what types of problems exist, or what the "fine print" contains.

Odd Pricing

This is a psychological pricing strategy that has long been used in the commercial sector. A program or

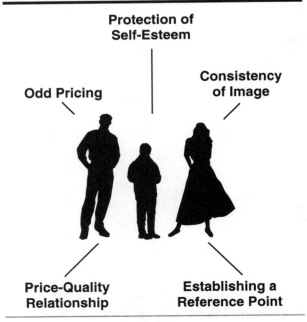

Figure 9.11   Psychological Dimensions

service may be said to carry an odd price if it costs 49¢ rather than 50¢, $9.95 instead of $10.00, or $19.96 rather than $20.00. Odd prices are thought to create the illusion of lower prices. While there is little concrete evidence to support this contention (Crompton & Lamb, 1986) it is used frequently.

Step Eight: Establish the Initial Price

The eighth step of the pricing process is to determine an actual price for the program or service. In the steps prior to this one, programmers were asked to understand and gather a wide range of information relevant to pricing. Thus, the first phase of the initial price setting step is to revisit step three of the pricing process by understanding the overall cost of the program. In addition, this phase also examines the price potential of programs based on the "going rate" charged by competitors or current demand. The second phase of setting the initial price involves considering how the cost could change as a result of the information presented in steps five, six, and seven. The last phase of determining the price is understanding how a servant leadership approach to programming might impact on pricing decisions.

Understanding Costs and the Price Potential of Programs

Establishing the initial price is based on cost-based pricing (discussed in step three) which identifies all costs of a program and then sets a price based on these costs. Cost-based pricing for individual programs is often presented using break-even analysis. This means that prices are determined by matching all costs. In this system, a program neither makes nor loses money. Alternatives to cost-based pricing include competition-based pricing and demand-based pricing.

Cost-Based Pricing: Using Break-Even Analysis

Cost-based pricing is based on all costs associated with offering a program. As discussed in step three of the pricing process this includes allocation of indirect costs, fixed costs, changing fixed costs, and variable costs. Cost-based analysis will provide valuable information to help establish prices. This information is often presented in two ways: by tabling the data or by placing them on a graph (Rossman, 1989). This allows programmers to visually understand the break-even point of their programs. To illustrate these techniques, the aerobics program cited

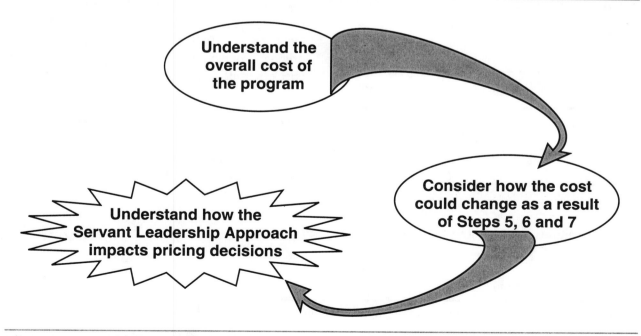

Figure 9.12   Establishing the initial price occurs in three phases.

in step three will be developed further. Table 9.1 presents the beginning set of facts regarding this program.

The information in Table 9.1 (costs of program) may be placed in a cost volume profit table. This is a table that illustrates the amount of cost in relation to the number of people in the program. Table 9.2 shows various costs based on different participation levels for an aerobics class. You'll remember that various participation levels reflected in the table represent the relevant range of the program. At the bottom end of the spectrum are eight participants

since this organization has a policy not to operate a program with fewer than eight participants. The top end of the range is 25 participants, which is the highest number of people the room will accommodate. The cost per participant, which is the final row in Table 9.2, is also known as the break-even point. As each volume is specified, the cost per participant represents the price that needs to be charged for the organization to break-even and cover all costs involved in the program.

The information presented in Table 9.2 can also be presented in a graph. This format allows programmers to include a revenue line which represents various levels of revenue as compared to the costs presented in the cost volume profit table. Plotting the revenue line also illustrates the potential loss or profit of a program at a specific price level. In Figure 9.13 using a price of $175 yields a break-even point between 13 and 14 participants.

Cost-based pricing allows programmers to isolate specific activities and to match their costs with the revenues they generate. As stated in step three of the pricing process, understanding all aspects of costs is an important starting point for actually identifying the price of a program or service.

Competition-Based Pricing

Unlike cost-based pricing, competition-based pricing has no relation to the actual cost of a program or service. Rather, it is based on the prices charged by competitors for similar programs and services (Montgomery, 1988). To establish competition-based pricing, programmers need to identify competitors, check their prices, and compare this information to

Table 9.1   Costs of an Aerobics Program

Cost Items Description	Total Costs
Indirect Costs	
Allocated %: Administrative Overhead	$200.00
Direct Fixed Costs	
Facility rent: 3x a week for 12 weeks	
Room rental: $30/hour at local fitness club ($30 x 36)	$1,080.00
Instructor salary: $25/class ($25 x 36)	900.00
Changing Fixed Costs	
Class aide for $7/class	
From the 16th–25th participant ($7 x 36)	$252.00
TOTAL FIXED COSTS	**$2,732.00**
Variable Costs	
Fitness manual	$4.00
T-shirt	5.00
TOTAL VARIABLE COST/PERSON	**$9.00**

Table 9.2 Cost Volume Profit Table for Aerobics Example

Cost Items	Number of Participants						
	8	10	12	15	16	20	25
Indirect Costs	200	200	200	200	200	200	200
Direct Fixed Costs	1,980	1,980	1,980	1,980	1,980	1,980	1,980
Changing Fixed Costs	0	0	0	0	252	252	252
Variable Costs ($9/person)	72	90	108	135	144	180	225
TOTAL COSTS	**2,252**	**2,270**	**2,288**	**2,315**	**2,576**	**2,612**	**2,657**
Cost per participant	*$281.50*	*$227.00*	*$190.66*	*$154.33*	*$161.00*	*$121.65*	*$106.28*

their own program or services. Taking this information into consideration, the price established for a program may be raised or lowered from the "prevailing market price" (i.e., what competitors are charging) based on a number of different variables. These variables include the unique characteristics of one's own program, the relative strengths or weaknesses of competitors, location, and the possible reaction of competitors to the price set by the programmer (Hanna & Dodge, 1995). This approach is popular with many organizations because prices for programs can be determined relatively easily and quickly. As you can see, whereas cost-based pricing works by identifying costs and then setting a price, competition-based pricing is a reverse approach where the price is set and the organization works backward to see if it can cover costs (Hanna & Dodge, 1995).

Demand-Based Pricing

A third method used to establish an initial price for a program or service is demand-based pricing. This method is based on setting a price with respect to buyers' expectations and needs (Montgomery, 1988). Under this approach the programmer looks beyond the costs connected to producing a program and instead considers the intensity of demand for the program or service. Thus, to make pricing decisions the programmer needs to have some idea of the possible demand for specific programs at various prices. This demand schedule then becomes the basis for determining which level of pricing would be most profitable for the organization (Hanna & Dodge, 1995).

Moving beyond simple cost-based pricing is important for parks, recreation, and leisure service organizations. By understanding what other organizations are charging for similar programs and services, programmers can develop a range of prices that are likely to be acceptable to users for a particular program or service. Determining this range

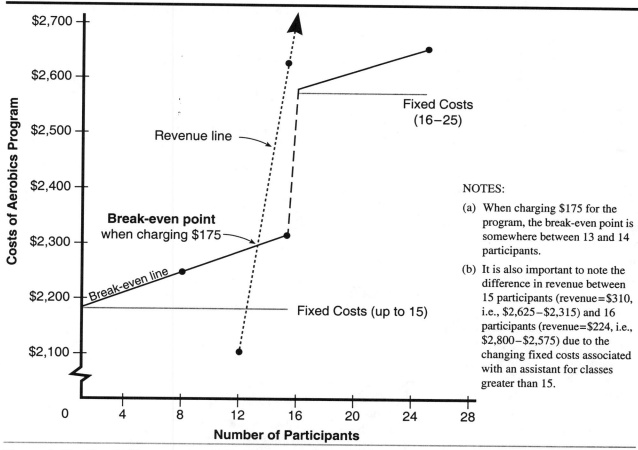

Figure 9.13 Break-Even Analysis Graph for Aerobics Example

requires that an organization addresses what potential customer groups are willing, or able, to pay for a particular service.

In addition to understanding the going rate of a program, programmers should also examine the expectations and needs of customers in terms of price. In some instances a price based on costs will be out of the price range of most constituents. For parks, recreation, and leisure service organizations this might mean not offering the program or looking for alternative funding sources to subsidize it. The point to be made here is that at times the going rate may not cover costs; especially for public and non-profit organizations. As a result, step four of the pricing process (i.e., determining the proportion of cost that the price should cover) becomes extremely important for programmers in that it gives them a strategy to build a price for their programs and services. Comparing this strategy to the actual cost of the program or service gives the programmer direction as to how to proceed in step five, six and seven of the pricing process.

For example, if the price of a six-week aerobics session is set at $120 the break-even point of providing the session is between 20 and 21 participants. However, an analysis of prices charged by competitors reveals an average cost of $80.00 for a similar series of classes. Further analysis of the demand for the program (perhaps through a needs assessment) indicates that potential customers are not willing to pay more than $80.00 to participate in this program. With this information programmers can begin to make decisions related to pricing, decide not to offer the program, or look for alternative funding sources.

These decisions may be influenced by the service orientation of the organization (e.g., public, nonprofit, commercial). A commercial organization may decide not to offer the program at all, or to offer it at a loss because it serves as a way to introduce new customers to their organization where they will spend their money on other programs, services, and goods. Public or nonprofit organizations may examine the program and feel it is a merit good (i.e., has value both to an individual and to society) and, as a result, decide to offer the program and set a price based on partial overhead recovery while looking for alternative funding sources. Public or nonprofit organizations may also decide to differentiate the price, set the price for the program at $80.00 (the

going rate), offer discounts for certain groups, and identify other funding sources.

Understanding how costs contribute to the break-even point of a program or service can also provide focus in lowering costs, thereby lowering prices. For instance, the bulk of the cost to offer this program lies in facility rental. As a result, we might search for a less expensive alternative location in which to hold the classes. Another venue might offer a better price or more space so we can add more participants. Furthermore, there might be a potential to share facilities with another organization or, the program might be offered at a different time when the price for renting the facility is reduced.

A Servant Leadership Approach to Pricing

A servant leadership approach to pricing is crucial if we are committed to empowering staff and customers in the creation, implementation, and evaluation of programs and services. It is easy to give lip service to a philosophy, but through the pricing process we have an opportunity to "put our money where our mouth is"—this can be a difficult task. One metaphor that we feel can help programmers understand a servant leadership approach to pricing is the image of a steward—someone who practices stewardship and cares for others and the environment.

In the opening chapter of this book we identified stewardship as holding something in trust for another. Historically, the concept of stewardship has often been thought about in terms of financial management; yet today we see the concept of stewardship being applied on a much larger scale. This larger vision of stewardship means that we consider all stockholders including future generations, and promote ways for participants to govern themselves, creating

> a strong sense of ownership and responsibility for outcomes at the bottom of the organization. It means giving control to customers and creating self-reliance on the part of all who are touched by the institution. (Block, 1996, p. 5)

In terms of pricing, this means programmers must hold themselves responsible for having a broad definition of costs, making sure we think through the impact of our programs not only on our finances, but also on the environment and larger society. In addition, programmers should involve customers as much as possible in pricing decisions through research, advisory boards, and customer advocate groups. Pricing does not have to be an adversarial process. Educating customers (especially in public and nonprofit organizations) about the costs, philosophy, and strategies in the pricing process can help customers become partners in very meaningful ways.

An excellent example of an organization taking a servant leadership approach to pricing is described by Emmett, Havitz and McCarville (1996). These authors document the pricing policies of a nonprofit recreation center operating in a large Canadian city. After a major capital campaign to renovate their facility, programmers realized that they would have to charge fees in order to offer and maintain their programs. They also wanted to ensure that the new fees and charges would not preclude anyone from using the facility. With this in mind, programmers developed a unique approach to customer subsidies for those who could not afford to pay membership fees. This approach enabled potential participants to personally negotiate with staff a mutually acceptable price level for the basic membership with staff. Consequently, no one is excluded from programs and services for financial reasons and everyone receives identical services.

What is unique about this process is how staff empower potential customers to make decisions related to the price they are able to pay. When staff meet with potential customers they may negotiate in terms of any number of relevant issues (e.g., family income, housing costs, living costs) that may influence their ability to pay. No proof of need is required, and honest disclosure is assumed by all applicants. The process is focused on specific needs rather than policies, criteria, and standards.

At this time the assisted member policy has had no negative effect on the Center's total revenues. In fact, revenues have risen consistently from 1989 to 1995. Most importantly, the policy is working as reflected in the following quote.

> The Center generously grants me membership assistance. You can't understand how important this is to me. I feel as though I can contribute to my community in a positive way even though I lie well below the poverty level and cannot always contribute

financially. The Center confirms my importance as a member of this community. . . by supporting me. I feel confident that one day I will be helping others in my position today. I intend on being a member for the rest of my life. Thank you." (Emmett, Havitz & McCarville, 1996, p. 74)

Step Nine: Understand Price Revision Decisions

Once a price has been established there is still a need to periodically review price and examine the need for revisions. In most cases, "revised" is synonymous with "increased;" thus, it is important to develop a systematic process for making price revisions. Figure 9.14 (page 202) provides an example of such a process used by a city parks and recreation department. The one additional consideration that an organization might consider in the price revision process would be to solicit participant input about potential price changes. This input helps to prepare constituents for a price change and can give programmers insights into various psychological considerations in price revision decisions. Crompton and Lamb (1986) identified four different psychological elements we should consider: tolerance zone, customer adjustment period, changing the perceived value of a service, and anchor pricing.

Tolerance Zone

The tolerance zone refers to the degree in which small price increases will not encounter client resistance and adversely impact involvement with the program or service. This concept suggests that a series of small incremental increases in price over a period of time are less likely to meet customer resistance than will a one-time major increase.

Customer Adjustment Period

When it is necessary to raise prices beyond the tolerance zone, organizations may encounter customer resistance. This often manifests itself in a decreased demand for the program. After an initial period, however, constituent groups will usually adjust, accept the new price, and return to the program or service.

Fee Review—Recreation Programs

Program: _____

Date: _____

1. Is this a public, merit service, or private service? _____

2. What are the total costs of the program? _____

3. What is the anticipated revenue at current prices? _____

4. Does the fee cover direct operating costs? ❏ Yes ❏ No

5. How much, if any, of the direct support costs are covered? _____

6. To what extent is the program tax supported? _____

7. Are fees, in general, comparable to those of other similar service providers in the area? ❏ Yes ❏ No

   Exceptions:

   _____   _____

   _____   _____

   _____   _____

   Comments:

   _____

   _____

   _____

8. Can we, or should we, charge "what the market will bear?" ❏ Can ❏ Should ❏ Are Now

   Why? _____

9. How does the fee of one program compare to the fee of like programs, i.e., adult ballet vs. adult tap?

   _____

   _____

   _____

   _____

Figure 9.14   Price Revision Analysis Form

Changing the Perceived Value of the Service

One means to reduce customer resistance when prices are raised beyond the tolerance zone is to (at the same time) raise customer's perceived quality of the program or service. If customers think that the quality of the program is commensurate with the new price being charged, they are less likely to react adversely to the price increase.

Anchor Pricing

Anchor pricing refers to identifying a price that exists between two already established prices—a high and low price (the anchors). Any time we charge a new price for a service or program we should assess the new price to see if it falls between the lowest and highest prices charged for other programs. Research has indicated that the lowest and highest prices charged for other programs are likely to be the most noticeable to constituents. Thus, these prices serve to *anchor* potential customers' judgments about the quality of services offered by the organization. Keeping prices within these two anchor points is less likely to arouse customer resistance than if prices are outside of these anchors.

Summary

Pricing has emerged as a important administrative tool for programmers in parks, recreation, and leisure services. As may be seen from this chapter the process of setting a price is complex, encompassing a variety of factors. To assist programmers in this process we have provided a nine-step process to determining a price for a program or service. This process includes understanding the overall environment of financing parks, recreation, and leisure service organizations, understanding the budget process, understanding the overall cost of programs, identifying the pricing objectives of the organization, examining the appropriateness of differential opportunities, considering the psychological dimensions of price, setting the initial price, and understanding price revision decisions.

Following this process does not give programmers a simple formula by which a price can be established. This process does, however, encourage programmers to consider the myriad of complex variables that must be addressed in establishing specific prices for programs and services. Lastly, we emphasized the need to maintain a servant leadership perspective when making pricing decisions.

References

Block, P. (1996). *Stewardship: Choosing service over self-interest.* San Francisco, CA: Berrett-Koehler.

Crompton, J. (1987). *Doing more with less in parks and recreation services.* State College, PA: Venture Publishing, Inc.

Crompton, J. and Lamb, C. (1987). Establishing a price for government services. In P. Kotler, O. Ferell and C. Lamb (Eds.), *Strategic marketing for nonprofit organizations: Cases and readings.* Englewood Cliffs, NJ: Prentice Hall.

Crompton, J. and Lamb, C. (1986). *Marketing government and social services.* New York, NY: John Wiley & Sons.

Crompton, J. and McGregor, B. (1994). Trends in financing and staffing local government park and recreation services 1964/65–1990/91. *Journal of Park and Recreation Administration, 12*(3), 19–37.

Delaney, P. (1991, July). Give a little...Receive a lot! *Resort and Commercial Recreation Association, 6.*

Deppe, T. (1983). *Management and strategies in financing parks and recreation.* New York, NY: John Wiley & Sons.

Drucker, P. (1992). *Managing for the future: The 1990s and beyond.* New York, NY: Truman Talley Books/Dutton.

Edginton, C., Hanson, C., Edginton, S. and Hudson, S. (1998). *Leisure programming: A service centered and benefits approach.* Boston, MA: McGraw-Hill.

Emmett, J., Havitz, M. and McCarville, R. (1996). A price subsidy policy for socioeconomically disadvantaged recreation participants. *Journal of Park and Recreation Administration, 14*(1), 63–80.

Gladwell, N. and Sellers, J. (1997, October). One way to pay for the places we play. *American City & County, 112,* 59–68.

Godbey, G. (1997). *Leisure and leisure services in the 21st century.* State College, PA: Venture Publishing, Inc.

Hall, M. (1988). *Getting funded: A complete guide to proposal writing, 3rd ed.* Portland, OR: Portland State University.

Hanna, N. and Dodge, H. (1995). *Pricing: Policies and procedures.* New York, NY: New York University Press.

Howard, D. and Crompton, J. (1980). *Financing, managing, and marketing recreation and park resources.* Dubuque, IA: Wm. C. Brown.

Hronek, B.R. and Spengler, J.O. (1997). *Legal liability.* Champaign, IL: Sagamore Publishing.

Jarvi, C.K. (1992). Leadership to meet the demands of today's changing needs. Bob Crawford Lecture Series at NRPA Conference, Cincinnati, Ohio, October 6.

Kotler, P. and Andreasen, A. (1996). *Strategic marketing for nonprofit organizations, 5th ed.* Englewood Cliffs, NJ: Prentice Hall.

McCarville, R. (1996). The importance of price last paid in developing price expectations for a public leisure service. *Journal of Park and Recreation Administration, 14*(4), 52–64.

McLean, D. (1993). Partnering: Extending resources and building networks. *Parks and Recreation, 28*(12), 48–51.

Montgomery, S. (1988). *Profitable pricing strategies.* New York, NY: McGraw-Hill.

Murtuza, A. (1993). Budgeting and the managerial process. In R. Rachlin and H. Sweeny (Eds.), *Handbook of budgeting.* New York, NY: John Wiley & Sons.

Osborne, D. and Gaebler, T. (1992). *Reinventing government.* New York, NY: Addison-Wesley.

Rossman, R. (1995) *Recreation programming: Designing leisure experiences, 2nd ed.* Champaign, IL: Sagamore Publishing.

Rossman, R. (1989). *Recreation programming: Designing leisure experiences.* Champaign, IL: Sagamore Publishing.

Sable, J. and Gravink, J. (1995). Partners: Promoting accessible recreation. *Parks & Recreation 30*(5), 34–40.

Sanction, T. A. (1989). Planet of the year. *Time, 133*(1), 26–30.

Spigner, C. and Havitz, M. (1992). Access to recreation activities by the unemployed: Implications for public health. *Journal of Recreation and Leisure, 12*(1), 106–123.

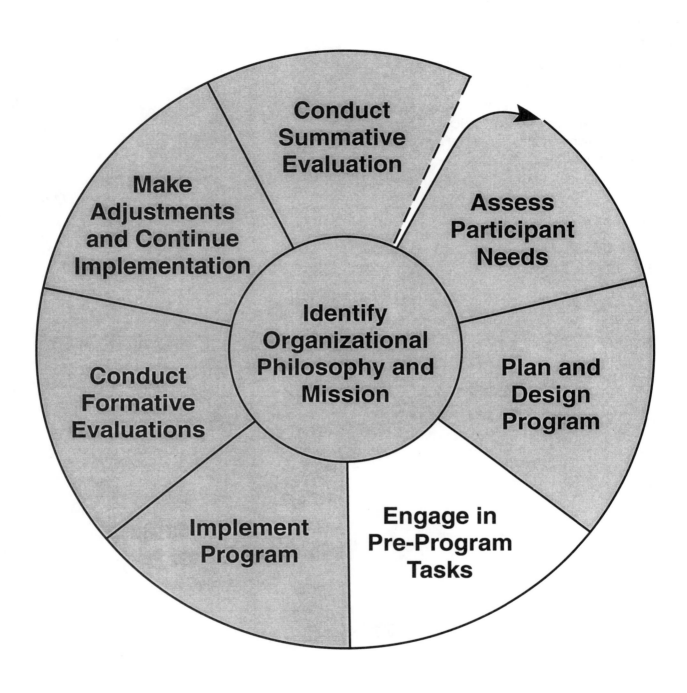

Chapter Ten

Facilitating the Participants' Pre-Program Experience

I long to accomplish a great and noble task, but it is my chief duty to accomplish small tasks as if they were great and noble.

Helen Keller

Albrecht (1992) identifies three components to providing quality services: a service strategy, customer-oriented front-line staff, and customer friendly systems (see Figure 10.1, page 208). The service strategy refers to understanding the vision and mission of an organization which we discussed in Chapter Four. Front-line staff refers to the importance of the customer-leader interaction which we will discuss in the next chapter. This chapter examines the area of customer friendly systems, especially during the customer's pre-program experience. The idea of a customer friendly system refers to a delivery system that is convenient, accessible, and pleasant for the customer. This may not always result in what might be easiest for the organization, however (O'Sullivan, 1991).

For most customers, involvement with an organization begins long before they participate in an actual program. In fact, the total customer experience may be thought of in terms of several distinct phases. Most often these phases or stages are labeled anticipation, travel to the site, participation in on-site experiences, travel back home, and recollection (Clawson & Knetsch, 1966). Within each of these phases an organization has the opportunity to enhance the customer experience. In this chapter emphasis will also be placed on ways to assist an organization in meeting its goals during each of the phases of the customer experiences. Specific emphasis is placed on creating and implementing systems that help customers anticipate and prepare to participate in leisure service programs.

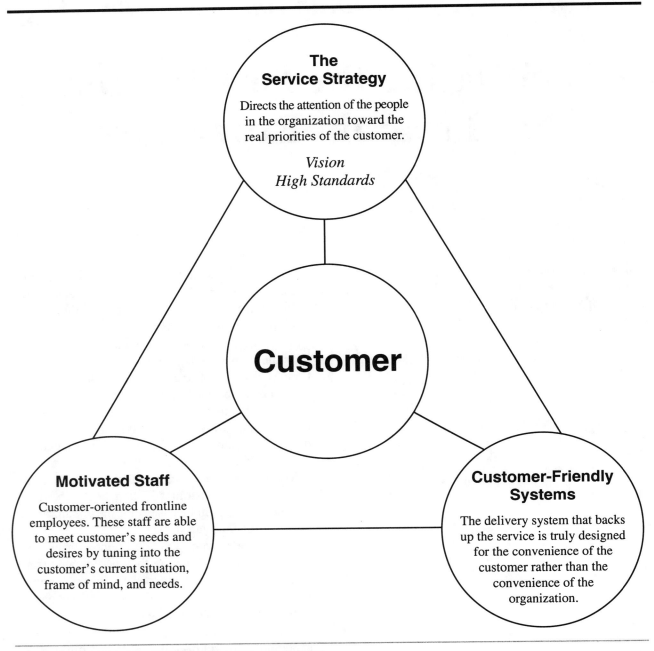

Figure 10.1   The Service Triangle (Albrecht, 1992)

Planning

Initially in the planning stage, potential customers must make decisions concerning their involvement. These questions usually start on a macro level asking many broad-based questions and gradually become more focused (see Figure 10.2). The consumer's excitement in making these decisions is usually high during the planning stage. At this point in the process, organizations should be providing potential customers with the information they need to make informed decisions. As mentioned in Chapter Eight, the process of educating potential customers is one of the goals of promotion. Additional considerations in facilitating the planning process for customers include serving as a general resource for customers and creating customer friendly registration procedures.

Promotional Materials

In managing the customer's pre-program experience programmers must identify how promotional materials can be used as well as how they will be distributed. Within a servant leadership perspective, we believe promotional materials should give potential customers the information they need to make informed decisions. In this regard it is important for promotional materials to *accurately* describe programs, services, and potential benefits. A critical element of facilitating the customer's pre-program experience is managing expectations. Promotional materials are the first step in this process and must set the stage for open and honest exchange between customers and program staff.

Serving as a General Resource for Customers

A servant leadership approach to programming goes beyond promoting an individual organization. Being responsive to customer demands means that we empower them to meet their own needs. This may mean recommending to customers that they try a different program which would better meet their needs even if the program is offered by a different organization. In the short run this customer resource approach may result in an occasional loss of a customer; however, in the long run the organization will develop a reputation based on integrity and customer responsiveness which will benefit both the customer and the organization.

Customer Friendly Registration Procedures

Organizations exist to meet the needs of customers, and to be successful at this organizations must become customer-oriented. Nowhere is the need to become customer-oriented more evident than in the registration process. Historically, registration procedures have been created to help organizations manage programs and services by developing a record of customers who want to, and are qualified to, participate in a specific program or service. The need for registration procedures is well-documented (see Figure 10.3, page 210). Customers generally recognize these requirements and are willing to go through the registration process. Yet, in many cases, registration procedures have been created for the ease of the organization rather than the customer. In today's competitive environment where the emphasis is on providing quality services, organizations must rethink the registration process with the needs and interests of the customer in mind. Today, customers want a registration process that is accurate, convenient, accessible, easy to understand, and works for them.

Desire
Identifies a need → **What desire do I want to satisfy?**

Generic
Selects a general activity → **How do I want to satisfy this desire?**

Service Form
Identifies a specific form of activity → **What specific activity can I do?**

Enterprise
Selects a specific delivery program → **What program should I choose?**

Figure 10.2   Planning Level Questions

Registration is necessary under the following conditions:

- When a fee needs to be collected.
- When the number of spaces in a program is limited.
- When the program has high variable costs and it is important for programmers to make informed decisions about supplies and equipment.
- When the program has qualifying criteria for admission. In outdoor programs, for example, certain qualifications may need to be demonstrated before an individual can participate in a program.

Figure 10.3   Need for Registration Procedures
(Adapted from Rossman, 1995)

Registration Methods

There are several basic registration methods used by parks, recreation, and leisure service organizations. These include registering at a central location, at a program location (the site where the program is being held), by mail, by telephone, via fax, over the Internet (World Wide Web), and through a combination of methods (Edginton, Hanson, Edginton & Hudson, 1998; Rossman, 1995). Each of these methods has advantages and disadvantages; it is up to the programmer to develop the method(s) that best serve the customer for various types of programs.

Central Location Method. In the central location method, participants registering for a program or service offered by an organization must go to one central location such as the organization's headquarters, a central facility, or a municipal hall. All the materials and information needed to register are found at this location. Oftentimes with this approach registration activities are offered only on specific dates and times. The advantages of this approach include a quick registration process, ease of advertisement and supervision of registration, the centralization of fee collections, and increased customer service due to a centralized flow of information. Disadvantages of the central location method are that programmers lose the opportunity to excite customers, customers are unable to become familiar

with the setting by seeing the program location, and due to conflicts, customers may be unable to visit the central location. In addition, the volume of customers may be high which can cause long lines and increase the chance of error in the registration process.

Program Location Method. In the program location method, registration takes place at the program site, such as a recreation center, swimming pool, golf course, or camp. This approach helps familiarize customers with the program site, and there is a greater probability that customers will have an opportunity to interact with program staff. As Rossman (1995) notes, these advantages are important features, particularly when registering young children. Youngsters are able to become comfortable with the location and staff during registration, and before returning to the site without their parents. Disadvantages of this method include extra time and effort, and the feeling of being given the "run around" if a customer is registering for several programs at different locations. In addition, this method makes supervision and cash control more difficult than the central location method.

Mail-In Method. As we might imagine, the mail-in method requires customers to complete a registration form and mail it to a centralized processing location. This is a very common registration process and is typical of public, private nonprofit, and commercial leisure service providers. Advantages of this method include that it is easy and time efficient for customers, it allows for flexibility of staff in processing the applications, and it centralizes the cash control element of registration. The major disadvantage of this method is it does not allow for any direct interaction between customers and staff, and as a result customers may experience a delay in knowing if they are registered for a specific program. Customers also lose the opportunity to see facilities prior to the start of the program.

Telephone Method. Telephone calls for registration purposes are usually directed to a central location which offers the advantages of centralized cash control, ease of supervision, and efficiency for customers. Disadvantages include lack of face-to-face interaction between staff and customers and the need for additional procedures to pay for programs and services especially when payment needs to be received before registration can be confirmed. In addition, there is no opportunity for customers to see the program location. Programmers must also realize that registering by phone can be very frustrating unless organizations have a method of managing a potentially high volume of calls and implementing a means of queuing phone calls as they are received.

Fax-In Method. This approach enables customers to register via facsimile and offers many of the same advantages and disadvantages of telephone registration. Added disadvantages of this method are the lack of interaction between customers and staff, and the limited availability of fax machines. An

additional advantage of this method, however, is that customers can register for programs 24 hours a day.

Internet (World Wide Web) Method. With the explosion of the World Wide Web in recent years many parks, recreation, and leisure service organizations are developing Web sites. These sites often include registration information and the forms needed to register for various programs. Figure 10.4 presents a reservation request form (found on the Internet) used as a first step in the registration

---

Registration Form

Parent/Guardian Name:_____

Address:_____

Home Phone:_____ Office Phone:_____ Total Fee Paid:$_____

Emergency Contact & Phone No. _____

Medical Insurance Co._____ Group Number:_____

Youth Registration

Participant's Name	Shirt Size	D.O.B.	Age	Grade	Program	Fee	Non-Res Fee

Adult Registration

Participant's Name	Program	Fee	Non-Res Fee

Are there any medical problems or medications that we should be aware of ? Yes _____ No _____

If so, please state _____

Adult-Parent/Guardian - Participant Release Waiver (to be signed on site)

The participant signed below knowing fully that the Kennebunk Parks and Recreation Department provides the program, activity and/or special event and all aspects associated with these being - Facility(s), Instructor(s), Equipment, and Supervision hereby: 1. Agree to furnish my own insurance in case of injury; 2. Assume all risks and responsibilities of possible injury involved with participating in this program, activity, and/or special event; 3. Testify that I am in sound health and capable of participating in the registered program; 4. I further agree to indemnify and hold harmless the Town of Kennebunk department or employees, to include volunteers, from liability resulting from my participation in this program, activity and/or special event.

I also fully understand that there is a charge if I am late picking up my child from any Parks and Recreation program. The fees are: 10-15 min. $5 15-25 min. $10 25-35 min. $15 35-45 min. $20 more than 45 min. $25 (child will be at the Recreation Dept. Office).

_____
Signature of Participant (if under 18 must be signed by parent/guardian)

Figure 10.4   Example of a Reservation Request Form Found on the Internet at the Kennebunk Parks and Recreation Department Web Site

process for a commercial outfitters organization. The major advantage of this method is flexibility for both the customer and the organization. People can peruse programs and register for them from the comfort of their home, it is inexpensive for both constituents and leisure service organizations, and materials can be updated quickly and easily.

Many of the disadvantages of the Internet method resemble those of registering by fax (e.g., no face-to-face interaction with staff, inability to see the program site, need for additional payment procedures). Additional disadvantages of the Internet are the potential lack of security involved in sending personal information over the Internet (e.g., credit card information, medical information), and the lack of computer access of many potential customers. As a result of these disadvantages, many organizations will likely view the Internet as a valuable component of their overall registration and promotional efforts, but will continue to rely on other methods of registration as alternatives.

Combination of Methods. The majority of parks, recreation, and leisure service organizations use a variety of registration methods to improve convenience and accessibility for customers. This fits well with a servant leadership approach to delivering programs as programmers strive to be open to the needs of customers and seek a variety of ways to meet these needs. For example, on the homepage of Ames (Iowa) Parks and Recreation Department the following registration methods are provided: mail in, drop-off, walk-in, and fax (see Figure 10.5).

Providing a variety of registration methods can be challenging for organizations and requires an organization to be well-organized and to think through the registration process. One way of doing this is through the use of computers. The increasing use of computers in the registration process is assisting organizations in coordinating various registration methods and information collection. Computers allow programmers in multiple locations to link to a centralized database, thus increasing the ability to manage the overall registration process. Various software packages are now available which maintain up-to-date program lists, provide programmers with demographic profiles of participants, manage financial information, and provide other information as programmed.

Issues Related to Registration

Regardless of the registration method(s) chosen by an organization, there are a number of issues or concerns that programmers must address to ensure the overall quality of programs and services. In examining the issue of quality, Parasuraman, Zeithaml and Berry (1985) identified five dimensions of quality across a number of different services. Listed in order of importance the five dimensions are reliability, responsiveness, assurance, empathy, and tangibles. McKay and Crompton (1988, 1990) examined these same dimensions of quality in public recreation facilities and programs and found similar results.

Reliability refers to the ability to perform the promised service consistently and accurately. *Responsiveness* is the willingness to help customers and provide prompt attention. And, *assurance* indicates courteous and knowledgeable staff who convey trust and confidence. The *empathy dimension* includes offering caring and individualized attention to customers. Lastly, the *tangible dimension* represents the physical facilities, equipment, and appearance of personnel. Many of these dimensions are relevant for programmers to address in the registration process and in preparing customers to participate in programs and services. Consider how staff treat customers in the registration process. By performing their duties accurately, being knowledgeable about programs and services, listening to customers, and making appropriate suggestions for improving programs staff exude an attitude of quality assurance.

By understanding what customers value in terms of service delivery, programmers are in a better position to identify the specific situations where problems may occur. To identify specific issues relative to service quality it may be helpful for staff to create a cycle of service (discussed in Chapter Six) specifically for the registration process. Once identified, staff can address the issues and ensure the process flows properly. Some critical points within the cycle of registration include: well-prepared staff, ease and accessibility of the registration process, additional paperwork, and payment methods.

Ames Parks & Recreation
Registration Information

Complete Registration Early!

Please register early! If your first choice is filled, you will automatically be placed on a waiting list. If you wish to attend the same class with a friend, please attach the registration forms together and enclose them in the same envelope.

Mail-in, Drop-off, Walk-in, Fax

The same priority is given to registrations received by mail as those delivered in person and are processed randomly on a daily basis. Postcards are mailed confirming your program registration. If a class is filled, you will be notified by postcard and placed on a waiting list. If confirmation is not received within ten (10) working days, please contact the **Parks and Recreation Office at 555-5350.** Updates and class status information may be obtained by calling **555-5350**; however, due to "computer lag," the Department cannot guarantee class openings quoted over the telephone.

Fees

All fees are payable at the time of registration. Checks should be made payable to "City of Ames." The Department now accepts MasterCard or Visa for payment. Please do not mail cash.

Cancellations/Inclement Weather

Announcements or cancellations due to inclement weather conditions will be on the **Information Line.** Please dial **555-5434 (Category #1)** for 24 hour recorded messages about program changes. Announcements will also be made on the local radio station KASI 1430. When possible, rainouts will be rescheduled, but refunds will not be given if a rain date is not possible. Where youth are involved, parents are asked to pick up their children from the program site as soon as possible if sudden, threatening weather conditions occur.

Scholarship Program

The Ames Parks and Recreation Department offers a scholarship program for all Ames elementary school-age youth. Eligible families must meet certification guidelines established by Mid-Iowa Community Action (MICA). Eligible youth can participate in up to 4 instructional programs per year at a discount of 50%. Available programs include swim lessons, volleyball, soccer, golf, baton, track, tennis, Tee-ball, gymnastics (not Tumbling Tots), basketball, dance, band, flag football, and ice skating lessons. Please contact MICA at **555-2736** for more information on how you can qualify for the scholarship program.

Figure 10.5   An Example of Registration Information from the Ames, Iowa Parks and Recreation Home Page

Prepared Staff

The most important relationship in the process of creating, implementing and evaluating leisure programs is that of the constituent and front-line staff member. The initial formation of this relationship occurs prior to the actual start of the program or service. Thus, the first impression that is created for customers as they interact with staff for the first time is critical to developing a positive relationship. As noted in the previous section, staff must be competent as they interact with customers. In addition, they must be knowledgeable about the organization and its programs. To be most successful, organizations will want to examine how they can train staff in ways that will prepare them to react to customers in a way that fosters a sense of reliability, responsiveness, assurance, and empathy.

In many parks, recreation, and leisure service organizations, programs and services are delivered by seasonal, part-time or volunteer staff. Preparing these staff to meet the demands of interacting with customers can be a challenge. Despite the importance of front-line staff and the fact that they constitute the majority of personnel recruited by parks, recreation and leisure service organizations, they are often the lowest paid and receive the least amount of training and development of all organizational staff. More needs to be done to enhance their preparation, training, and status within organizations.

Many organizations fail to produce benefits to the customer because they fail to realize the importance of developing and supporting their front-line staff. We should all strive to redraw the organizational chart with a fresh look to include customer benefits as a fundamental part of what goes on in successful organizations. Such a chart should also reflect benefits staff will receive from working within an organization (see Figure 10.6). In this approach values or benefits flow outward. Internal service departments deliver value to the front-line staff, who then deliver value to the customer.

In working through such a structure programmers can begin to work with staff to identify ways the interactions between customers and staff can be improved. Staff development opportunities to learn more about the organization, customers, and how to effectively communicate with the public should be created on a regular basis. During training organizations might also acknowledge the difficulty of interacting with customers, answering the same questions a hundred times each day (seemingly), and dealing with the problems of others. By acknowledging these difficulties and working through them *with* staff the organization fosters a servant leadership perspective for delivering programs and services, and meets the customer's needs relative to the five dimensions of quality identified by Parasuraman, Zeithaml, and Berry (1985).

Ease and Accessibility of the Registration Process

In addition to preparing, training, and maintaining quality front-line staff, we also impact participants' pre-program experiences through the actual registration process. When adopting a method or methods

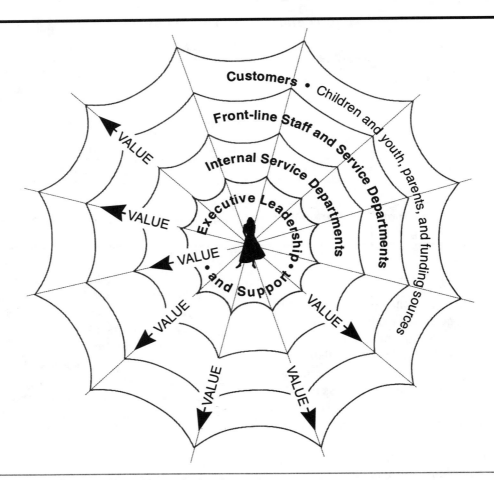

Figure 10.6   Web-shaped Organization Chart (Adapted from Albrecht, 1992)

of registration, ease and accessibility for customers are important dimensions to keep in mind. Customers are, after all, the reason we offer leisure programs and services. Their perceptions are paramount to an organization's success. Suggestions for making the registration process "user-friendly" include:

- Provide enough (in terms of numbers) knowledgeable staff to handle the registration process;

- Schedule registration at times that are convenient for customers;

- Make all forms and other information readily available for all potential constituents (perhaps in multiple languages);

- Establish well-organized queuing systems to make sure customers are served in the order they arrive (or call). Queuing refers to standing in line while waiting for a turn to be served or being on hold on the telephone. There are a number of different types of queues that can be established: single line with single service, multiple lines with multiple service, single line with multiple service, and station-to-station service (Rossman, 1995);

- Provide clear and easy to follow registration forms. Arrange the form in such a way that customers can complete as much of the registration form as possible before needing assistance from staff. Consider aesthetics, language, reading comprehension level, length of form, use of words, and any other factors of communication that may arise.

Use of Forms

Once an individual has registered for a specific program or service, there are a number of other tasks which need to be completed during the registration process. These tasks often involve filling out additional forms such as informed consent forms, waivers, power of attorney forms, medical history forms, and photo release forms. We will now turn our attention to discussing each of these forms in more detail.

Informed Consent Forms or Agreements to Participate

These forms are used to help constituents understand the risks and responsibilities associated with participating in certain activities. Both forms usually explain that accidents may occur and the organization cannot totally guarantee the safety of participants. In addition, participants are reminded that they must assume elements of responsibility for their own. An Agreement to Participate form formalizes the fact that customers agree to participate and assume the inherent risks associated with the activity. When using the agreement to participate forms with children, programmers should properly inform both children and parents or guardians about the activity, its risks, and expectations of participants. Such forms should be signed by both the child and the parent or guardian (Hronek & Spengler, 1997).

Parental Permission Slips, Power of Attorney Forms, and Medical Release Forms

A permission slip is a signed statement saying parents agree that their minor children (under age 18) may participate in a specific program or service. Permission slips are usually used in conjunction with power of attorney or medical release forms which allow program staff to authorize emergency medical care in the case of a medical emergency. Parental permission forms do not substitute for a participant's informed consent form, and in some cases, both should be used. Medical release forms are also used for adults, which in case of emergency, allows medical attention to be given if the participant is unconscious or unable to make a medical decision (Jordan, 1996).

Medical History Forms

Some programs may require participants to complete a medical history form prior to participation. For instance, many high-impact aerobics classes, aquatic programs, highly active programs for seniors, or programs for those recovering from medical procedures typically require medical releases and physician signatures. Medical release forms may be simple health disclosure forms used to collect basic information such as name, address, emergency contact phone numbers, sex, birth date, height, weight, age, blood type, social security number, medical insurance policy type and number, and physician information (e.g., phone, address). The form may also include questions about health histories and prior injuries, fears, medications, allergies, and so on. This depends on the nature of the activity or program. For instance, if a program is going to be held outside at a park it would be wise to know (and be prepared for) someone who is allergic to bee or insect stings. More complex medical forms may include a form signed by a doctor which documents the health of a participant and indicates their fitness to participate in certain programs or activities. When using medical and health forms, participants should be assured that information will remain confidential and that only medical personnel staff who have a need will have access to the information.

Waivers

Waivers are agreements between the organization and the participant which state that participants will not hold the organization liable for any damages if ordinary negligence is the reason for participant injuries or damages (Hronek & Spengler, 1997). Waivers have a higher likelihood of being validated by the courts if they are specific and related to high-risk activities such as whitewater rafting, mountain climbing, hang gliding, and scuba diving than if they are overly broad in scope (Peterson & Hronek, 1997). Parents cannot waive the rights of their children since children may sue once they reach the age of legal consent; therefore, waivers should be used along with other forms for minors.

Photo Release Forms. Organizations are always looking for photo opportunities to promote their organizations. Photographs might be used in brochures, calendars, television commercials, and other promotional opportunities. To ensure that the "once in a lifetime" photo may be used by an organization, everyone in the picture must agree to allow the organization to use the picture. This is especially true when photographing people with disabilities (especially minors) and others who have particular concerns about privacy. To simplify the process of using photos, many organizations ask all participants to sign a photo release prior to participating in programs and services. Failure to sign a photo release would not preclude participants from participating; however, programmers must be aware of those participants and honor their wishes not to be photographed.

In addition to all the forms and registration information, organizations will want to examine their programs and decide if any other paperwork is needed. Many organizations combine several forms into one. This can create problems, however, because participants may be willing to sign one aspect of the form, but not another. For example, an individual may agree to sign a waiver, but not consent to a photo release. If these two components are wrapped into one form this could create undue problems for both the agency and the individual.

We have talked about the registration process and the many forms that might be completed as a part of that process. To foster and maintain a servant leadership approach to all aspects of programming we try to build customer orientation into all program cycle elements. Cost and payment for programs and services is an integral part of this process.

No matter an organization's orientation (i.e., commercial, nonprofit, public) payment of some sort usually accompanies the delivery of a program or service. Costs across and within programs can be flexible. For example, one program might cost more than another, and two different constituents could pay different amounts for the same program. Some of these individuals might be on a flexible pay scale, while others might barter for an exchange of services.

Payment Methods

Ease of registration includes resolving several questions concerning payment methods. In their efforts to best serve constituents, Lovelock (1996) suggests that organizations answer the following questions about payments:

Who Should Collect Payments?

To facilitate positive interactions between programmers and participants, programmers will want to make it as easy as possible for constituents to obtain information, make reservations, and offer payment for programs and services. In most cases parks, recreation, and leisure service organizations handle these arrangements themselves, yet some organizations delegate some of these tasks to intermediaries, thus freeing the organization to focus on program or service delivery. Examples of intermediaries include travel agents who make hotel and transportation arrangements, ticket agents who sell seats for a variety of events, and businesses that sell trail passes for bicycles or cross-country skiing. Although the

**CHALLENGE COURSE INSTRUCTOR'S
MEDICAL INFORMATION
THIS IS TO REMAIN AT CAMP REDLAND'S CC**

OUTDOOR ADVENTURE
OKLAHOMA STATE UNIVERSITY

**CHALLENGE COURSE
INFORMED CONSENT AND
MEDICAL RELEASE**

Any person using the
it to the Instructor. N

WHEREAS, the u
HOMA STATE UN
conducted by:

and in consid

Assumption of Risk and Liability / Photo Release

I, (please print) _____, have been advised that participating in live action
role-playing games and activities of the type run by the International Fantasy Gaming Society
(IFGS) necessarily involves risks, and that accidents, even serious or fatal accidents, can occur.
While I understand that IFGS enco___ ty, an accident may occur involving me or my
property. In return for being ___ ate in an IFGS game, I fully and knowingly assume
the risks and agre ___ the IFGS, game participants and observers, and
any oth ___ er activities, form any claims, including those for
___ ulting in my death. I understand the substantial
___ to participate. I understand the assumption and
___ will be binding on anyone acting on my behalf
___ sign this assumption waiver, and that the only
___ articipate in this IFGS game or other activity.
___ d for several purposes including publicity,
___ via photography, video, and audio recordings,
___ d to participate in this game or other activity,
___ s, recordings, documents, artwork, or other
___ ty in any manner it chooses, and without

___ ss you are at least 18 years of age, you

___ ame Dates: _____

**Pima County
Community
Resources**

Parks & Recreation

EL DEPARTAMENTO DE PIMA COUNTY PARQUES Y RECREACION
PACTO Y LIBRERO DE RESPONSIBILIDAD

Yo, (nombre)_____, quiero participar en el evento,
actividad, o programa escrito abajo, por este medio yo renuncio y descargo por siempre
cualquier y todos los derechos a y/o reclamaciones por daños que pueden ser sufridos de
mi, de resultas de mi preparación para, el participación en, o viajando a o de el evento,
actividad, o programa escrito abajo. Yo reconozco los riesgos asociados con mi participación
en este evento, actividad, o programa y especificamente consento a indemnizar y ocupa
Pima County, Arizona infensivo sus oficiales, agentes, empleados, juntas directivas y
comisiones, y cualquieras otras personas portando en beneficio o promovedores, contratista
o, subcontratista quienes facilidades o servicios están relatados para este evento, actividad,
o programa, de y contra cualquier y todas heridas o daños, incluyendo muerte, surgiendo
de o en cualquier manera relatado o atribuido con mi participación en este evento, actividad,
o programa.

Además yo atestigo que no tengo ningun menoscabo fisico, enfermedad o defecto, ni latente
o patente, que támpoco me preludia de o sube los riesgos a mi participando en este evento,
actividad, o programa. Además yo atestiao que soy en buena salud y tengo capaz a participar
en este evento, actividad, o programa y soy educado suficientemente para participar en este
evento, actividad, o programa.

Evento/Actividad/Programa:_____

Fecha(s) del evento:_____

Yo he leido éste pacto cuidadosamente y yo comprende completamente su contenido. Yo
sé que esto es un librero de responsibilidad y un contrato entre Pima County, Arizona y yo
y firmo de mi libre albedrío.

Fechas: _____

Edad: _____

Firma: _____

Imprime su numbre: _____

Fecha del nacimieno: _____

PERSONAS MENOR LAS EDADES DE 18 NECESITAN PERMISO DE LOS PADRES.

Yo, el pariente, o guardián legal de la persona menor que firmó arriba por este medio asento
al pacto arriba y el librero de responsibilidad y convengo que estoy ligado de todos sus
condiciones explicado arriba.

Fechas: _____

Firma: _____

PERMISSION SLIP

Telephone _____

State _____ Zip _____

Location _____

pproval for their participation
reation program listed above.
s the Urban County Division
l of them. In case of injury
on-Fayette Urban County
f the supervisors appointed
arks and Recreation will
ed as a result of an injury
e responsibility of the
upervisors any or all of
the Division of Parks

Emergency Phone Number

Figure 10.7   Examples of Forms

organization may have to pay a commission for this service intermediaries are able to offer customers greater convenience in terms of where, when, and how the program cost should be paid. Even after commissions, the use of intermediaries often offers a net savings in administrative costs to the organization (Lovelock, 1996).

When Should Payments Be Made?

There are four basic options related to when payments for services or programs should be made. Customers can be asked to:

1. Pay in advance of the program,
2. At the onset of the program,
3. After the program is completed, or
4. With some combination of methods (e.g., a deposit may be required prior to the program starting with the balance due at the completion of the program).

Asking customers to pay prior to a program beginning often builds customer commitment and provides the organization with needed capital to finance programs and services. Other approaches may also be initiated to assist customers in the payment process. One approach that offers customers flexibility and encourages early payment is when an organization offers discounts for early payments and for payment in full.

How Should Payments Be Made?

There are a variety of different ways of paying for programs and services including cash, checks, credit cards, debit cards, prepayment cards, and vouchers. Cash may appear to be the simplest form, but it can raise questions about security and may be inconvenient when exact change is required. Accepting payment by check is commonly practiced, but there are concerns of accepting checks from individuals who do not have sufficient funds. Credit cards are also widely accepted although they can create additional paperwork for the leisure services organization.

Debit cards are quickly becoming a very popular means for paying for services. Debit cards look like credit cards but act more like plastic checks because the money comes directly for the customer's checking account. Related to both debit cards and credit cards are prepayment cards. These are based on cards that store a dollar value on a magnetic strip or in a microchip imbedded in the card (a prepaid calling card for telephone use is an example). As services are purchased the card is scanned and a specific amount is deducted from the total value of the card. Another form of payment, vouchers, can also be used effectively in certain situations, especially when organizations wish to subsidize the cost of a specific program. Whatever the method of payment, programmers must remember that for many transactions, the simplicity and speed with which payment is made may influence the customer's perception of overall service quality (Lovelock, 1996).

Anticipation

Once an individual makes a decision and commits to a specific program or service she or he begins to anticipate the upcoming experience. Organizations have an opportunity to use this time to prepare customers for upcoming programs, thereby enhancing the total customer experience. A critical component of this process is managing the expectations of customers—these play a crucial role in the evaluation of the overall quality of a program or service.

Quality—a perception of excellence—is the extent to which the services received by a customer equal or exceed expectations. Customer expectations for programs and services are developed in many ways. Factors that influence customer expectations include word-of-mouth communications from other customers, personal needs, past experiences, external communication (such as promotional materials), and the concept of equity (primarily applicable in the public and nonprofit sectors) (Crompton & Lamb, 1986; Parasuraman, Zeithaml & Berry, 1985).

Within this list of factors the way organizations can have the most direct impact on customer expectations is through external communication. As noted in Chapter Eight on program promotion, external communications may be used to inform, persuade, educate, and remind customers about all elements of programs. To be most successful within the anticipation phase of an experience organizations should attempt to inform and educate customers about the upcoming experience.

Organizations accomplish these tasks in a variety of ways. For example, Figure 10.8 presents a Web page from the Itasca Park District which outlines policies and procedures related to the registration

Itasca Park District - How to Register

How to Register

Registration will begin on Monday, August 17. Registration will continue until the class is filled or needs to be cancelled due to insufficient enrollment. Mail-in registration for the Fitness Center and aerobics classes will not be accepted. Mail-in, drop-off, and walk-in registration all begin Monday, August 17 at the Itasca Park District, 350 E. Irving Park Road, Itasca, IL 60143.

Waivers

In accordance with Recreation Department policy, all program participants must sign a hold harmless agreement prior to participation in Department sponsored programs. The waivers are on the reverse side of the program registration form and must be signed by adults participating in adult programs, and by a parent or legal guardian for children under 18 years of age.

In Case of Oops!

Complete details of program policies, procedures and guidelines are sometimes omitted from program brochures because of space limitations. Also, errors in days, times, registration requirements and fees may occur as well. We apologize for any errors that may occur in the brochure. When such errors do occur, we will advise you of the change as quickly as possible. We thank you for your patience and understanding when these situations arise.

Go to Online Forms

Definition of Residency

Anyone living within the geographic boundaries of the Itasca Park District. If there are any questions about your reisdency, please call the Park District office, where a complete list and map is maintained.

Refund Policy

A. All requests for refunds must be submitted in person or by phone two days prior to the first class meeting, practice of program, or trips.

B. Individuals requesting refunds with two or more days notice prior to the first class, meeting or practice will receive a 100% refund (less $5 for administration costs).

C. No refunds will be issued for any programs after the first meeting, unless a physician's excuse is presented. Refunds requested for medical reasons will be prorated from the time the request is received.

Insurance Policy

The Itasca Park District does not provide medical coverage for injuries suffered while participating in Park District programs, or while using park facilities. The Park District, therefore, cannot assume responsibility for personal injury for persons participating in recreation programs or using facilities. Persons are advised to make provisions to provide this coverage in their family insurance program.

Fee Information

Due to liability concerns all individuals wishing to participate in any Park District program must pay the registration fee in the brochure prior to the start of the first class. Any individual who is unable to pay the registration fee must contact the Superintendent of Recreation to set up a payment plan. No phone registration will be accepted. **Individuals not paying full program registration fee or those on payment plans will be assessed a 10% service charge if any payment is late.**

Itasca Recreation Center Rental

The Itasca Recreation Center may be reserved by Park District residents for private use during non-program hours. This facility is available to groups and individuals at nominal rates. Interested residents should contact the Park District at 555-2257. A security deposit is required in order to hold a date. If cancellation occurs within three (3) weeks prior to rental, deposit will be retained.

Cooperation

The Park District wishes to acknowledge the cooperation of the Village of Itasca and the Itsaca School District #10 for enabling the Park District to provide year-round recreational activities. The Park District is permitted to use the school facilities when not used by the schools. For this reason, there may be occasional changes in the schedule.

Senior Citizens

Senior Citizens (60 and older) who are residents of Itasca Park District are entitled to enroll in some of the Park District classes free of charge. For details on specific classes, call us at 555-2257.

Figure 10.8   Example of Registration Guidelines from Itasca Park District's Web Site

process. This Web page informs customers about how to register, and provides information about refunds, cancellation, insurance, and fees. In addition, many organizations use other means of preparing customers for programs and services. Program packets might be mailed to participants and include such things as packing lists, an explanation of policies and procedures, a welcoming letter from program staff, and material that explains the logistics of programs so customers begin to know what to expect. A good rule of thumb in developing program packets is to be realistic in program information and description and then overdeliver during the actual program. By being realistic and overdelivering organizations exceed the expectations of customers. This ultimately aids in producing quality programs.

Travel-To

The travel-to stage of a parks, recreation, or leisure program occurs after the planning is complete (or nearly so) and serves as a transition into the anticipation phase of a leisure experience. There are times when recreation programmers will provide transportation to a special event (e.g., a bus is utilized to transport seniors to a festival) and other times when individual constituents transport themselves to a recreation experience or event (e.g., by foot, bicycle, vehicle). In this case the travel-to phase of a leisure experience occurs outside of the immediate realm of the parks, recreation, and leisure services programmer. Nonetheless, we should recognize that travel-to does have an impact on the upcoming experience for most constituents.

If we are providing the transportation to a leisure experience we should recognize that the transportation itself is a stand-alone programming opportunity. The tone is set and the entire experience impacted by the music played, songs led, drinks and food provided, decorations used, and games and activities engaged in while in transport. Participants are strongly impacted by these events. They are also impacted by the scenery viewed during the trip. In the case where participants provide their own transportation we can influence that experience by providing routing suggestions for scenic routes and/or the quickest routes with the approximate travel time for each, ideas for activities to be played while enroute, and audio stimulation (e.g., songs and audio tapes).

Participation

By addressing several areas of elements of planning, programmers can use the time prior to the program to enhance the experience of constituents in a number of ways. Thinking about and manipulating the physical environment of a program

facilitates the ability of constituents to receive the benefits they desire. A second area directly related to participation that programmers should address prior to the actual start of a program or service is risk management. How customer problems and complaints are going to be handled is another area programmers should discuss with staff before a program begins. Thinking these through beforehand can serve to create a program environment which enhances a constituent's actual experience.

Creation and Management of the Physical Environment

As noted earlier in this chapter, the physical environment or "tangibles" of an organization is one of the major dimensions of providing quality services (McKay & Crompton, 1990; Parasuraman, Zeithaml & Berry, 1985). As a result, there are a number of areas related to an organization's physical environment that programmers can address in both managing a customer's pre-program experience and facilitating an individual's participation in a program or service.

The overall aesthetics of a facility or area provides subtle messages to customers about the

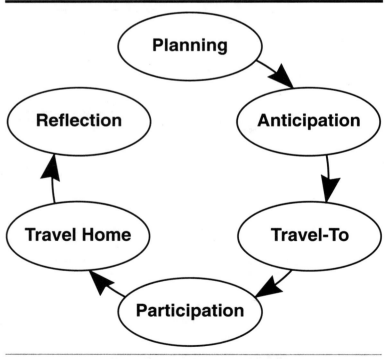

Figure 10.9 A program experience is typically considered to have six stages.

organization. The appearance of the reception or registration area, the cleanliness of the bathrooms and the condition and level of repair of exercise equipment all present the organization in a positive or negative light. As one airline executive lamented, "if our bathrooms are dirty, people think our planes will not fly." This is also the case for parks, recreation, and leisure service programs. When the environment is not clean and well-maintained, constituents may have questions about the quality of programs and services. It is important to note that equipment and facility do not necessarily have to be new; a clean and well-maintained area will present a positive image for an organization. This is especially relevant from a servant leadership approach to programming which encourages programmers to be good stewards of resources and equipment. This attitude often spills onto participants, and they tend to take good care of the equipment and resources, also.

O'Sullivan (1991) has noted that many of the benefits sought from leisure experiences are intangible. People seeking benefits seem to know intuitively when benefits occur and will assess the physical environment of a proposed program or service in light of the probability that their needs can be met. Thus, the physical environment of program and services is a crucial component of the overall customer experience. Tangibles include such things as lighting, plants, music, signage, and tablecloths. They may be related to socialization, relaxation, or provide tangible evidence of accomplishment or recognition (e.g., receiving a T-shirt following participation in a 5K run). These peripheral images can substantially impact upon the success of a program or service and should be addressed while planning a program or service.

Different lighting, colors, sounds, and spatial arrangements create different moods within programs and each may be manipulated by programmers to accomplish specific objectives. For example, rock-and-roll music, informal dress, bright lights, and brightly colored malt shop decorations can be used to create one type of mood, whereas classical music, formal dress, intimate lighting, and European cafe decorations will create a different type of mood. In setting the mood for programs and services, programmers must work hard to create the appropriate atmosphere. This includes having all props and equipment ready prior to customers arriving for a specific program or event.

Pre-Program Checklists

Many organizations utilize checklists immediately prior to beginning programs. Checklists may focus on a variety of areas. For example, adventure education programs that utilize ropes courses have facilitators/leaders conduct a walk-through of the course and complete a checklist to ensure that the structures and equipment are safe and ready to use. This type of checklist is related to good risk management. Other checklists may be used to ensure that the programmer or leader did not leave any task undone prior to the start of a program, thus serving as a reminder about maintaining the quality of the overall program. Still other checklists may fill a combination of these functions and direct programmers through the program design and implementation process. Figure 10.10 (page 222) presents a comprehensive checklist for organizations developing an outdoor trip program.

Dealing with Customer Dissatisfaction

Pre-program checklists serve to aid programmers in minimizing customer complaints, yet no matter how well-planned leisure programs may be there will be times when a customer is not satisfied with the service provided. One early study into customer complaint behavior found that the average business never hears from 96% of its unhappy customers; and, for every complaint received, the average company has twenty-six customers with problems, six of which are serious (Albrecht & Zemke, 1985). Therefore, it is important for organizations to take a two-prong approach to dealing with customer complaints. First, organizations must examine how they can encourage customers to share their dissatisfaction with program staff. Second, an organization needs to provide staff with direction and the authority to handle customer dissatisfaction as it arises or is brought to the staff's attention.

Parks, recreation, and leisure service organizations can encourage comments and possible complaints from customers in a variety of ways. Many of these are discussed in Chapters Twelve and Thirteen on program evaluation. In addition, many organizations utilize customer complaint/suggestion forms (see Figure 10.11, page 223). A written approach to complaints is favored by many organizations for several reasons. First, it allows information to be organized in a way that allows for an orderly, well-thought-out response. Second, it provides a safety valve, or buffer, for customer complaints, enabling the organization to handle concerns at the earliest possible time. This minimizes the concern that complaints won't be addressed until much later, when the situation may become more volatile. Third, a written complaint system is accurate and quantifiable (Edginton, Hanson, Edginton & Hudson, 1998).

One difficulty with written complaint forms is that they can be long and time-consuming which may discourage customers from giving feedback. A second problem with complaint forms is that organizational response is not immediate and this is

---

Rationale

Is there a rationale, reason for going on the trip? What are the goals and objectives for the trip? Do these goals and objectives fit into the overall philosophy of the organization?

Participants

Who are the participants? What are needs of the participants? Do meeting these needs fit into the rationale and philosophy of the organization? Do the participants match the needs as established by the trip rationale? Are they compatible with routing, scheduling, activities and location?

Activities

Does the chosen activity or activities match the needs of participants as established by the trip rationale?

Location

Does the chosen location match the needs of participants as established by the trip rationale? Is the location compatible with the types of activities we want to do while on the trip?

Route

Does the chosen route and schedule match the needs of participants as established by the trip rationale? Are the route and schedule compatible with the activities and the location on the trip?

Group

Do the groups formed match the needs of participants as established by the trip rationale? Are the groups compatible with the routing, scheduling, activities, and location of the trip?

Staff

Do the staff match the needs of participants as established by the trip rationale? Are they compatible with the routing, scheduling, activities, and location of the trip? Are staff compatible with each other?

Equipment

Do the equipment lists match the needs of participants as established by the trip rationale? Are they compatible with the staff, routing, scheduling, activities, and location of the trip?

Food and Water

Does the food and water provision match the needs of the participants as established by the trip rationale? Are the provisions compatible with the equipment, staff, routing, scheduling, activities, and location of the trip? Are meals balanced? What kind of water purification system will be used?

Accommodations

Do the accommodations match the needs of the participants as established by the trip rationale? Are the accommodations compatible with the provisions, equipment, staff, routing, scheduling, activities, and location of the trip? Have advanced reservations been made where necessary? Have payments been made in advance?

Transportation

Does the chosen means of transportation match the needs of the participants as established by the trip rationale? Are the methods of transportation compatible with the accommodations, provisions, equipment, staff, routing, scheduling, activities, and location of the trip?

Communication

Does the chosen means of communication match the needs of the participants as established by the trip rationale? Is the method of communication compatible with the transportation, accommodations, provisions, equipment, staff, routing, scheduling, activities, and location of the trip?

Budgeting

Do the financial arrangements meet the needs of the participants as established by the trip rationale? Is the method of budgeting compatible with the communication, transportation, accommodations, provisions, equipment, staff, routing, scheduling, activities, and location of the trip?

Risk Management

Is the method of risk management compatible with all the above elements of the trip? Has a risk management plan been developed? Are staff familiar with the risk management plan? Do staff have all necessary certifications and skills to lead the trip?

Figure 10.10 Pre-program Checklist for an Outdoor Program (Adapted from Priest & Gass, 1997)

frustrating for customers. As a result, all staff must be prepared *prior to programs and services* to deal with customer dissatisfaction in later aspects of the program.

If we are serious about developing programs and services to be customer-centered, staff must avoid simply responding to constituent complaints—they must actively seek them out. Each complaint offers an opportunity for organizations to recover from the problem or concern and improve their weaknesses. Staff should also understand what they are authorized and not authorized to do to resolve a customer complaint. In some organizations staff have the authority to offer refunds for programs or vouchers for another program without seeking approval from administration. This helps with addressing the need for immediacy when working directly with constituents. In other situations staff are authorized to offer discounts on merchandise to apologize for a mistake. From a servant leadership perspective program leaders want to avoid having to pacify or make irate customers wait until a supervisor can review the situation.

When examining these types of questions it is helpful for staff to consider the priorities to be managed in each situation. Albrecht (1992) has identified five critical priorities that organizations should discuss with staff as a means of helping them decide how to focus their energies in situations related to customer complaints. These priorities, which form the acronym SPACE, include:

- *Speed*. How time-critical is the response to the customer? To the organization?

- *Personal Touch*. How important is it to manage the constituent's state of mind?

- *Accuracy*. How important is precision, conformance to specifications, safety, security, information clarity, and error prevention?

- *Cooperation*. How important is it to dovetail with another person's task or with what the customer is doing?

- *Economy*. How important is it to minimize the resource cost involved to the organization?

For example, if a disgruntled constituent complains to a staff member about an unexpected change

To Our Valued Guests,
We would appreciate your taking the time to fill out this card to let us know how we are doing in our effort to make this a first-class facility.

52

	Much Better Than Expected	About As Expected	Worse Than Expected
GENERAL FACILITIES			
Building Exterior			
Lobby			
Meeting Rooms			
Pool/Recreation Areas			
GUEST ROOM			
Price Value			
Appearance			
Overall Cleanliness			
Carpet			
Television			
Heat/Air Conditioning			
Hot Water			
Bed			
Quietness			
Bathroom			
How did everything work			
HOTEL STAFF			
Check-In			
Check-Out			
Friendliness			
Efficiency			
Services (Wake-up, etc.)			
RESTAURANT			
Price Value			
Food Quality			
Service Quality			
Appearance			
OVERALL RATING			

If you were back in the area, what are the chances you would stay in this hotel again?
0%___ 20%___ 40%___ 60%___ 80%___ 100%___
Have you stayed here before? Yes___ No___
Are you here on Business___ Pleasure___
COMMENTS_____
_____
_____
Date of Stay_____ Room#____ # People in Room____
Name (optional) _____
Address _____
City _____ State ____ Zip _____
Male___ Female___
Age: Under 21___ 21-34___ 35-44___ 45-54___ over 65___

Figure 10.11 Sample Suggestion/Complaint Form

in the program schedule, the staff member and her or his program supervisor might have already agreed that the sequence of priorities in addressing this complaint will be using a personal touch first, then economy, followed by cooperation with the constituent, speed (to avoid wasting the customer's time), and accuracy. It's not that accuracy is not important, but it holds less importance on the priority list, which is keyed to keeping the customer's good will within the resources of the organization.

In addition to deciding on a sequence for addressing complaints, the programmer will need to identify what steps exist within the staff member's priority for solving the problems. In the example stated above, the staff member will need to:

1. Listen to the customer,

2. Apologize for the change in the schedule while explaining why the change took place, *then*

3. Look for other alternatives with the customer while offering a $10.00 discount on a new registration fee,

4. Assist the customer with registration, and

5. Ensure that all new information is accurate and up-to-date.

In this case, all five of the SPACE considerations are important, but agreeing to a sequence for the priorities gives the staff member a focus for dealing with the complaint. If these priorities are discussed between program supervisors and staff, it allows for employee input into what is important. It also helps supervisors inform staff about their expectations in various situations.

Travel Home

The travel-home phase is similar to the travel-to phase in that it may or may not be within the purview of the parks, recreation, and leisure services programmer. As with travel-to the site of the experience, travel home is an opportunity for additional programming. Typically, we want this programming to assist in the reflection process of the experience. It tends to be less active than the travel-to phase (in part because participants are tired) and can aid in the transition from an enjoyable activity to warm and positive remembrances of that event. If we have direct impact on this phase we might ask participants to respond to questions about the activity verbally, or in writing (trip journals are used by many groups). In this way, we can help constituents

SPEED→ of response to constituent(s)

PERSONAL TOUCH→ to let constituent(s) know we care

ACCURACY→ of information

COOPERATION→ with other staff members

ECONOMY→ of time, money and resources

Figure 10.12 SPACE considerations in helping staff to focus on customer complaints.

capture their thoughts, feelings, and memories in such a way as to prolong the leisure experience.

Reflection

As stated previously, the focus of this chapter is on the pre-program experience of the customer. However, the reflection phase of the customer experience is closely related. We want to encourage programmers to think about how they can create mechanisms that foster positive reflections about an experience offered by a parks, recreation, and leisure service organization. The importance of the reflection stage is often neglected in program planning, even though it often provides the customer the most long-lasting satisfaction. One person's experience can be lived again and again, and through such memories, participants keep the experience alive. In addition to enhancing the memories of an experience, enhancing the customer's program reflections can encourage excellent word-of-mouth promotion for the organization. Figure 10.13 presents several techniques to enhance the reflection aspect of a customer's experience.

Use Photographs

Take pictures and send them to participants following the program.

Help Participants Create Remembrances

Children's art projects are often kept by parents and children to provide a visual symbol by which to remember programs.

Provide Promotional Items such as T-shirts, Stickers, or Pins

Hurricane Outward Bound ends their courses with participants pinning fellow classmates while telling the person what they enjoyed about her or him during the course.

Journals

Encourage participants to keep a journal during their program experience.

Sponsor Program Reunions

This can be done at locations and times convenient to different groups of participants.

Send Out Newsletters

Ask participants to contribute poems, stories, and photos of the event and paste it together in a newsletter to send out.

Letters

Have participants write themselves a letter during the program experience and then mail it to them three to six months after the program.

Figure 10.13 Techniques to Enhance the Reflection Stage of the Customer Experience

Summary

In the process of creating, implementing, and evaluating recreation programs programmers must pay attention to creating customer friendly systems that enhance all phases of a customers experience— planning, anticipation, travel-to, participation, travel home, and reflection. In facilitating the pre-program experience, organizations must pay attention to a variety of factors recognizing that everything the organization does communicates to customers. The look of promotional material, the "feel" of the registration process, the paperwork that is required before participating in a program, the set-up of the environment when participants arrive for the start of a program, and the interactions with staff all contribute to the expectations and perceptions of customers before the actual program ever begins. As a result, programmers must not only be concerned with developing a program, but must also plan the events leading up to the program. This chapter has presented a number of key areas which programmers should address in an effort to improve the quality of the overall experience for the customer.

References

Albrecht, K. (1992). *The only thing that matters.* New York, NY: Harper Business.

Albrecht, K. and Zemke, R. (1985). *Service America: Doing business in the new economy.* Homewood, IL: Dow Jones-Irwin.

Clawson, M. and Knetsch, J. (1966). *Economics of outdoor recreation.* Baltimore, MD: Johns Hopkins Press.

Crompton, J. and Lamb, C. (1986). *Marketing government and social services.* New York, NY: John Wiley & Sons.

Edginton, C., Hanson, C., Edginton, S. and Hudson, S. (1998*). Leisure programming: A service centered and benefits approach.* Boston, MA: McGraw-Hill.

Hronek, B. and Spengler, J. (1997). *Legal liability in recreation and sports.* Champaign, IL: Sagamore Publishing.

Jordan, D. (1996). *Leadership in leisure services: Making a difference.* State College, PA: Venture Publishing, Inc.

Lovelock, C. (1996). *Services marketing, 3rd ed.* Upper Saddle River, NJ: Prentice Hall.

MacKay, K.J. and Crompton, J. L. (1990) Measuring the quality of recreation services. *Journal of Park and Recreation Administration, 8*(3), 47–57.

MacKay, K.J. and Crompton, J. L. (1988). A conceptual model of consumer evaluation of recreation service quality. *Leisure Studies, 7*(1), 41–49.

O'Sullivan, E. (1991). *Marketing for parks, recreation and leisure.* State College, PA: Venture Publishing, Inc.

Parasuraman, A., Zeithaml, V. and Berry, L. (1985). A conceptual model of service quality and its implementation for future research. *Journal of Marketing, 49,* 41–50.

Peterson, J. and Hronek, B. (1997). *Risk management for park, recreation, and leisure services, 3rd ed.* Champaign, IL: Sagamore Publishing.

Priest, S. and Gass, M. (1997). *Effective leadership in adventure programming.* Champaign, IL: Human Kinetics.

Rossman, R. (1995). *Recreation programming: Designing leisure experiences, 2nd ed.* Champaign, IL: Sagamore Publishing.

Chapter Eleven

The Programmer

Those striving to be principle-centered see life as a mission, not as a career. Their nurturing sources have armed and prepared them for service. In effect, every morning they "yoke up" and put on the harness of service, thinking of others. See yourself each morning yoking up, putting on the harness of service in your various stewardships. See yourself taking the straps and connecting them around your shoulders as your prepare to do the work assigned to you that day. See yourself allowing someone else to adjust the yoke or harness. See yourself yoked up to another person at your side—a coworker or spouse— and learning to pull together with that person.

Covey, 1991, p. 34.

The leisure services programmer is an individual who is involved with an event or activity from needs assessments into implementation and through the evaluation process. Programmers work with people in every aspect of their duties—planning, designing, creating, implementing, evaluating, and so on. Sometimes this occurs within a supervisory role where the programmer oversees other staff (typically direct-line staff such as craft instructors and camp counselors) in the delivery of services. Other times the programmer does all the program development and is also the one who delivers the program to constituents.

The role of the programmer is determined by size of the organization, qualifications of available staff, organizational goals, budgetary constraints, and other issues. In any case, programmers will fulfill roles that benefit the community, organization, fellow staff, and constituents. Thus, having an orientation to others is necessary for success in this field.

Servant Leadership

As we have mentioned throughout the text, this other-orientation is a hallmark of servant leadership. To provide quality programs we have to be able to put ourselves in the shoes of others and respond to their needs. There are many ways for us to do this. Larry Spears, executive director of the Greenleaf Center for Servant Leadership, has identified ten key elements of servant leadership which we offer as personal goals toward which each one of us should strive in our role as parks, recreation, and leisure services programmers.

1. *Listening receptively about what others have to say* [Parks, recreation, and leisure services programmers do this through needs assessments and informal avenues of data collection];

2. *Accepting others and having empathy for them* [A goal that helps us to understand others; our similarities and differences];

3. *Using foresight and intuition* [These two traits are used extensively in the program design stage of the program cycle, and for safety and risk management purposes];

4. *Exhibiting awareness and perception* [By being aware of subtle nuances, we can provide the quality our constituents desire. By using these skills we can also go beyond expectations in our delivery of programs and services];

5. *Practicing highly developed powers of persuasion* [Used in moderation, this trait enables us to best serve our constituent groups outside of politics and other extraneous issues];

6. *Enhancing our ability to conceptualize and communicate concepts* [Program design and the use of our creative powers require that we be able to explain to others what we are doing, and why.];

7. *Exerting a healing influence on individuals and institutions* [This is the very essence of parks, recreation, and leisure services—it speaks to the benefits of our field];

8. *Building community in the workplace* [The role we share with colleagues and the relationships we develop spill over into the work we do for others];

9. *Practicing the art of contemplation* [Reflection and contemplation are avenues we use to better ourselves, our programs and services, and the way we reach others]; and

10. *Recognizing that servant leadership begins with the desire to change oneself* [When we change, grow, and develop we promote our humanity and that of those around us]. (1994, p. 2)

Servant leadership is the framework around which we can build our professional selves. By operating from the assumptions underlying servant

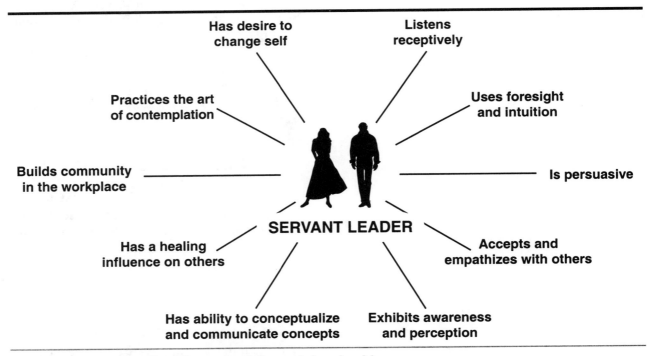

Figure 11.1   The Ten Key Elements of Servant Leadership

leadership we strive to design and implement high-quality, community-benefiting programs and services for all of our constituents. This framework establishes the structure that provides shape to who and what we are as practitioners.

Professionalism

Parks, recreation, and leisure services programmers are professionals. This is true to the extent that we are members of a profession which has a statement or code of ethics, an accreditation process for practitioner preparation programs, a professional association which seeks to provide continuing education and establish standards (NRPA), and individual certification (e.g., CLP, CTRS, CPO, CPR). We also exhibit various qualities that reflect our professionalism, including taking initiative, having integrity, and following through with all tasks related to programs and services.

Qualities or traits of a high-quality programmer mirror many of those traits identified for skilled leaders and professionals—honesty, integrity, competence, responsibility, creativity, authenticity, persistence, courage, maturity, and a willingness to take risks (Jordan, 1996). We know that our constituents (both program users and nonusers), supervisors, those who work for us, local businesses, and the general public all have expectations of who we should be and what we should do. It is up to each one of us to exceed those expectations and do all we can, within our organizational values and mission, for each group. This chapter will discuss the different ways we provide service to the community, our organization, fellow staff, and constituents in our roles as programmers.

Service to Community

Whether we work in a rural, urban, or suburban community and whether our organization is representative of a commercial, public, or nonprofit sector, by the very nature of what we do, we serve the community. Quality parks, recreation, and leisure services in and of themselves, increase the quality of life in a community. The provision of open space (e.g., parks, golf courses) as well as the opportunities to engage in active programs (e.g., festivals, athletic leagues) are commonly viewed as positive services

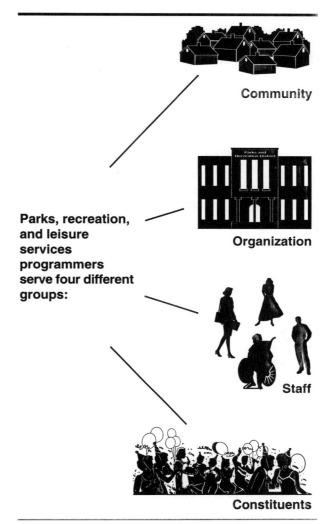

Parks, recreation, and leisure services programmers serve four different groups:

Community

Organization

Staff

Constituents

Figure 11.2 As programmers we provide a service to the community, our organization, fellow staff, and constituents.

for a community. For instance, to gain a competitive edge in recruiting new employees, many businesses advertise the parks, recreation, and leisure service opportunities in the community and use them as drawing cards. Some companies even offer memberships to fitness and social clubs as perks to employees. Because our profession is integral to community life, roles that we can fill in service to communities include that of a problem solver, creative catalyst, and benefits provider.

Problem Solver

Parks, recreation, and leisure service programmers serve in a problem-solving capacity to communities through much of what we do. We are called upon (and usually respond) to help in community efforts to reduce teen drug abuse, cut the juvenile crime rate, teach English to new immigrants, conduct health/wellness screenings at community health fairs, serve the elderly, increase the economic base of the community, and so on. In addition, because leisure services can be offered almost anywhere, we are sometimes looked to as a way to create new jobs and/or respond to needs of those who are under-employed or unemployed. For instance, many parks, recreation, and leisure service organizations provide jobs to unemployed youth during the sum-mer. In addition, many nonprofit and public parks and recreation organizations serve as venues where individuals who have gone through the court system can fulfill their requirement for hours of commu-nity service.

A national example of a recreation organization fulfilling a problem-solving role is the National Youth Sports Program (NYSP). This is a program that began in 1969 with federal monies to establish a sports program for economically disadvantaged youth. It is a partnership between the U.S. Depart-ment of Health and many colleges and universities through the National Collegiate Athletic Associa-tion (NCAA).

In the NYSP, economically disadvantaged youth receive free sports-skill instruction, opportunities to engage in competition, and opportunities to improve their levels of physical fitness. As a part of the special services provided, all youth in the program receive a free medical examination before participating in NYSP. If a medical condition is found, that young-ster receives follow-up treatment. In addition, one USDA approved meal is served each day to aid in meeting the nutritional requirements of the youth. Lastly, each participant is covered by accident-medical insurance, and the sponsoring institution (university or college) is provided liability insurance. Since 1969 the NYSP has served nearly 1.5 million youth (National Youth Sports Program, 1998).

As we can see, the services we offer and the skills we have as leisure professionals serve a large role in community problem solving. In addition to taking direct action, parks, recreation, and leisure service personnel often serve on community boards (e.g., the town council, police board), and indirectly help a community respond to existing needs. Part-nerships with schools, health departments, and other

community services enable us to make a difference in the lives of individuals, and thus, the community.

Creativity Catalyst

Another service we provide as professional program-mers is to help with the creative aspects of commu-nity life. Again, no matter our profit orientation, we are often the community group that enhances and provides opportunities for individuals to express their creativity through such avenues as community theater, music, and art exhibitions. We also use our ability to think and respond creatively to help local businesses and entire communities develop the creative sides of themselves. Through our creative programs and services we serve as a creative cata-lyst to other community efforts.

For example, Vision Us, Inc., a corporate chal-lenge course provider, utilizes parks, recreation, and leisure experiences out-of-doors to help businesses and corporations use creativity in communication, problem-solving efforts, rethinking organizational structure, the manufacturing process, and other as-pects integral to a successful business. By engaging people in creative processes, Vision Us, Inc. helps corporate leaders to understand and integrate cre-ativity in the workplace as well as other aspects of their lives.

Benefits Provider

We mentioned early on in the text that communities benefit from parks, recreation, and leisure programs and services through a variety of mechanisms. In-dividuals, as well as the community as a whole, benefit from involvement in leisure opportunities including mental and emotional health (e.g., stress reduction), physical health (e.g., increased endurance and cardiovascular functioning), spiritual health (e.g., through nature-based recreation and church activi-ties), and social skill development (e.g., learning to live well with others).

Through our programming efforts programmers in parks, recreation, and leisure services provide a healthy outlet for daily stresses and contribute to the community in a meaningful way. Other community benefits include a direct positive impact on the local economy through such profit-generating events as festivals, and indirectly through a healthy popula-tion (i.e., healthy people contribute positively to the economy). Furthermore, parks, recreation, and

For 30 years, the National Youth Sports Program (NYSP) has combined sports instruction with exciting educational programs for youths ages 10-16. Enrollment is free and open to all youngsters in the community whose parent(s) or guardian(s) meet(s) Department of Health and Human Services income guidelines.

NYSP participants also receive — at no cost — (1) a NYSP T-shirt, (2) a daily USDA-approved meal, (3) transportation to campus (if necessary), (4) a medical examination, (5) accident-medical insurance coverage, and (6) interaction with college students and staff.

Youth practice standard sports and learn new ones!

✔ Activities include swimming and a variety of other sports which may include basketball, football (touch or flag), softball, tennis, track and field, soccer, volleyball, dance/aerobics, badminton, gymnastics, and wrestling.

✔ Top-quality sports equipment is provided by the program.

Community leaders bring information to youth on:

✔ Alcohol- and other drug-abuse prevention,

✔ Nutrition and personal health,

✔ Career opportunities and job responsibilities, and

✔ Higher education and community concerns.

Figure 11.3   An Example of Problem Solving—The National Youth Sports Program

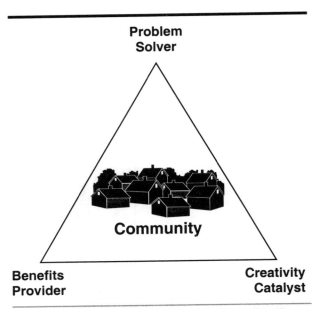

Figure 11.4 Programmers fulfil three primary goals in service to the community.

leisure services are wonderful mechanisms to transmit culture and cultural values. We see this through the efforts of leisure service providers such as museums, local artisans and craftspeople, and in music and other media. It is through these mechanisms that we learn about cultural norms, traditions, and values. Other benefits of parks, recreation, and leisure include a positive impact on community morale (this is a strong emphasis of armed forces recreation programs, for example) and ongoing lessons in citizenship—many sports leagues promote ideals of fair play and teach participants and spectators how to lose gracefully.

Service to Organization

In addition to providing services to a community, parks, recreation, and leisure service programmers also provide services to the organization for which they work. As employees, we are integral to the functioning of the organization in which we work. This is true whether we are the only employee (very small public recreation programs often have only one employee and rely heavily on volunteers) or one of several hundred employees (large resort and theme parks often have extremely large staffs). In our role as programmer we enhance the organizational mission, vision, and philosophy, and facilitate the achievement of its goals and objectives. We do this through service in several capacities—planner, budgeter, public relations specialist, and risk manager.

Planner

Programmers tend to be good planners. We are skilled at understanding our constituents, creative design, logistics, and foresight; we are also flexible. These various skills use both sides of our brains (i.e., the linear/logical and the creative/abstract) enabling us to contribute to a variety of areas within an organization. Planning skills put us in position to provide direction to the organization and those who work within it. Solid planning establishes a positive image for the organization.

The planning role we undertake involves many different elements. We plan for staffing needs—by being involved in the selection and hiring process, training, and scheduling of staff and volunteers. We plan for appropriate facilities and ensure their maintenance and safety. Concern for equipment for which we are responsible is another task under this role. We must consider its condition, availability, and appropriateness to the activity. Of course, the activity itself is of utmost importance in our planning function. Promotion and program delivery, as well as recordkeeping, complete the many aspects of planning for which we are responsible.

Budgeting and Recordkeeping

Budgeting is one aspect of planning that has direct and easily recognizable impact on the larger organization. Because it is necessary for us to budget for individual programs, quality programmers know and understand budgeting issues on a specific level (program by program, as well as by program area). By being astute and financially responsible in this area, we aid the entire organization in utilizing resources wisely and meeting budgetary goals. Thus, we provide an important service to our organization.

Recordkeeping in general is one role we fulfill that can help our organization be successful in ongoing efforts. As programmers we are responsible for maintaining a whole series of accurate records. Some of the more common recordkeeping duties include personnel records (our own as well as those working for us including résumés, copies of certifications and training, and letters and documentation related to job performance).

Program records also fall within our purview. These records are used in evaluation and future planning efforts. Examples of program records include: general program records (such as describing and outlining the nature of the program, staffing needs, budget, facility and equipment needs, demographics of participants), registration and attendance records (i.e., who signed up for what, when), and documentation of promotional efforts (i.e., copies of flyers, ads, and public service announcements). Other common records we maintain include inventory and maintenance records of equipment and facilities, petty cash records, and telephone records. Records related to risk management are always important. Some of the more common records we keep include permission forms (for minors, signed by guardians), medical release forms (for all participants, particularly if the activity is moving off-site), and accident/incident reports.

Public Relations Specialist

Programs and services are very often the most visible and recognized aspect of parks, recreation, and leisure service organizations. Thus, if done well, our programs and services are wonderful opportunities for positive organizational promotion. Through our efforts (and the efforts of our staff) the programs and services we offer impact public support of what our organization does. This is true no matter our service orientation—commercial, public, or nonprofit. If people perceive what we are doing as valuable to the community, our organization will be valued and community efforts will support those of the organization. Thus, our individual physical appearance (i.e., dress and demeanor), the manner in which we respond to constituent needs and concerns, the values we promote, how we utilize information gathered on evaluations, and the behaviors we model are all important to us as public relations specialists.

Risk Manager

An additional role we have in relation to our organization is in risk management. We have a responsibility to minimize risks to the community, participants, staff, and our organization which might result from providing programs and services. This means that we must have a solid understanding of the risks involved in our programming efforts and how to best manage those risks. This has been

addressed in some detail in an earlier chapter. Being a risk manager includes being prepared for all contingencies, following maintenance protocols, assigning staff to activities appropriately, choosing activities and events wisely (utilizing both needs assessments and activity analysis), and conducting thorough evaluations.

Service to Staff

In addition to serving the community and our organization we also have a role in serving fellow staff members. In this capacity we might be team members, supervisors, trainers, mentors, and/or subordinates. In each of these roles we provide service to our colleagues in ways that enhance the work environment and individual as well as group success. In this way we put our colleagues first and our work habits and tasks facilitate their success.

The type of goal orientation where one person's goal enhances or supports another person's goal is considered a *cooperative goal structure* (Tjosvold, 1989). For instance, consider a program supervisor who has a goal of becoming the highest quality parks, recreation, and leisure services provider in the region and a staff member who has a goal of

Figure 11.5   In serving the organization, programmers act as planners, budgeters, public relations specialists, and risk managers.

putting constituent needs first in all program efforts. It is likely that by one of these people achieving her or his goal, the other individual would be supported in their goal attainment as well. This is a cooperative goal structure.

If, however, the staff member has a goal of cutting corners whenever possible to save money, the two goals might be in competition, or conflict with one another. Cutting corners would likely be antithetical to becoming the highest quality program in the region. The opposite would also be true—if the goal of becoming the highest quality were reached, cutting corners would not occur. This is known as a *competitive goal structure* (Tjosvold, 1989). Lastly, if the staff member's goal was to learn how to budget, this may not have anything to do with the programmer's goal of becoming the highest quality program. If this is the case (the goals have nothing to do with one another), then the goals would be said to be independent of one another— it is an *independent goal structure* (Tjosvold, 1989). Cooperative goal structures enhance the ability of all staff to serve one another's needs, as well as those of the organization. From a servant leadership perspective, we should strive for a cooperative goal structure with our colleagues. The reality is, however, that there are times when our goals will compete or be independent from others with whom we work. In these instances, we must do our best to remain professional and collegial in all we do.

Supervisor

Parks, recreation, and leisure service programmers serve in a supervisory role when they are responsible for the work and success of individuals who are "below" them in an organizational hierarchy. These individuals may be paid or volunteer staff and tend to be direct-line staff who deliver the program and interact with participants in a face-to-face situation. As a supervisor to others, programmers provide job descriptions to staff, inform them about ongoing training opportunities and relevant evaluation processes, and assist them in the performance of their jobs.

Job descriptions for program staff are typically developed and provided to staff from the administrative unit of the organization. Informing about training opportunities and conducting staff training are responsibilities that fall within the realm of program supervisors who serve staff. All new staff

require orientation to the organization. This typically includes learning about and buying into the philosophy, mission, and vision of the organization. It also involves physically orienting staff to the facility and grounds which are a part of the organization, its operational policies and procedures, and expectations of staff members. Training may also be content specific and focus on critical issues such as blood-borne pathogens, child and elder abuse, and skills such as CPR and basic first aid.

In addition to orientation and training, supervisors are actively involved in scheduling and matching staff to appropriate programs, assisting with securing equipment and facility space, and providing support as needed during all programming stages. These efforts have been described in previous chapters of this text. Being a servant to one's staff is the orientation of a programmer who follows the servant leadership model.

Mentor/Evaluator

Furthering the role of trainer, program supervisors also have responsibilities to mentor staff to help them maximize their success as professionals in the field. Mentoring involves taking on a coaching, supportive role for staff. It is a friendly facilitator role and is focused on helping individuals to become the best parks, recreation, and leisure services professional they can be. Mentors listen, make suggestions for action, guide staff into positions and situations where they will stretch and grow, know when to push and when to step back, and are pleased in the growth and development of the individual staff member—often above their own.

In order for programmers and other staff members to improve and develop all of their skills, they need to receive periodic evaluations. Those in supervisory roles usually have this responsibility. Often, an employee will be reviewed after a probationary period of time (typically three to six months) and every year thereafter. By being open, honest, reflective, and sensitive to the feelings of the individual being evaluated, a supervisor can take on a servant leadership demeanor when discussing an evaluation. From this perspective, evaluations are used as a developmental opportunity, rather than simply for punitive or remunerative (for pay raises) purposes.

Team Player

While programmers may serve as supervisors and mentors, they always are part of the larger organization, and in that respect fill a role as a member of a team. Being a team player is important in that people who are a team work well together, support one another's efforts, communicate openly, and move the organization forward in its efforts. Programmers (as are all staff members) are important team members. They are deeply involved in the service component of the organization. A team has been defined as a group that

> has a particular process of working together, one in which members identify and fully use one another's resources and facilitate their mutual interdependence toward more effective problem solving and task accomplishment. (Reddy & Jamison, 1988, p. 77)

This definition of team expresses the ideas of cohesion and mutual trust within a group of people which help move a group forward in attaining its goals. Jordan (1996) suggested that building a team is a process which involves ten essential elements:

1. Taking care of ourselves;
2. Taking care of each other;
3. Taking care of facilities, equipment and supplies;
4. Having balance in our lives;
5. Giving the other person the benefit of the doubt;
6. Bringing our best to each situation;
7. Putting the other person first;
8. Thinking "We" and supporting other group members;
9. Melding our goals with the group's goals; and
10. Appreciating the strengths, diversity, and limitations each person brings to the team.

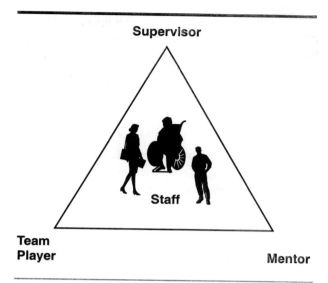

Figure 11.6   In their service orientation to fellow staff, programmers serve as supervisors, mentors, and team players.

Service to Constituents (Users and Nonusers)

Program personnel provide services and programs to the community, the organization, staff, and, perhaps most importantly, to individual constituents. We emphasize that this aspect of service is to *all* constituents—users and nonusers alike. The services we provide to constituents are visible in the goals and objectives we develop and strive to meet through our programs and services. In this way we meet the needs and desires of the members of the community. The roles we fill in this aspect of our jobs may be most easily understood in terms of functions. One function we undertake is that of analyzing activities—to help us develop and provide appropriate programs to appropriate groups. Other functions of our service to constituents are those of sequencing, preparation, and interfacing with customers.

Activity Analysis

Activity analysis is an important task for programmers to undertake. It is a systematic process through which we learn the nuances of activities so that we can design, implement, and evaluate appropriate programs for various constituent groups. We use it in conjunction with needs assessments and other forms of information gathering, and it is used during many phases of the programming cycle. Because of the impact the utilization of this information can have on the design and implementation of programs and services, the function of analyzing an activity is a very important one.

Activity Analysis by Domain

Activity analysis has been approached from several different perspectives. One way to analyze activities (i.e., to break them down into understandable parts) is to examine the requirements of different domains for participant success. These domains include examining the *psychomotor (physical), cognitive (intellectual), affective (emotional),* and *social interaction* demands of an activity. Peterson and Gunn (1984) offer descriptions of what might fall within each of the domains. Within the *psychomotor domain* we might look at what body parts are involved (e.g., feet, hands, legs, eyes), the types of movements required by those body parts (e.g., kicking, throwing, twisting, bending, standing), the types of locomotion required (e.g., scooting, walking, crawling, skipping), level of exertion, degree of fitness, required skill level, endurance, rhythm, and sensory demands.

The *cognitive* domain requirements might include the rule complexity level, required academic skills (e.g., reading, writing, math), level of concentration, level of factual knowledge/understanding/ evaluation/analysis/synthesis required, ability to think quickly, abstract thinking, and use of verbal skills.

Affective requirements of an activity include opportunities to communicate feelings, level of potential enjoyment, opportunities to display creativity, control over one's environment, self-discipline, self-esteem, and teamwork.

Finally, all activities require some degree of *social interaction*. In this domain, we examine the levels of competition/cooperation, the ability to work within rules, individual or small group involvement, level of structure in activity, the mix of participants (in terms of age, gender, ethnicity, abilities, and so forth), interaction levels, proximity, and touching.

Activity Analysis by Social Interactions

Another way of conducting an activity analysis is to focus solely on *examining the social interactions* required in the activity. This was first developed and presented in 1974 by Avedon. The different interaction possibilities, with examples of each, follow:

Psychomotor

Social Interaction

Affective

Cognitive

Figure 11.7 **Activity analysis may be conducted by examining four domains.**

- Intraindividual—within one person; the activity involves no outside person or object (e.g., running or jogging);

- Extraindividual—directed to an outside object; no interaction with another person is involved (e.g., art project or reading);

- Aggregate—a number of people all concentrate on an object with no interaction between them (e.g., group bicycle ride, riding on a roller coaster);

- Interindividual—dyad (two people interacting) in a competition format (e.g., board games, tennis);

- Unilateral—three or more people in a competition where one of them is 'it' (e.g., tag, keep away);

- Multilateral—three or more people in a competition where there is no 'it' (e.g., golf match, swim meet);

- Intragroup—two or more people cooperating toward the same goal (e.g., barbershop quartet, relay teams);

- Intergroup—two or more intragroups engaged in competition (e.g., team sports).

Activity Analysis by Activity Dimensions

A third way of conducting an activity analysis is to *look at the various dimensions of different leisure activities and search for commonalties.* These dimensions have included: body contact, element of chance, kind and intensity of competition, space required, time required, kinds and use of props, role-taking functions, rules and their complexity, levels of participation, leeway for emergent leadership, respite opportunities, suspense, role switching, pleasure/pain (win/lose), use of rewards and punishments, obstacles, trust, real-life themes, amount of ritual, genderizing games, humor, challenge, locomotion, movement of body parts, competency required, and interactiveness (Farrell & Lundegren, 1991).

Whichever method (or combination) of activity analysis is utilized the key point is to examine the different pieces of the activity so that they can be easily understood and matched to constituent needs, desires, and capabilities. When we consider program elements in this way we can best determine if and what types of modifications are necessary for optimum participant and programmatic success.

Modifications as a Result of Activity Analysis

One important reason for conducting activity analyses is to most appropriately match activities with potential constituents. As a result of conducting an activity analysis we can also see how to best modify or adapt an activity for maximum participation, enjoyment, and success—especially for people with special needs. There are general guidelines for use in adapting or modifying programs and activities for people with special needs. First, we should review the results of the activity analysis to identify the particular needs of the activity or event. Through this process we also identify environmental and equipment needs so that we can determine how much and what type(s) of modification are needed for anticipated participants.

Kraus and Shank (1992) suggested several overall guidelines for adapting activities for full inclusion of all participants. They include:

1. Programs should include enjoyable activities that are suitable for the chronological age of participants;

2. Activities should be selected to include a wide variety of leisure pursuits;

3. Activities should resemble those found in community-based settings as much as possible, to permit learning that can be used in other settings;

4. Programs should include instructional, organized, and free-play kinds of opportunities with emphasis on pursuits that stimulate motivation and provide enjoyment; and

5. Difficulty levels should be such that self-confidence is instilled through repeated success in different environments.

More specifically, we should examine activities and events (in a task analysis process) and modify only that component necessary to insure inclusion. In addition, Smith, Austin and Kennedy (1996) offered the following guidelines for modifying activities:

1. Change as little as necessary;

2. Where possible, involve the person in the modification process;

3. Avoid making assumptions about a person's abilities based on a disability;

4. Consider all levels of competition (a person with a special need might be able to compete at one level, but not another);

5. Offer activities that are characteristic of what everyone else is being offered;

6. Develop ways for people to participate rather than watch or help the leader; and

7. Give individuals opportunities of free choice.

Generally, there are four categories of modification for specific activities (Smith, Austin & Kennedy, 1996): procedural and operational adaptations (e.g., modify the rules, walk rather than run, shorten the time for the game, use buddies); environmental adaptations (e.g., adjust boundaries, change playing surfaces, use bright lighting); equipment adaptations (e.g., add aids to existing equipment, use special equipment), change equipment (e.g., use a beachball in place of a volleyball); and human intervention (e.g., a person might physically assist individuals by pushing their wheelchairs or by verbally guiding a person through a task). By considering all of these modification opportunities and then following the general guidelines as suggested previously, we can provide recreation and leisure programs with dignity for all.

Sequencing/Pacing

Two other functions we fill in our roles as programmers are sequencing and pacing. When sequencing we accept the responsibility for ordering activities in ways to enhance participant success and enjoyment. In this way we continue our commitment to servant leadership by putting the needs of participants first, and doing what is best for them. This role requires that we consider what we know about the audience (e.g., age, abilities, skills), resources (e.g., available equipment and facilities), activity (e.g., complexity of rules, physical and other domain requirements), and our own skills to conduct activities in an order that enhances program goals.

We can sequence *within* an activity (e.g., begin a painting workshop by mixing paints before moving on to putting paint on a canvas) and within a program (e.g., early in a t'ai chi class we teach simple, easy-on-the-body exercises before moving on to more complex, physically demanding elements). It is usually appropriate that we utilize both forms of sequencing in programming. In some cases, sequencing is critically important for safety reasons. For instance, in swimming, gymnastics, skiing, scuba diving, and in facilitating ropes courses, sequencing is very important to the safety and well-being of participants. If we move to advanced skills before participants have a clear understanding of foundational skills, people could get hurt (physically and/or psychologically).

Closely related to sequencing is pacing. Programmers and activity leaders pace activities by manipulating the tempo (some activities are full of quick movements while others are much slower in their movements and pace); and by sequencing, or scheduling activities in a certain order (e.g., by

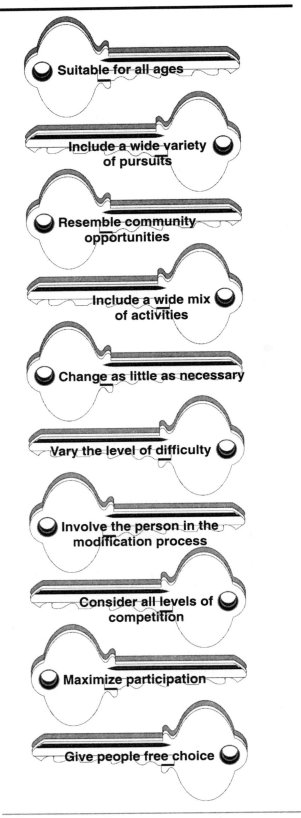

Figure 11.8 Key elements to successful modifications of activities.

alternating fast-paced and slow-paced activities). Pacing is important to managing fatigue levels of participants and to respond to learner readiness (particularly in skill-based activities such as learning to play soccer). This is important because different individuals need different pacing in order to learn certain skills. If people are overstimulated and/or fatigued, learning and attending to task drop off. Thus, pacing and sequencing are designed to match the readiness of participants with activities.

Preparation (Equipment, Staff, Facilities)

The roles of a programmer that directly interact with participants are necessary to illustrate a participant focus. One of the functions that arises out of direct interactions includes being prepared in all programming and service efforts. In earlier chapters we have emphasized the need for preparation in various stages of the programming cycle. By visualizing ourselves engaging in this function we remind ourselves of one important aspect of professionalism. Being prepared includes such basic things as having enough equipment and staff for the program, utilizing a facility that enhances the program goals, and beginning and ending on time. Other more subtle aspects of being prepared include having a complete understanding of risk management, being prepared to subgroup people within the program (especially needed for tournaments and other formal participant groupings), and knowing who will be in attendance and anticipating their needs.

Interfacing with Constituents

This function of a parks, recreation, and leisure services programmer is perhaps the most critical to organizational success. Being available and responsive to customers are tasks involved in the customer interface role. As mentioned in an earlier chapter, interfacing with constituents begins the first time the programmer and customer (constituent) come into contact with one another. This may be in passing as the programmer greets participants, at registration, on the telephone, through promotional materials, or any other time the "long arm" of the programmer reaches out and touches a constituent. Thus, we must always be aware of how others might perceive us.

Different aspects of customer interfacing involve different skills. All interfacing, however, involves treating people with respect, exhibiting an attitude of service to others, and doing what is necessary to maintain human dignity. When we interface with constituents we display our leadership capabilities. In this role we may need to remind ourselves that rather than being an end in itself, leadership is a vehicle or a means to an end—it helps us to help others.

Good leaders have a whole host of skills. We would like to suggest that leaders in programming focus on the following skills:

1. Listening effectively and communicating clearly;
2. Seeking out and enabling great ideas in others—empowering them to be the best people possible;

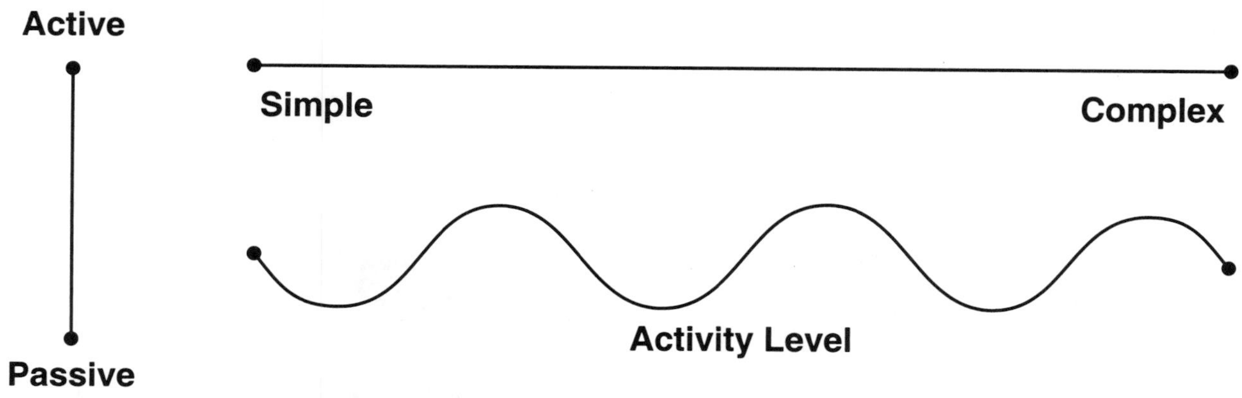

Figure 11.9 Sequencing and pacing involve considering issues of complexity and activity level (passive to highly active).

3. Engaging in creative thinking and other risk-taking behaviors;

4. Having courage to stand in the face of conflict and confusion;

5. Sharing and drawing others into the organizational vision and mission;

6. Practicing an orientation toward others, putting others' needs ahead of one's own;

7. Selling the benefits of involvement in parks, recreation, and leisure services;

8. Being willing to support and defend a moral position;

9. Knowing and understanding the role of our profession in the quality of life; and

10. Being a servant to others.

With these as a focus, interfacing with constituents is a positive experience.

Summary

This chapter has reemphasized the importance of servant leadership for those in roles as parks, recreation, and leisure services programmers. We offered ten essential elements of servant leadership as a way of seeing ourselves. We then examined the avenues through which we serve others; we provide a service to the community, our organization, fellow staff, and constituents. In each of these areas we fill several roles.

When we provide service to the community we do so by serving as a problem solver, creativity catalyst, and benefits provider. Several examples of how we do this were presented. We then presented material related to the service we give to our organization. The roles we fill in that area include planner, budgeting and recordkeeping, public relations specialist, and risk manager. In our service to fellow staff we look to link goals in a cooperative goal structure. This is done whether we are serving as a supervisor, mentor/evaluator, or team player. Finally, we looked at the functions we engage in relative to our role with constituents. In this capacity we are responsible for activity analysis, sequencing and pacing of activities, preparation, and interfacing with customers.

Preparation Checklist

✓ **Enough equipment?**

✓ **Enough staff?**

✓ **Facility that enhances program goals?**

✓ **Begin on time?**

✓ **End on time?**

✓ **Risk management?**

✓ **Prepared to subgroup?**

✓ **Know attendee list?**

✓ **Needs of attendees anticipated?**

Figure 11.10 Preparation and Interfacing

References

Avedon, E. (1974). *Therapeutic recreation service: An applied behavioral science approach.* Englewood Cliffs, NJ: Prentice Hall.

Covey, S. (1991). *Principle-centered leadership.* New York, NY: Fireside.

Farrell, P. and Lundegren, H. (1991). *The process of recreation programming: Theory and technique, 3rd ed.* State College, PA: Venture Publishing, Inc.

Jordan, D. (1996). *Leadership in leisure services: Making a difference.* State College, PA: Venture Publishing, Inc.

Kraus, R. and Shank, J. (1992). *Therapeutic recreation service: Principles and practices, 4th ed.* Dubuque, IA: Wm. C. Brown.

National Youth Sports Program. (1998). *1998 Calendar.* Available from NCAA, 6201 College Blvd., Overland Park, KS, 66211-2422.

Peterson, C. and Gunn, S. (1984). *Therapeutic recreation program design: Principles and procedures, 2nd ed.* Englewood Cliffs: Prentice Hall.

Reddy, W. and Jamison, W. (Eds.) (1988). *Team building: Blueprints for productivity and satisfaction.* Alexandria, VA: NTL Institute for Applied Behavioral Science and University Associates.

Spears, L. (1994). *Servant leadership: Quest for caring leadership. Report #2.* Indianapolis, IN: The Greenleaf Center for Servant Leadership.

Smith, R., Austin, D. and Kennedy, D. (1996). *Inclusive and special recreation: Opportunities for persons with disabilities, 3rd ed.* Dubuque, IA: Brown & Benchmark.

Tjosvold, D. (1989). Interdependence and power between managers and employees: A study of the leader relationship. *Journal of Management, 15,* 49–64.

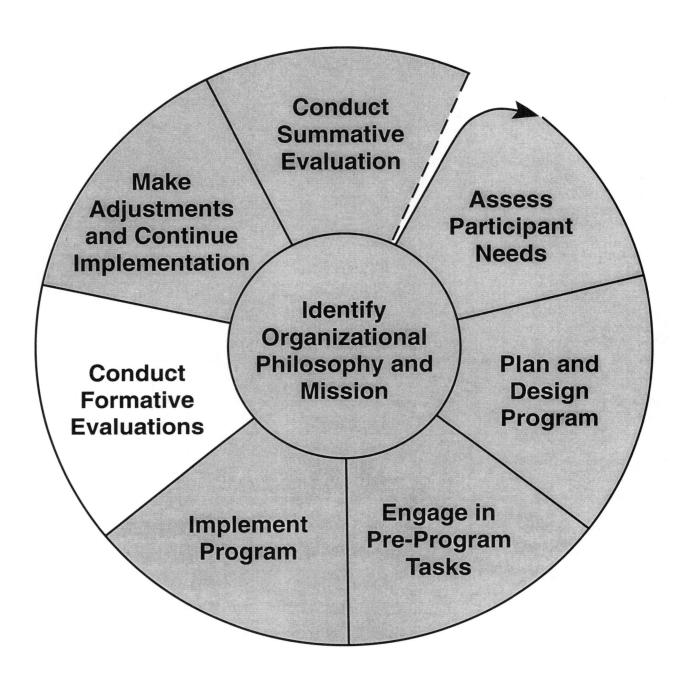

Chapter Twelve

The Essence of Program Evaluation

People perform what they measure—help the performers to measure the "right" stuff.

Belasco and Stayer, 1993, p. 222

Many people cringe when they hear the word *evaluation*. For those who have not participated in the process of evaluation, it often conjures up images of tedious statistics that no one understands (or cares about). Evaluation, however, is an integral component of the program cycle; it is NOT a distinct and separate concern that someone else must deal with. We must constantly remind ourselves that programming does not stop with implementation of a program. Indeed, it is through evaluation that parks, recreation, and leisure service professionals engage in a continuous learning process about the delivery of leisure services. Among other things, we learn how to better prepare, implement, and provide programs and services to our constituents. As such, evaluation is a very important component of the servant leadership approach to programming.

Graham and Klar (1979) said, "Program evaluation is considered to be one of the most important aspects of the leisure service delivery system" (p. 45)—and we agree. As an integral element of programming, evaluation is considered in the program planning cycle well *before* a program is implemented. This enables leisure professionals to seek out continuous feedback about programs, facilities, staff, organization, and participants and make adjustments as needed throughout the programming process. Thus, evaluation becomes a process within a larger process.

The evaluation process is systematic. This means that there are defined steps and tasks to accomplishing evaluation goals. Obviously, leisure programmers want the evaluation to result in useful and usable information. To make sure this happens, first learn about what evaluation is, how to do it, and how to use it. Therefore, this chapter will present information about terms, the components of evaluation, evaluation models, and selected evaluation techniques.

Definitions

As we've mentioned in earlier chapters when learning new material, it is wise to begin with a presentation of terms and their definitions. This enables everyone to understand the use of the terms and concepts as they come up later in the chapter—it also helps in making sense of the material. There are multiple definitions for many terms related to evaluation and in this section we present the most inclusive and commonly used definitions. These will help set the stage for the remainder of the chapter and give us a common frame of reference as we discuss evaluation in more depth.

Evaluation

Every author cited in this chapter agrees that evaluation is about *judging the value or worth of something*—in our case—leisure services and programs. The other common element to the many definitions of evaluation is that evaluation is a *way to determine if program goals and objectives have been met.* In addition to these two elements, *evaluation is a systematic process* (meaning that it can be followed and understood, is purposeful, and has a discernible shape) *of collecting information* about activities, characteristics, and outcomes of programs to make judgments about the program, improve the program effectiveness, and/or inform decision making (Patton, 1997). In addition, Patton has suggested an approach to evaluation called *utilization–focused* evaluation. It strongly emphasizes that evaluation is done "for and with specific, intended primary users for specific intended primary uses" (1997, p. 23).

We, too, believe that evaluation should be done for specific people (users) and for specific reasons (uses). Knowing this ahead of time helps to define the evaluation process, focuses the evaluation questions, and provides direction to the evaluation report. It makes the evaluation process have real life meaning and ensures its usefulness to the agency. It also lends support to our emphasis on servant leadership in programming.

Assessment

Commonly related to identifying needs, this is a *process of gathering information and data about people, places, and things* so that appropriate leisure services might be provided to aid in meeting individual's needs. Assessment is the act of collecting information about what is or what exists—and then using this information in program and facility planning. Space, facility, and equipment inventories are common examples of assessments. We dealt with needs assessments in depth in Chapter Five.

Measurement

A loosely used term, measurement typically refers to assigning a number to an attribute or characteristic that provides a way of quantifying that element. When conducting both assessments and evaluations, measurement is used to help us understand what we are examining. For example, when measuring levels of satisfaction among participants, we often assign a range of arbitrary numbers to levels of satisfaction (1, not at all satisfied, to 5, extremely satisfied). In this way we can measure levels of satisfaction.

There are primarily two ways to view evaluation—by the timing of it (i.e., when in the program life cycle it occurs) and by what is evaluated (i.e., the content of the evaluation). The terminology associated with these two views can be confusing; therefore, in the next section of the text we address the terms related to these two views.

Terms Related to the Timing of Evaluation

Formative Evaluation

Formative evaluation is conducted during the implementation process or delivery of an event or service. It may be thought of as evaluation that helps to *form* an event as it occurs. It is continuous and ongoing. Through using formative evaluation, adjustments can be made in programs and services along the way. This is a very responsive type of evaluation that helps refocus things as the programmer sees the need. For example, imagine an arts-and-crafts session for five to seven years olds in which they are working on a nature art project. You observe that some of the children are idle and seem to be disassociated from the project. In fact, they are beginning to engage in undesirable behaviors. A formative evaluation, using direct observations as a technique, would direct that staff first determine what the problem is: Are there insufficient supplies? Is room lacking at the work table? Do the children lack the skills needed to do this activity? Do the children need staff attention? Once the issues are determined (and this is done quickly), the staff could then act to rectify the situation. This "in the midst" type of evaluation is considered formative because it occurs during the program event. Be aware that formative evaluation does not always occur "on-site" during a program or event. It often occurs at staff meetings and at informal times while the program is being conducted elsewhere.

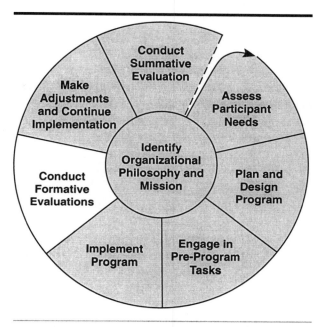

Figure 12.1   Formative Evaluation Within the Programming Cycle

Summative Evaluation

Since formative evaluation is conducted throughout the implementation of the program it makes sense that summative evaluation occurs once the program is over. It is like a *summary* evaluation—conducted when the program or service delivery has been implemented and is completed. Staff might sit down and discuss how the event went and take notes about adjustments to be made the next time the program occurs (whether it be tomorrow or next year). In the above example of the arts-and-crafts program, if only summative evaluation were used nothing would be done to help the children at the time of the problem.

Observations would be made and notes taken for the next day, week, or year to suggest adjustments in how the nature art program would be presented. With summative evaluation, levels of customer satisfaction issues are not fully addressed until after the program ends.

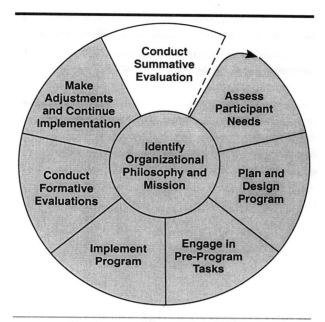

Figure 12.2   Summative Evaluation Within the Programming Cycle

Terms Related to the Content of Evaluation

Process Evaluation

As mentioned earlier, it is easy to confuse the terms used to describe timing and content issues of evaluation. In fact, process evaluation is sometimes confused with formative evaluation, but it is not an issue of timing; rather process evaluation addresses what is to be evaluated. As the name suggests, process evaluation is about evaluating the process—the *how was it done*—of a program. So, if we were to conduct a process evaluation of a wheelchair basketball league, we would evaluate how it was put together and how it was implemented. In this type of evaluation we would look at how the facilities were lined up, how teams were formed, how coaches and officials were recruited, how registration was handled, how the team scheduling occurred, and so on. In process evaluation we are concerned with the efficiency and effectiveness of how we did things to get the league underway.

Product Evaluation

The other half of the content component to be evaluated is product evaluation. Product evaluation is sometimes confused with summative evaluation because it occurs at the end of a program. Product evaluation, however, is about evaluating the outcome or product of an event, program, or service; not the timing of the evaluation. In our wheelchair basketball example, if we were to conduct a product evaluation at the end of the season we might look at the league itself—how many teams were active, did it meet the needs of the players, how was it perceived by those not involved with the league, what was the quality of the league, and so on. We would summarize these ideas and be better prepared for next season.

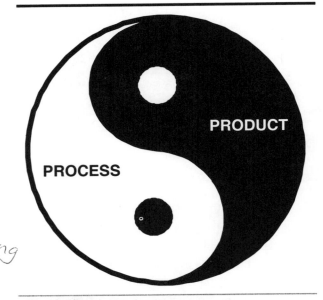

Yin
Yang

Figure 12.3   The content of evaluation consists of both process and product.

The Need to Conduct Evaluations

As mentioned at the outset of this chapter, evaluation is often avoided by practitioners. Sometimes it appears as though a form of "evaluation phobia" exists where people will do just about anything to avoid becoming involved with the process. It is important to reiterate, however, that evaluation is not a stand-alone process—it is integral to the entire programming cycle. As such, it can be helpful to look at the reasons people put forward for not doing evaluations so that we can address and overcome these concerns.

The reasons for avoiding and dismissing program evaluation as unimportant are many; yet none of them outweigh the benefits. Evaluation is crucial to well-run programs because it is through evaluation that we improve. It is also important to a servant leadership approach to programming since we empower constituents to participate in the program process through evaluations. We have all heard (and sometimes perpetuated) the reasons some programmers use to avoid program evaluation. Some practitioners believe that evaluation is not vital to an event or service—after all, "No one uses evaluation results anyway." Others firmly believe that the intuitive approach commonly used to evaluate programs is perfectly adequate to meet organizational needs. In this approach we have a gut feeling for what worked and what didn't, and make changes as we feel a need for them. After all, "We have been doing leisure services programming for *x* number of years and know a good program when we see one, right?

Evaluation phobia also manifests itself in the following reasons: We have no time for a long drawn-out evaluation process (evaluation *can* occur in a short time period); we cannot spare any staff to conduct the evaluation; or we have no money, copying equipment, or other resources to undertake a thorough evaluation. Others acknowledge that deep down inside they are fearful because they lack the confidence and knowledge about how to conduct evaluations; still others are less than enthusiastic about what to do with all those statistics. We have heard other practitioners say they prefer to avoid systematic evaluations because "the programs seem to work, so why rock the boat?" Still others believe that evaluation can stifle creativity, and some are fearful of potential change.

In response to these reasons (and others you might have thought of while reading this) for not doing evaluation, we say again—*evaluation is a critical element of the programming cycle*. A program is not complete until an evaluation has been undertaken and the information which has been learned is utilized in adapting or planning upcoming programs and services. Even then, the programming cycle begins anew—thus, the cyclical nature of programming and of evaluation.

Benefits of Evaluation

The ostrich syndrome of putting our heads in the sand when it comes to evaluation of programs and services is counterproductive. It doesn't help the situation, we don't learn from it, and it can hurt us when something we should have noticed (e.g., a safety hazard) ends up hurting someone. Consequences of avoiding evaluation range from losing participants/customers and the revenue they would have generated, to causing serious injury and/or cessation of services. If designed and conducted properly, there is nothing to lose from undertaking evaluations, and quite a bit to gain. There are many reasons for conducting evaluations and some of those are presented in the following section.

To Improve Programs, Events, and Services

If we were to ask people why program evaluations are conducted, improving programs and services would likely be the most common response. People generally understand the relationship between an evaluation and intent to improve programs and services. From evaluations we learn if something needs to be stopped, changed, or augmented to positively impact the perceived quality of services. By conducting an evaluation, we can assess quality and then make changes to better a program. We are being short-sighted, however, if this is the only reason we think evaluations have any merit. In fact, evaluation helps parks, recreation, and leisure programs and services in many ways.

To Seek Out and Eliminate Detrimental Elements

Similar to improving programs, seeking out and eliminating detrimental elements to services and programs is another reason for conducting evaluations. Improving programs often entails discovering and eliminating elements that detract from full participant satisfaction and program quality. These detrimental elements may include staffing (e.g., lack of interpersonal skills), facilities and grounds (e.g., poor maintenance and cleanliness), participants (e.g., with conflicting goals), agency organization (e.g., tedious and unwieldy registration process), and program delivery (e.g., insufficient equipment). To minimize factors that detract from quality experiences we need to ask questions related to omission (e.g., what we did not include) as well as commission (e.g., what we did include that needs to be changed or dropped).

For Risk Management and Safety Reasons

Evaluating areas, facilities, staff conduct, and program implementation on a continuous basis is part of a strong risk management plan. For instance, if there is a deficiency in a piece of equipment or structure (e.g., broken swing), it can be tended to and repaired within a reasonable time period. If staff are conducting themselves in a manner that may prove hazardous to participant safety, that too can be addressed in a timely fashion. Evaluation can also help in recognizing if any agency policies are contradictory to local, state, or federal laws and regulations (e.g., if registration procedures inadvertently discriminate against people with disabilities this would violate the Americans with Disabilities Act). Being "in the know" with regard to one's agency will help keep programs operational, effective, and efficient.

To See If the Program Meets Predetermined Goals and Objectives

For most of us, our common world experience tells us that evaluation is somehow related to the goals and objectives of an organization. That is, we have a need to know if an organization and its programs and services are doing what they set out to do. Indeed, in some fashion, parks, recreation, and leisure service professionals attempt to answer questions related to how well programs and services meet the stated goals and objectives for those programs. This requires a solid understanding of the organization philosophy, mission, vision, and goals and objectives. It also requires an understanding of potential constituents.

To Improve Decision Making

No agency can offer programs and services to meet the needs and desires of all constituents. Decisions have to be made about what to offer where, to whom, when, how much of it, and at what cost. We can design and conduct evaluations to help us in this very complex decision-making process. Evaluations can provide information that will help set priorities so that we might make wise choices relative to program ideas, staffing, budgeting, facility use, and equipment purchases.

To Justify Expenditures, Accountability, and Documentation

Determining benefits and costs of programs and services is one way to accommodate needs of policymakers and those who hold the budgetary purse

strings. While this is not easily done, it is required of organizations in commercial, nonprofit, and public sectors. Measuring the benefits of parks, recreation, and leisure services has long been an enigma for those in the profession. How do we know if our programs and services are helping to reduce the local crime rate? How do we know that participation in parks, recreation, and leisure services contributes to the emotional and mental health of participants? Recent evaluative efforts in Canada addressing the measurement and dissemination of leisure participation benefits are beginning to answer these types of questions (*Benefits Catalogue*, 1997).

Accountability and documentation are two related concepts that have existed in the leisure services profession for quite some time and recently have been taking on new and stronger meanings. All those impacted by expenditures in our field (e.g.,

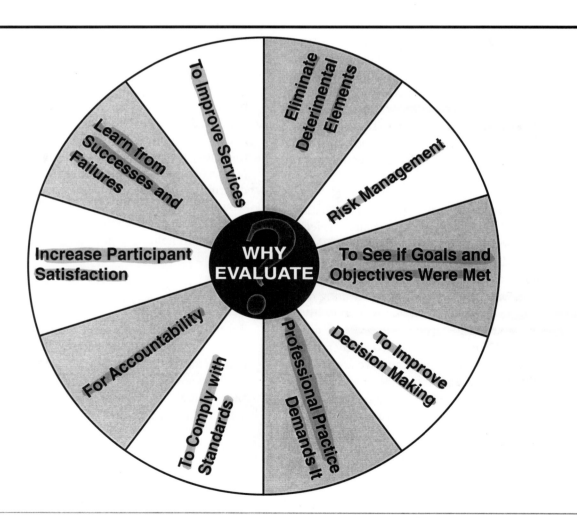

Figure 12.4   There are a multitude of benefits and reasons for conducting evaluations.

the public, politicians, investors, healthcare professionals) are asking questions about where money is spent, for whom, and the impact it is having. In fact, on the clinical side of therapeutic recreation third-party payments to insurance companies demand accountability and documentation of recreation services and their impacts provided to patients. Completing intake assessments, progress notes, and weekly charting are all forms of evaluation that address documentation and accountability. Non-therapeutic recreation agencies are also being mandated to provide documentation and accountability as monies become tighter and resources fewer.

To Increase Participant Satisfaction

Presumably, a reason many of us have for going into parks, recreation, and leisure services is to positively impact the lives of others. Through leisure and recreation we have an opportunity to influence the quality of peoples' lives. Thus, it becomes very important to know if our programs and services are having a positive impact on participants. To maintain high levels of participant satisfaction, we must learn about the impact of our programs on quality of life and make necessary adjustments—this is done through assessment and evaluation throughout the programming cycle. Another way participant satisfaction is increased through evaluation is through the very process of asking for input—participants like to be involved in meaningful decision-making processes. This opportunity for input is necessary to maintain a servant leadership foundation to programming.

To Explain Key Successes and Failures— and Learn from Them

Leisure services and programs are as diverse as the individuals we serve. The impacts of those programs and services on various constituents also differ tremendously. Some programs succeed beyond our wildest expectations while others fail miserably and we are stumped as to why. Evaluations can be designed to help leisure providers understand why certain programs succeeded while others failed so that we can incorporate these desirable elements into future efforts. Programs and services often fail, not because the entire event was flawed, but because one or two key elements were lacking. Evaluation helps us to identify those key elements to adjust for continued and future success in all our programming efforts.

To Comply with Internal or External Standards

In parks, recreation, and leisure services academic programs, we utilize external standards (e.g., NRPA/AALR Accreditation) to help monitor and document that curricula are complying with nationally established standards of minimum competency. These standards indicate that each accredited university program meets or exceeds standards set by the profession for professional competence. Similar forms of external standards exist in several program areas of our field—clinical therapeutic recreation sites are often accredited by the Joint Commission for the Accreditation of Health Care Organizations (JCAHO), and organized camping organizations adhere to standards established by the American Camping Association. These certifications and accreditations speak to our concern for quality; they also serve as a mechanism for recruiting staff and marketing to potential constituents.

Professional Practice Demands Ongoing Evaluation

One of the hallmarks of a professional is the concern for and involvement in ongoing evaluation—of self as well as those program and agency elements with which one is affiliated. Every professional in parks, recreation, and leisure should be intensely interested in her or his skills, competencies, and abilities to impact other's lives through program and service delivery in parks, recreation, and leisure services. Good professional practice means following through the entire program cycle by conducting evaluations and using that information in program development.

It is clear that there are many excellent reasons to conduct program evaluations and a few reasons explaining why some people avoid them. It is now time to examine a few issues that can influence the evaluation process and its outcomes. These influences affect all of us and should be acknowledged so that we can minimize the negative effect they have on the evaluation process and our findings.

Influences on the Evaluation Process and Outcomes

As in all spheres of life, evaluation does not occur in a vacuum. It is influenced by the many internal and external events that affect all leisure service organizations. Local politics, ethical issues, and cultural biases are a few of the concerns that need to be addressed early in the program planning evaluation cycle. These elements can affect both the evaluation process as well as outcomes. For instance, in the evaluation process ethical issues arise whenever other people are involved—How much should we push and insist that participants complete evaluation forms? When does encouragement become harassment? or coercion? In another vein, outcomes often are affected by local politics—for instance, the evaluation report might be softened so as not to offend the mayor who has a pet program she or he has been advocating. Additionally, cultural biases affect us at our core, influencing the way we view the world and the assumptions we make about what people do and do not like.

Ethics and Professionalism in Evaluation

The essence of ethics is knowing right from wrong; this strikes at the core of who we each are as a person. Ethics are not something that occur once, nor are they something that a person does. A person either behaves and lives in an ethical fashion, or she or he is willing to be compromised. Ethics are ongoing behaviors and attitudes that protect the rights of others while upholding standards. An ethical person is reliable and has a sense of professionalism and integrity. This means that an ethical individual consistently acts in a certain way when faced with difficult decisions, and others can count on this type of behavior.

In evaluation (as well as other elements of programming) an ethical person works in such a way as to promote the ideals of the profession while ensuring participant safety and positive experiences (Rossman, 1995). When doing evaluations, ethical issues might arise relative to how the people who are selected to participate in the evaluation process (i.e., the sample)

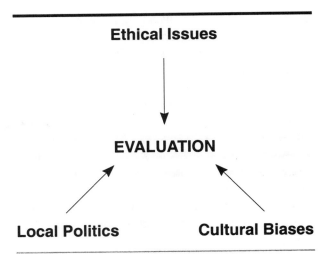

Figure 12.5   Evaluation is impacted by a variety of internal and external influences.

are treated. Some participants try to avoid completing evaluations because in the past they were harassed, not believed, and otherwise treated poorly. Some have even reported feeling manipulated or pressured into answering questions in a certain way. This is unethical behavior by the individual conducting the evaluation. Programmers need to have the utmost respect and care for constituents in all respects, and particularly when in the midst of an evaluation.

Another example of unethical behavior related to program evaluation may occur when evaluating by standards. If an organization typically operates below standards, yet during the two weeks prior to an evaluation visit, organizational staff frantically scurry about to appear as though they do meet standards only to fall back into substandard behaviors once the evaluation is completed, this is unethical.

A third example is changing the results or writing a report that misrepresents the findings of an evaluation. This sometimes occurs when an individual is fearful of an unflattering evaluation.

Politics in Evaluation

Those who are involved in evaluation often strive to be free of political influences so they can state that the evaluation was unbiased and free from external pressures. However, every evaluation is influenced by internal and/or external politics. Politics are inevitable and should be acknowledged and addressed as forthrightly as possible. Political maneuvering might come in the form of executives from the head office demanding that only certain types of questions be asked to ensure a positive evaluation. Or, it might be evident in pressure to present a report in a less-than-truthful fashion to ensure third-party payment in a clinical therapeutic setting. We should all address the political issues and stay true to reliable, valid, and usable evaluations—in this way, evaluation will be an effective component of the programming process in spite of political influences.

Cultural Biases in Evaluation

Cultural biases are inherent in every society. In the United States, the dominant cultural group is representative of people who are white, middle-class, and educated. Therefore, the way most people in the U.S. view the world is influenced by attitudes, beliefs, and values held by this group of people. Partly due to this, most people in our society know very little about the way program participants who represent minority groups look at the world, the appropriateness of various program interventions in meeting their needs, or the personal consequences of program participation for minority group members (Madison, 1992). Programmers who have little contact with people who are affiliated with minority groups, therefore, may not be the best people to determine the appropriateness of program and evaluation strategies for these groups (Madison, 1992).

Davis (1992) has suggested that evaluators tend to homogenize groups of participants—they either select people who are more alike than different, or they report findings as though respondents were very much alike. This is often done with the underlying assumption that evaluation respondents are reflective of the dominant cultural group in the United States. This homogenization can result in poor program conceptualization, insensitive measures and evaluation, and inappropriate generalizations of findings. It is important that the entire program process, including evaluations, be contextually relevant to the geographic area and culture of the constituents. In other words, evaluations should involve a diverse group of constituents.

According to Davis (1992) there are five steps programmers can take to be more culturally sensitive in evaluating programs:

1. Conduct within-group and between-group comparisons (i.e., to observe and note that all people of one minority group are not necessarily alike in their thoughts, values, and opinions);

2. Use culturally sensitive evaluators who understand themselves as well as other cultural viewpoints;

3. Solicit feedback about interpretations of evaluations before reporting them (i.e., ask those who participated in the evaluation process if your interpretation accurately portrays what they meant);

4. Analyze the program in context—look at the whole picture—to serve as a basis for different results (i.e., identifying the context or situation helps because context is likely to have more impact on differences in responses than a person's cultural background or skin color); and

5. Use multiple variables to determine if there is difference in evaluation results based on various demographic characteristics (e.g., socioeconomic status, age, religious affiliation, marital status, geographic area) (Murphy, Niepoth, Jamieson & Williams, 1991).

Evaluators need to consider culture and cultural biases in conceptualizing the evaluation process, collecting data, and interpreting findings. If a target population's cooperation is expected, then its values, beliefs, and traditions need to be taken into consideration during the evaluation design process, implementation, and the dissemination of evaluation findings and recommendations.

Having addressed some of the concerns related to evaluation, it is now time to examine evaluation on a conceptual level. This entails considering two views of evaluation: the generic evaluation process and several specific evaluation models. Understanding the "big picture" as well as the relationships between the many elements is helpful in understanding how we go about actually conducting an evaluation.

Defining Our World-View

Before deciding on a particular evaluation model or technique we should identify and articulate our preferences relative to how we look at the world. A world-view is also known as a paradigm. In evaluation, there are two primary paradigms—qualitative and quantitative. Most of us grew up learning and practicing tasks that reflect a quantitative world-view; and for many of us, this has been quite comfortable. In evaluation the quantitative paradigm means that we try to quantify, or assign numerical values, to different attributes in life. Generally speaking, we are trying to crunch numbers in such a way as to reduce multiple responses to one that is easily understandable. From a qualitative paradigm, we look at targets of evaluation in a holistic framework and use words as data sources, rather than numbers. This makes a great deal of sense in many respects and enables us to present multiple perspectives in context. We can find a deep, rich "truth" to the ways respondents perceive a program through a qualitative paradigm.

Quantitative Paradigm

Those who prefer a quantitative world-view generally perceive evaluation as a time to collect information that can be reduced to numbers for analysis. The quantitative paradigm examines one or more program attributes or characteristics in isolation

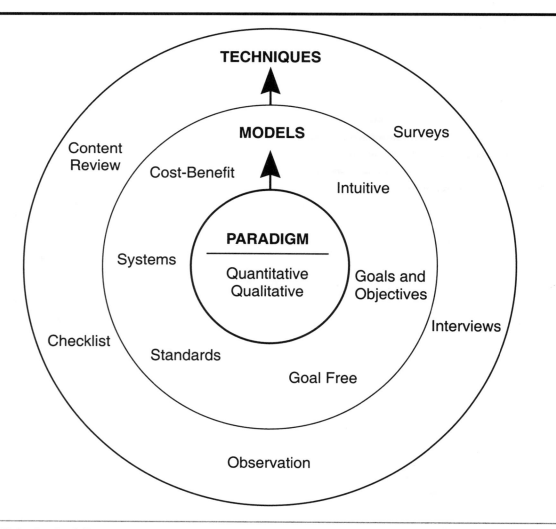

Figure 12.6 **In deciding upon an approach to evaluation, programmers must first decide on a world-view, then a model, and then techniques to collect data.**

from the entirety of the program. For example, we might evaluate individual staff members and *not* consider their experience, hours, pay scale, training, or access to resources. Depending on the intended use of the evaluation and the disparity among staff based on these traits, this could result in a biased evaluation. Quantitative evaluations typically occur with paper and pencil and everyone is measured in the same way on the same attributes. When we ask about levels of satisfaction relative to a program, everyone answers the same question on the same scale with the same response choices. This allows us to examine responses in a uniform fashion, and collapse the data into readily analyzed numbers.

Qualitative Paradigm

The qualitative paradigm is one where the evaluator examines the program to describe what was (or is being) done and to determine overall program quality. People who prefer this paradigm recognize that there are multiple truths and that people have different perspectives of the same experience. Determining overall program quality is accomplished through gathering information which are words (e.g., from interviews, written responses to open-ended questions, observations). The strength of this world-view is that it allows us to evaluate the interrelationships found throughout the programming cycle. It can be used as exploratory evaluation whereby the programmer looks at the big picture, and after noting areas of interest conducts a more narrowly focused quantitative evaluation. On the other hand, qualitative evaluation can be used to add details, depth, and meaning to what was found in an earlier quantitative analysis (Patton, 1987).

The qualitative paradigm is particularly useful in evaluation when examining program effectiveness (Henderson & Bialeschki, 1995; Howe, 1993). Using a qualitative perspective, for instance, programmers learn why participation (or nonparticipation) in a program was meaningful to people. If we were to ask individuals about levels of satisfaction with a program, we would do so in such a way that would allow them to answer in their own words. In this way, one person's answer may or may not look like anyone else's answer. We gain a tremendous amount of information from this process.

Patton (1990; 1997) provided a sampling of examples describing when a qualitative paradigm is the most appropriate choice for program evaluation. Adapted, those examples include the following:

- To look at the internal dynamics of a program—how something was accomplished;
- To evaluate individual outcomes—as in therapeutic recreation and in skill development programs;
- To document unusual cases—such as successes/failures/oddities;
- To describe diversity across program sites;
- To conduct a formative evaluation—to provide a holistic picture of existing interrelationships;
- To emphasize detected problems within a complex structure;
- To add depth to quantitative analyses and to increase quantitative understanding;
- To generate new insights and creativity in program and service delivery ideas; and
- To evaluate a setting where it is extremely difficult to develop a quantitative instrument to measure the attributes with which we are concerned.

While most people favor either the quantitative or qualitative paradigms in terms of conducting evaluations, the two can be integrated. For instance,

QUANTITATIVE PARADIGM	QUALITATIVE PARADIGM
• Data consist of numbers • Examines one component of a program • Uniform in appearance and in data collection • Typically use paper and pencil as instrument • Effective to examine program product	• Data consist of words • Looks at a program from a holistic perspective • Appearance can change based on sample • The evaluator is the instrument • Effective to examine program effectiveness

Figure 12.7 Qualitative and Quantitative Paradigms

we might conduct an evaluation that includes two data collection techniques—interviews and paper-and-pencil surveys. Another approach would be to use a paper survey that includes both closed-ended and open-ended questions. The open-ended items, if worded well, can result in rich word data that are then treated as qualitative data. Once we have decided upon an evaluation paradigm, we can then move forward in the evaluation process. An integrated approach to evaluation often provides the strongest form of measurement for a program or service.

The Evaluation Process

Before we get into the specifics of different evaluation models, it is appropriate to consider a generic evaluation process. The generic process, or framework, remains the same no matter which model is used to formulate the evaluation plan. It serves to remind us about the needed steps to complete evaluation within the programming cycle. Just like the larger process of programming, the process of evaluation is cyclical. And, as mentioned several times, evaluation is an integral part of the complete program process. Therefore, evaluation is a cycle within the cycle of programming.

The evaluation cycle begins early on in program design. The users and uses, paradigm, model, and techniques of evaluation are clearly spelled out *while the program is being designed and planned*. In other words, the evaluation for a particular program is designed at the same time that program implementation is designed.

Evaluation involves first understanding the agency and the people who will be using the evaluation results. This information helps to form a value orientation (i.e., how we know something is considered good or bad) relative to program characteristics. A decision then has to be made about world-view (i.e., qualitative or quantitative) and the most appropriate evaluation model (based on several factors, e.g., personal preference, programmer skills, desired information, resources available). Next, an evaluation tool or technique must be selected. Lastly, the program is implemented. Because formative evaluation allows us to make corrections in midcourse, some level of evaluation is conducted shortly after the program is introduced and periodically through-

out the implementation process. Adjustments are made, and the program is continued. Upon program completion a summative evaluation is conducted, the data are collapsed and analyzed, a report is written, and the information is disseminated to those who will use it in future programming efforts.

As a reminder, we are advocating a utilization-focused evaluation process, no matter the paradigm or model utilized. According to Patton (1982; 1997) the essence of this orientation is twofold: first, those people who will use the evaluation results must be identified as real people, preferably by name; and second, evaluators must work with those individuals to make decisions about the evaluation process. The utilization focus is based on ten basic premises.

1. A concern for use should be the driving force in the evaluation;
2. The concern for use is ongoing and continuous from the very beginning;
3. Evaluations should be user-oriented;
4. Once identified, the users of the evaluation results should be active in the entire evaluation process;
5. There are multiple and diverse interests surrounding the evaluation;
6. Careful selection of those who will use the results will allow for high-quality participation;
7. Evaluators have a responsibility to train users in evaluation processes and the use of information;
8. There are many ways in which evaluation processes and findings are used;
9. A variety of situational factors affect evaluation; and
10. Serious attention to utilization involves financial and staff time costs.

By adhering to these ten premises and bearing in mind the use of the evaluation, a programmer will collect useful data which have real meaning in terms of program and participant satisfaction. Remember, no matter which of the following models or techniques is used to conduct program evaluation, it is the orientation toward users that sets utilization-focused evaluation apart from other types of evaluation.

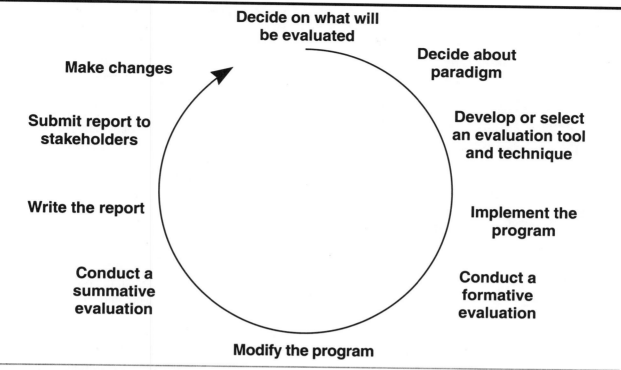

Figure 12.8   The evaluation process is cyclical.

Evaluation Models

As you might imagine for a profession that relies on the effective and efficient delivery of programs and services for its livelihood, there are quite a few models and approaches describing how we might evaluate the quality of our work. While most programmers tend to have a favorite model or two, having a look at several of them helps put perspective on things and may help in better understanding this element of the programming cycle. You are encouraged to work to fully understand each model, and begin to examine different situations when it might be most useful to apply each model. Each approach has certain strengths and weaknesses that make it more or less suitable in certain conditions.

Intuitive Model

We can venture to say that intuitive evaluation is used by everyone at one time or another. In fact, it is a method of discrimination (i.e., sorting through) and evaluation used by each of us in various aspects of our lives. The intuitive model is what we use when we have "a feel" or gut reaction to something. For instance, we "know" a program is going well or not

based on our feelings which are based on receiving all kinds of sensory input.

Intuition has been described as being the culmination of various stimuli, both conscious and subconscious, that form an impression on our subconscious. For instance, when we informally observe a program we notice participant reactions, the setting, numbers of participants, types of equipment used, numbers and reactions of staff, and so on. This information enters our subconscious and is compared with our expectations of what the program "should" be like. The judgment we make based on this comparison is intuitive evaluation; we are involved with discernible elements of evaluation (i.e., judging value or worth), we are simply unable to articulate what they are. While this model is not based on scientific methods, it is easy-to-use, is used on a day-to-day basis, and is low-cost in terms of time and money. Unfortunately, it is also low in reliability (consistency) and the evaluator might not address the issues of real concern.

Application. Intuitive evaluation is most appropriate when a quick overview of the program is needed; or, if there are no funds, staff, or the time to do a more in-depth evaluation. In addition, intuitive evaluation is often used between the periodic

Figure 12.9   The evaluation toolbox includes all models.

structured formative evaluation efforts. Intuitive evaluation provides a general sense of things which may then lead to a more structured form of evaluation. To maximize the usefulness of this model, several people should be invited to share their intuition about the success or failure of a program. This allows for triangulation (i.e., using several data sources to verify information) and strengthens the reliability of the evaluation.

When to avoid. The intuitive model of evaluation should not be utilized when it is the only evaluation method intended—the lack of systematic process and reliability cause it to be too weak to be used alone. Intuition is not a strong alternative for a comprehensive summative evaluation, nor does it work particularly well in process evaluation. In addition, if formal documentation of evaluation is required, this model would not be sufficient; too much is done in a "casual" fashion.

Evaluation by Goals and Objectives

Evaluating by goals and objectives is a clear cut method to determine if a program or service has accomplished what it said it would. It is also the most commonly used method of evaluation in parks, recreation, and leisure services (Henderson & Bialeschki, 1995; Kraus, 1997). This is one aspect of almost all evaluation efforts—someone in the organization or evaluation hierarchy wants to know if an agency or program has met its goals and objectives. This model is sometimes referred to as the goal attainment model (Theobald, 1979). It begins with an articulation of the organization philosophy, mission and vision. Next, program specific goals and objectives are developed; the program is implemented, and those goals and objectives are measured.

To many in the profession of parks, recreation, and leisure services, writing program goals and objectives is as unappetizing as conducting evaluations. This is because writing meaningful goals and objectives can be difficult and requires a good deal of practice. Students are encouraged to begin practicing writing goals and objectives early in their studies as they will find them to be extremely useful in a variety of classes, as well as in the profession. Because programs and services should reflect the mission and underlying philosophy of the organization, we should have a solid understanding of these elements upon which to base the goals and objectives.

Goals

A goal may be short-term or long-term. It is a course of action that one intends to follow—an aim. It is broad-based and rather global in nature. Objectives are the steps to reaching the goal. They are very specific and measurable. Poorly written or a total lack of goals and objectives may result in activities and programs without focus, unsatisfied participants, ineffective leadership, and evaluation limited in usefulness (Jordan, 1996). Examples of program goals include:

- To aid in participant skill development;
- To increase the health and well-being of community members;
- To provide healthy and wholesome recreation opportunities for adolescents;

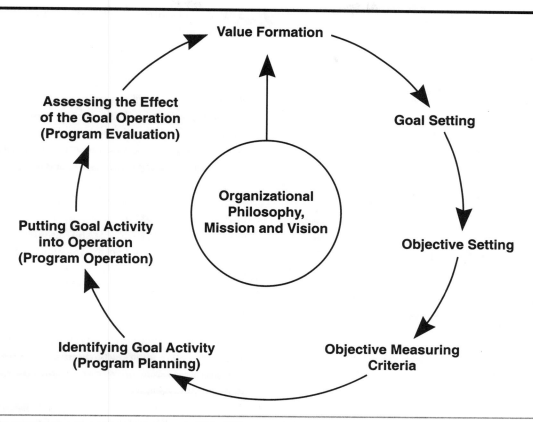

Figure 12.10 Evaluation by Goals and Objectives (Adapted from Theobald, 1979)

- To encourage social interaction among participants; and
- To maximize participant fun and enjoyment while also maximizing profit.

A programmer identifies the goals and objectives for each program to provide structure and focus to leisure experiences—this is done during the planning stages and is related to the anticipated evaluation process. Goals are broad statements that describe the intent of a particular program or event.

Objectives

Objectives are the steps to reaching goals. If one were to picture a staircase, objectives would be the individual steps and the goal would be at the top of the stairs. Each step can have three different types of objectives: *cognitive*, *behavioral*, and *affective*. *Cognitive* objectives are those that deal with thinking, *behavioral* objectives deal with physical actions and skills, and *affective* objectives deal with feelings and emotions. In parks, recreation, and leisure services all three objectives are addressed through

programs and services, although one may be more emphasized than another. To utilize evaluation by goals and objectives we would ask questions designed to determine if the stated goals and objectives had been met.

Application. Evaluation by goals and objectives can be very useful in a variety of situations. When a formal, relatively objective evaluation is desired, this is a useful model to follow. In addition, when goals and objectives are well-written and related to the agency mission this model can be particularly enlightening. As far as program settings go, evaluation by goals and objectives fits in well with therapeutic recreation since typically, each client is evaluated on her or his progress toward specific goals and objectives. It also works well with commercial recreation ventures where goals and objectives are often clearly spelled out.

When to avoid. This form of evaluation is not the best choice when poorly written goals and objectives exist (or there are none). In addition, because the evaluation closely follows the establishment of goals and objectives, someone will need to develop

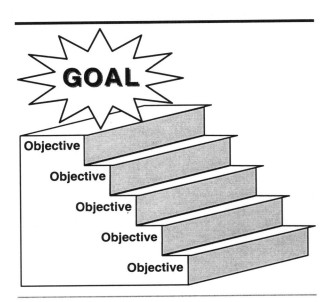

Figure 12.11 Objectives are the steps to reaching a goal.

an instrument to measure the specific goals and objectives for each program. This can be time-consuming. Therefore, if staffing concerns exist, another model might be a wiser choice.

Goal-Free Model

The goal-free (or black box) model of evaluation (Henderson & Bialeschki, 1995; Theobald, 1979) is one where the evaluator is unaware of the program goals and objectives before undertaking the evaluation. This often requires the use of an evaluator from outside of the organization. The idea is that the evaluator will examine the program in its totality and evaluate all that is observed. This allows for a very holistic approach to the evaluation process. In fact, because of the holistic approach, this model relies heavily on qualitative methods to gather information. It can provide a wealth of information about the interrelationships of the various factors affecting a program or service.

Application. The goal-free model of evaluation is increasing in popularity among parks, recreation, and leisure service programmers. It is rich in data and provides an excellent overview of the entire organization or program in process. If we want to see how various elements of a program interact, the goal-free model provides this type of information. In addition, it elicits a fresh look at efforts of the organization, in part, because it is usually done by a person external

to the organization. Because of its richness and open view, the goal-free model is a very solid choice to use when interested in process evaluation and formative evaluation. It can also be used to provide general information and clues as to what aspects of the program or service need closer inspection.

When to avoid. There are times when we would not want to use a goal-free model of evaluation. For instance, it can be time-consuming and costly, especially if an outside evaluator is used. In addition, it is not the best method to use when we want to examine one small element of the organization. Furthermore, the data that result from this model are words—qualitative data. If staff are unskilled in qualitative methods and techniques, or the users of the evaluation want numbers (i.e., quantitative data), then another model would be a better choice.

Evaluation by Standards

Evaluation by standards has been mentioned earlier in this chapter. It refers to the use of external standards against which a program or agency is measured to determine quality. If standards are met, the program is said to be a quality program. This model provides an objective approach to evaluation—the standards are usually developed and the program monitored by an outside agency or group of professionals. This model is often used in conjunction with the "expert judgment approach" to evaluation. Criteria are established as standards, agency personnel engage in a verification process (indicating which standards are met and which are not), and outside experts come in to review the efforts of the agency in this regard.

Application. This model of evaluation is appropriate when it is mandated by law to meet external standards (i.e., the ADA). It is also a good model when it is desirable to comply with industry standards (common practice in the field) as this is an indicator of quality. In addition, meeting standards is often good documentation for a risk management plan, and can aid in professional networking.

When to avoid. Standards should not be used as a basis for evaluation when the standards do not reflect agency practice, mission, or philosophy. Misapplying standards to a program or agency can be detrimental in the long run. In addition, it can be expensive, so if expenses are a concern, this might not be the best evaluation model to follow. Furthermore, standards are a minimum, and if we do not intend to exceed most standards we may be doing our agency and constituents a disservice by solely relying on this technique.

Systems Models

Systems models to evaluation are commonly used for special events and other programs or services that tend to follow a well-defined path or timeline. We mentioned these earlier in Chapter Three as bases for theories of programming—they help in decision-making processes and provide graphic representation of the programming process. They also serve as evaluation models or techniques. Because these models are visual and detailed relative to what needs to be done and in what period of time, they are favored by many in our field. Several models fall within the general systems category—Gantt, Performance Evaluation Review Technique (PERT), and Critical Path Method (CPM).

Gantt Chart

A Gantt chart (named after the person who developed the model) is essentially a bar chart that depicts a timeline of events which comprise a program. To use this model, we need to first break down the program into the components that need to occur to make it happen (program task analysis). When these

elements are identified they are placed on a calendar and the time for completion is noted by use of a bar chart. If all timelines are met, the program design process is said to be successful (see Figure 12.12).

Program Evaluation Review Technique (PERT)

The PERT process builds on the Gantt model. In addition to the timeline graphically represented by the Gantt chart, PERT includes a flow chart that depicts how a program will occur from the establishment of objectives through the evaluation process. Time estimates to complete the event components are identified and links between events are noted with the flow chart. This model provides a very detailed look at the logistical elements of a program. This type of system is particularly appropriate for process evaluation, because it can tell us how we planned an event, and if that planning process was effective (see Figure 12.13, page 262).

Critical Path Method (CPM)

Taking the systems approach to evaluation one step further, CPM, or Critical Path Method, adds one more element to the PERT system. In addition to the timeline and flow chart of events, we now add the factor of how each program component

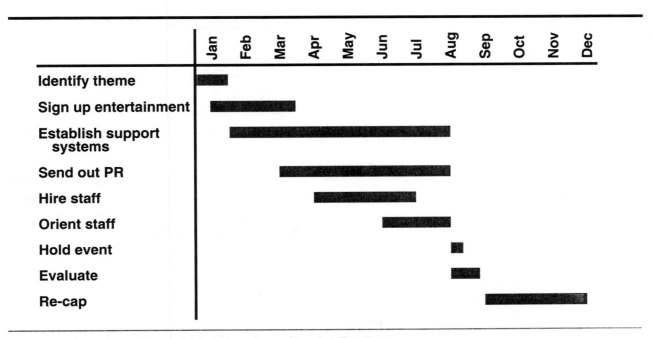

Figure 12.12 Example of a Gantt Chart for a Special Event

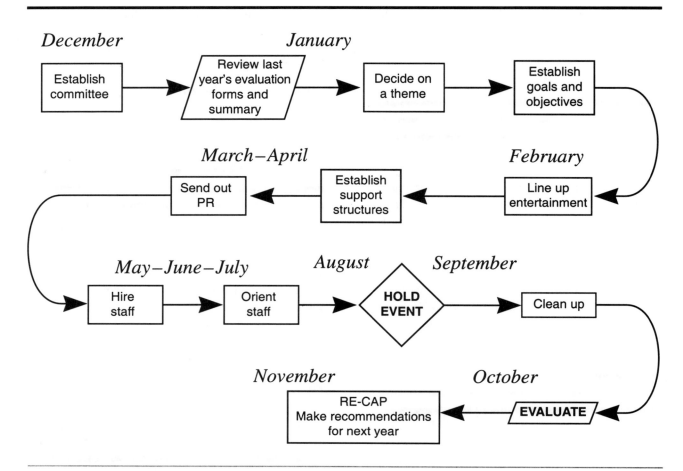

Figure 12.13 A PERT Chart identifies tasks and a timeline in a flow chart format.

relates to another. In the flow chart, arrows are drawn to graphically represent the most efficient path to accomplish objectives (see Figure 12.14). With CPM we have:

1. A breakdown of each component necessary for the program cycle;

2. An estimated timeline for completion of each component;

3. A flow chart of when each component should be addressed and how it relates to other program components; and

4. Arrows indicating the most efficient path to take to successfully implement the program.

As with PERT, CPM is useful in process evaluation because it provides so much process information.

Application. Systems models to evaluation are appropriate for use when we either need or desire a business-like orientation. Because they are systematic and include three broad steps—input, process, output—they are relatively easy to follow. They provide a clear path of checkpoints and timelines for programmers. Another strong suit of these models is that they are process-oriented. At a glance, we can see where the program is in the cycle of development, and make changes as program implementation is anticipated.

When to avoid. Systems models of evaluation are best avoided when we want to learn about issues of quality such as participant satisfaction or facility appropriateness for the event. The very nature of systems models of evaluation (quantitative) limits the type of information gained through their use. In addition, a special event or program may be too large or convoluted to maximize the use of these models in evaluating an event. Systems models are quite broad and may not allow for in-depth measurements of quality.

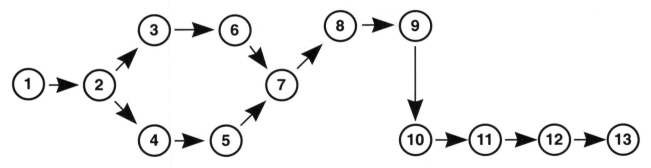

1. Establish committee
2. Review past evaluations
3. Decide theme
4. Establish goals and objectives
5. Line up entertainment
6. Establish support structures
7. Send out PR
8. Hire staff
9. Orient staff
10. Hold event
11. Clean up
12. Evaluate
13. Re-cap

Figure 12.14 The critical path method (CPM) utilizes a basic structure to provide a visual representation of what tasks are done when.

Cost-Benefit Analysis

As an evaluation model cost-benefit analysis is often used in commercial recreation settings and other instances when budgeting is a bottom-line concern. It examines the relative effectiveness of alternative programs and strategies in terms of costs (Farrell & Lundegren, 1991; Lundegren & Farrell, 1985). In addition, it determines the relationship of costs to benefits derived from the program (Theobald, 1979). The types of costs that are examined include direct costs (e.g., staff salary, promotion, equipment) as well as indirect costs (e.g., insurance, utilities, maintenance). These are weighed against direct benefits (e.g., revenue generated, customer loyalty) and indirect benefits (e.g., decrease in social problems, the concomitant decrease in property taxes) (Hendon, 1981). Much of this was discussed earlier in the pricing chapter.

Application. The cost-benefit model of evaluation is beneficial if we need to adhere to a business approach where money and profit are of primary concern. Also, in a situation where budgetary constraints and the need for cost or benefit documentation exists, this is an appropriate model of evaluation. This model is particularly useful when trying to decide between program priorities as it helps to clearly identify financial advantages and disadvantages of various issues.

When to avoid. Because cost-benefit analysis is concerned with the financial bottom line, it measures monetary efficiency more so than program effectiveness or quality. This model is often most useful when used in conjunction with other types of evaluation that do a better job of measuring actual program quality. We should avoid using cost-benefit analysis as an only method of evaluation when we

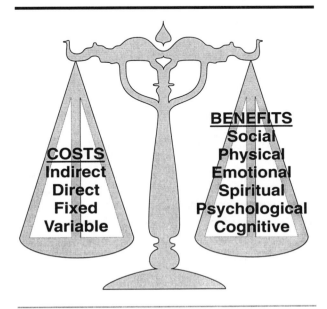

Figure 12.15 Cost-benefit analysis involves weighing the identifiable costs with benefits of a program.

want to know about participant satisfaction, program leader effectiveness, or overall program quality.

As we can see, there are a variety of models that can be used in planning the program evaluation process. Some of them fit better with the quantitative paradigm, others fit best with the qualitative paradigm, and others fit either view equally well. It is up to each program evaluator to decide among the models based on several factors. In utilization-focused evaluation, two primary considerations are the user and uses of the evaluation findings. The most appropriate model, then, will be partly determined by these two factors. In addition, the primary and secondary purposes of evaluation have a great deal of influence on the evaluation model selected, as do the skills and preferences of the individual(s) conducting the evaluation.

We have discussed evaluation paradigms, evaluation models, and evaluation techniques. To move further along the evaluation process and begin to design the actual evaluation we look to guiding questions to help focus our evaluation. If, in the evaluation process, we answer the following six key questions, we will have put together a very viable evaluation system to aid in program development.

Guiding Questions

Why?

First, we must decide why we are doing this evaluation. *What are the primary and secondary purposes of this evaluation?* Bearing in mind that the ultimate purpose includes the goal of using the evaluation findings (e.g., utilization-focused evaluation), we still need to articulate other aims of every evaluation. Is it for program improvement? to satisfy external standards? to assuage fears of money being wasted? to compare to other similar programs? or to document the impacts of programs on participants? There are many reasons for conducting evaluations and we need to be clear about why we are conducting each one.

Who?

The who question consists of several subquestions: *Who* is to conduct the evaluation? *Who* will be impacted by the evaluation? *For whom* is the evaluation designed? *Who* will have an impact on the evaluation? *Who* will participate in the evaluation

process (as part of the sample)? Answers to these questions help us in terms of choosing an evaluation model, and provide guidance in terms of how we implement the evaluation and how we treat the results.

What?

What answers the question of what we will evaluate. We need to identify the attributes or characteristics that reflect the stated purposes of the evaluation. There are typically five elements of a program open to evaluation: *areas and facilities, personnel, participants, policies and procedures,* and the *program itself (activity)* (Henderson & Bialeschki, 1995). We might decide to conduct a comprehensive evaluation or only examine one component—this is dependent upon time, staffing, money, and other organizational factors.

When?

When will the evaluation be conducted? During what season, which week, and what time of day? *Timing* is very important to several types of evaluation and should be considered in every evaluation design. In addition to asking about when the evaluation will be conducted, it is equally important to have a sense of the programming and evaluation cycle timelines. This includes when the report will be written and disseminated.

Where?

At which *physical location* will the evaluation be conducted? The area should be conducive to the type of evaluation being administered and should help to reflect the primary and secondary aims of the evaluation. Consideration should be given to addressing location concerns such as accessibility, weather, traffic flow, and so on. For instance, if we wanted to evaluate a swimming or boating program we would want to make sure respondents had a dry, warm place in which to complete the evaluation form. Sometimes we mail evaluations to constituent's homes, in which case the location is somewhat out of our control.

How?

How will the evaluation be conducted? Which *paradigm* (qualitative or quantitative) will be utilized? Which *model* of evaluation is best-suited to get at the types of data desired? Which *techniques* are most appropriate considering all of the pertinent issues (e.g., time, money, programmer experience).

Answering the questions of why, who, what, when, where, and how helps to provide substantive information to the evaluator. By writing down our intentions relative to each of these questions we provide ourselves with a comprehensive view of the evaluation process and enhance our evaluation success.

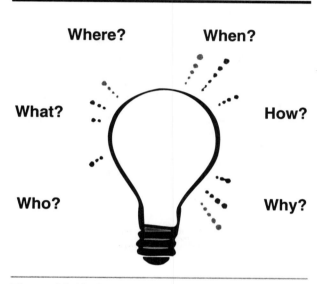

Where? When?

What? How?

Who? Why?

Figure 12.16 Answering several questions helps to guide a programmer in the evaluation process.

Summary

It is very clear—program evaluation is one element of the larger programming cycle. It is integral to program development and aids in many ways. Evaluation can be used to improve programs and services, for risk management and safety reasons, and to ascertain whether or not predetermined goals and objectives have been met. In addition, program evaluation is used to aid in decision making, to justify expenditures, and to increase participant satisfaction. Furthermore, program evaluation can be used to explain keys to success, comply with standards, and is evidence of a commitment to the profession.

Ethical and political issues can influence program evaluation as can cultural biases held by the evaluator. These need to be addressed in the planning of the program evaluation process. Some people involved in evaluation prefer to adhere to a quantitative world-view, while others utilize a qualitative world-view. No matter one's perspective, several different evaluation models may be utilized in the evaluation process. These models include the intuitive model, evaluation by goals and objectives, as well as by standards; the goal-free model, and several systems models. Deciding which paradigm and model to follow is based on many factors inherent in the planning process.

References

Belasco, J. and Stayer, R. (1993). *Flight of the buffalo*. New York, NY: Warner Books.

The Benefits Catalogue. (1997). Canadian Parks and Recreation Association, 1600 James Naismith Drive, Gloucester, Ontario, Canada K1B 5N4.

Davis, J. (1992). Reconsidering the use of race as an explanatory variable in program evaluation. In A. Madison (Ed.), *New Directions in Program Evaluation, Vol. 53, Spring 1992*, pp. 55–67. San Francisco, CA: Jossey-Bass.

Farrell, P. and Lundegren, H. (1991). *The process of recreation programming: Theory and technique, 3rd ed.* State College, PA: Venture Publishing, Inc.

Graham, P. and Klar, L. (1979). *Planning and delivering leisure services*. Dubuque, IA: Brown & Benchmark.

Henderson, K. and Bialeschki, M. D. (1995). *Evaluating leisure services: Making enlightened decisions*. State College, PA: Venture Publishing, Inc.

Hendon, W. (1981). *Evaluating urban parks and recreation*. New York, NY: Praeger.

Howe, C. (1993). The evaluation of leisure programs: Applying qualitative methods. *Journal of Physical Education, Recreation and Dance, 64*(8), 43–46.

Jordan, D. (1996). *Leadership in leisure services: Making a difference*. State College, PA: Venture Publishing, Inc.

Kraus, R. (1997). *Recreation programming: A benefits-driven approach*. Boston, MA: Allyn & Bacon.

Lundegren, H. and Farrell, P. (1985). *Evaluation for leisure service managers: A dynamic approach*. Philadelphia, PA: CBS College Publishing.

Madison, A. (1992). Primary inclusion of culturally diverse minority program participants in the evaluation process. In A. Madison (Ed.), *New Directions in Program Evaluation, Vol. 53, Spring 1992*, pp. 35–44. San Francisco, CA: Jossey-Bass.

Murphy, J., Niepoth, E. W., Jamieson, L. and Williams, J. (1991). *Leisure systems: Critical concepts and applications*. Champaign, IL: Sagamore Publishing.

Patton, M. (1982). *Practical evaluation*. Newbury Park, CA: Sage.

Patton, M. (1987). *How to use qualitative methods in evaluation*. Newbury Park, CA: Sage.

Patton, M. (1990). *Qualitative evaluation and research methods, 2nd ed.* Newbury Park, CA: Sage.

Patton, M. (1997). *Utilization-focused evaluation: The new century text*. Newbury Park, CA: Sage.

Rossman, J. R. (1995). *Recreation programming: Designing leisure experiences, 2nd ed.* Champaign, IL: Sagamore Publishing.

Theobald, W. (1979). *Evaluation of recreation and parks programs*. New York, NY: John Wiley and Sons.

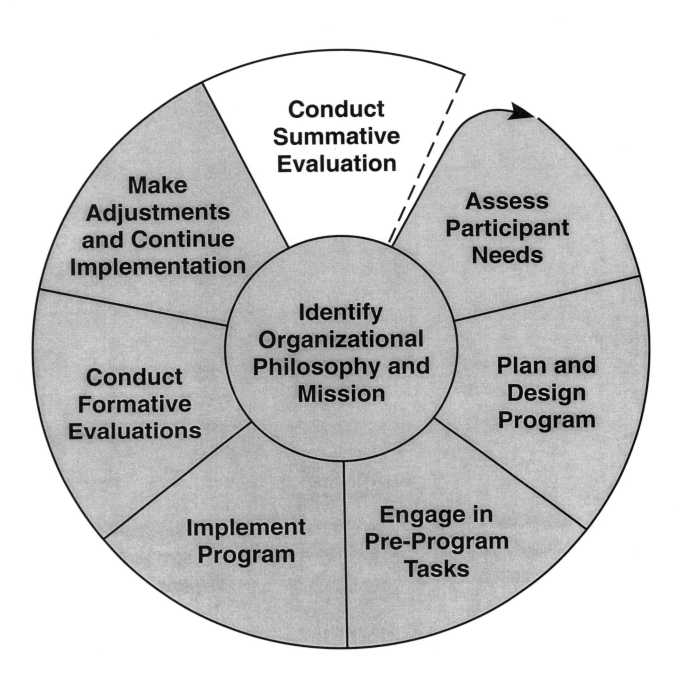

Chapter Thirteen

Evaluation Tools, Techniques, and Data Analysis

A "mere" perception problem. The real problem is that perception is all there is. There is no reality as such. There is only perceived reality, the way each of us chooses to perceive a communication, the value of a service, the value of a particular product feature, the quality of a product. The real is what we perceive.

Peters, 1985, p. 83

Learning about models, tools, and techniques to collect information for program evaluation is essential. The same is true for data analysis. While we might prefer the quantitative paradigm over the qualitative or vice versa, and we might have a particular model in mind that will answer the evaluation questions we have, we still need to know how to go about gathering that information. There are techniques that are appropriate for each paradigm, and several that are suitable for each evaluation model. Each programmer must decide which is most appropriate for the existing circumstances and then put it into action. This chapter will provide an overview of selected sampling techniques, several data collection techniques, and data analysis procedures all of which are necessary elements of evaluation.

Sampling

Sampling, or choosing which people will participate in an evaluation, is a concern any time we want to systematically collect data from a group of people. Part of the expectation of a systematic process is that with enough information, another person can replicate (copy) what we did and come up with information against which we can compare our results. While we will not offer a comprehensive look at sampling procedures here, we will offer enough background for you to have a general understanding of how to go about choosing individuals to participate in the program evaluation process.

In evaluation terms, a *population* consists of all constituents in one's service zone—they are all people who potentially could be a part of the evaluation process, and they might be users or nonusers. We say potentially, because very few agencies have the time, money, or staff to include every possible constituent in an evaluation. In addition, statistically, after a certain number of people, it becomes redundant to include everyone.

A *sample* is a subset of the larger population who will participate in the evaluation process. We usually try to identify a sample that is representative of the larger population, but there are times when this is not possible. By selecting a representative sample we can generalize our findings to the larger population and make broad statements about overall program quality. For instance, if we asked people who were a representative sample to rank their five favorite activities, after analyzing the data we could say that V, W, X, Y, and Z were likely the five favorite activities of the entire population. If the sample was not representative of the population, we could not make such a global statement.

Bearing in mind that we need to be systematic in our sampling methods, we need to clearly state the procedures we use to select the people who participate in the evaluation process. If representation to the larger population is desirable, we will want to use some form of random selection. *Random sampling* is a method that relies on the premise that *every person in the population has the same chance as every other person to be selected for the sample.*

For example, if the population is the entire community, we need to find a way to identify *every* community member (e.g., including those with and without permanent addresses, those with and without telephones, those who have or have not registered for our programs).

Once the entire population has been identified, we then choose a method to select individuals from among the larger group so that every person has the same chance of being selected as every other person. This is commonly done by computer or by hand using a random numbers table; it may also be done with a technique called "fishbowl with replacement." In this technique, every name is placed in a fishbowl and drawn one at a time. In order to ensure the equal chance rule, once drawn and the name recorded, the name is replaced in the fishbowl and another name drawn. This continues until we have the desired number of names.

Systematic random sampling is a method that first generates a random list of all members of the population, then systematically chooses every *n*th name from that list (Farrell & Lundegren, 1991; Henderson & Bialeschki, 1995; Kraus & Allen, 1987; Lundegren & Farrell, 1985; Rossman, 1995). Knowing the size of the population and the desired size of the sample will determine what figure is used for *n*. For instance, if our population is 10,000 and we want 100 people in our sample, we would select every 100th name from our list. An example of this

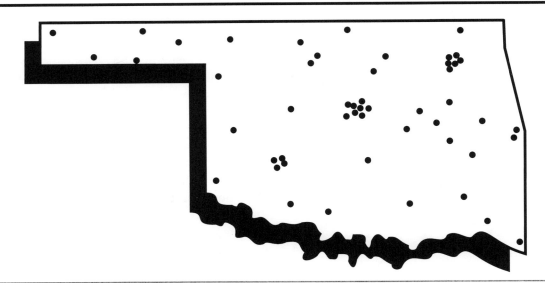

Figure 13.1   A random sample would select people who represent the entire population.

technique is to use a membership or mailing list, randomly point to a name on that list, then identify every *n*th name after that to be in our sample.

A couple of nonrepresentative sampling techniques include *convenience sampling* and *purposive sampling*. These techniques do not allow us to make generalized statements about the evaluation findings to the larger population. As you might suspect, convenience sampling is based on the ready availability of people to participate in the evaluation process. For instance, at a festival the sample might be chosen based on individuals who were approached and agreed to participate. This convenience sample offers no representation to the larger population. For example, we might discover at the festival that only adults who were dressed well and looked friendly were approached. Therefore, the visibly less friendly individuals at the festival were eliminated because they did not look as open to being approached by those conducting the evaluation. When we report our evaluation findings we will only be able to say that the *people who were approached* thought such and so. We can *not* say that *all* festival attendees felt that way.

Purposive sampling is a technique that results in individuals being chosen from the larger population based on predetermined criteria. Criteria might include participation in a particular program or that individuals represent a particular group (e.g., female, over 65 years old, ethnic minority). If used, the criteria chosen for sample selection must be made explicit in the final evaluation report so that others have a clear understanding of how evaluation participants were selected. In both convenience and purposive selection, the ability to generalize findings to the larger population is limited. For instance, if either of these two sampling techniques were used we could not say that "from this evaluation it is apparent that the community felt the program was a success." We could only say that the individuals who responded to the evaluation felt the program was a success.

Concerns with Tools

Once we know the population and have decided on a sampling technique we are ready to select a technique or tool for collecting program evaluation data. Evaluation techniques or tools are varied and offer different strengths and limitations for their use. Instrumentation refers to the actual tool or instrument used to gather information for an evaluation. Most commonly used are paper-and-pencil surveys, but people can also be instruments when they are interviewers. In either case, we need to be concerned with three elements related to the instrument: reliability, validity, and usability.

Reliability

Reliability refers to just what it sounds like—How reliable is the instrument? Can it be counted on to elicit similar information if used again? Another word for reliability is consistency. Does the instrument measure a phenomenon consistently over time? If we cannot count on the instrument to be stable and reliable, then it is of limited use in evaluation. To determine reliability, we often administer the instrument to two different groups or to the same group at two different times, and compare answers. If the responses are similar, we can say the instrument is reliable.

According to Henderson and Bialeschki (1995), to increase reliability in quantitative evaluation

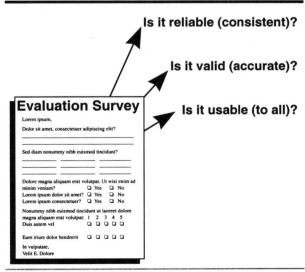

Figure 13.2   Three Concerns about Evaluation Instruments

techniques we should have well-written items, lengthen the instrument, pilot test the instrument before using it on a large-scale, provide clear directions, and be sure the instrument is appropriate for the individuals completing it. If we are using a qualitative paradigm, we would want to be sure to use an audit trail. We do this by documenting everything we did so that others might follow our steps without difficulty. The audit trail becomes a record of the entire data collection process. It should be extremely detailed and follow accepted practice relative to the chosen data collection technique.

Validity

Not only are we concerned with consistency of responses, but we are also concerned with whether or not the instrument measures what we intended it to measure (Henderson & Bialeschki, 1995; Howe, 1989; King, Morris & Fitz-Gibbon, 1987; Kraus & Allen, 1987; Lundegren & Farrell, 1985; Patton, 1982; Rossman, 1995; Sanders, 1992). This is validity. There are several forms of validity, three of which directly relate to evaluation techniques: construct validity, content validity, and face validity. *Construct validity* refers to the overall question of whether or not an instrument measures what it set out to measure—Is it evaluating the appropriate construct or attribute of the program? For instance, if we set out to evaluate the safety of a facility, questions about aesthetics would not be valid items. *Content validity* refers to the actual content of the instrument—Does the content found on the instrument cover all the areas we want to evaluate? Are the items inclusive—is the instrument thorough? Lastly, *face validity* refers to whether or not "on-the-face-of-it," it looks like the instrument measures what it says it measures (Patton, 1997). Having several different people make this assessment is important to ensure accuracy.

Henderson and Bialeschki (1995) suggest that to improve instrument validity we should use subjective evaluation, choose an appropriate evaluation instrument to match a particular model, use a pilot test prior to expanded use, and ensure clear directions are given for use. If we have utilized a qualitative paradigm where the evaluator is the instrument we can increase validity through prolonged engagement (i.e., observing the program over an extended period of time), use of examples and negative cases (i.e., to add to and confirm our written descriptions), and

provide thick (rich-detailed) descriptions of our observations and experiences (the more detailed and thorough, the better).

Usability

In program evaluation, usability (and utility) is an important concern for an instrument. This refers to how easy and convenient respondents find the evaluation process, and to the usefulness of the evaluation report upon completion (Henderson & Bialeschki, 1995; Patton, 1982, 1986, 1997; Rossman, 1995). It directly relates to utilization-focused evaluation. If an instrument is not usable, it is of limited value.

Usability of a quantitative instrument can be enhanced by ensuring ease of administration (giving a paper-and-pencil evaluation outdoors in a rainstorm is not reflective of usability), designing the instrument to take a reasonable amount to time for completion (i.e., most evaluations should be able to be completed in 15 minutes or less), making the instrument easy to score and interpret, and keeping the evaluation process at a reasonable cost (Henderson & Bialeschki, 1995; Patton, 1987; 1990). In the case of qualitative evaluation methods, to increase usability we should make sure we have a trained and competent evaluator, be sure we have the time commitment to complete the process, use triangulation (i.e., use multiple evaluators, ask both staff and participants, and/or use more than one data collection tool), and explain all variances in our findings. In both cases the final report should be well-written and the information in it easy to use.

Tools and Techniques of Data Collection

Quantitative Techniques

As a reminder, the quantitative *paradigm* takes thoughts, attitudes, and opinions held by respondents and converts them to numbers. This is also true of quantitative *data collection techniques*. By assigning number values to standard items on a survey, comparisons within and between groups can be made and numerical norms can be established. For instance, we can say that levels of participant satisfaction with a particular program are above average. In fact, with quantitative data, if we use the right statistical techniques we can even say how much above average a certain program is rated. There are several quantitative techniques and tools to collect evaluation information, a few of which are mentioned here.

Head Counts

Head counting is a method used quite frequently in parks, recreation, and leisure services (in fact, it is often overused). It refers to the counting procedures used in program evaluation. Head counting may include counting participants in attendance at an event, or may use some other unit of participation measurement such as participant hours or participant days (commonly used in park settings) (Mull, Bayliss & Ross, 1987). It is fast, easy to do, and easy to understand. At the same time, however, head counts fall short in terms of measuring program quality, effectiveness, and efficiency. For example, if a person were to ask how successful a program was and the answer was, "Very successful! We had over 100 people show up!" The number of people in attendance is designated as the evaluation criteria, however, those 100 people may have been extremely dissatisfied with the program quality. In addition, if only ten people were in attendance (and we expected 100) that information is not enough to judge the program as a failure. Those ten people might have had a very positive experience. It could be that the need for such a program was limited, there was a conflict with another large event, publicity was poor, or some other reason. As Theobald (1979) indicated, head counting in and of itself does not address levels of satisfaction or quality.

Questionnaires

Questionnaires, or surveys, are another common method of data collection for program evaluation. They consist of written (i.e., paper or electronic form) standardized items (i.e., everyone is asked the same things in the same format) and can be relatively quick to administer and analyze. They can be administered by:

1. Handing them out to participants and asking them to drop them in a box;

2. Mailing them and providing a self-addressed, stamped-envelope for return;

3. Conducting them through e-mail or some other electronic medium;

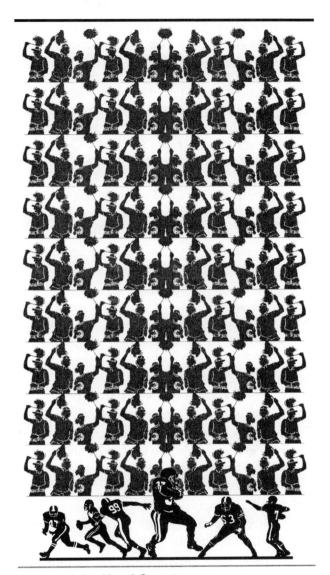

Figure 13.3   Head Counts

4. Asking the survey questions verbally over the telephone; and

5. By administering them to a group of people all at once.

When designing questionnaires, there are several considerations to bear in mind to enhance reliability, validity, and usability. The following information comes from much practice and working with evaluation questionnaires over a long period of time. You are encouraged to add to the list as you learn more about constructing surveys over the course of your academic and professional careers. The following suggestions are adapted from Farrell and Lundegren

(1991), Henderson and Bialeschki (1995), and Lundegren and Farrell (1985):

Design and Layout Concerns. Design and layout concerns have to do with the aesthetics of a questionnaire. A well-designed questionnaire or survey can aid in completion and return rates, and enhances professionalism. There are several issues to bear in mind (see Figure 13.4a and 13.4b for examples as marked in brackets):

a. Minimize the use of white space (empty space) on a survey. Be sure the questionnaire looks aesthetically balanced [A].

b. As much as possible, put items that address the same general topic together on the survey [B].

c. Put items that are of the same format (i.e., Likert scale items, semantic differentials) together. This helps minimize confusion with multiple and repeated instructions [C].

d. Use a typeface that is a 10 to 12 point font or larger for ease of readability [D].

e. If using both sides of the paper, be sure to give directions on the bottom of the page to turn the page over and respond to all items [E].

f. Ask the most nonthreatening questions first; save demographic questions for the end of the questionnaire [F].

g. Typographical errors, blotches, light ink, or other unsightly printing errors are *not* acceptable—the questionnaire should look clean, sharp, and inviting,

h. If you have a long list of items, visually separate them with extra white space by groups of five (i.e., insert an extra wide line between items 5 and 6).

i. If same-format items carry over to another page, repeat the instructions and any acronyms (e.g., SA = strongly agree, A = agree, D = disagree, SD = strongly disagree, and NA = not applicable) to remind respondents about the abbreviation.

j. If the survey has open-ended items, leave enough room for the type and length of response you would like [G].

Wording Issues. How questionnaire items are worded directly impacts not only the cooperation of respondents, but also the types of responses received. Poorly worded items may result in the item being skipped over (i.e., not answered), or the answer may not match the intended outcome. Helpful hints with wording include:

a. Use wording appropriate to the intended evaluation respondents (i.e., items written for children should differ from those written for adults).

b. The directions should be clear, concise, and repeated if the questionnaire is lengthy. In addition, each section of items should have its own directions.

c. Use only one idea per item so that the entire question is answerable.

d. Be as clear, brief, and simple as possible with each item.

e. Avoid leading questions that suggest a response.

f. Avoid technical jargon and unfamiliar language. Try to write at a sixth grade level since this is the average reading level of people in the United States.

g. If using closed-ended items, be sure all possible responses are provided. By using the category "other," an individual can fill in the blank if their response is different than those provided.

h. Avoid questions that are worded negatively (e.g., Do you not agree that we need a new swimming pool?).

i. Be sure the questions are relevant to the intent of the questionnaire.

j. The questionnaire should be easy to prepare, administer, and score.

Question Formats

There are three basic types of formats that can be used in writing survey questions: closed-ended items, forced-choice items, and open-ended items. The type of format used depends, in part, upon the type of desired responses (see Figure 13.5, page 277). *Closed-ended* items are those that have a limited number of choices, but may offer a middle ground

Date: _____   Course Title: _____

D

Course Evaluation

The purpose of this course evaluation is to aid the instructor in making decisions related to the course. Your input will be utilized to determine course content, use of the textbook, how the course is taught in the future, assignments and other methods of student evaluation (e.g., exams), and other elements of this course. Your feedback is greatly appreciated!!

Section I: Semantic Differential

Please make an X in the space which best describes how you feel about this course.

THE COURSE MATERIAL IS/WAS:	— **B**					**A**

C

highly interesting	__|__|__|__|__					quite boring
very valuable	__|__|__|__|__					worthless
too difficult	__|__|__|__|__					too easy
too slow paced	__|__|__|__|__					too fast paced
very relevant	__|__|__|__|__					irrelevant
clear, easy to follow	__|__|__|__|__					confusing, hard to follow
very practical	__|__|__|__|__					very philosophical
current, up-to-date	__|__|__|__|__					old, out-of-date

THE INSTRUCTOR:	— **B**

cared about students	__|__|__|__|__	didn't care about students
was fair to all students	__|__|__|__|__	appeared to have favorites
was difficult to understand	__|__|__|__|__	was easy to understand
had high expectations	__|__|__|__|__	had low expectations
was closed to new ideas	__|__|__|__|__	was open to new ideas
was very knowledgeable	__|__|__|__|__	didn't appear to know the subject
helped me to understand	__|__|__|__|__	did not care if I understood
was boring, lost my interest	__|__|__|__|__	was able to keep my interest

Section II: Open Feedback

Please be *as specific as possible* and make suggestions for change as you think of them.

1. What aspects of this course have been most beneficial to you (such as topics, techniques, assignments, interaction with classmates)?

PLEASE COMPLETE OTHER SIDE	— **E**

Figure 13.4a Sample Survey—Side A

2. What do you suggest to change this course (such as length of class, prerequisites, textbook, teaching techniques)?

G

3. Comment on the grading system (such as number of assignments, consistency in grading, assignments match course goals).

4. In what areas should the instructor improve (such as dealing with students one-on-one, communication, enthusiasm)?

5. What characteristics of the instructor were most helpful (such as explanations, gestures, progression)?

6. Overall, how would you grade this course? (circle one grade)

      A   B   C   D   F

Please explain why you assigned this grade:

7. Any other comments?

8. What year in school are you? (circle one)   1st   2nd   3rd   4th   5th   6th+

F

9. What is your sex?   Female   Male

10. What is your major? _____

Figure 13.4b Sample Survey—Side B

response, such as a Likert scale item or a semantic differential item.

Forced-choice items are a special type of closed-ended question that have limited response choices and respondents are forced to select one of the alternatives. These might be yes/no or true/false questions, checklist, or rank order items. They tend to be either/or types of questions with no middle ground. Closed-ended and forced-choice items can be difficult to write, but tend to be easy to score, analyze, and interpret.

Open-ended questions are written in such a way as to encourage wordy responses. They are least restrictive in terms of possible responses and can yield a wide variety of answers. Questions that can be answered with a yes or no should be designed as closed-ended items rather than open-ended. Open-ended questions require some thought and time to answer, and some respondents skip right over them.

In addition to being concerned with questionnaire layout and question format, a program evaluator must also decide what *type* of questions to ask.

Likert Scale Item

For each of the following items, please rate your level of satisfaction (1 is low and 5 is high).

	not at all satisfied				extremely satisfied
Registration process	1	2	3	4	5
Staff courtesy on the telephone	1	2	3	4	5
Appearance of the reception area	1	2	3	4	5

Semantic Differential Item

Please think about your experience with our agency staff. On the scales below, please place an X indicating your opinions.

Agency Staff

warm _____ cold
happy _____ grumpy
can't be bothered _____ helpful
positive attitudes _____ negative attitudes

Checklist Item

Please circle all of the sports you would participate in, if they were available.

basketball   volleyball   scoop ball
wallyball   soccer   disc golf
double dutch   rugby   softball

Ranking Item

Please rank the following issues by level of importance to you. A number 1 ranking means that item is of the most importance; a 5 is the lowest importance.

____ constructing a new community swimming pool
____ maintenance at our county parks
____ safety for evening and night programs
____ childcare for center activities
____ purchasing new resources for the community library

Open Ended—Single Stage

In the space below, please describe one new activity, service, or program you would like to see us provide.

Open Ended—Multiple Stage

Please describe your concerns about accessibility of this facility.

What suggestions do you have for improvement?

Figure 13.5   Question Formats

For instance, closed-ended items might include Likert scale items, semantic differential items where opposite words are placed on a continuum and respondents are asked to mark on the continuum where their opinions lay, checklists, and ranking items. Open-ended items might be simple (single stage) or compound (multiple stage). Each item elicits slightly different types of information. When deciding on question type, keep in mind the users and uses of the evaluation. You are encouraged to examine the figure depicting each type of item closely to better understand the nature of the type of question.

Importance-Performance Analysis

As the name implies, this technique for data collection involves asking questions about both the importance of certain program attributes as well as how well an agency is doing related to the performance of that attribute. It is an effective measure of participant satisfaction with an actual program, service, or product (Henderson & Bialeschki, 1995; Rossman, 1995). First, a set of attributes to be measured are identified and questions are written that will measure how important participants think those attributes are. On this portion of the survey we might ask participants about the *importance* of features such as clean facilities, skilled leaders, new equipment, smooth registration procedures, and family activities.

On the next section of the instrument, we would ask the same questions, only this time, we ask participants about their level of satisfaction with the organization's performance on each feature. Therefore, in the example above, participants would be asked to rate their *level of satisfaction* with clean facilities, skilled leaders, new equipment, smooth registration procedures, and family activities. By using a grid to compare the importance and performance items we can see which areas need improvement, which are doing well, which should be moved to a lower priority, and which areas are apparently being stressed more than they need to be (see Figure 13.6).

Qualitative Techniques

Following the qualitative paradigm, qualitative techniques are those efforts that elicit rich descriptions and use words to explain the data. They collect information from several different sources to learn about multiple perspectives. The data are not as easily reduced as numerical data, but they do provide a holistic and rich explanation of what is occurring. There are a whole host of data collection tools that are qualitative in nature, and a few of the more common techniques are described here.

Review Documents and Records

In program evaluation reviewing documents and records is done fairly regularly on an informal basis. It refers to the *systematic* review and examination of records and documents related to a program (King, Morris & Fitz-Gibbon, 1987). In program evaluation we might study past program plans, reports, and other documents related to an event or service. We might look at registration forms, attendance records, trip permission slips, agency files, sign-in sheets, client treatment plans, and so on. By studying records we can gather information without putting undue demands on participant time and energies.

Observation

Observation is a tool for gathering data about a program or activity that utilizes the program evaluator as the data collection instrument. The program evaluator might be an *open observer* where it is obvious to everyone that she or he is observing the event, or she or he might act as a *covert participant observer* where she or he would engage in the program or activity just like a participant and no one would know an evaluation was being conducted. From either position, the observer makes in-depth observations about her or his experiences and documents what was noted. The aim of observation as an evaluation tool is to see the program through the eyes of participants and make detailed notes about behaviors, the setting, comments people make, and so on. Observation provides detailed descriptions about peoples' activities, behaviors, actions, and interpersonal relationships that are a part of all human relationships (Patton, 1990). It can yield fascinating information.

Observation may be a structured form of evaluation meaning that in advance, the program evaluator knows the answers to the six guiding questions (i.e., why, what, who, when, where, how) or it may be more flexible. This technique fits well within the goal-free model of evaluation. It can also be used

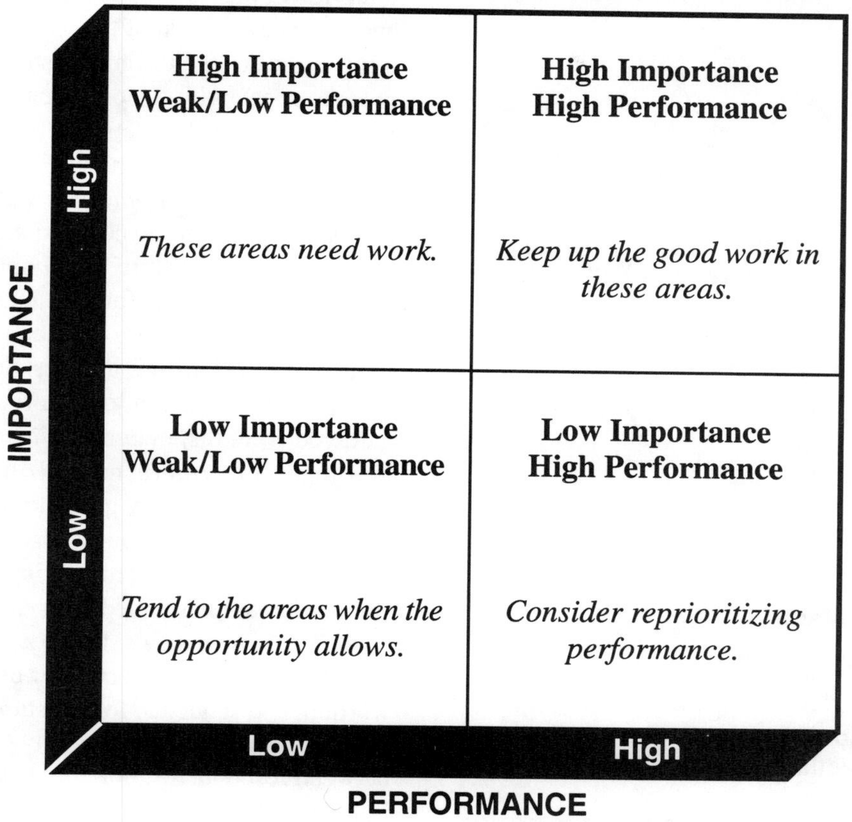

IMPORTANCE High	**High Importance Weak/Low Performance** *These areas need work.*	**High Importance High Performance** *Keep up the good work in these areas.*
Low	**Low Importance Weak/Low Performance** *Tend to the areas when the opportunity allows.*	**Low Importance High Performance** *Consider reprioritizing performance.*
	Low	High

PERFORMANCE

Figure 13.6   Importance-Performance Grid

with a more restrictive checklist of criteria for quality (King, Morris & Fitz-Gibbon, 1987).

A *case study* is a study of observations related to a specific case—a case might be a person or an activity/program. This type of evaluation enables us to make comparisons between cases. We might note the diversity of participants and programs involved at a particular organization, or the extreme or unusual cases we see (Compton, 1989; Henderson & Bialeschki, 1995; Howe, 1989; Huston, 1987; Kraus & Shank, 1992; Patton, 1990; Peterson & Gunn, 1984; Sanders, 1992; Wright, 1987). Case studies are used quite frequently in therapeutic recreation settings with individual clients as well as in commercial and tourism-focused recreation to identify and highlight examples of excellent business practices.

Sociometry

Sociometry is a technique that examines relationships among and between people—participants, leaders, and spectators. It results in a graphic representation of how people interact with one another, and sometimes, how they interact with equipment or structures (Henderson & Bialeschki, 1995; Kraus & Allen, 1987; Russell, 1982; Sanders, 1992). This is done by drawing lines between interacting elements as seen in Figure 13.7 (page 280). From this information we can examine how our program facilitates relationship building, social skills, and leadership development.

Focus Groups

Focus groups are a special form of group interviewing. When using this technique we assemble a group of people based on preselected criteria. They might be representative of larger constituent groups or they might have certain background knowledge that makes them particularly useful for responding to pointed evaluation questions. A focus group usually consists of eight to twelve people and examines all aspects of one broad question. In groups, the program evaluator can get multiple perspectives and respondents tend to "play off of each other" resulting in

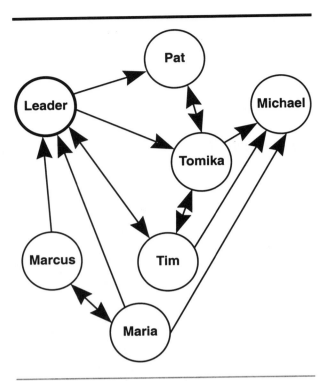

Figure 13.7   A sociometric diagram indicates direction of interactions between people.

diverse and rich responses. Focus groups can be helpful in needs assessment as well as program or organizational evaluation.

Interviews

Interviews can be time-consuming tools for data collection, but they result in a richness of data and understanding not found with many other techniques. There are four primary methods of interviewing that differ based on amount of structure to the interview process. The *informal conversational interview* is one that occurs when individuals are readily accessible to be engaged in conversation (Henderson & Bialeschki, 1995; Lundegren & Farrell, 1985; Patton, 1987, 1990). The interviews might occur in the hallway, between programs, at a park, or any time and place participants and programmers meet. Interview questions are developed as the conversation flows and in-depth information can be elicited from each participant. Of course, with this technique, different people might be asked different questions, so it could be difficult to compare responses. In addition, because it is done on an informal basis,

interviewer biases may creep into the questions and the interpretation of the responses. Furthermore, if this is the desired technique, strong efforts must be made to speak with a representative sample of the population.

The second least structured interview format is the *interview guide approach*. With this technique topics and issues to be covered are predetermined, but the sequence differs based on the flow of the interview. This allows for a bit more consistency in terms of response categories than the informal approach, but still allows the free-flowing nature of a conversation. Again, a lot of information can be gathered from respondents using this form of interviewing. Furthermore, multiple interviewers can use the same interview guide to ask large numbers of individuals similar questions.

More structured forms of interviewing include standardized open-ended interviews and the closed quantitative interviews. In the *standardized open-ended interview* the interviewer uses the exact same wording and sequence for questions with each interviewee. This enhances the ability to compare answers between respondents, but may result in a "stiffness" in the interview process. The *closed quantitative interview* is similar to an oral survey where individuals are asked questions and select answers from among choices. The analysis of data is much simpler for closed quantitative interviews than in other forms of interviewing, but this type of interviewing is very constraining to respondents. It can result in distorted meanings because it doesn't allow for probing or expanding on answers.

Triangulation

Triangulation means to use more than one source of information (i.e., ask questions of participants, staff and observers), multiple evaluators, or several types of evaluation models or tools in the search of "the truth" relative to what is being evaluated. Certainly, it makes sense that if participants, leaders, and spectators were asked to evaluate the same program we would receive more detailed and complete information than if just one of those groups were asked the questions. Similarly, if two or three program leaders or supervisors were asked to conduct an evaluation of the same program, we would get a more complete picture of that event than if only one person conducted the evaluation. Lastly, if multiple tools were

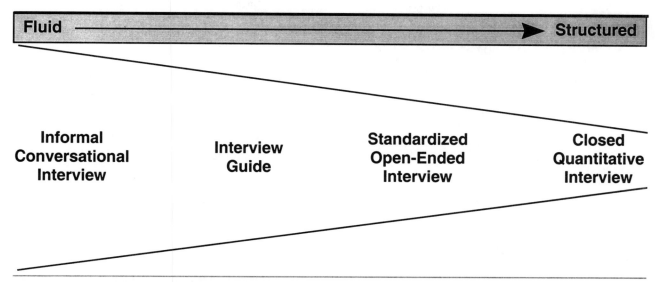

Figure 13.8   Interview methods move from being very fluid to highly structured.

utilized to collect data, we would also enrich our findings. Often, triangulation is constrained by a shortage of resources (e.g., staff, time, money). As much as possible, however, we should try to utilize triangulation in evaluation.

As we can see, there are a wide variety of qualitative and quantitative evaluation techniques. Each has its own advantages and disadvantages, and each can result in data about programs and services. Data are the information we collect from our constituents. Once we have collected data, we must do what we can to collapse them into something meaningful. That is the role of data analysis.

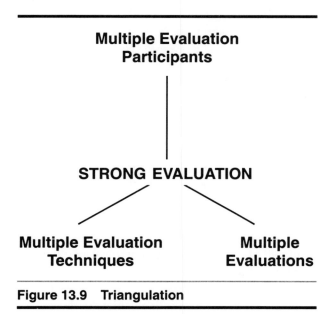

Figure 13.9   Triangulation

Data Analysis

Imagine that we've recently conducted a program evaluation and a sample of 75 people responded to 25 different items on an evaluation form. This results in a potential of 1,875 different pieces of information gathered for one small evaluation! The human brain is not designed to make sense of close to 2,000 pieces of individual information at once. Therefore, we must collapse these data into smaller, more manageable sizes. This is the purpose of data analysis—to reduce the many individual responses we've gathered so the evaluation will make sense and be relatively easy to utilize. When we collapse the individual pieces of data in the analysis process, this is referred to as *data reduction*. We simply reduce large volumes of information into a smaller, more understandable set of data. This process differs depending on whether one used quantitative or qualitative techniques to collect data.

In quantitative techniques of data collection there are two primary analysis techniques used to reduce data. These provide two different types of general information. *Inferential statistics* are mathematical techniques that allow us to make generalizable statements about the population's (i.e., all constituents') thoughts, feelings, and attitudes. *Descriptive statistics* are mathematical techniques that give enough broad information to provide a general overview or description of the sample's (respondents') thoughts, feelings, and attitudes.

Figure 13.10 Data analysis is a method of reducing large amounts of individual data into a few meaningful pieces of data.

Inferential Analysis

As mentioned above, inferential data analysis allows us to study the evaluation results and make general statements that relate to the entire population, rather than just the sample. Thus, these techniques are more sophisticated than descriptive techniques, and require additional understanding of mathematical processes. Because most evaluations tend to be descriptive in nature, we will cover only descriptive data analysis techniques here. Inferential statistical analysis techniques are usually covered in other academic courses concerned with evaluation and research.

Descriptive Analysis

Descriptive analysis is what most program evaluators attempt to do—provide a description of the feelings, thoughts, and attitudes of respondents. This can be accomplished through following qualitative or quantitative paradigms and/or data collection techniques—both can provide a description of respondents' feelings, thoughts, and attitudes. Before we can provide a general description about how respondents felt about the program, however, we must do something to reduce the large set of data. Techniques for analyzing data for descriptive analysis are found in the following sections.

Techniques for Quantitative Evaluation

A quantitative paradigm and quantitative data collection techniques result in numbers. These might be on a Likert scale, in rank order items, or arbitrarily assigned numbers, as in the case of demographic variables (e.g., female = 1, male = 2). Numbers are relatively easy to reduce to more manageable and understandable terms and we do it all the time in our daily lives. We calculate batting averages, bowling scores, median home costs, and other numbers when we work and play.

Frequencies

Calculating frequencies is the simplest of descriptive data analysis techniques. We simply count the number of "whatever" we have. For instance, when we indicate that we have four apples, three oranges, and three bananas, we are reporting the frequency of each occurrence of apples, oranges, and bananas. In evaluation, we might indicate that 12 people answered 'Yes', 47 answered 'No', and 7 did not respond to a particular item. These are frequencies. See Table 13.1 for a sample of how frequencies are typically represented in a written report.

Percentages

You can see the usefulness of calculating frequencies—it takes (in the example above) 66 individual responses and reduces them to three easy-to-understand categories. By themselves, however, frequencies are not always useful. For instance, if we had 175 total responses and 85 people answered 'Yes' while 90 said 'No', this does not translate into very meaningful information—the numbers are too big and too close for our brains to really make sense of things. Therefore, we might calculate percentages

---

Table 13.1   Calculating Frequencies

Frequencies are calculated by simply counting the number of one score. On the following item, people identified their level of satisfaction with the registration process.

On the following scale, please indicate your level of satisfaction with the registration process (1 = extremely low, 5 = extremely high).

Twenty-one people responded to this item and their scores were:

2	3	4
3	2	3
1	4	4
2	1	2
3	2	3
2	1	1
1	1	2

A frequency table for these scores would look like this:

score	frequency
1	6
2	7
3	5
4	3
5	0

Table 13.2   Calculating Percentages

Percentages are calculated by dividing the frequency of one score by the total number of responses—in this case, 21. Using the same example of satisfaction with the registration process, the percentages are calculated below.

On the following scale, please indicate your level of satisfaction with the registration process (1 = extremely low, 5 = extremely high).

Twenty-one people responded to this item and their scores were:

2	3	4
3	2	3
1	4	4
2	1	2
3	2	3
2	1	1
1	1	2

A frequency and percentages table for these scores would look like this:

score	frequency	%
1	6	28.6
2	7	33.3
3	5	23.8
4	3	14.3
5	0	0

---

of each possible response. Percentages are calculated by dividing the number of one response by the total number possible. Thus, continuing our example of 175 respondents, we find that 45.6% of respondents (85/175) answered this item 'Yes' while the other 54.4% (90/175) responded 'No.' This presents the responses in a slightly different light and allows us to make statements about the "majority" and "minority" of respondents. Percentages are often reported in conjunction with frequencies to provide an additional dimension of understanding.

Measures of Central Tendency

Getting a bit more sophisticated in terms of reducing or analyzing quantitative data, we can also calculate measures of central tendency. This information informs us about how and where scores fall relative to the "middle" of the data set. By examining "middle" scores we get a little more information about relative positioning of data. There are three measures of central tendency which describe the "middle" score—mean, median, and mode. They may or may not be the same number for any one data set, although the numbers are typically close to one another.

Mean

The mean is another term for mathematical average. Remembering from early years of school math, the mean is calculated by adding all the scores and then dividing by the total number of responses. Therefore, with a Likert scale item where respondents could answer on a scale from one to five, we could calculate the average score. See Table 13.3 (page 284). When presented along with frequencies and percentages, this information provides a deeper understanding of how individuals responded to a particular item. Do be careful not to try and get an

Table 13.3   Calculating the Mean

The mean is calculated by dividing the total of all the scores by the total number of responses. Continuing with our example with satisfaction of the registration process we calculate the mean below.

On the following scale, please indicate your level of satisfaction with the registration process (1 = extremely low, 5 = extremely high).

Twenty-one people responded to this item and their scores were:

2	3	4
3	2	3
1	4	4
2	1	2
3	2	3
2	1	1
1	1	2

First, we add all the scores above (sum=47). Next, we divide that by the number of respondents (21) resulting in a mean of 2.24.

---

average of arbitrarily assigned numbers (e.g., female = 1, male = 2) as we should not calculate means of items that are categorical and not number-based since these numbers won't add to understanding the constituent base.

Median

The median is another measure of central tendency that provides a slightly different perspective in understanding data. The median is calculated by finding the middle of a series of scores by counting up or down the column. First, we list all the scores individually in descending order (this makes it easier to do additional calculations). If there are 15 total scores, the eighth one in the column is at the middle—that is, it is in the middle of the column whether we count from the top or the bottom. See Table 13.4 for an example of this. Median scores are reported, usually in conjunction with the mean, to help better understand how people answered a particular item. When interpreting the median we report that half of the respondents scored higher than *n* and half of the respondents scored lower than *n*.

Table 13.4   Calculating the Median and Mode

The median is calculated by finding the halfway mark between the scores. Continuing with the example with satisfaction of the registration process we identify the median below.

On the following scale, please indicate your level of satisfaction with the registration process (1 = extremely low, 5 = extremely high).

First, arrange the scores in descending order:

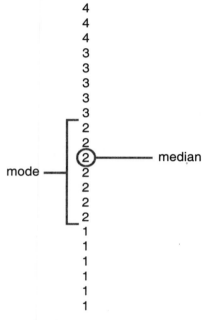

There are 21 scores, so divide 21 by 2 to find the halfway mark. This number is 10.5. Then, starting at the top, count down 10.5 scores. In this case, that places us in the midst of the 2 scores; thus, 2 is the *median*.

The *mode* is the most frequently occurring score. We can see from the frequencies table and by looking at the table above that the most frequently occurring score is 2. Thus, 2 is the mode.

Mode

Calculating the mode is the simplest of the three measures of central tendency and is also the roughest estimate of where the middle score is found. The mode is the most frequently occurring score. There can be multiple modes—if there are two, the data are considered to be bimodal, if there are three modes, the data are trimodal, and so on.

Measures of Dispersion

Measures of dispersion refer to describing how spread out the data are. This is helpful to know because even though measures of central tendency might be similar (or even the same), the scores might look different. For instance, if we were evaluating the safety and risk management aspects of a program facility using a standard evaluation tool with Likert scale items, we might find that two different areas in the building had a mean score of 3.5 on a 5.0 scale. In looking at the individual items that were used in the calculation of these means, however, we might find that one facility received mixed scores of one and fives, while the other facility received a score of three or four on every item. Obviously, one facility is "okay" on all areas, while the other is excellent in some areas and severely deficient in others. This information would lead us to take different forms of action in these two facilities.

Range

The *range* is the easiest form of dispersion to calculate. It is determined by calculating the difference between the highest and lowest scores and adding one. For example, in the facility safety check above, the range of the first program area with scores of ones and fives would be five; the range of the second program area where scores were all threes or fours would be two. Each quantitative item on an evaluation instrument has a range. It gives us an idea about how spread out the scores are. See Table 13.5.

Standard Deviation

Standard deviation is the most commonly used measure of dispersion, or spread, of data (Henderson & Bialeschki, 1995). It is the average of how much the scores differ from the mean. The smaller the standard deviation, the more closely the scores are clustered around the mean and the more alike are peoples' responses. The higher the standard deviation, the more spread out the scores are from the mean, and the more dissimilar peoples' responses. See Table 13.6 (page 286).

Table 13.5   Calculating the Range

The range is calculated by subtracting the lowest score from the highest score and adding one. Continuing with our example with satisfaction of the registration process we calculate the range below.

> On the following scale, please indicate your level of satisfaction with the registration process (1 = extremely low, 5 = extremely high).

Twenty-one people responded to this item and their scores were:

2	3	4
3	2	3
1	4	4
2	1	2
3	2	3
2	1	1
1	1	2

The highest score (4) minus the lowest score (1) equals 3; then add 1. The range for the above scores is 4.

Techniques for Qualitative Evaluation Analysis

We've already mentioned that using a qualitative paradigm and qualitative data collection techniques results in words rather than numbers (for example, words are data on open-ended items on a questionnaire or in an interview, and are considered data). These words provide a rich data set that enables us to gain understanding of what people thought in relation to the items we asked. In analyzing *quantitative* data, we try to reduce the data into smaller, more manageable categories or, even, single numerical descriptors (e.g., the mean).

In analyzing *qualitative* data, rather than reducing the data to one word, we attempt to understand and report the various perspectives that people shared (Henderson & Bialeschki, 1995; Patton, 1987, 1990). We work to bring order to the data and organize "words into patterns, categories, and basic

Table 13.6   Calculating Standard Deviation

The standard deviation is calculated by following several steps. Continuing with the example of satisfaction with the registration process, we can identify the standard deviation below.

On the following scale, please indicate your level of satisfaction with the registration process (1 = extremely low, 5 = extremely high).

①
First, arrange the scores in descending order:

score	deviation (s)	squared differences (s^2)
4	1.76	3.10
4	1.76	3.10
4	1.76	3.10
3	0.76	0.58
3	0.76	0.58
3	0.76	0.58
3	0.76	0.58
3	0.76	0.58
2	−0.24	0.06
2	−0.24	0.06
2	−0.24	0.06
2	−0.24	0.06
2	−0.24	0.06
2	−0.24	0.06
2	−0.24	0.06
1	−1.24	1.54
1	−1.24	1.54
1	−1.24	1.54
1	−1.24	1.54
1	−1.24	1.54
1	−1.24	1.54

② Second, determine the mean—in this case, the mean is 2.24. (See Table 13.4, page 284.)

③ Third, determine the difference between each of the individual scores and the mean—those calculations are the "deviation" column.

④ Once the deviation is determined, square each of the deviation scores and place that value in the squared differences column.

⑤ Then, sum the column of squared differences.

$$\Sigma s^2 = 21.86$$

⑥ Next, we divide the sum of the squared differences by the total number of respondents less one.

$$21.81 \div 20 = 1.093$$

⑦ Finally, we take the square root of that figure—this is the standard deviation.

$$\sqrt{1.09} = 1.05$$

Standard deviation (steps 5 through 7) can also be represented by the statistical formula:

$$\sqrt{\frac{\Sigma (s)^2}{(n - 1)}}$$

where Σ = "sum of"
s = deviation from mean
n = number of responses, measurements (data)

descriptive units. Interpretation involves attaching meaning and significance to the analysis, explaining descriptive patterns, and looking for relationships and linkages within the data" (Henderson & Bialeschki, 1995, p. 261). Thus, analyzing data of any type involves both analysis and interpretation.

Open Coding

Open coding is a process used to organize qualitative data so that emerging patterns and themes become evident. This is the process of reducing data into smaller, more manageable pieces and coding it so we can easily find it again later. To begin, we must read and reread the data several times. As we go through this process we can place a code word next to the data to aid us in focusing on our findings. These initial codings are not firm; they will change based on our growing understanding as we read through the responses several times (Patton, 1987; 1990). Some people put the data (words) on index cards and sort them into like categories and patterns. Others use the cut-and-paste function of word processing programs and computers to move the data around as codes are being developed.

Enumeration

Enumeration is a relatively straightforward technique of bringing some sense to qualitative data. It is the coding and *counting* of words, themes, or patterns based on the code we have assigned (Henderson &

Bialeschki, 1995). The use of numbers in this analysis technique helps in understanding the strength and frequency of feelings. For instance, if a question asked individuals to identify the strengths of a program, we might get the following responses: great staff!; stale food; staff were warm and inviting; facilities were clean; staff were enthusiastic; I liked the way the staff treated me and my family—we felt very welcomed to this event; good facilities; and facilities were easy to get to. Enumeration might lead us to say that there were three positive responses about staff, three positive comments about the facilities, and one negative response related to the food.

In qualitative analysis we would not want to only rely on the use of enumeration as this greatly reduces the richness of the responses. To counter the potential for an overreliance on the use of enumeration, in

---

Table 13.7   Coding and Enumeration

In the example below respondents were asked to

"Please comment on the environmental policies of this recreation center."

This was an open-ended item and resulted in diverse responses. Responses are identified below, as is the initial *coding*.

Code	Response
negative—no know	I didn't know there were any!
negative/good	It seems a litttle carried away at times. I mean, having to reuse paper plates is ridiculous!
positive	I like the concern for the environment
negative—no know	I never really noticed
positive	It seems to make sense to me!
positive	In this day and age it is critical to have pro-environment policies everywhere—thank goodness, someone is doing it!
neutral	It's messy to use a compost pile (it smells too)
positive	I like recycling whatever we could
positive	It's good to get up awareness
negative/neutral	The area around the can collection place is always sticky
positive	I'm glad it's happening!
negative—no know	Don't know what they are
neutral	Okay

Enumeration involves calculating a frequency for the codes. In this case, it would look like this:

3   Negative—no know(ledge)
1   Negative/Netural
1   Negative/Good
2   Neutral
6   Positive

evaluation reports we often provide direct quotes from the responses to help address the depth of feeling and the various aspects of what it was people enjoyed. In this way, various perspectives are shared in the words of the respondents, and most accurately understood by those using the evaluation report.

Constant Comparison

Constant comparison as a data analysis technique offers a systematic way of seeking out the meanings in peoples' responses (Henderson, 1991; Henderson & Bialeschki, 1995; Patton, 1987; 1990). It is particularly useful in dealing with interview or focus group data because there is so much of it. In this technique the data are recorded (all verbal interview or focus group data must be transcribed as quickly as possible after the initial interview), read, coded, reread, themes are developed, the data are reread and recoded, and themes are checked for fit. In fact, in this effort, other colleagues may be asked to read, code, and identify themes to see if there is consistency in interpretation. This is important to ensure accurate interpretation of raw data.

According to Henderson (1991), there are three stages involved in the constant comparison process. Stage one involves the initial coding, reducing, and organizing of the data into categories. Stage two includes comparing the various categories with one another and with the original data set to ensure appropriate interpretation. The third stage involves reworking the categories (if necessary) to talk about the data and how they fit or don't fit with evaluation criteria. At this stage it is important to ensure that no categories or important data are missed. If new themes are discovered at this stage, the process begins again.

Content Analysis

Content analysis is used when examining old records, documents, photographs, electronic media, and anything else in printed form. In program evaluation we might utilize this technique to examine reports from previous years, to better understand the community, and/or to enable accurate portrayals of things such as historic themes. In this form of analysis we use a systematic process to examine printed documents in a fashion similar to constant comparison. We look for similarities, differences, and outstanding elements.

Interpreting the Analysis

Once we've analyzed qualitative data we need to interpret it for the users of the evaluation. This tends to be a cyclical process where we look at the results of our analysis, make an interpretive statement, then look again at our results to be sure the interpretation fits. In this effort we look for negative cases that would cause us to rework the analysis, or redefine our interpretation. To ensure accurate interpretations we must take our time with the entire coding, analysis, and interpretation process. Evaluators using qualitative analysis need to remain open to changes in the midst of the analysis process. This is how qualitative data bring us to emergent ideas (i.e., notions that develop as we work), and it is one of the strengths of qualitative evaluation.

As we become more familiar and comfortable with qualitative data we will come to understand it as it was meant by the respondents. To help users of the evaluation to know it as well without going through the entire data analysis process, we need to present the findings and interpretation in a relatively straightforward fashion. This is done, in part, by making statements about the data and supporting our comments with quotes and anecdotes directly

| **1** Initial coding into categories | → | **2** Comparing categories with each other and other data | → | **3** Rework and redefine the categories |

Figure 13.11 The constant comparison process involves three stages.

from the data set. We try to present a balance of our description with the actual words of the respondents to provide the depth and richness qualitative data have to offer.

Report Writing

Once we've completed our analysis of the data we must present it in a meaningful fashion to potential users. Bearing in mind that we are proponents of utilization-focused evaluation, we want to present a written report in such a way as to maximize its usefulness. Therefore, we must consider writing style and format, as well as the content. In some cases an executive summary might be sufficient (i.e., a three to five page summary of the process and major findings with recommendations); in other situations, a full blown report might be required complete with graphics, figures, and appendices.

Generally, in a written report of an evaluation we will present background information about the evaluation explaining the why, who, what, when, where and how questions; findings (i.e., factual information learned from the data analysis); interpretations (i.e., our understanding of the reduced data based on background and other information); judgments (i.e., values and criteria used with the data); and recommendations (i.e., suggested courses of action based on the findings, interpretation, and judgments) (Henderson & Bialeschki, 1995; Morris, Fitz-Gibbon & Freeman, 1987; Rossman, 1995; Theobald, 1979). A typical report format follows.

Front Cover

The front cover of any evaluation report should include the following:

- Title of program and its location
- Time period covered by the report or date of event
- Name of evaluator(s) and how she or he can be contacted
- Information about to whom the report is submitted
- Date report is submitted

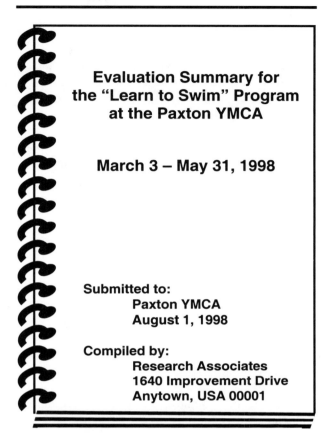

> **Evaluation Summary for the "Learn to Swim" Program at the Paxton YMCA**
>
> **March 3 – May 31, 1998**
>
> **Submitted to:**
> **Paxton YMCA**
> **August 1, 1998**
>
> **Compiled by:**
> **Research Associates**
> **1640 Improvement Drive**
> **Anytown, USA 00001**

Figure 13.12 Example of a Report Cover

Section 1: Summary

This section of a written evaluation report is a brief summary of the evaluation explaining why the evaluation was undertaken and reporting the major findings and recommendations. Sometimes this is called the executive summary. Usually, the summary is kept to fewer than 500 words and is designed for the individual who wants a quick overview of the evaluation. Although this comes first in a written report, it is actually written last (Morris, Fitz-Gibbon & Freeman, 1987).

Table of Contents

Depending upon the length of the report, a table of contents may or may not be necessary. For any report over eight pages in length, a table of contents is helpful for those searching for particular pieces of information.

Section 2: Background Information

This is the section of the evaluation report that provides the context to help readers understand all that is to follow. The amount of information and detail will depend upon the targeted audience of the report. Some will require a great deal of information, while others may already have a thorough understanding of the program being evaluated. This section also serves to keep things in context as the report is being written and helps the program evaluator to stay well-focused.

Typical information found in this section (although in varying amounts of depth) includes: general information about the organization, its philosophy, goals, mission, and vision. Also, material about the origin of the program (e.g., What was the impetus and process for program development? Who are the constituents?), philosophy and goals of the program, demographic information about the participants of the program, characteristics of the program (e.g., facilities, location, equipment, activities, program format and structure), and staffing information are included.

Section 3: Methods and Procedures

This section of the report focuses on explaining the evaluation process to the reader. The language should be such that the intended reader understands what is explained. In this section, the report writer describes the paradigm followed (i.e., quantitative or qualitative); how the sample was chosen; and what evaluation model and data collection techniques were used. In addition, information about how the instrument was developed or selected as well as information about its validity, reliability, and usability is found in this section. Other information to include relates to data collection procedures and an explanation of how the data were analyzed. A reader should have enough information from reading this section, that if she or he so desired, she or he could conduct a similar evaluation by following the information given.

Section 4: Results

This section of the evaluation report is the most straightforward, and often the most difficult to write. It should present the results of the data analysis. This is where the results of the data reduction process are presented along with graphs, tables, and figures which help explain what was found.

General Organizational Information
- History
- Philosophy
- Mission
- Vision
- Goals

Participant Information
- Demographics
- Historical Involvement
- Other Knowledge

General Program Information
- Philosophy
- Purpose
- Goals
- Target Population
- Location and Facilities

Program Description
- Event
- Staffing
- Process
- Budget

Figure 13.13 Background information in an evaluation report helps provide context for increased understanding.

Section 5: Interpretations, Conclusions, and Recommendations

The interpretations, conclusions, and recommendations section is where the program evaluator has an opportunity to explain why she or he thinks the findings came out as they did. Taking time to explain program results, utilizing the information found in "Section 2: Background Information," is helpful in putting things in context. Providing alternative reasoning is helpful. For instance, we may have found that participants were concerned about a lack of pre-event information, but we are unclear as to why. By looking at all the information we have we might speculate that the problem was due to poor event planning, a snafu with the mailing process, a poor printing job, poor selection of evaluation techniques, or some other reason. In the recommendations

subsection, the program evaluator makes suggestions relative to changes in the program based on the interpretation of the results. This should be worded clearly and in action statements. See Figure 13.14 for an example of this.

Appendices

Appendices provide a place to include additional explanatory information which serves to enhance the material found in the report. Often included in this section is a copy of the evaluation instrument (sometimes with descriptive statistics included—if appropriate), a copy of the cover letter if a mail survey was used, summaries of needs assessments or evaluations from past years, promotional material for the program, cost information, and a list of references from which community information was gathered.

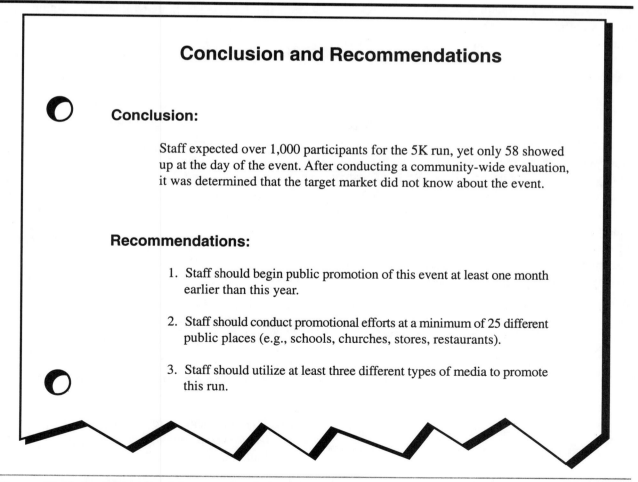

Conclusion and Recommendations

Conclusion:

Staff expected over 1,000 participants for the 5K run, yet only 58 showed up at the day of the event. After conducting a community-wide evaluation, it was determined that the target market did not know about the event.

Recommendations:

1. Staff should begin public promotion of this event at least one month earlier than this year.

2. Staff should conduct promotional efforts at a minimum of 25 different public places (e.g., schools, churches, stores, restaurants).

3. Staff should utilize at least three different types of media to promote this run.

Figure 13.14 An Example of Conclusions and Recommendations

Summary

There is much to be learned about program evaluation. We can utilize a qualitative or quantitative paradigm and associated tools for gathering data. Prior to beginning the evaluation, however, we must select a sampling technique appropriate to the intent of the evaluation process. We have choices of random and nonrandom methods to do this. Once the sample is selected we then turn our attention to instrumentation. We are concerned with the reliability, validity, and usability of the tools we are using to collect data to ensure a worthwhile evaluation process.

There are many quantitative techniques to use in collecting data, each of which has its strengths and weaknesses. Head counts and questionnaires of some sort are the two most common techniques for gathering information. Head counts do not address quality elements, and there are many issues to be concerned with when designing a written questionnaire. Qualitative techniques such as reviewing documents and records, observation, sociometry, and interviewing are used to elicit in-depth information from respondents. These tools are often used to augment the quantitative data we have collected.

Finally, reducing the data gathered is necessary to make sense of all the individual answers that have been collected. With quantitative data we commonly use descriptive analysis which includes calculating frequencies, percentages, measures of central tendency, and measures of dispersion. With qualitative data we utilize open coding, enumeration, constant comparison, and content analysis to reduce the word data we have collected. This all leads to the writing of the report. This final report includes several sections, each designed to bring understanding to what we learned from the evaluation.

References

Compton, D. (Ed.). (1989). *Issues in therapeutic recreation: A profession in transition.* Champaign, IL: Sagamore Publishing.

Farrell, P. and Lundegren, H. (1991). *The process of recreation programming: Theory and technique, 3rd ed.* State College, PA: Venture Publishing, Inc.

Henderson, K. (1991). *Dimensions of choice: A qualitative approach to recreation, parks, and leisure research.* State College, PA: Venture Publishing, Inc.

Henderson, K. (1992). Camper surveys: A tool for program planning and marketing. *Camping Magazine, 64*(3), 42–43.

Henderson, K. and Bialeschki, M.D. (1995). *Evaluating leisure services: Making enlightened decisions.* State College, PA: Venture Publishing, Inc.

Howe, C. (1989). Assessment instruments in therapeutic recreation: To what extent do they work? In D. Compton (Ed.), *Issues in therapeutic recreation: A profession in transition* (pp. 205–221). Champaign, IL: Sagamore Publishing.

Huston, A. (1987). Clinical application of quality assurance in the therapeutic recreation setting. In B. Riley (Ed.), *Evaluation of therapeutic recreation through quality assurance* (pp. 67–75). State College, PA: Venture Publishing, Inc.

King, J., Morris, L. and Fitz-Gibbon, C. (1987). *How to assess program implementation.* Newbury Park, CA: Sage.

Kraus, R. and Allen, L. (1987). *Research and evaluation in recreation, parks, and leisure studies.* Columbus, OH: Publishing Horizons.

Kraus, R. and Shank, J. (1992). *Therapeutic recreation services: Principles and practices, 4th ed.* Dubuque, IA: Wm. C. Brown.

Lundegren, H. and Farrell, P. (1985). *Evaluation for leisure service managers: A dynamic approach.* Philadelphia, PA: CBS College Publishing.

Morris, L., Fitz-Gibbon, C. and Freeman, M. (1987). *How to communicate evaluation findings.* Newbury Park, CA: Sage.

Mull, R., Bayliss, K. and Ross, C. (1987). *Recreational sports programming.* North Palm Beach, FL: The Athletic Institute.

Patton, M. (1982). *Practical evaluation.* Newbury Park, CA: Sage.

Patton, M. (1986). *Utilization-focused evaluation.* Newbury Park, CA: Sage.

Patton, M. (1987). *How to use qualitative methods in evaluation.* Newbury Park, CA: Sage.

Patton, M. (1990). *Qualitative evaluation and research methods, 2nd ed.* Newbury Park, CA: Sage.

Patton, M. (1997). *Utilization-focused evaluation: The new century text.* Newbury Park, CA: Sage.

Peters, T. (1985). *A passion for excellence.* New York, NY: Warner Books.

Peterson, C. and Gunn, S. (1984). *Therapeutic recreation program design: Principles and procedures, 2nd ed.* Englewood Cliffs, NJ: Prentice Hall.

Rossman, J. R. (1995). *Recreation programming: Designing leisure experiences, 2nd ed.* Champaign, IL: Sagamore Publishing.

Russell, R. (1982). *Planning programs in recreation.* St. Louis, MO: Mosby.

Sanders, J. (1992). *Evaluating school programs: An educator's guide.* Newbury Park, CA: Corwin Press.

Theobald, W. (1979). *Evaluation of recreation and parks programs.* New York, NY: John Wiley and Sons.

Wright, S. (1987). Quality assessment: Practical approaches in therapeutic recreation. In B. Riley (Ed.), *Evaluation of therapeutic recreation through quality assurance* (pp. 55–66). State College, PA: Venture Publishing, Inc.

Chapter Fourteen

Innovation
(and How to Find Inspiration)

Unless someone like you cares a whole awful lot, nothing is going to get better, it's not.

Dr. Seuss, 1971

It is easy to understand that as a student approaches the end of a textbook or college course, the breadth and complexity of information presented may appear overwhelming. Programmers are often faced with this dilemma as well. It may be difficult for a programmer to step into the field and immediately apply this knowledge to the programming cycle. To facilitate this we believe that it is helpful to remember that programming is not an act—it is a process. The task of programming becomes manageable when we realize that we simply need to start the process and then continue on our journey, working on one aspect at time, toward constant improvement. In Chapter Seven, we looked at the key elements of designing programs and gave particular attention to the importance of creativity and passion to that phase of the programming cycle. We will now revisit these two concepts in this last chapter as we apply them to how the recreation programmer conducts research and utilizes resources.

The acronym CPR—Creativity, Passion and Research—developed by Clark (1995) is helpful as it suggests that these three concepts are intertwined and are responsible for breathing life into programs. We believe that if every programmer practices CPR in their programming efforts, programs will remain vital, contemporary, and desirable. In addition, the process and product of programming will benefit both the programmer and constituents. We will discuss each of the CPR elements in the following section.

Creativity and Passion

Creativity and passion are integral to the conduct of research. This might seem contradictory because for many of us, the idea of research is limited to traditional views of white lab coats, endless forms, and overwhelming statistics. Therefore, the idea that research can be vital and creative rather than dry and boring can be a stretch of the imagination. For this reason, we often find that recreation programmers are less committed to this aspect of service delivery than it merits. As discussed previously, creativity is the ability to make something out of nothing, or to use something in a new or innovative way. The recreation programmer who approaches research with passion and thinks creatively is likely to find the process both productive *and* enjoyable.

Within this context it is important that we take a step back and identify what we mean by the concept of passion. Passion carries with it a connotation of being dramatic, powerful, and emotional. While these characteristics may indicate how we express passion, passion itself is more accurately characterized as an unfailing dedication to an ideal. Thus, the idea that passion is something rare and not sustainable is more myth than reality. Passion is often demonstrated by intensity and duration. For instance, when programmers make a long-term commitment to gradual and continuous improvement of programs and the organization, they demonstrate a strong sense of passion. One way in which this passion can be demonstrated is a commitment to research. This includes a new look at resources which are currently part of the programmer's "bag of tricks," as well as searching for new ideas.

It is difficult to argue with the benefit of gaining practical experience in the professional development of a recreation programmer. It is always a confidence booster to be able to conduct or adapt a program "on the spot" with little or no preparation. Acquiring this skill allows programmers to respond spontaneously to people and situations, making us more responsive to the individual needs of constituents. Leisure professionals who become too comfortable with their current level of programming knowledge tend to do a disservice to participants, the organization, program, and themselves.

No one questions the need for health professionals to continually educate themselves about current and changing medical techniques and practices. While the consequences of being comfortable with the status quo in leisure services is not generally a matter of life or death as it can be with health issues, the vitality and life of a program may be put in serious jeopardy if research is neglected. Furthermore, the programmer who is not actively involved in expanding her or his "bag of tricks" may very well experience a resulting decrease in enthusiasm and passion for the program by staff and participants as activities become stale and tedious through repetition and a lack of energy. Consequently, even programs that have a high turnover in participants need to reflect a commitment to expanding ideas and implementing change.

Research and Resources

Research goes far beyond conducting a survey or an experiment of some sort. *Webster's Encyclopedic Unabridged Dictionary of the English Language* (1996) refers to research as a diligent and systematic investigation into a subject to discover or revise facts, theories, or applications. This implies that *all* avenues of gaining knowledge and gathering resources should be utilized. This includes looking to disciplines beyond leisure services for information and ideas. Related human service disciplines and fields which may prove valuable in this search include education, psychology, social work, health services, parenting/childcare, and business. As servant leaders concerned with maximizing our abilities to meet our constituents' varied needs, we need to undertake an exhaustive search for new viewpoints and material. This requires expanding our own thinking as well as looking to other people, organizations, media, written materials, and other potential sources for assistance and guidance throughout the programming cycle.

Adapting Resources

A logical starting point when approaching research creatively is to challenge ourselves to look at the resources we already have in new ways. This includes:

1. Finding unique and different uses for equipment we possess;
2. Expanding the target group, changing locations, and/or altering timing for particular programs; and

3. Adapting activities to meet different objectives.

Sometimes it's a very minor adjustment or change that precipitates the most dramatic results.

Equipment

Introducing familiar equipment in a new way addresses the issue of "blind spots" (see Chapter Seven) because we tend to associate things with previous experiences. Consequently, if we present participants with a basketball, soccer ball, or football and give no instructions, we can predict with a fair amount of certainty how participants will use these pieces of equipment. Those with the basketball will dribble and pretend to shoot a basket; those with the soccer ball will kick it or bounce it off their heads; and those given the football will pass it back and forth. If we give them rules that are incompatible with the conventional uses of these balls, however, we suddenly create a new game or sport. To venture even further from tradition, we could give participants access to art supplies and tell them they need to use the balls in some way to create an art project. Although the equipment remains the same, by changing other variables, the possibilities suddenly seem limitless.

Another strategy is to introduce new equipment to a familiar activity. At *The Caring Connection,* a child development center in Cedar Falls, Iowa, a wading pool is filled with rice and used in place of a sand box. This provides easier clean up and stimulates the children with a different medium to explore that they don't have at home or in playgrounds at public parks. Leaders can also vary activities by altering the number of pieces of equipment generally used. Imagine what would happen when a doubles tennis game is suddenly played using two balls.

Equipment may also be adapted to create a homemade version which is often simpler and more cost-effective than the commercial alternative. For example, if our program does not own an earth ball, we could fill a garbage bag with inflated balloons for a similar effect. Another consideration is to look at new products and determine if they can be easily duplicated with existing resources. For example, Trak Paks™ are an innovative product in terms of how they are "packaged." They are small fanny packs that contain objects which represent abstract characteristics and concepts to be used when working

with groups. For instance, among the 24 "starter" items, each pack contains a key (What was the key to our success?), a bragging stone (Talk about what you did that contributed positively to the group.), and a battery (What about this activity gave us a charge?). The idea of using small objects as symbols and metaphors in group processing is the real innovation, and the idea can be borrowed and expanded upon by creating a customized Trak Pak™ for your own use. All of these strategies improve programs by increasing variety and innovation. A guideline for making equipment and resources for attaining inexpensive equipment is presented in Figure 14.1 (page 298).

People, Places, Timing

We can also be creative programmers by rethinking what we offer, where we offer it, to whom, and when. While it is a valuable skill to think in terms of developmentally appropriate activities (see Chapter Six), it is also true that we often think too narrowly in terms of individual skills and interests. By expanding our thinking, we begin to realize that we may want to offer an activity we have traditionally targeted for a particular age group to someone else. For example, we typically think about playgrounds being a resource for young children. However, a playground may also be incorporated into an obstacle course for teens or adults. Recreation programmers trying to involve senior citizens in a fitness activity by utilizing a playground as part of an obstacle course could tap into the popularity of *Bingo* with this population. *Bingo* cards could be placed at strategic places on the obstacle course to be used subsequently in the game of *Bingo*, or BINGO could be used as an acronym during promotion for a different program (e.g., Be Involved Now—GO fitness!!). Programmers do need to take care that when trying to increase the appeal of a program the program is not misrepresented to the target audience.

Changing settings can also serve as a way to create enthusiasm in participants and staff. Moving a football game to a mud hole or swimming pool adds a whole new and exciting dimension to the game. Changing the time for an activity is also a factor—both daily and seasonally. A barbecue on the beach may appeal to teens; schedule it for midnight under the stars and participation may soar (however, excellent crowd control and chaperones are a necessity). Those seeking to appeal to the more

Design Considerations

1. Concerns in deciding between "homemade" versus manufactured: quality, safety, and versatility.
2. Are materials easily obtained and in sufficient quantities?
3. Is it safe for age level/maturity level of those using it?
4. How durable is it? Maintenance required?
5. Will it be interesting and challenging plus aid in meeting the goals of the program?

Helpful Hints

1. Make one sample model before you mass-produce. You may decide on alteration.
2. Whenever feasible make enough for each participant to have one (small apparatus) or at least one piece for every group of 3–5 participants (medium to large apparatus).
3. Wood apparatus should be sanded and painted to avoid splinters; corners should be rounded off when feasible.
4. Use resources in the community to help you construct the equipment.
5. Use bolts in place of nails whenever possible, especially if equipment is to be dismantled or stored after use.
6. When soliciting for "new materials" take a sample model with you and explain how your participants will benefit by using the donor's gracious gift.
7. Allow yourself ample time to construct the equipment to ensure a quality product.
8. Trips to toy or sporting goods stores (or magazine browsing) may prove useful in obtaining ideas concerning a variety of equipment available for creative modification or utilization.

Safety and Legal Liability

The importance of maintaining a safe and healthful environment cannot be over-emphasized both from a humanistic and from a legal point of view. The use of homemade equipment places an additional responsibility on the individual who utilizes such equipment that each piece of homemade equipment be built at least to required specifications with effort being made to improve upon its design in terms of safety. The equipment should be regularly inspected and defects immediately corrected. A program of preventative maintenance that anticipates and removes potential hazards before they arise is the best way to avoid the hazards of legal liability.

Resource Banks for Inexpensive Equipment and Supplies

- Sporting goods businesses (e.g., old bike tires, old bowling pins, damaged products)
- Telephone companies (e.g., colored wires, large/small spools)
- Stores (e.g., feed sacks, plastic flags, barrels, fruit crates, large baskets, old displays)
- Tennis or golf clubs (e.g., old tennis balls, old golf balls, old nets)
- Card stores (such as Hallmark; e.g., mailing envelopes, old wrapping paper and ribbon)
- Auctions, garage/rummage sales, and pawn shops (any number of miscellaneous items)
- Furniture/appliance stores (e.g., large cardboard boxes, packing material, old mattresses)
- Travel agents (e.g., old travel posters)
- Art stores (e.g., leftover or damaged paper and other merchandise)
- Churches (e.g., old candles)
- Garment factories (e.g., old buttons, ribbon, yarn, fabric scraps)
- Building supply companies (e.g., wood and lumber, tiles, wallpaper books, color samples)
- Hardware/paint stores (e.g., linoleum, rope, chain, wood, leftover paint, end rolls of wallpaper)
- Carpet companies (e.g., remnants and scraps)

Figure 14.1 Equipment Development and Modification (Adapted from Marston, 1997)

adventurous spirits don't need to start building a ropes course; just follow the lead of the Darien (IL) Park District by offering Spikecicle Volleyball, which is outdoor volleyball held in January (NRPA, 1997).

Rules and Procedures

Changing objectives or rules of familiar games can also create excitement and enthusiasm among participants. Using the example of the *baseball*, imagine if we made a rule that players could run the bases in any order they desire (Morris & Stiehl, 1989), or use a larger or smaller or a different type of ball for the game. Think about the changing dynamics of playing *Capture the Flag* if the rules included any of the following:

- If half of any team is captured, then play is discontinued while negotiations for release are held;

- Persons who are jailed may get "early release" by performing a talent for the "parole board" made up of impartial judges; or

- Players must hold hands with at least one other player on their team at all times; any time players fail to do this, they must join the other team.

Introducing such elements to a game teaches flexibility and openness and is often used to foster cooperation rather competition. It can also be used as the means to include players of varying abilities as seen in the case example presented in Sidebar 14.1. The importance in this situation was not whether adjustments were made for Lenny or whether all players changed how they were going to play, but the fact that these children helped Lenny redefine how he saw himself. We can certainly hope that it is only a matter of time before Lenny becomes active in determining his own game adaptations.

PACE (Patience, Alternatives, Creativity, Enthusiasm)

The acronym, PACE, developed by York and Jordan (1992) incorporates all of these areas when looking specifically at programming for persons with disabilities. The underlying idea is that to be successful, a programmer must consider and meet the individual needs of participants. The key to this effort is:

Sidebar 14.1 A Case Example of Adapting Games (Adapted from Morris & Stiehl, 1989)

The fifth-grade students at Adamsville Elementary had been modifying games for quite a while when Lenny first arrived. That day they happened to be playing a variation of kickball. Lenny had never played kickball. In fact, he had not played many games because most people agreed that a boy who used a wheelchair could not participate in vigorous activities.

The children immediately began to introduce themselves to Lenny and invited him to participate in the game. Lenny was frightened—he had been alone before, but never in this sense. This time he was alone in his belief that he could not participate in such a game. The other children were already embracing a "can do" spirit and were determined to include this newcomer.

Lenny was assigned to the team at bat, some members of which had been deciding on a strategy of including him in a manner equal with his abilities. Instead of kicking the ball and running bases, Lenny had to maneuver his wheelchair through some obstacles and then squirt a water pistol at a paper cup, knock it over, and return home without colliding with any of the obstacles. If he did so, he was pronounced "safe."

Sometimes Lenny succeeded, and sometimes he did not. His classmates and he determined what he could do, verified their strategy with teachers, and then agreed that this was an acceptable option. Lenny was no longer merely a spectator. His was not a case of token involvement, but of genuine participation—of inclusion.

P. having the Patience to accept progress at any rate;

A. seeking Alternatives by modifying activities, skills, equipment, rules, and presentation;

C. acting Creatively through improvisation, modification, and adjustment; and

E. being Enthusiastic.

Figure 14.2 (page 300) suggests several specific ways programmers can modify programs and may prove helpful to those working with all populations.

Programming with PACE

Using the chart below, combine one or more pieces of equipment with one or more actions/movements to form a new activity. Add your own actions and equipment, too.

EQUIPMENT

ACTIONS/MOVEMENT	Pins	Balls	Hoops	Scooters	Bats	Tires	Ropes		
Run									
Hop									
Skip									
Jump									
Roll									
Slide									
Kick									
Throw									
Strike									
Catch									
Pass									
Crabwalk									
Balance									

Figure 14.2   Programming with PACE (Adapted from York & Jordan, 1992)

People

We often hear managers talk about people being their most important resource. While actions speak louder than words as to whether this belief is put into practice, it is an ideal that servant leaders should be passionate about making a reality. We appreciate that one benefit of this approach is that people feel valued, but the real purpose of utilizing people as resources is because they can truly help us. Trying to provide quality leisure services in a vacuum is like trying to make a pizza with only flour, water, and oregano. It is unnecessarily limiting, nearly impossible, and certainly frustrating. There is nothing so gratifying as realizing that "we are all in this together." If we are thinking and acting creatively, we will diligently utilize people within our organization as well as in the community at large.

Within Our Own Organizations

With the onset of technology came a widening of our world—we now live in an era in which even young children are aware of events which occur across the globe. While it is a good thing to broaden our horizons, particularly from the perspective of becoming more culturally sensitive, it is a huge mistake to overlook all of the resources available in "our own backyard." Even before our first day on a job, the networking process within the organization has begun; initial contacts with staff and constituents become the foundation for future relationships.

Management. If our organization is structured in such a way as to support the needs of constituents, then it is also likely that it is responsive to personnel who are functioning in direct service and middle management roles since they are the key to success. However, even in organizations that are not effectively supporting programmers and activity leaders, upper management can be a valuable resource. Therefore, even if it is difficult to get past obstacles, such as political posturing or inaccessibility, recreation programmers need to be proactive about tapping the knowledge and experience of management personnel. These are often people who have walked in your shoes and are willing to tell about it. Find out the strengths of different managers in your organization and start to build your own expertise by learning from theirs.

Constituents. We have already talked about the servant leader's desire to empower constituents and this commitment usually proves to be mutually beneficial. Not only do participants gain a sense of program ownership, but programs and programmers also benefit in a variety of ways. First of all, participants are a source of ideas. Put simply, they expand the volume of input *if given the opportunity.* They also improve the quality of ideas since they are in touch with the needs and desires of the population to be served (themselves), are often highly invested in the program and committed to the organization. Third, they serve as a link for programmers trying to network in the community—an important resource discussed below.

Colleagues. One of the real joys of working in the leisure services profession is that it is very people-oriented. So much job satisfaction comes from the people we serve, but also from the people with whom we work. The experiential nature of our education programs and the practical side of our field enable us to collaborate with coworkers. At the minimum, we should make the time to share ideas with other staff on a regular basis. This process inevitably leads to new ideas which no one would have conceptualized on their own, but result from the building of one idea upon another—creativity at its best. It is also helpful to actually work with colleagues throughout the programming cycle on specific projects or areas of development.

Community: Partnerships and Networking

One of the most important tools of resource attainment is the ability to network and establish partnerships with other entities. Minimally, this requires strong and effective social skills in order to meet new people and build relationships; ideally, this requires the ability to envision how two entities can share resources for their mutual benefit.

Businesses (Partnerships, Mentors, Donations). Forming a partnership can take many forms. One example is mentoring programs that exist in urban areas between youth serving organizations and businesses. These programs often require members of the business community to donate time on a weekly basis to a youth who is identified "at risk" and in need of positive adult role models. Another example of a partnership is soliciting sponsorship in the form of cash or product donations from businesses for a program or organization. In exchange, the leisure organization typically offers free publicity or advertisement of the products, test marketing, or service recognition in the community.

An example of a program that involved some rather complex partnerships is the A-Billy-Tea [ability] Day event conducted in Redcliffe, Queensland, Australia on December 3, 1997, the International Day of Disabled People. This celebration included visual arts, theater presentations, and a challenge course to recognize the contributions, abilities, and needs of persons with disabilities as well as to increase public awareness. A flow chart documenting steps taken in planning the event (see Figure 14.3) highlights the high level of collaboration involved including the city government, private businesses, and many nonprofit organizations.

Leisure Organizations. Just as we want to broaden our knowledge base into other disciplines, we also want to expand our resources by networking with professionals in other leisure service organizations. Possible strategies to facilitate this information exchange include:

1. Telephoning directors of similar programs and inquiring about their most successful programs and traditions;

2. Mixing business with pleasure by visiting museums, amusements parks, outdoor recreation areas and other parks, recreation, and leisure settings, and taking notes about innovative programs or ideas we can utilize; and

3. Participating in a staff exchange for whatever time or distance is feasible—this could be as little as one day at a local organization or as much as one year in another country.

While it is important to talk with professionals who work in similar settings or with similar populations, we unnecessarily limit our programs and creativity by maintaining these contacts exclusively. We can learn a great deal by collaborating across the lines that have historically served as barriers. These include parameters such as whether the organizations are:

*   Private, commercial, or public nonprofit;

*   Youth serving or adult focused;

*   Therapeutic or nontherapeutic;

*   Urban or rural;

*   Outdoor or indoor; and so on.

The complexity of our world requires us to compartmentalize; we should use this to aid us in delivering quality services, not limit our potential. We need to find out what others are doing (and not doing) in our local communities as well as nationally and internationally. Think about the possibilities if staff at museums, amusement parks, libraries, youth organizations, parks and recreation districts, daycare centers, golf courses, travel agencies, and nature centers networked successfully.

Professional Associations

Professional associations serve as a means to advance the interests of their memberships. This overall mission involves benefits to both professionals and the association. Membership in the association entitles members to certain benefits such as subscriptions to journals, trade magazines, and newsletters; reduced costs for conferences and workshops; special mailings of information and so on. Associations, in turn, are sustained by members sharing their time, talents and ideas. Thus, professional associations can be viewed from the dual perspective that they are a resource as well as an opportunity to serve (Edginton, Jordan, DeGraaf, Edginton, 1998).

Professional associations vary a great deal in their scope, geographic parameters and size. Some associations such as the Association for Challenge Course Technology (ACCT) are very specific while others like the American Association for Health, Physical Education, Recreation, and Dance (AAHPERD) have a much broader appeal. Within a particular association, such as the National Recreation and Park Association (NRPA), there are different levels of the association that serve specific locations. NRPA serves the entire country, for example, while separate, related branches serve geographic regions, states, or cities. Both the scope and level of the association affect the size that it attains which also affects the benefits that can be provided to members (due to varied resources). Parks, recreation, and leisure service professionals often begin their involvement at the local level and build on this as they become involved in and serve the parent organization.

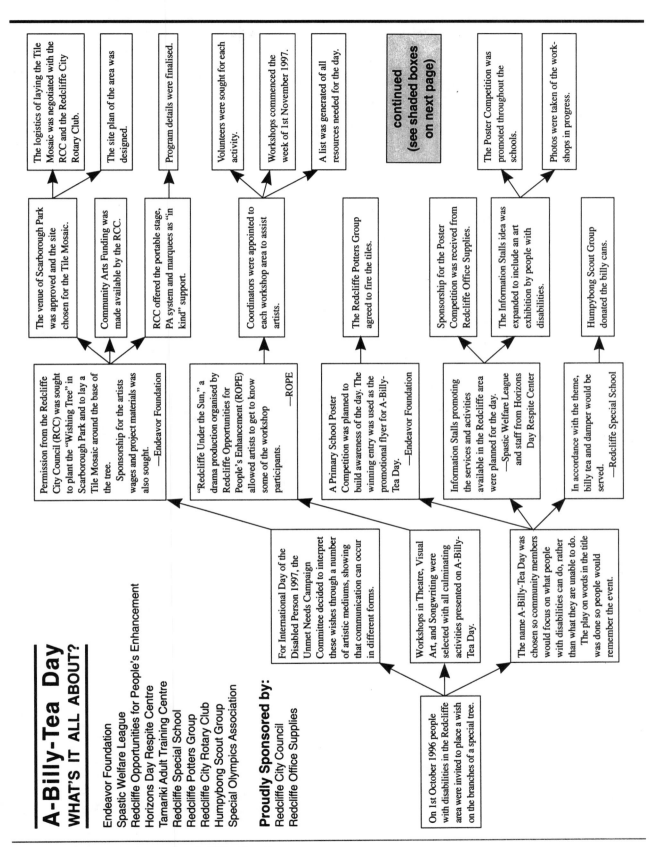

Figure 14.3a   Flow Chart for A-Billy-Tea Day

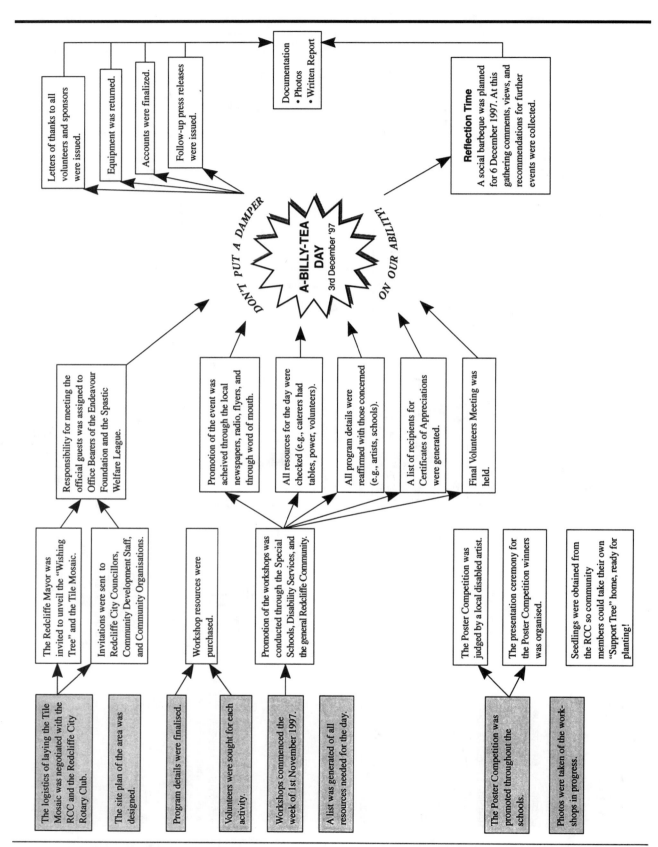

Figure 14.3b   Flow Chart for A-Billy-Tea Day (continued)

Examining professional associations more closely, we find that they serve eight basic functions as represented in Figure 14.4. They are:

- Advocacy—promoting the profession to the public at large, including legislative interests;

- Promotion of standards—promoting high quality of service and ethics by establishing standards;

- Research—the study and dissemination of trends and issues related to the profession;

- Education—providing opportunities for ongoing education and training, usually through the form of conferences, workshops, seminars, or institutes;

- Communication—disseminating information regarding association activities, as well as current research and job opportunities via magazines, journals, newsletters, and computer technology;

- Networking—by providing opportunities for people with similar interests to meet, those individuals can jointly problem solve, share resources, and reaffirm their commitment to the profession;

- Recognition—acknowledging the contributions and efforts of individual members, influential people outside of the membership and students via certificates, plaques, scholarships, and prizes; and

- Insurance and retirement benefits—tangible benefits such as health insurance, liability insurance, and retirement are often provided to members and organizations at reduced rates (Edginton et al., 1998).

The first three of these functions involve the profession as a whole while the remaining five focus on individuals. These benefits of participation in leisure services professional associations are also applicable to professional organizations in other fields. Whether it be personal contacts, conference or workshop attendance, or written resources, many valuable ideas can be borrowed from the organizations listed in Figure 14.5.

Figure 14.4 Professional organizations serve eight primary functions.

Written Materials

The wealth of written information available to leisure service professionals should be a source of great comfort in our research efforts. Because of the many resources, programmers can realize that they do not have to work in isolation or without easily available resources. Written materials are often fairly compact and can be easily transported from place to place. We also realize, however, that the breadth of written materials (even before the technology explosion) might seem overwhelming to parks, recreation, and leisure programmers. For most organizations, limitations of time and money require that research be focused and efficient. From the thousands of materials available, decisions need to be made about which to access, read, purchase, and use in programming efforts. In addition, one of the disadvantages of written materials is that they become outdated in a fairly short period of time; therefore, we need to remember to update the books most helpful to us, and supplement information from other resources.

The recreation programmer who is searching with passion and creativity should think broadly

Professional Associations

American Alliance for Health, Physical Education, Recreation and Dance (AAHPERD)
1900 Association Drive
Reston, VA 22091
703–476–3400 ☎ 703–476–9527 🖹

American Camping Association (ACA)
Bradford Woods
5000 SR 67N
Martinsville, IN 46151-7902
765–342–8456 ☎ 765–342–2065 🖹

Association for Challenge Course Technology (ACCT)
P.O. Box 970
Purcellville, VA 20134
540–668–6634 ☎ 540–668–6634 🖹

Association of Experiential Education (AEE)
2305 Canyon Blvd., Suite 100
Boulder, CO 80302
303–440–8844 ☎ 303–440–9581 🖹

Canadian Parks/Recreation Association (CPRA)
1600 James Naismith Drive, Suite 306
Gloucester, Ontario K1B 5N4
Canada
613–748–5651 ☎ 613–748–5854 🖹

International Festivals Association (IFA)
P.O. Box 2950
Port Angeles, WA 98362-0336
206–457–3141 ☎ 206–452–4695 🖹

National Employee Services and Recreation Association (NESRA)
2211 York Road, Suite 207
Oak Brook, IL 60521-2371
630–368–1280 ☎ 630–368–1286 🖹

National Intramural Recreation and Sports Association (NIRSA)
850 S.W. 15th Street
Corvallis, OR 97333-4145
503–737–2088 ☎ 503–737–2026 🖹

National Recreation and Park Association (NRPA)
22377 Belmont Ridge Road
Ashburn, VA 20148
703–858–0784 ☎ 703–858–0794 🖹

Resort and Commercial Recreation Association (RCRA)
P.O. Box 1208
New Port Richey, FL 34656-1208
813–845–7373 ☎

The Ecotourism Society
801 Devon Place
Alexandria, VA 22314

World Leisure and Recreation Association (WLRA)
P.O. Box 309
Sharbot Lake, Ontario K0H 2P0
Canada
613–279–3172 ☎ 613–279–3372 🖹

Education

National Association for the Education of Young Children (NAEYC)
1509 16th Street, NW
Washington, DC 20036

National Education Association (NEA)
1201 16th Street, NW
Washington, DC 20036
202–833–4000 ☎

Social Work

National Association of Social Workers (NASW)
750 1st Street NE, Suite 700
Washington, DC 20002

Psychology

American Psychological Association (APA)
10 Industrial Ave.
Mahwah, NJ 07430

Figure 14.5   A Selection of Professional Associations

and of both traditional and nontraditional sources of information. These include strategies that stretch our thinking beyond convention such as looking to unpublished works and how they can be accessed. This may seem difficult on the surface, but it opens a wonderful opportunity to tap into student work

efforts being made at local universities and colleges. Many times students conduct research which is valuable, yet not publishable. Educators in colleges and universities may be willing, with student permission, to make available activity files, book reviews, and special projects to the practitioner. One example of such a project was developed by a student at University of Northern Iowa. Using a text about "minute mysteries," she created science experiments which correlate with the mysteries.

Textbooks

As leisure services students, you are required to purchase and read many textbooks to prepare for your future profession. While many of these end up back at the bookstore for their resale value, some will prove helpful to you as you enter the workforce as a programmer. In particular, those texts that address leadership, programming, and ethics may be good sources of information and guidance in specific situations and under certain conditions. These types of books often address the overall questions of "How?" and "Why?" which can be helpful in job-related situations. For instance, we might learn or be reminded about how we can determine what our constituents need and want; and why we should make our building accessible if it means we don't have funds to provide childcare. Utilizing texts and class notes as resources provide many entry level practitioners with an edge over others.

Program Books

Program books are often helpful in answering the question "What?" as in "What are we going to do?" "What are we going to need?" and "What are we going to accomplish?" While we all have our favorite activities and programs that we can offer without relying on books or additional research, we also need to develop systems to help us access specific information about activities we don't know as well. In this way, research helps us to expand our programming repertoire and incorporate new ideas into familiar programs. This may be something as simple as designating a bookshelf in our office for the latest programming books which can be purchased in bookstores or ordered through a variety of catalogues. Efforts may also prove to be more time-consuming such as creating a personal file which contains details for conducting activities that have been successful in the past, or attending sessions and exhibitions at professional conferences to find out what current resources and products are available. Figure 14.6 (pages 307–309) provides bibliographical information for recommended books under specific program area headings.

Recommended Program Books

Aquatics

Adapted Aquatics: A Professional Guide. (1998). M. Lepore, G. W. Gayle and S. Stevens. Champaign, IL: Human Kinetics.

Aquatic Fitness Everyone. (1993). T. Elder and K. Campbell. Winston-Salem, NC: Hunter.

Swimming Everyone. (1989). Y. Messner and N. Assmann. Winston-Salem, NC: Hunter.

Waterplay: Games and Activities for Everyone. (1990). M. Humphrey. Dubuque, IA: William C. Brown.

Adventure Education

Adapted Adventure Activities: A Rehabilitation Model for Adventure Programming and Group Initiatives. (1994). W. Elmo and J Graser. Dubuque, IA: Kendall Hunt.

Bridges to Accessibility: A Primer for Including Persons with Disability in Adventure Curricula. (1992). M. Havens. Dubuque, IA: Kendall Hunt.

Cowstails and Cobras II: A Guide to Games, Initiatives, Ropes Courses, and Adventure Curricula. (1989). K. Rohnke. Dubuque, IA: Kendall Hunt.

Processing the Experience: Strategies to Enhance and Generalize Learning. (1997). J. Luckner and R. Nadler. Dubuque, IA: Kendall Hunt.

Quicksilver. (1995). K. Rohnke and S. Butler. Dubuque, IA: Kendall Hunt.

The Complete Ropes Course Manual. (1997). K. Rohnke. Dubuque, IA: Kendall Hunt.

Safety Practices in Adventure Programming. (1990). S. Priest and T. Dixon. Boulder, CO: Association for Experiential Education.

Silver Bullets. (1984). K. Rohnke. Dubuque, IA: Kendall Hunt.

Teamwork and Teamplay. (1998). Cain, J. and Jolliff, B. Dubuque IA: Kendall Hunt.

Arts and Crafts

The Kids Multicultural Art Book. (1993). A. Terzian. Charlotte, VT: Williamson Publishing.

The Little Hands Art Book. (1994). J. Press. Charlotte, VT: Williamson Pub.

Multicultural Art Activities. (1994). B. Cavanaugh. Huntington Beach, CA: Teacher Created Materials, Inc.

Nature Crafts for Kids: 50 Fantastic Things to Make with Mother Nature's Help. G. Diehn and T. Krautwurst. New York, NY: Sterling.

Figure 14.6   A Bibliography of Recreation Resources >>

Recommended Program Books (continued)

Arts and Crafts (continued)

Snips and Snails and Walnut Whales: Nature Crafts for Children. (1975). P. Fiarotta. New York, NY: Workman Publishing Company.

Cooking

Extending the Table ... A World Community Cookbook. (1991). J. Handrich Schlabach, P. Longacre and K. Hiebert. Waterloo, ON: Herald Press.

The Kids' Around the World Cookbook. (1994). D. Robbins. Greenville, SC: Kingfisher LKC.

The Kids Multicultural Cookbook: Food and Fun Around the World. (1995). D. Cook. Charlotte, VT: Williamson Publishing.

More with Less Cookbook. (1997). D. Longacre. Scottsdale, PA: Herald Press.

Drama

The Greatest Skits on Earth. (1986). W. Rice and M. Yaconelli. Grand Rapids, MI: Zondervan Publishing House.

The Handbook of Skits and Stunts. (1953). H. Eisenberg and L. Eisenberg. New York, NY: Association Press.

Environmental Activities

Detective Science. (1996). J. Wiese. New York, NY: John Wiley and Sons.

Good Earth Art: Environmental Art for Kids. (1991). M.A. Kohl and C. Gainer. Bellingham, WA: Bright Ring.

Problem-Solving Science Investigations. (1989). J. Carratello and P. Carratello. Huntington Beach, CA: Teacher Created Materials.

Project Wild K-12 Activity Guide. (1992). Bethesda, MD: Project Wild.

Ready, Set, Explore. (1996). M. Barron with K. Romano Young. New York, NY: John Wiley and Sons.

Sharing the Joy of Nature: Nature Activities for All Ages. (1989). J. Cornell. Nevada City, CA: Dawn Publications.

Teaching Kids to Love the Earth. (1991). M. Herman, J. Passineau, A. Schimpf and P. Treuer. Duluth, MN: Pfiefer Hamilton.

The Unbelievable Bubble Book. (1987). J. Cassidy and D. Stein. Palo Alto, CA: Klutz.

The Usborne Book of Science Experiments. (1991). J. Bingham. London, UK: Usborne Publishing, Ltd.

The Usborne Rainy Day Book. (1994). A. Smith. London, UK: Usborne Publishing, Ltd.

Fitness/Wellness Activities

The Complete Walker III. (1984). C. Fletcher. New York, NY: Knopf.

Exercise Activities for the Elderly. (1988) K. Flatten, B. Wilhite and E. Reyes-Watson. New York, NY: Springer Publishing Company.

Teaching Your Child Basic Body Confidence. (1988). P. Carmichael Gerard with M. Cohn. Boston, MA: Houghton Mifflin.

Literary

Celebrating Diversity: Using Multicultural Literature to Promote Cultural Awareness. (1993). M. Abbott and B. Polk. New York, NY: Simon and Schuster.

Classroom Close-ups: A Guide to Using Video Technology in the Classroom. (1996). B. Bug. Parsippany, NJ: Good Apple.

Crossing the Bridge: A Journal in Self-Esteem, Relationships, and Life Balance. (1997). S. Negley. Beachwood, OH: Wellness Reproductions.

Journal Activities Throughout the Year. (1996). K. Zaun. Grand Rapids, MI: Instructional Fair.

Ready, Set, Read and Write. (1995). M. Barron with K. Romano Young. New York, NY: Skylight Press.

Still More Two-Minute Mysteries. (1975). D. Sobol. New York, NY: Scholastic.

Tales with a Twist: Ethics, Dilemmas and Points of View. (1991). G. Barclay Lipson. Carthage, IL: Good Apple.

Miscellaneous

Activity Experiences and Programming within Long-Term Care. (1995). T. Tedrick and E. Green. State College, PA: Venture Publishing, Inc.

Creative Play Activities for Children with Disabilities. (1989). L. Rappaport, Morris, and L. Schultz. Champaign, IL: Human Kinetics.

Hands Around the World. (1992). S. Milord. Charlotte, VT: Williamson Publishing.

Inclusive Leisure Services: Responding to the Rights of People with Disabilities. (1994). J. Dattilo. State College, PA: Venture Publishing, Inc.

Figure 14.6   A Bibliography of Recreation Resources (continued)   >>

Recommended Program Books (continued)

Miscellaneous (continued)

Leisure Education Program Planning. (1991). J. Dattilo and W. Murphy. State College, PA: Venture Publishing, Inc.

Leisure Lifestyles: A Resource for Community Agencies and Organizations to Encourage Education for Leisure. (1988). B. Ballantyne. Kitchener, Canada: Parks and Recreation Department, City of Kitchener.

Life Management Skills: Reproducible Act Handouts Created for Facilitators. (1991). K. Korb, S. Azok, and E. Leutenberg. Beachwood, OH: Wellness Reproductions.

Making the Peace: A 15 Session Violence Prevention Curriculum for Young People. (1997). P. Kivel and A. Creighton. Alameda, CA: Hunter House.

More Than a Game: A New Focus on Senior Activity Services. (1998). B. Corbett. State College, PA: Venture Publishing, Inc.

Rainy Day Play. (1997). Surrey, England: Zig Zag Publications.

Recreation Programs that Work for At-Risk Youth: The Challenge of Shaping the Future. (1996). P. Witt and J. Crompton. State College, PA: Venture Publishing, Inc.

Music

Brown Girl in the Ring: An Anthology of Song Games from the Eastern Caribbean. (1997). Collected and documented by A. Lomax., J.D. Elder and Bess Lomax Hawes. New York, NY: Pantheon Books.

First Steps in Teaching Creative Dance to Children. (1980). M. Joyce. Palo Alto, CA: Mayfield.

Special Events

Creative Socials and Special Events. (1986). M. Yoconelli and W. Rice.

Great Special Events. (1991). A. Morton, A. Prosser and S. Spangler. State College, PA: Venture Publishing, Inc.

Special Events Inside and Out. (1997). R. Jackson and S. Wood. Champaign, IL: Sagamore.

Sports and Games

Changing Kids Games. (1989). D. Morris and J. Stiehl. Champaign, IL: Human Kinetics.

Children's Games from Around the World. (1991). G. Kirchner. Dubuque, IA: WCB

Dynamic Physical Education for Elementary School Children. (1995). R. Pangrazi and V. Dauer. Boston, MA: Allyn and Bacon

Dynamic Physical Education for Secondary School Students. (1997). R. Pangrazi and P. Darst. Boston, MA: Allyn and Bacon.

The Encyclopedia of Group Activities. (1989). J. W. Pfeiffer. San Diego, CA: University Associates.

Everybody Wins. (1983). J. Sobel. New York, NY: Walker.

Games Games Games. (1980). M. Hohenstein. Minneapolis, MN: Bethany Fellowship.

Inclusive Games. (1995). S. Kasser. Champaign, IL: Human Kinetics.

International Playtime: Classroom Games and Dances From Around the World. (1992). W. Nelson and H. Glass. New York, NY: Simon and Schuster.

More New Games. (1982). D. Leonard. San Francisco: New Games Foundation.

Mutlicultural Games. (1997). L. Barbarash. Champaign, IL: Human Kinetics.

Parachute Games. (1996). T. Strong and D. LeFevre. Champaign, IL: Human Kinetics.

The Sport Rules Book. (1998). T. Halon. Champaign, IL: Human Kinetics.

Sports and Recreation for the Disabled. (1995). M. Paciorek and J. Jones. Champaign, IL: Sagamore.

Teaching Cues for Sport Skills. (1997). H. Fronske. Boston, MA: Allyn and Bacon.

Travel and Tourism

Coast to Coast Games. (1996). B. Smutnik. Rand McNally and Company, USA

Kids U.S. Road Atlas. (1992). Rand McNally and Company.

Figure 14.6   A Bibliography of Recreation Resources (continued)

Children's Literature

Children's literature can provide a wealth of ideas and information for recreation programming. Books that may prove helpful for particular programs fall into a variety of categories. Classics include individual books such as *Charlottes' Web*, as well as series such as *The Hardy Boys Mysteries*. Many times it is the author, such as Dr. Seuss, who makes a work of literature stand out as a potential resource. In a similar vein, a popular character, such as Curious George, may offer ideas for programs. Many children's books can be utilized in programs which serve all ages. For example, Dr. Seuss's 1996 book, *The Places We'll Go....* makes a wonderful banquet theme for a variety of occasions. If we are to think creatively about children's literature, we need to work on breaking away from the idea that its value is restricted to children. We also need to think beyond the typical "story time" approach, although this certainly is a valuable activity. By using our imagination and including participants in program design we open up a wide variety of possibilities.

Journals

Professional journals may be categorized into two groups based on the audience targeted. One type of journal includes those that target practitioners and promote best professional practice in a specific area. These types of journals are often connected with a specific professional association and are sent to members as one of the benefits of their membership. For example, *Camping Magazine*, produced by the American Camping Association, offers camp directors a variety of current information on such topics as programming, managing areas and facilities, supervising staff, meeting professional standards, dealing with risk management, and working with children.

A second type of journal is research-based and is targeted at university professors and researchers within the parks, recreation, and leisure field as well as practitioners who are interested in practical applications of completed research. Research journals are connected to professional associations and provide readers with current information about issues related to parks, recreation, and leisure services. Figure 14.7 (pages 311–312) provides a list of selected research and professional journals related to our field.

Trade Books

Much of the information available on parenting and childcare, for example, is not in the form of textbooks or program resources, but is typically categorized as a trade book. These are books published by individuals who sell to the general public through bookstores. While some trade books are available in public and university libraries, many of the current and most helpful sources of information for programs that serve children, youth, families, and are about leadership, sports and games, educational activities, and nature are found in bookstores. Resources focused on families or youth will commonly provide guidance and ideas in the form of activities, behavior management strategies, and developmental milestones. Other types of trade books that often prove helpful are health and medical guides, cookbooks, and travel books.

Periodicals

We define periodicals as magazines and newspapers which are circulated to businesses, public agencies, and residential households. They may be published as infrequently as quarterly, or as frequently as weekly. Periodicals that programmers may wish to consult include national newspapers (e.g., *USA Today, The Washington Post, The New York Times*), local newspapers, news magazines (i.e., *Time, Newsweek, U.S. News and World Report*), hobby magazines (e.g., *Better Homes and Gardens, Computer Digest*), magazines of general scope with wide circulation (e.g., *Reader's Digest*), and specialty magazines (e.g., *American Demographics, Backpacker*).

Articles. Articles in periodicals often prove to be good indicators of trends and issues in our culture. This provides the leisure professional with a window to the topics that are important to constituents now and in the near future. For example, one of the front page articles of the April 7, 1998 issue of *The New York Times* examined the impacts of the elimination of recess at elementary schools throughout the nation. Although Atlanta was cited as one of the few districts to totally cut recess from the curriculum and built new schools without playgrounds, many districts are now making that decision independently. The reasons cited included a fear of lawsuits, vulnerability to unsavory characters while on playgrounds, lack of personnel willing to supervise recess, and

Research and Professional Journals and Magazines

Professional Journals

Camping Magazine. Bimonthly; published by the American Camping Association, 5000 State Road 67N, Martinsville, IN 46151-7902.

NIRSA Journal. Three issues/year; published by the National Intramural Recreation and Sport Association, 850 SW 15th Street, Corvallis, OR 97333.

Journal of Experiential Education. Three issues/year; published by the Association of Experiential Education, 2305 Canyon Blvd., Suite 100, Boulder, CO 80302

Journal of International Council for Health, Physical Education and Recreation. Quarterly; published by the International Council for Health, Physical Education and Recreation, 1990 Association Drive, Reston, VA 22091.

Journal of Physical Education, Recreation and Dance. Bimonthly; published by the American Alliance of Health, Physical Education, Recreation, and Dance (AAHPERD), 1990 Association Drive, Reston, VA 22091.

Parks and Recreation Magazine. Bimonthly; published by the National Recreation and Park Association (NRPA), 22377 Belmont Ridge Road, Ashburn, VA 20148.

World Leisure and Recreation. Quarterly; published by the World Leisure and Recreation Association (WLRA), P.O. Box 309, Sharbot Lake, Ontario, K0H 2P0, Canada.

Research Journals

Journal of Applied Recreation Research. Quarterly; published by the University of Waterloo Press, Porter Library, Waterloo, Ontario N2L 3G1, Canada.

Journal of Leisure Research. Quarterly; published by the National Recreation and Park Association (NRPA), 22377 Belmont Ridge Road, Ashburn, VA 20148.

Journal of Park and Recreation Administration. Quarterly; published by the American Academy for Parks and Recreation Administration. Available from Sagamore Publishing, P.O. Box 673, Champaign, IL 61824-0673.

Leisure Sciences. Quarterly; published by Taylor & Francis, 1101 Vermont Avenue, Suite 200, Washington, DC 20005.

Leisure Studies. Quarterly; published by E. & F.N. Spon, 2-6 Boundary Row, London, SE1 8HN, United Kingdom.

Therapeutic Recreation Journal. Quarterly; published by the National Recreation and Park Association (NRPA), 22377 Belmont Ridge Road, Ashburn, VA 20148.

SCHOLE: A Journal of Leisure Studies and Recreation Education. Annual; published by the Society for Park and Recreation Educators. Available from the National Recreation and Park Association (NRPA), 22377 Belmont Ridge Road, Ashburn, VA 20148.

Magazines

Backpacker. Published nine times annually by Rodale Press, 33 E. Minor St., Emmaus, PA 18098.

Climbing. Published nine times annually by Climbing, Inc., 1101 Village Road Ste. LL-1B, Carbondale, CO 81623.

Creative Forecasting. Published by Creative Forecasting, P.O. Box 7789, Colorado Springs, CO 80933.

Dance. Published monthly by Dance Magazine, Inc., 33 West 60th St., New York, NY 10023.

Islands. Published six times annually by Islands Publishing Company, P.O. Box 4728, Santa Barbara, CA 93140.

Outside Magazine. Published monthly by Outside Magazine, P.O. Box 54715, Boulder, CO 80322.

Education

Child Education. Monthly; published by Scholastic, Ltd., Villeirs House, Clarendon Ave, Leamington Spa, Warwickshire, United Kingdom.

Education. Quarterly; published by Project Innovation, Inc., 1362 Santa Cruz, Court Chula Vitas, CA 91910.

Journal of School Psychology. Quarterly; published by Elsevier Science, Inc., 655 Avenue of the Americas, New York, NY 10010.

Our Children: The National PTA Magazine. Monthly; published by The National PTA, 330 N. Wabash, Suite 1200, Chicago, IL 60611.

Young Children: Journal of the National Association for the Education of Young Children. Monthly; published by the National Association for the Education of Young Children, 1509 16th St., Washington, DC 20036-1426.

Figure 14.7   Research and Professional Journals and Magazines Related to Recreation   >>

Research and Professional Journals and Magazines (continued)

Parenting and Childcare

Child Care Information Exchange. Bimonthly; published by Exchange Press, Inc., 17916 NE 103rd Court, Redmond, WA 98052.

Children Today. Three or four issues/year; published by the U.S. Department of Health and Human Services—Administration for Children and Families, 7th Floor, 370 L'Enfant Promenade SW, Washington, DC 20447.

Family Fun. Monthly; published by Glen Rosenbloom, P.O. Box 37032, Boone, IA 50037-0032.

Parenting. Monthly; published by Time Publishing Ventures, 1325 Avenue of the Americas, 27th Floor, New York, NY 10019.

Psychology

The Journal of Social Psychology. Bimonthly; published by Heldruf Pub, 1319 18th St. NW, Washington, DC 20036.

Human Development. Bimonthly; published by S. Karger AG, P.O. Box CH-4009, Basel, Switzerland.

Psychological Bulletin. Bimonthly; published by the American Psychological Association, 10 Industrial Ave., Mahwah, NJ 07430.

Social Psychology Quarterly. Quarterly; published by the American Sociological Association, 1722 N. Street NW, Washington, DC 20036.

Social Work

Affilia: The Journal of Women and Social Work. Quarterly; published by Sage Publications, 2455 Teller Rd., Thousand Oaks, CA 91320.

Families in Society: Journal of Contemporary Human Services. Bimonthly; published by Family Service America, 11700 W. Lake Park Dr., Milwaukee, WI 53224.

Journal of Gay and Lesbian Social Services. Quarterly; published by Haworth Press, 10 Alice St., Binghamton, NY 13094.

The Journal of Multicultural Social Work. Quarterly; published by Haworth Press, 10 Alice St., Binghamton, NY 13094.

Special Populations

The Braille Monitor. Monthly; published by The National Federation of the Blind, 1800 Johnson St., Baltimore, MD 21230.

Education and Training in Mental Retardation and Developmental Disabilities. Quarterly; published by The Council for Exceptional Children, 1920 Association Dr., Reston, VA 22019.

JADARA. Quarterly; The American Deafness and Rehabilitation Association, P.O. Box 55369, Little Rock, AR 72225.

Modern Maturity. Bimonthly; published by the American Association of Retired Persons (AARP), 3200 E. Carson St., Lakewood, CA 90712.

Figure 14.7   Research and Professional Journals and Magazines Related to Recreation (continued)

pressure from parents to provide only academics and structured time.

This trend in public schools has many implications for parks, recreation, and leisure service programmers. The decrease in physical activity in a time when obesity in American children is higher than ever is problematic for life-long wellness. In addition, the lack of unstructured play time and subsequent lack of opportunities for problem solving and conflict resolution are also issues to be considered. As a profession, we may wish to educate parents and school personnel about the benefits of leisure. Furthermore, this may serve as a call to parks, recreation, and leisure services programmers to offer additional forms and formats of recreation for children.

In addition to articles informing us about national, state, and local trends, they also serve as a good source of evaluative information about products and programs. For instance, each year *Good Housekeeping* magazine rates the safety and educational level of children's toys. Programmers can use these sources to prioritize equipment expenditures and as a basis for making decisions. Furthermore, programs of excellence are sometimes featured in periodicals such as *World Traveler*. This magazine recently highlighted the *Entros* nightclub in Seattle which bills itself as "the world's first intelligent Amusement Park." This establishment features high-tech, socially interactive games designed to promote group participation and be intellectually stimulating, while maintaining high-quality food service (Gallo, 1998). Reading about such programs provides recreation programmers with concrete information as well as inspiration, increasing the programmer's own sense of passion and commitment.

Comic Strips. While reproducing comic strips for publication can prove prohibitive due to copyrights and the cost of reproducing them, comic strips can be used in a variety of ways at very little expense. One obvious example is to use them as a springboard to a comic strip drawing/writing activity as part of an arts program or session related to self-expression. This might take the form of a book of original comic strips that participants compile for their own enjoyment or to sell to raise financial support for a program, agency, event, or particular purchase. Another idea might be to hold a comic strip contest between participants—perhaps all entries could be printed in newsletters and/or displayed for public enjoyment while the winning cartoon could be incorporated into a program brochure or T-shirt design. A creative use of comic strips developed into an activity which became a tradition at the Recreation Center at Camp Walker, an army base located in Taegu, South Korea. During the eighties when *Garfield* was extremely popular, programmers held Garfield birthday parties which incorporated the character as well as characteristics he possessed. The menu always included lasagna and activities such as Garfield trivia and "Pin the Nose on Odie." As we move into the next millennium, we find may find program ideas and activities built around *Far Side* animals.

Pamphlets and Newsletters

Pamphlets and newsletters are not as accessible to programmers as other written materials from the standpoint that they are not indexed or catalogued in the same way as books, journals, and periodicals. However, they are easy to access from the standpoint that they are often free or available at a minimal cost, and may be obtained easily through the mail. We recommend that programmers ask for such things from staff at various organizations when meeting in person, talking on the phone, or corresponding via the Internet or e-mail. A starting point could be to obtain the newsletter published by NRPA entitled, "PIN—Programmers Information Network." This publication is an informal document which highlights programs throughout the United States, offers advice and tips, advertises upcoming

educational opportunities, and provides creative ideas for new programs. Another valuable resource are the Public Affairs Pamphlets published by the government and available from the Consumer Information Center in Pueblo, Colorado, which contain information about a wide range of topics.

Calendars

Calendars come in all shapes, sizes, and levels of detail. In programming efforts we might use the pictures and graphics calendars offer or for the information they contain. Many businesses make calendars available free of charge to those who ask, and they often contain wonderful pictures of wildlife and scenery that can be used for collages, making puzzles, decorating, and other art projects. Furthermore, calendars contain information about specific dates of importance or recognition for a variety of cultural groups.

For many years, recreation programmers have been incorporating this information by celebrating the changes in seasons and specific holidays such as Thanksgiving, Chanukah, Halloween, and Martin Luther King Jr., Day. These widely known holidays only scratch the surface of potential ideas. Many calendars include information about less publicized anniversaries, birthdays, and other significant events that can provide new ideas for creative programming. The 1998 National Recreation and Park Association Calendar lists a variety of these less widely known dates such as Dr. Seuss's birthday (March 2), Random Acts of Kindness Week (2nd week of February), International Day for the Elderly (October 1), and Peanut Butter Lover's Month (November). As we can see, calendar information varies considerably and may be viewed as humorous and frivolous, or important and meaningful. Programmers may also want to research significant dates relating to their particular field or specific program, as well.

Television and Radio

All of us in parks, recreation, and leisure would be wise to remember that one source of ideas for themes and activities may be found in television and radio. Often referred to as a "drug" due to its powerful appeal, we have learned that one of four Americans indicate they would not trade their televisions for a million dollars, and the average child watches almost four hours daily (Wallace, 1996). Radio is also widely utilized and has the added attraction of being mobile and offering a wide variety of stations in most locations without additional costs to the listener. Both of these mediums offer programming ideas that could be easily implemented or adapted for individual needs.

A good starting point when examining modern television and radio media are PBS (Public Broadcasting System) and NPR (National Public Radio) stations. Focusing on educational topics, the quality of content in programming is generally high and varied. These programs can serve as a source of positive fads in the listening and viewing realm of the public. On the radio, interesting current trends and issues are often reported, as well as presentations which capture aspects of daily living. Examples of this are Garrison Keillor's, *A Prairie Home Companion* or Robert Fulgrahm's, *All I Ever Needed to Know I Learned in Kindergarten.* On television, the popularity of *The Magic School Bus* may be capitalized on by incorporating it into existing or new programs. One example of this happening is the Saturday Kids' Club program at the Grout Museum in Cedar Falls, Iowa. Children can sign up for the entire season (12 weeks) or "drop-in" to programs that teach a concept of science through Magic School Bus videos, experiments, crafts, and snacks that fit the weekly themes. Day camp staff might dress up like Ms. Frizzle to transport participants on field trips or program areas within the facility.

Ideas for science experiments may also be gleaned from television figure, *Bill Nye the Science Guy.* This show is broadcast on both PBS and on major networks. He presents instructions for science experiments as well as fun science facts. This information is also available on the World Wide Web, using the keywords: "Nye Labs." Adults are also avid television viewers in our society and may enjoy special events designed around popular television shows. Examples include (1) a Star Trek party where the *U.S.S. Enterprise* is re-created, complete with food simulators, holodecks, and space creatures from a variety of galaxies; and (2) a Jeopardy quiz show where staff could elicit category topics from participants to reflect their interests or design category topics to cross a wide range of knowledge (e.g., answers within a music category might vary from Boyz II Men to Frank Sinatra). This would result in an intergenerational event to facilitate interaction between team members of varying ages and build respect for what each individual has to offer.

Cable television has also opened up a vast array of possibilities for programming ideas. Nickelodeon and Disney channels often broadcast shows appropriate for children and general family viewing. In addition, science and nature specials are a frequent fare on the Discovery channel and, used judiciously, may be a wonderful supplement for programs that utilize particular themes or maintain a "Science Zone" in their facility.

Television and radio can also be sources of songs to teach children and adults. PBS shows like *Barney* and *Sesame Street* present songs which can easily be learned and taught to preschool and school-age children. Theme songs for shows such as *Arthur* and *The Magic School Bus* will have appeal to older children. Theme songs (past and present) can also provide content for talent shows and trivia contests for participants of all ages. Videos of the show can often be purchased from the network, retail stores, or catalogues.

In making decisions about television and radio shows to utilize as ideas, programmers need to be careful to utilize content that will appeal to participants and will not conflict with values of constituents and the organization. For example, *Power Rangers* is a very popular television show among children today, and recreation programmers should be concerned about the content of violence since it tops the charts with 211 violent incidents per hour (Boyatzis, 1997). Our concerns should revolve around how the violence might affect participants, be received by parents, and conflict with our organization's mission and vision. Even animated movies rated "G" may be objectionable for images that may be too frightening for children of certain ages. Furthermore, since television viewing is widely overused in American households, we would caution against utilizing this resource too frequently. A creative programmer can develop a memorable experience by involving participants in creating a theater or environment complete with refreshments, ushers carrying flashlights, tickets, "live" previews or commercials presented by staff or participants, and other elements of this medium.

Electronic Media

The category of electronic media includes avenues that communicate information via electricity as well as computer technology. These resources have several advantages, one of which is that these resources tend to be more current than written materials, with the exception of newspapers. They are also very accessible to most constituents; computers are found in many homes and most businesses. If someone doesn't have home access to services such as e-mail and the World Wide Web it is often available at nearby public libraries, county court houses, and Internet cafés. Electronic media minimize paper waste and the need for physical storage space such as book shelves or filing cabinets. This resource category is critical to the recreation programmer who wishes to keep informed of fast-paced trends and changes as well maximize resources available via electronic communication.

Videotapes, Audiotapes, and Compact Discs

Videotapes, audiotapes, and compact discs provide recreation programmers with a good deal of flexibility to utilize electronic media at a time that best fits a program. One service that is commonly provided to constituents is making sports, fitness, and instructional videotapes available for individual viewing. This enables participants to do several things:

- Continue their fitness and conditioning at home;
- Learn new skills and techniques for a particular activity at an appropriate pace;
- Learn safety techniques;
- View and evaluate videotapes for personal purchase; and
- Become interested in new activities.

Many organizations (especially those that are nonprofit in orientation) provide educational videotapes for youngsters (e.g., conflict resolution skills, antidrug messages), and adults (e.g., parenting skills, behavior management). In this fashion, constituents are being provided an important service related to continuing education.

Tapes and compact discs may also be utilized by an organization as a promotional tool, and to enhance a particular program. For instance, tapes of sound effects are often used to set the mood for a party (e.g., spooky noises at Halloween, nature sounds during a yoga class). In addition, music from audiotapes and compact discs are commonly used in programming.

Computer (WWW)

The Internet is becoming so accessible and informative that it is hardly considered new technology anymore. Resources that can be accessed range from product information to activity ideas to international networking. While specific Web addresses can be useful and efficient, they do become outdated rather quickly. A more time-consuming and pragmatic approach is to search for information, referred to as "surfing the Web," by using keywords. This opens up many different links of information from which to choose.

One particular home page which provides innovative activity ideas can be accessed by using the keywords: "Donna's Day." Organized by category, Donna Erickson presents ideas for activities for parents to do with their children at home. She is extremely creative and many ideas are suitable for all ages and can be used in a wide variety of parks, recreation, and leisure settings. Supplies are often easy to acquire and inexpensive, making them very practical in spite of their uniqueness. Other strengths of Erickson include her follow-through on how creations can be used later (e.g., gift wrap, neighborhood art fair.). She is also a firm believer that presentation and enthusiasm of the parent or leader adds a great deal to the degree of fun and enthusiasm which children or participants possess when presented with an activity. In addition, her home page has merchandise for sale which includes books, videotapes of her PBS television show, and preschool activity kits. By reviewing some of her ideas presented in Figure 14.8 (page 316) we can easily see that many of them would be fun for adults as well as children.

Other sources of ideas for a wide range of topics can be found by accessing Recreation (keywords: Therapeutic Recreation, Recreation Therapy) and Fitness (keywords: exercise, fitness). In the education field a wide range of activity information is found in Kathy Schrock's Guide for Educators (keywords: Kathy Schrock), Teach 2000 Physical Education/Sports (keywords: physical education central) and ERIC lesson plans (keywords: teacher's curriculum). Activities and resources for children may be accessed thorough Berit's Best Sites for Children (keywords: kid's stuff berits' best), and Interesting Places for Kids (keywords: interesting places for kids), Internet for Kids (keywords: Kidscom) and Children's On-line Stories (keywords: children's storybooks on-line).

Donna Erickson Program Sampler

Recipes

Italian Pasta—Make fresh pasta using just flour, water and eggs

Chocolate Roses—Edible clay molds into ornate flowers for plate or basket decoration

English Shepherd's Pie—Turn leftovers into a culinary masterpiece

German Soft Pretzels—A real "twist" with ordinary bread dough

Smoothie Fruit Drink—Tasty and nutritious drink that comes together in two shakes

African Groundnut Stew—Serve from cooking pot with traditional African story

Native American Fry Bread—Makes a great dessert or festive treat

French Marzipan Potato—Whimsical treat made out of marzipan and chocolate cake

Activities

Gooey Goop—Stretch, pull, and play with this glue-based concoction

Sand Goop Frames/Fossils—Sand mixture for photo frames or "fossil" with toy inside

Wacky Bubble Brew—Household utensils can form magnificent bubbles from easy brew

Gelatin Plastic—Simple concoction dries hard and shiny for jewelry and decorations

Mancala Game—Collect beads, beans, or buttons for this traditional African game

Homemade Butter—Shake cream in a jar, spread on muffins, have a tea party

Homemade Ice Cream—Using two cans, rock salt, crushed ice, and favorite ingredients

Oatmeal Soup—Turn leftover scraps of soap from "old duds" into "new suds"

Figure 14.8 Donna's Day (Erickson, 1998)

Summary

This chapter focuses on how recreation programmers can apply their creativity and passion to the process of research. By thinking and acting innovatively, we find a vast number of resources not available through traditional methods. This requires that we utilize people, organizations, written materials and electronic technology across disciplines. By persevering in our quest for constant improvement, we take the most important step in delivering quality services to our constituents. As servant leaders we must remember that equipping ourselves with the best resources available, within the financial constraints of our organization, is imperative to provide quality programs. The greatest resource inherent to all organizations to make this happen is the creativity and passion of its staff. While creativity and passion take many different forms and vary from individual to individual, key elements include open-mindedness, perseverance, collaboration, resourcefulness, and commitment. Violin virtuoso, Anne Aikiko Meyers, captures the essence of this as she reflects on her own passion for music:

> *I have to practice for a couple of hours every day, or my fingers will get stiff. But I don't overdo it. It's like that in life, too… If you concentrate too hard on school, work or whatever, you run the risk of extinguishing what you love about it. But if you take a step back every now and then, it can grow beyond your dreams.*

Akers, 1998, p. 65

References

Akers, P. (1998). Note of distinction. *World Traveler*, April, 44-48, 64-65.

Boyatzis, C. (1997). Of Power Rangers and V-chips. *Young Children, 52*(7), 74-79.

Clark, S. (1995) *Innovative programming: How to survive the jungle*. Speech given at Academy for Youth Leaders, October 10, 1994, University of Northern Iowa, Cedar Falls, IA.

Edginton, C., Jordan, D., DeGraaf, D. and Edginton, S. (1998). *Leisure and life satisfaction*. Dubuque, IA: McGraw-Hill.

Erickson, D. (1997). *Activity Index* [On-line]. Available: http://www.ktca.org/donnasday/creative/activndx.html

Gallo, N. (1998). Seattle's quirky dozen. *World Traveler,* April, 33-42, 74-75.

Johnson, D. (1998, April 7). Many schools putting end to child's play, *New York Times, 147*(31), pp. 1,16.

Marston, R. (1997). Personal Interview. University of Northern Iowa.

Morris, G.S. and J. Stiehl. (1989). *Changing kids' games*. Champaign, IL: Human Kinetics.

National Recreation and Park Association. (1997, October). *Programmers Information Network, 9*(4). Ashburn, VA: NRPA.

Seuss, Dr. (1971). *The lorax*. New York, NY: Random House.

Wallace, S. (1996). *The TV Book: The kid's guide to talking back*. Toronto, ON: Annick Press, Ltd.

Webster's Encyclopedic Unabridged Dictionary (1996)

York, S. and Jordan, D. (1992). "Programming With PACE." Presented at the Central District AAHPERD Conference, May 23, Des Moines, Iowa.

Appendix

Tournament Scheduling

Ladder Tournament

The ladder tournament is designed to encourage participants to generate their own play through a challenge system organized by the programmer. Participants or teams are ranked initially by skill level. The time and place of the actual playing is agreed upon by the two participants. Officiating is usually done on the honor system. In its simplest form, the ladder is a straight, single-unit, step-by-step listing of ranks. The challenger may contest the person in the step immediately above her or him. Failure to arrange a contest, avoiding a challenge, or not meeting a legitimate challenge within a prescribed period, such as 48 hours after its issue, can be considered a forfeit and the challenger trades places on the ladder with the player above.

Advantages to this type of tournament is that it is easy for a programmer to arrange, and encourages participants to interact. It doesn't matter how many contestants participate since "rungs" are easily added or removed (although anything over 10 is not recommended). Disadvantages are that participants are limited to playing those on neighboring rungs, and since skills and abilities can change over the course of time, a predetermined date or time of finish is required. Also, when large numbers of participants are involved, the ladder tournament breaks down.

This type of tournament, however, can be a useful tool. When used throughout scheduled practices (e.g., youth tennis league), players can be added if they join after the start of the season. It is also handy in helping to determine the seeding for end-of-season tournaments. Paperwork is minimal since keeping track of this tournament can be as simple as using a bulletin board and index cards with each contestant's name.

Isaac
Rochelle
Jonathon
Jenna
Daniel
Ian
Matthew

Pyramid Tournament

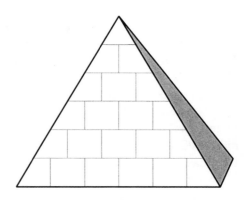

As mentioned earlier, when larger numbers of participants are involved, the ladder tournament breaks down. The solution is to create additional subpatterns that create many different opportunities to play frequently. The pyramid tournament is the next logical step as it creates a number of different opportunities for playing graduating from a broad, lower ranked base to a number one person at the peak. Any player in the lowest level may challenge anyone in the second layer, anyone in the second layer can challenge anyone in the third layer, and so on. Specific procedures must be created which identify how often a player must participate and against what level players she or he needs to participate.

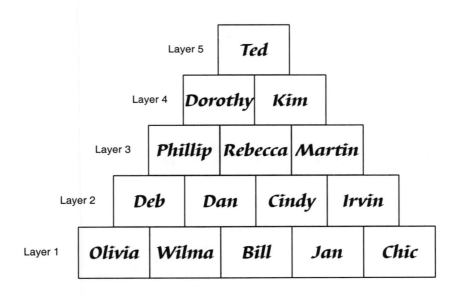

Single Elimination Tournament

The single elimination tournament is efficient, but it does not maximize the play opportunities of contestants. Individuals or teams are paired randomly, asked to challenge another contestant, or through a mechanism that assigns contestants through rankings or seeds. The system of bracketing the teams or players into paired contests is easily accomplished as long as the number of players is a power of two. Any other number means a rigged first round using byes until the power of 2 is reached. For example, a six or twelve team tournament requires 2 and 4 byes respectively in order to assure that four or eight teams progress to the second round. Byes can be given by random picks or through a seeded approach with the top teams receiving the byes.

Eight Contestant Single Elimination Tournament

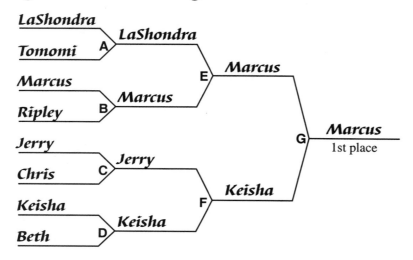

Sixteen Contestant Single Elimination Tournament

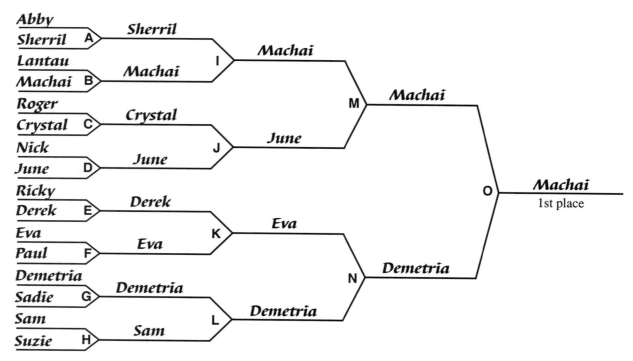

Single Elimination with Placement

Within this tournament structure, final placement is determined by contest. It allows for more play than the traditional single elimination structure, and may also be used to determine seeding for a future tournament. Programmers may opt to use this chart to rank the final eight teams in any size single elimination, or reduce it to place only four teams by using just the G and K brackets. It may be modified to determine placement of larger tournaments, also.

As results come in, move the "eliminated" team to the lower brackets where indicated, for example, contest A winner moves to bracket E while the eliminated contestant takes the slot in bracket H (marked A2). If the programmer wishes to heighten suspense, she or he may choose to play out the lower placement brackets first (i.e., L, J, K then G).

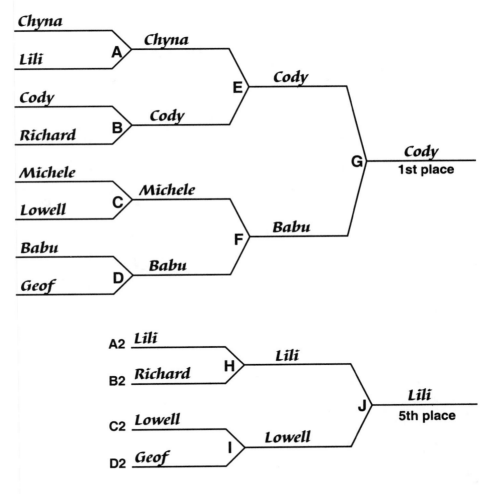

Order of Finish

First Place — Winner of G
Second Place — Loser of G
Third Place — Winner of K
Fourth Place — Loser of K
Fifth Place — Winner of J
Sixth Place — Loser of J
Seventh Place — Winner of L
Eighth Place — Loser of L

Double Elimination Tournament

The double elimination tournament extends play of every team or individual since no one is eliminated from winning until they have lost two contests. Upon the first loss, the player moves over to the consolation bracket; a second loss eliminates them from play. If the contestant makes it through the consolation bracket without a second loss, she/he/they eventually play the winner of the winners' bracket for the championship.

The double elimination tournament is a popular structure since it allows more play for all players. When run well, it is a fair evaluation of skill level. However, if care is not taken during set up and while transferring contestants from the winners' bracket into the consolation bracket, contestants may feel cheated if they are defeated by the same opponent who knocked them into the consolation bracket in the first place. This occurrence can be avoided until the final rounds by using a crossover method.

To use this sixteen-contestant chart, place the first round players in the A-H brackets. Proceed by moving winners to the right and consolation contestants to the left. Players added to the consolation bracket in later rounds are placed in the indicated bracket (e.g., loser of J moves to J2). This crossover pattern within the tree avoids having players eliminated by the same team that put them into the consolation bracket until the semifinal round. Note that in the final round, the consolation finalist needs to defeat the winners' finalist twice to win the tournament since a double elimination isn't over until all contestants except one accumulate two losses.

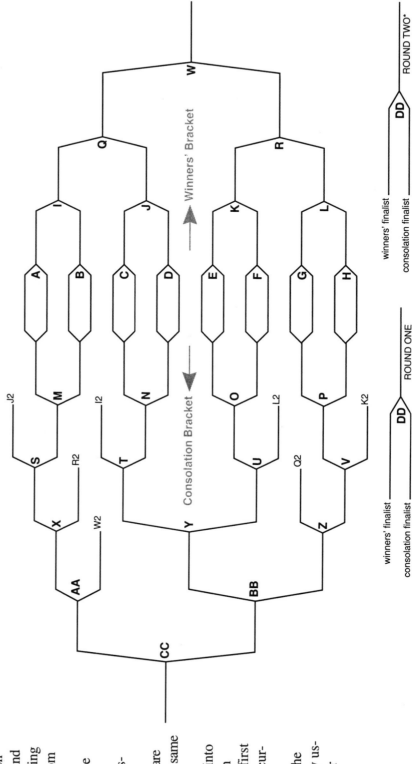

EXAMPLE 1

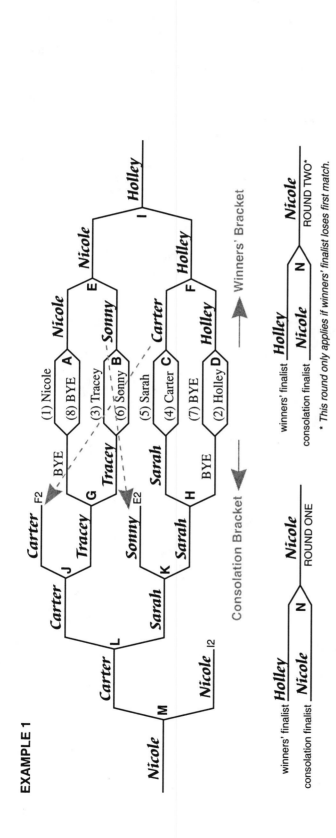

EXAMPLE 2

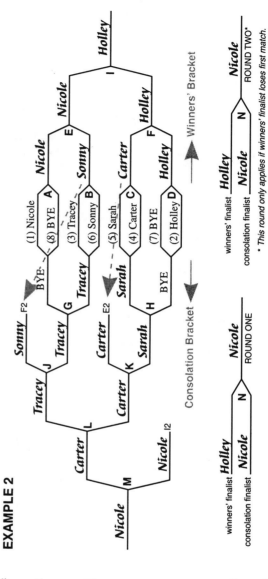

Note in these examples the positioning of the byes, seeding, and "crossover" pattern of the double elimination. Had the crossover pattern (indicated by the dotted arrow) not occurred, Sarah and Carter would have met a second time in bracket K as would have Tracey and Sonny (see Example 2). This would have left Sarah feeling shortchanged since not only did the same individual who knocked her into the consolation bracket eliminate her, she also played against only that individual. This crossover pattern is effective and should be used in any size double elimination tournament. Compare this eight-person tournament, to the sixteen person pattern on the opposite page. Note the crossover happens in the nearby "branches."

Double Elimination with Limited Placement

In this eight contestant example, there is some play beyond two losses to determine overall placement within a tournament. Complete this as a traditional double elimination (bracket finalists play until one has accumulated two losses) with extra play for the losers of the G, H, J and K matches to determine placement. Even if the consolation bracket finalist defeats the winners' bracket finalist, it will not affect the overall placement because each of the bracket finalists would have met the third place finisher in play (see bracket I and compare to the position of I2). If time is limited, this tournament can "give" the title to the undefeated winners' bracket finalist without necessarily meeting the consolation bracket finalist (see Order of Finish). Tournament staff should follow the alphabetical order of play for this tournament to run smoothly.

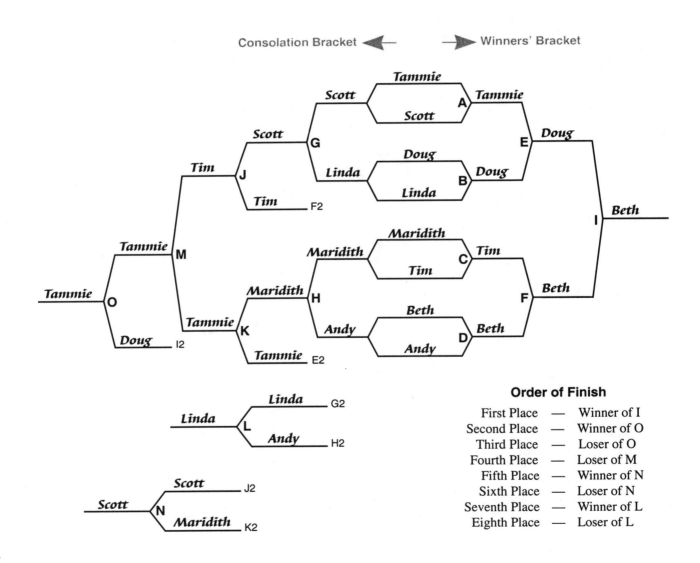

Order of Finish

First Place	—	Winner of I
Second Place	—	Winner of O
Third Place	—	Loser of O
Fourth Place	—	Loser of M
Fifth Place	—	Winner of N
Sixth Place	—	Loser of N
Seventh Place	—	Winner of L
Eighth Place	—	Loser of L

Setting Up Elimination Tournaments

There are several common ways to set up an elimination tournament schedule: *random draw*, *controlled draw*, *seeding*, and *challenge*.

For a *random draw*, it is best to write the name of each contestant on an index card, place all the cards together, shuffle them, and then select cards randomly to determine first round pairings on the elimination tree. The advantage is that no one knows who they will meet in the first round and there is no basis on skill level or past performance. The drawback is that if you have a group of people in attendance who regularly practice together or meet each other in competition elsewhere, they may run into someone with whom they practice in the first round.

The *controlled draw* takes care of this disadvantage in the random draw. In this case, keep the contestants who play together regularly separated in the tournament tree. Whether it involves several teams that meet in league play throughout the region or a group of karate students from a particular trainer or class, these contestants can be spread through the tree first, then the other contestants can be added to the tree. The advantage is that contestants get the chance to compete against others who they would seldom see otherwise, at least in the first round. The disadvantage is that sometimes this is perceived by people as "stacking the deck."

The *seeded tournament* usually involves a group of contestants who compete against each other regularly, or "earned" their slots in the tournament. Whether the contestants' ranking (seed) comes from past performance, polls, intuition or statistics, seeding spreads the contestants apart by perceived abilities. For example, you are given a list of sixteen teams in the order they are expected to place at the end of the tournament according to a coaches' poll. The teams should then be paired on the tournament tree as follows:

1 v. 16
5 v. 12
3 v. 14
7 v. 10
8 v. 9
4 v. 13
6 v. 11
2 v. 15

The theory is that if teams or players are seeded appropriately, the number one and number two seeds will meet in the final round, resulting in an exciting match. Usually placement in a seeded tournament is earned through a season of play, so byes are rare. It is up to the programmer to decide how to handle "no shows" in the case of a double elimination. If a contestant drops out for any reason before a day-long tournament where contestants are required to prequalify, an alternate is usually in attendance to take their seed. This may involve shifting the seeds before the tournament begins since the alternate had not qualified for the tournament and, therefore, would have the lowest seed. For example, seed number four cannot attend due to an injury, but seed number seventeen is in attendance and ready to play. Seeds five through sixteen move up one seed and seed seventeen becomes seed sixteen.

It is also the programmer's option to set the tree and rule that if a contestant doesn't meet their challenger for any reason, it is considered a forfeit. The forfeit moves through the tree as a bye would if it occurs in the first round; the contestant who wins the forfeit advances.

A servant leader should consider all options and decide how to handle such scenarios well before the tournament. This allows potential contestants to understand the guidelines and procedures related to how the tournament is being run, and whether or not a hopeful contestant should bring any equipment or clothing. It can be a good idea to encourage hopefuls to attend; especially if you expect to use byes. Hopeful contestants are usually more than willing to play the byes just for the experience, even if regulations don't permit last minute substitutions.

First-round *challenge* format allows competitors to select who they will compete with in the first round. This, however, is a bit tricky to set up properly on a tree. It can allow byes to occur late in the elimination tree's structure and should be avoided unless you are only a few competitors shy of a "perfect" tree. For example, twelve competitors wish to begin a tournament with a challenge-up. There are two fair ways of handling such a situation and eliminate byes by the end of the second round.

Using the twelve competitor example, the first step is to spread the pairs equally through the sixteen-contestant tree. You will have two branches where bye meets bye on opposite sides of the tree. Since there is no seeding in such a tournament, a random draw of cards can allow you to determine which two of the first pairs will meet the "bye pair" in the second round. Another alternative is to have each pair draw one of six cards, two of which will be marked BYE. Those pairs will then be spread out into the singles slots accordingly. By doing this the byes are eliminated by the end of the first round, but the initial challenge match results don't count. If the competitors choose to start from their challenges, you will have byes until the end of the second round.

Placement of Byes

It is rare to have an elimination tournament that doesn't involve byes, especially when preregistration for the tournament is not required. Byes can and should be played out during one-day tournaments so that all the competitors are exposed to an equal amount of physical and/or mental exertion. This can be done two ways: (a) ask a few experienced players to attend to play the "byes," or (b) pair up the competitors who drew the byes to play a match where their results won't count (although this only works if you have an even amount of byes to start). Whether or not to "play" the byes depends upon if the organizer has enough time scheduled to

complete the tournament, and what the traditional consensus of the competitors or group of competitors involves.

If using the random draw or controlled draw method of setting up the first round, space the "byes" throughout the tree first. As the names are drawn, they fall randomly down the tree giving everyone an equal chance to obtain a bye in the first round.

In the case of byes within a seeded tournament, the top ranked teams "earn" the byes and the placement shifts accordingly. For example, thirteen teams would result in this set up:

1 v. bye
5 v. 12
3 v. bye
7 v. 10
8 v. 9
4 v. 13
6 v. 11
2 v. bye

Even in a situation where a league only has enough people sign up for five teams, byes, when placed in the tree correctly, are eliminated by the end of the second round. Since the "perfect" elimination tournament occurs at four and eight contestants, five teams bumps the tree structure to eight, leaving three byes in the first round and three byes in the consolation bracket of the second round. After that there should be no byes, and the tournament is played out until a winner prevails. For example:

Correct Set Up	Incorrect Set Up
1 v. bye	1 v. bye
3 v. bye	2 v. 5
4 v. 5	3 v. 4
2 v. bye	bye v. bye

Elimination Tournaments and Servant Leadership

A successfully run elimination tournament: (a) rids itself of all byes as soon as possible; (b) avoids contestants meeting twice (double elimination); and (c) keeps competitors and spectators informed.

Competitors will always be curious and ask who or what team they will meet up with next. To avoid this and keep the central coordination area clear, place a sign in a public area where it is updated regularly. In a fast-paced, day-long tournament, it is especially helpful to have a volunteer keep this sign up-to-date for both spectators and competitors so that curious individuals are not tempted to bother those coordinating the tournament. This way the coordinators can concentrate on the organization of the tournament tree, confirm results when needed, and keep communications open to officials and staff resulting in a successful and pleasant tournament experience for everybody.

Round Robin Tournaments

The round robin tournament enables all individuals or teams to play every other individual or team. It can be used in a day-long competition, or over a longer time period. The advantage of this format is that no team or individual is eliminated, so everyone plays an equal number of games. Sometimes, three-way ties occur in a round robin tournament (e.g., players 1, 3 and four all won three matches, 1 beat 3, 3 beat 4, and 4 beat 1), so procedures (i.e., if or what kind of tie-breaker should occur) need to be settled on in advance if prizes or trophies are being awarded.

The round robin is a very versatile tournament, since it can be run with or without a formal structure. For a self-directed approach, make a grid with the contestant's names in the rows and columns. When each game is complete the winner's name is written in the box along with each individual or team representative's initials. Here is an example of a six contestant, self-directed round robin grid. Note that the black squares are where players would meet themselves, and that the lower half of the grid is shaded. Usually, competitors only meet

	Lowell	Don	Deb	Kathy	Sherril	Lynne
Lowell	■	Don	Deb	Kathy	Lowell	Lynne
Don	Court A 1 p.m. 2/14	■	Deb	Don	Sherril	Don
Deb	Court A 7 p.m. 2/16	Court C 1 p.m. 2/21	■	Deb	Sherril	Lynne
Kathy	Court C 7 p.m. 2/23	Court B 7 p.m. 2/18	Court B 1 p.m. 2/14	■	Sherril	Kathy
Sherril	Court C 7 p.m. 2/18	Court B 7 p.m. 2/16	Court B 7 p.m. 2/23	Court A 1 p.m. 2/21	■	Sherril
Lynne	Court B 1 p.m. 2/21	Court A 7 p.m. 2/23	Court A 7 p.m. 2/18	Court C 7 p.m. 2/16	Court C 1 p.m. 2/14	■

once in a round robin so in a self-directed structure, players should note the results in the white boxes. Time and place of the meetings may be placed on the shaded grid. Tally by counting how many times each competitor's name is indicated as a winner on the grid.

When a more structured approach is preferred, such as when facility time is limited, the tournament organizer should direct the play more. In this case, using a numbers table may be the better option especially when the time it takes to complete a round of play is short (e.g., less than 15 minutes), or if the organizers are using more than one play area (e.g., racquetball courts). In this case, the competitors or an official should approach the person handling the results; she/he will record the results, then inform the players who they will meet next. The list is ordered so that games are spaced out to provide equal rest time for each competitor as much as possible. Here is an sample table for a six competitor round robin using the more structured number table.

Assign each competitor a number	Direct competitors to play in this order and circle winner's number:			Circle Winner's Number					
1. Christopher // (5)	**R-1**	**R-2**	**R-3**		1	2	3	4	5	6
2. Nicole /// (2)	(1)-2	1-(3)	1-(5)	1	—	(1)-2	1-(3)	1-(4)	1-(5)	(1)-6
3. Carter // (4)	3-(4)	(2)-5	3-(6)	2		—	2-(3)	(2)-4	(2)-5	(2)-6
4. Holley /// (3)	(5)-6	(4)-6	(2)-4	3			—	3-(4)	3-(5)	3-(6)
★5. Matthew //// (1)				4				—	4-(5)	(4)-6
6. Sarah / (6)	**R-4**	**R-5**		5					—	(5)-6
	(1)-6	1-(4)		6						—
	4-(5)	(2)-6								
	2-(3)	3-(5)								

Tally Wins

Follow rows and columns to tally circled wins for each player (e.g., shading for player 3). Usually when ties occur, two-way ties can be broken by referring to who won the contest where the "tied" players met.

Index

Other Books from Venture Publishing, Inc.

The A•B•Cs of Behavior Change: Skills for Working With
Behavior Problems in Nursing Homes
by Margaret D. Cohn, Michael A. Smyer and Ann L. Horgas

Activity Experiences and Programming Within Long-Term Care
by Ted Tedrick and Elaine R. Green

The Activity Gourmet
by Peggy Powers

Advanced Concepts for Geriatric Nursing Assistants
by Carolyn A. McDonald

Adventure Education
edited by John C. Miles and Simon Priest

Aerobics of the Mind: Keeping the Mind Active in Aging—A New
Perspective on Programming for Older Adults
by Marge Engleman

Assessment: The Cornerstone of Activity Programs
by Ruth Perschbacher

At-Risk Youth and Gangs—A Resource Manual for the Parks
and Recreation Professional—Expanded and Updated
by The California Park and Recreation Society

Behavior Modification in Therapeutic Recreation: An
Introductory Learning Manual
by John Dattilo and William D. Murphy

Benefits of Leisure
edited by B. L. Driver, Perry J. Brown and George L. Peterson

Benefits of Recreation Research Update
by Judy M. Sefton and W. Kerry Mummery

Beyond Bingo: Innovative Programs for the New Senior
by Sal Arrigo, Jr., Ann Lewis and Hank Mattimore

Beyond Bingo 2: More Innovative Programs for the New Senior
by Sal Arrigo, Jr.

Both Gains and Gaps: Feminist Perspectives on Women's Leisure
by Karla Henderson, M. Deborah Bialeschki, Susan M. Shaw
and Valeria J. Freysinger

Effective Management in Therapeutic Recreation Service
by Gerald S. O'Morrow and Marcia Jean Carter

Evaluating Leisure Services: Making Enlightened Decisions
by Karla A. Henderson with M. Deborah Bialeschki

The Evolution of Leisure: Historical and Philosophical
Perspectives (Second Printing)
by Thomas Goodale and Geoffrey Godbey

Experience Marketing: Strategies for the New Millennium
by Ellen L. O'Sullivan and Kathy J. Spangler

File o' Fun: A Recreation Planner for Games and Activities,
Third Edition
by Jane Harris Ericson and Diane Ruth Albright

The Game Finder—A Leader's Guide to Great Activities
by Annette C. Moore

Getting People Involved in Life and Activities: Effective
Motivating Techniques
by Jeanne Adams

Great Special Events and Activities
by Annie Morton, Angie Prosser and Sue Spangler

Inclusive Leisure Services: Responding to the Rights of
People with Disabilities
by John Dattilo

Internships in Recreation and Leisure Services: A Practical
Guide for Students, Second Edition
by Edward E. Seagle, Jr., Ralph W. Smith and Lola M.
Dalton

Interpretation of Cultural and Natural Resources
by Douglas M. Knudson, Ted T. Cable and Larry Beck

Introduction to Leisure Services—7th Edition
by H. Douglas Sessoms and Karla A. Henderson

Leadership and Administration of Outdoor Pursuits, Second
Edition
by Phyllis Ford and James Blanchard

Leadership in Leisure Services: Making a Difference
by Debra J. Jordan

Leisure and Family Fun (LAFF)
by Mary Atteberry-Rogers

Leisure and Leisure Services in the 21st Century
by Geoffrey Godbey

The Leisure Diagnostic Battery: Users Manual and Sample
Forms
by Peter A. Witt and Gary Ellis

Leisure Education: A Manual of Activities and Resources
by Norma J. Stumbo and Steven R. Thompson

Leisure Education II: More Activities and Resources
by Norma J. Stumbo

Leisure Education III: More Goal-Oriented Activities
by Norma J. Stumbo

Leisure Education IV: Activities for Individuals With
Substance Addictions
by Norma J. Stumbo

Leisure Education Program Planning: A Systematic Approach
by John Dattilo and William D. Murphy

Leisure in Your Life: An Exploration, Fourth Edition
by Geoffrey Godbey

Leisure Services in Canada: An Introduction
by Mark S. Searle and Russell E. Brayley

Leveraging the Benefits of Parks and Recreation: The
Phoenix Project
by The California Park and Recreation Society

Other Books from Venture Publishing, Inc.

The Lifestory Re-Play Circle: A Manual of Activities and Techniques
   by Rosilyn Wilder

Marketing for Parks, Recreation, and Leisure
   by Ellen L. O'Sullivan

Models of Change in Municipal Parks and Recreation: A Book of Innovative Case Studies
   edited by Mark E. Havitz

More Than A Game: A New Focus on Senior Activity Services
   by Brenda Corbett

Nature and the Human Spirit: Toward an Expanded Land Management Ethic
   edited by B. L. Driver, Daniel Dustin, Tony Baltic, Gary Elsner and George Peterson

Outdoor Recreation Management: Theory and Application, Third Edition
   by Alan Jubenville and Ben Twight

Planning Parks for People, Second Edition
   by John Hultsman, Richard L. Cottrell and Wendy Zales Hultsman

The Process of Recreation Programming Theory and Technique, Third Edition
   by Patricia Farrell and Herberta M. Lundegren

Protocols for Recreation Therapy Programs
   edited by Jill Kelland, along with the Recreation Therapy Staff at Alberta Hospital Edmonton

Quality Management: Applications for Therapeutic Recreation
   edited by Bob Riley

Recreation and Leisure: Issues in an Era of Change, Third Edition
   edited by Thomas Goodale and Peter A. Witt

The Recreation Connection to Self-Esteem—A Resource Manual for the Park, Recreation and Community Services Professionals
   by The California Park and Recreation Society

Recreation Economic Decisions: Comparing Benefits and Costs, Second Edition
   by John B. Loomis and Richard G. Walsh

Recreation Programming and Activities for Older Adults
   by Jerold E. Elliott and Judith A. Sorg-Elliott

Recreation Programs That Work for At-Risk Youth: The Challenge of Shaping the Future
   edited by Peter A. Witt and John L. Crompton

Reference Manual for Writing Rehabilitation Therapy Treatment Plans
   by Penny Hogberg and Mary Johnson

Research in Therapeutic Recreation: Concepts and Methods
   edited by Marjorie J. Malkin and Christine Z. Howe

Simple Expressions: Creative and Therapeutic Arts for the Elderly in Long-Term Care
   by Vicki Parsons

A Social History of Leisure Since 1600
   by Gary Cross

A Social Psychology of Leisure
   by Roger C. Mannell and Douglas A. Kleiber

The Sociology of Leisure
   by John R. Kelly and Geoffrey Godbey

Therapeutic Activity Intervention with the Elderly: Foundations and Practices
   by Barbara A. Hawkins, Marti E. May and Nancy Brattain Rogers

Therapeutic Recreation: Cases and Exercises
   by Barbara C. Wilhite and M. Jean Keller

Therapeutic Recreation in the Nursing Home
   by Linda Buettner and Shelley L. Martin

Therapeutic Recreation Protocol for Treatment of Substance Addictions
   by Rozanne W. Faulkner

Time for Life—The Surprising Ways Americans Use Their Time
   by John P. Robinson and Geoffrey Godbey

A Training Manual for Americans With Disabilities Act Compliance in Parks and Recreation Settings
   by Carol Stensrud

Venture Publishing, Inc.
1999 Cato Avenue
State College, PA 16801

Phone: (814) 234-4561
Fax: (814) 234-1651
E-mail: vpublish@venturepublish.com
On the Web: www.venturepublish.com